MAKING ANGLO-SAXON DEVON
Emergence of a Shire

MAKING ANGLO-SAXON DEVON
Emergence of a Shire

Robert Higham

First published in Great Britain by The Mint Press, 2008

© R. A. Higham and The Mint Press, 2008

The right of R. A. Higham to be identified as author of this work
has been asserted by him in accordance with the
the Copyright, Designs and Patents Act 1988.

Cover: Part-views of a silver penny of Aethelred II minted at Lydford
(by permission of the Royal Albert Memorial Museum and Art Gallery, Exeter)
and of text from the poem *Widsith* in the Exeter Book (by permission of the
Dean and Chapter of Exeter Cathedral).

All rights reserved. No part of this publication may be
reproduced in any form or by any means without
the prior permission of the copyright holders.

ISBN 978 1 903356 57 9

Cataloguing in Publication Data
CIP record for this title is available from the British Library.

The Mint Press
Taddyforde House South
Taddyforde Estate
New North Road
Exeter, Devon
England EX4 4AT

Typeset in 11/14pt Times by
Kestrel Data, Exeter, Devon

Cover design by Delphine Jones

Printed and bound in Great Britain by
Short Run Press Ltd, Exeter, Devon

Contents

Acknowledgements	vii
List of Illustrations	xi
Notes on Some Primary Historical Sources	xv
Preface	xxi
1 Prologue: Dumnonian and Saxon Foundations	1
2 People and Place	13
3 Church and Society	73
4 Government and Towns	139
5 Land and Rural Folk	204
6 Epilogue: The Legacy of Anglo-Saxon Devon	260
Appendices	269
1: St Boniface – Devon's best-known Saxon	
2: The Minster church at Crediton before and after 909	
3: Some influential people in pre-Norman Devon	
Bibliography	281
Indices	299

Acknowledgements

This book owes much to friends and colleagues with Exeter associations. Frank Barlow taught me Anglo-Saxon history at the University many years ago and I owe much to him. Mary Ann O'Donovan, editor of crucial Sherborne records, once taught at Exeter University, as did the late George Greenaway, who wrote about Saint Boniface. The late Aileen Fox and Ann Hamlin introduced me, as a student, to the post-Roman archaeology of the Celtic-speaking regions. Ian Burrow, a fellow undergraduate from those days, pioneered the mapping of dark-age archaeological data in Devon. One of the editions of the *Anglo-Saxon Chronicle* consulted was produced by Michael Swanton. My debt to the archaeologically-based studies of the south west by Malcolm Todd, Charles Thomas and Susan Pearce is great, as is my debt to Oliver Padel for his place-name studies. Several contributions to the *Historical Atlas of South West England*, an Exeter University publication edited by Roger Kain and the late William Ravenhill, have proved most helpful.

I have benefitted over the years also from discussions with other Exeter colleagues (past and present) sharing early Devonian interests, notably Oliver Creighton, the late Audrey Erskine, Derek Gore, Christopher Holdsworth, Gill Juleff, Nicholas Orme, Henrietta Quinnell, the late Timothy Reuter, Stephen Rippon and Howard Williams (amongst whom OC, DG, SR and HW also read and commented helpfully upon drafts of individual chapters, for which thanks are due). Undergraduate and postgraduate students have also contributed to my knowledge of this period over many years through the writing of their dissertations and theses. Stephen Price, a friend from my student days, as well as my sons, Ben and

Joe, kindly drove me to various places in Devon during the writing of this book, providing congenial and enquiring company on the way.

I am grateful to the late Christopher Henderson, and more recently Peter Weddell and Stuart Blaylock, of Exeter Archaeology (formerly Exeter Archaeological Field Unit), who have generously shared their knowledge of Exeter and Devon and made the results of their various projects available to me, sometimes in advance of publication. Frances Griffith and Bill Horner (Devon County Council Historic Environment Service) have shared the knowledge gained from aerial photography over many years which has added so much to our understanding of Devon landscapes and the settlements, abandoned and living, within them.

I am grateful to John Allan, another friend from student days in Exeter and a colleague ever since, for sharing his extensive knowledge of south-western coinage, pottery, building traditions and urban archaeology acquired during many years at the Royal Albert Memorial Museum (Exeter) and at Exeter Archaeology. He also read my first (very short) draft text and made helpful suggestions. The developing text of the main chapters was scrutinized by Julia Crick, a most supportive friend at Exeter University, who was concurrently researching parts of this subject, and to whom I am much indebted for her general encouragement. The text of the book was read at an advanced (but not complete or illustrated) stage in its development by Barbara Yorke (another Exeter friend from student days, now at the University of Winchester) on behalf of myself and the publisher. I am very grateful for her improving comments, for her suggestions on reading as well as for invaluable personal discussion of her published and unpublished ideas. The outcome owes much more to her than is apparent from occasional references to her name in the text and bibliography.

I thank sincerely the authors of the numerous articles and specialist works on the south west, and on England generally, which I have consulted. I hope I have construed their ideas accurately, and that authors will forgive the absence, within my chapter texts, of direct references: these I felt would not be helpful to my anticipated readership. I have, however, frequently quoted the names of relevant authors in order to indicate the large number of people who have contributed to this subject as well as their areas of expertise. I know that useful unpublished material lies in recent postgraduate theses (outside Exeter) as well as in archaeological repositories, but these I have not generally consulted, limiting my reading mainly to published primary and secondary material.

This book was written during a period as an Honorary Fellow of

Acknowledgements

Exeter University. I am grateful for the help of the staff at the University Library, the Devon and Exeter Institution Library, Exeter Cathedral Library and Archives, and the Devon Record Office. The Department of Archaeology at the University very kindly provided me with some working space and facilities, as well as enjoyable society, during the book's final writing and assembly. Technical advice came from my friends and collaborators on earlier projects, Seán Goddard and Mike Rouillard, especially the latter who generously gave his time to preparing illustrations.

I owe warm thanks to the postgraduates and undergraduates of the Department of Archaeology, who welcomed me into their lively culture and whose own experiences reminded me so vividly of my own student days. As well as providing much moral support throughout, my friend and sometime co-author Oliver Creighton produced several computer-compiled maps for me, for which I am very grateful. In July 2007, I took part in a symposium at Exeter, organised by Stephen Rippon and Oliver Creighton, which examined the links between landscape history and cultural perception. I am grateful for this invitation and benefitted from much helpful discussion on that occasion, especially with Nicholas Higham and Rosamund Faith.

Photographs and permission for their reproduction have been provided by various institutions including: Exeter Archaeology, Devon County Council, Exeter Cathedral Archives, Royal Albert Memorial Museum and Art Gallery (Exeter). Many authors and publishers have given permission for reproduction of their already-published illustrations. To all of them I am very grateful and acknowledgement of provenance is given in the captions. In a few cases, all going back about fifty years, published sources are stated but correspondence revealed that copyright lay only with authors no longer alive. I am grateful to George Fox and Susan Hewitt for permission relating to items published by Aileen Fox and W.G. Hoskins.

The book was written at the suggestion of its publisher, Todd Gray (The Mint Press). He waited patiently while it evolved from a very short to a somewhat longer study and also scrutinized my final text for editorial errors. Longer than originally anticipated though it is, the battle involved in its authorship has still been one of compression and some casualties will have been inevitable. If I have not always taken the advice of those who have kindly offered it, then any mistakes and bizarre ideas arising are entirely my own fault.

I am grateful to Paul and Anne (Kestrel Data) for their patience and skill in typesetting my material, and to Delphine Jones for a most attractive cover design.

As this book was entering production stage in August 2007, one of Devon's finest medieval historians died. With much sadness, but also with much gratitude for the sharing of both his scholarship and his friendship over many years, I dedicate this book to the memory of Professor Harold Fox of Leicester University.

List of Illustrations

1. Prologue

1.1.	Physical geography: coasts, main rivers and higher land	3

2. People and Place

2.1.	Map of central and eastern Dumnonia (with modern shire bounds)	17
2.2.	Two *Civitas Dumnoniorum* inscriptions	18
2.3.	Distribution map of inscribed memorial stones	20
2.4.	(a) Inscribed memorial stone from Buckland Monachorum (now in Tavistock) (b) inscription originally from Fardel, Ivybridge (now in British Museum)	22
2.5.	Early Devon: map of "events"	29
2.6.	Early Devon: map of "processes"	31
2.7.	The Galford area	33
2.8.	High Peak: aerial photograph	34
2.9.	Bantham Ham: aerial photograph	35
2.10.	Imported amphora from Bantham	36
2.11.	Map of recorded British-English conflicts	40
2.12.	Map of Brittonic place-names in Devon	50
2.13.	Map of British river-names	53
2.14.	Map of Treable	56
2.15.	Map of place-names with the element *tre*	58
2.16.	Maps of other place-name elements	60-61
2.17.	Map of documented English-Viking conflicts	64
2.18.	Viking-period armlet from Goodrington	66

2.19.	Pottery from (a) Northern France (b) Exeter (c) Devon/Somerset border	68
2.20.	Bonework (a) comb (b) spindle whorls and needles	70
2.21.	Metalwork (a) finger-ring (b) stirrup mounts (c) hooked fasteners	71

3. Church and Society

3.1.	A late Roman sherd from Exeter with Chi-Rho symbol	74
3.2.	The evolution Exeter's early medieval cemetery	75
3.3.	Burials in Exeter (a) sub-Roman (b) late Saxon	76
3.4.	The early Christian cemetery at Kenn	78
3.5.	Map of *lann*, *stow* and related names	84
3.6.	Reconstructions of some early minster territories	91
3.7.	Map of some churches in early Devon	96-7
3.8.	Exeter Cathedral's eleventh-century foundation charter	106
3.9.	Map of Exeter's medieval parishes and churches	117
3.10.	Exeter minster's apse after excavation	120
3.11.	St. Olave's church, Exeter	121
3.12.	St George's church, Exeter (a) plan (b) elevation	122-3
3.13.	Plan of the crypt at Sidbury church	124
3.14.	An antiquarian sketch of Teignmouth church	125
3.15.	Cross-shaft in Exeter	129
3.16.	Cross at Colyton	129
3.17.	Cross at Copplestone	131
3.18.	Cross/font at Dolton	133
3.19.	The Exeter Book	136

4. Government and Towns

4.1.	Map of royal interests in Saxon Devon	141
4.2.	Map of Devon's Hundreds	146-7
4.3.	Map of Anglo-Saxon land-grants in Devon and Cornwall	158
4.4.	King Cnut's charter for Stoke Canon	161
4.5.	The evolution of early Exeter	168
4.6.	Map of Exeter's late Saxon environs	170
4.7.	The evolution of Exeter's south gate	172
4.8.	Late Saxon crenellations in Exeter's city wall (Northernhay)	173
4.9.	Aerial photographs (a-d) of Devon's four urban *burhs*	176-7
4.10.	Map of hundreds and *burhs*	180
4.11.	Profile of the *burh* defences at Totnes	182
4.12.	Plans of the *burhs* at (a) Barnstaple (b) Totnes	184-5

List of Illustrations

4.13.	Plan of the *burh* at Lydford	186
4.14.	Plan of Oldaport	190
4.15.	Map of towns and mints in Devon	192
4.16.	The careers (a, b) of two Devon moneyers	194
4.17.	Late Saxon silver pennies from Devon mints (a) Lydford (b) Exeter	195
4.18.	Eleventh-century pits excavated in Princesshay, Exeter	199
4.19.	Exeter in the Eleventh Century	200
4.20.	The Norman castle gatehouse in Exeter	202

5. Land and Rural Folk

5.1.	Map of some places mentioned in Chapter 5	205
5.2.	The *Exon* Domesday Book	206
5.3.	Map of hedges mentioned in Anglo-Saxon charters	216
5.4.	Domesday Devon (a) named places (b) population	220-1
5.5.	Development (a, b) of field-systems at Holne Moor	224-5
5.6.	Aerial photograph of crop-mark enclosure near Buckfastleigh	230
5.7.	Map of early settlement in Devon	231
5.8.	Maps of (a) Bowley and (b) Sampford Courtenay	238
5.9.	Hartland: a study of hamlet shrinkage	239
5.10.	Aerial photograph of South Hole hamlet, Hartland	241
5.11.	Plans of village morphology (a) Bradworthy (b) Ugborough	242
5.12.	Aerial photograph of Ugborough village	243
5.13.	Strip fields at (a) Kenton (b) Down St. Thomas	246
5.14.	Kemacott hamlet and fields, near Martinhoe	247
5.15.	Braunton Great Field	249
5.16.	Kingsteignton: church and curvilinear settlement topography	251
5.17.	Crediton: church and rectilinear settlement topography	253
5.18.	Excavation of an iron-smelting site at Blacklake Wood	256

6. Epilogue

6.1.	Nymed charter boundary	262
6.2.	(a) Stoke Canon charter boundary (b) aerial photograph of Stoke Hill camp	263
6.3.	The Crediton charter boundary	264

Notes on Some Primary Historical Sources

Many sources relevant to Devon explicitly, or by implication, are to be found in D. Whitelock (ed), *English Historical Documents, I, c. 500–1042* (London. Eyre and Spottiswood. 1955 etc). This includes selections from Bede's *Ecclesiastical History*, the *Anglo-Saxon Chronicle*, Asser's *Life* of King Alfred, law-codes, land charters, wills and letters. A most valuable compendium of related material, with much useful commentary, is S. Keynes and M. Lapidge, *Alfred the Great: Asser's Life of King Alfred and other contemporary sources* (Harmondsworth. Penguin. 1983). The *Anglo-Saxon Chronicle* is also conveniently available in the edition by M. Swanton (London. Dent. 1996). *The Chronicle of Aethelweard*, well-informed on the south west, is available in the edition by A. Campbell (London. Nelson. 1962).

Gildas's *The Ruin of Britain* has been published by Phillimore (ed. M. Winterbottom, 1978). The places of Gildas's origin and of his writing have been subject to much debate. Northern Britain and Wales have often been favoured, but a very good case has been made (especially by N. Higham) for just outside the eastern edge of Dumnonia, in Wiltshire or Dorset, as the location of his writing, helping to explain his familiarity with Dumnonia. Dates suggested for this source by various commentators range from the later fifth to the mid-sixth centuries. The "Welsh Annals", which include some Dumnonian and Cornish matters, are in J. Morris (ed), *Nennius: British History and the Welsh Annals* (Chichester. Phillimore. 1980).

Domesday data (the *Exchequer* version with additions from *Exon*) is accessible in C. & F. Thorn, *Domesday Book: Devon* (2 vols;

Chichester.Phillimore. 1985). The DB text (in English) by O.J. Reichel in *Victoria History of the County of Devon, Vol I.* (ed. W. Page. London. 1906) is based on *Exon*. For the full Latin texts of *Exon* and of the Geld Inquisition of similar date, the *Additamenta* volume of the Record Commission edition (1816) must be consulted. In my own end-of-chapter references I have listed simply the Phillimore edition.

Much is revealed about the topography of Saxon Devon in D. Hooke, *Pre-Conquest Charter Bounds of Devon and Cornwall* (Woodbridge. Boydell. 1994), and the south-western charter material was gathered in H.P.R. Finberg's *Early Charters of Devon and Cornwall* (Leicester. 1953). Charters are indexed nationally in P.H. Sawyer, *Anglo-Saxon Charters. An Annotated List and Bibliography* (London. Royal Historical Society. 1968). Many texts, in the original Latin and Old English, are given in J.M. Kemble, *Codex Diplomaticus Aevi Saxonici* (6 vols. London. 1839-1848) and W. de Gray Birch, *Cartularium Saxonicum* (4 vols. London. Whiting & Company. 1885-1899). Some original texts with modern English translations are provided in A.J. Robertson, *Anglo-Saxon Charters* (Cambridge University Press. 1939). The charters of the wider region to which the south west belongs have been treated most recently in H. Edwards, *The Charters of the Early West Saxon Kingdom* (British Archaeological Reports, British Series 198, 1988). Where using charter evidence, I have sometimes noted the difference between dates of charters and dates of grants they describe, as well as the difference between dates of charters and their boundary clauses. Such differences do not necessarily make their content unreliable. I have, however, largely avoided analysis of the "authenticity" of individual charters, a subject inappropriate for a general book of this sort, but whose complexity is illustrated in the Devon studies by P. Chaplais (1966), H.P.R. Finberg (1968) and C. Insley (1998). The interpretation of charter boundaries can also be contentious. A Devon example which has given rise to much debate is king Aethelwulf's grant of 20 hides of land to himself in the South Hams (in 847). Again, I have avoided discussions of such problems, largely following the published work of Della Hooke (1994) on boundary identification.

The two volumes of the *The Place-Names of Devon* (eds. Gover, Mawer & Stenton) were published early (1931–32), lacking the depth and breadth found in later studies of some other counties. They contain, nevertheless, a huge amount of helpful data and I have made considerable use of them, hopefully to good effect.

One source needs particular comment, that is William of Malmesbury's *History of the English Kings*, whose first version was completed around

Notes on Some Primary Historical Sources

1125. William was from south-west England, born near the Somerset-Wiltshire border to an English mother and Norman father. His account of the reign of Aethelstan (925–940), though written long after the event, is held by historians to be especially valuable because, as William reveals in his own narrative, it was based on "a certain ancient book" whose content was clearly a panegyric of Aethelstan written soon after the king's death. This source adds greatly to the narrative of the reign given in the *Anglo-Saxon Chronicle*. It no longer survives independently, so William's use of it provides a major illumination of the period. The relevant parts of his narrative are available in D. Whitelock (ed), *English Historical Documents,* Vol I (1955), 121, 277-283; and in the more recent edition of William's *History* (eds. Mynors, Thompson, Winterbottom 1998–99, Vol. II, chs. 132,134), where the varied views of historians concerning the reliability of William's claim are also discussed (Vol. I, 116-118). These circumstances are relevant to the history of south west Britain, since it is only from William of Malmesbury's account that we know of Aethelstan's Cornish campaign, his expulsion of the remaining British population from Exeter, his additions to the fortifications of Exeter city, and his fixing of the Devon-Cornwall boundary along the river Tamar. These events comprised a very significant stage in the evolution of the region's political geography, and I have regarded these details as reliable. Aethelstan's reign was marked by significant warfare: against the Scandinavians in the north and the British in Wales and the south west: William of Malmesbury called the latter *Cornewalenses*. The most likely timing of Aethelstan's south-western campaign, as suggested by Stenton (*Anglo-Saxon England*, 1947, 337) was the period spanned by the great council he held in Exeter in 928 and the one held in 931, much further west in Lifton. Stenton thought it was prompted by a Cornish revolt which received support from the British population in Devon, especially in Exeter. Aethelstan's creation of a see, subordinate to Crediton, at St German's in Cornwall makes sense in the context of events described by William of Malmesbury. Changes in secular administrative arrangements within Cornwall may also have taken place. William noted that memories of Aethelstan's impact on Exeter and Devon were very much alive, and in later traditions Aethelstan was regarded as a benefactor of south-western churches, including Exeter's minster. Exeter was one of the places visited by William when collecting information for his various works: see R.M. Thompson, *William of Malmesbury* (Woodbridge. Boydell Press. 2003). It is tempting to suggest that his knowledge of south-western history, drawn primarily from the written source which he quoted, was supplemented by information acquired in person at this time. Hopefully, the foregoing information will avoid a need for further explanation at points in this book where William's narrative of Aethelstan occurs. Following several earlier authors, I have regarded his treatment of Aethelstan to be, in effect, a near-contemporary source.

Since it forms such a major source for early English history, some comment on the *Anglo-Saxon Chronicle* is appropriate for readers who may be misled by its apparently simple title. This source, which actually takes the form of a series of annals, first emerged late in the reign of Alfred of Wessex. Its compilers made use of a variety of earlier written sources, including Bede's *Ecclesiastical History*, royal genealogies and annals (not now surviving), as well as of immediate personal knowledge of recent events. Although Alfred himself was a notable patron of education and writing, it is thought that the *Chronicle* was not his own personal inspiration, but the work of his learned circle: it has been noted that one contributor was well-informed about western Wessex and may have come from the eastern parts of the south west region. In his edition of the work (see above), Michael Swanton has called it "the first continuous national history of any western people in their own language". It was certainly written at a time when the English had felt seriously challenged by viking incursions: there was thus an element of "nationalism" in its compilation and certainly a bias towards the position of the West Saxon dynasty. But it should not be seen simply as crude Alfredian propaganda, but rather as a means to bolster a sense of English unity, in the vernacular tongue, under West Saxon leadership. It was subsequently circulated, probably at Alfred's direction, to a number of ecclesiastical centres in different parts of the country, where it was continued through to the eleventh century (and in one case, the twelfth). In its surviving form it is thus not a single source, but a group of sources which display differences of content and regional emphasis. In its original form, it was used immediately by Asser as a source for his (Latin) *Life* of Alfred, a work intended for a more restricted readership (including perhaps the Welsh courtly circles of his homeland). In the late tenth century, it was the basis of the Latin chronicle written by the Anglo-Saxon nobleman Aethelweard. It was also used by Anglo-Norman chroniclers in the twelfth century, some of whom had access to versions no longer surviving. In its immediate impact and its on-going influence, the *Anglo-Saxon Chronicle* was very successful.

Finally, readers should note that the past which I have written about is one derived from the modern methodologies of history and archaeology.

Although the scope of the known data and of the questions which we ask of it have grown greatly in the last hundred years, the framework of this study would be recognisable to all who have written about the south-west during very recent centuries. But if we go back further, we find a shift of emphasis. For example, John Hooker, Exeter's sixteenth-century Chamberlain and its first historian, wrote that Devon had been ruled by Britons, Saxons, Danes and Normans: he knew the cultural sequence which produced successive royal dynasties. But he also believed that, centuries earlier, Britain had been founded by Brutus, who had given the south west to his ally Corineus, and that these men had founded Exeter and Totnes. This version of the south-western past derived from Geoffrey of Monmouth's *History of the Kings of Britain*, written in the early twelfth century, which narrated the history of Britain from its foundation by Brutus to its domination by the Saxons. It was an immensely popular and influential work. In its treatment of the post-Roman period, it contained themes which are clearly recognisable to us (from our later tradition of history writing) involving the struggle between the British and their Germanic enemy (during which period Cornwall had its own kings), emigration of some of the Britons to Armorica, and the English subjugation of all but the western British extremities. Real places in the south west occurred in this narrative, including Tintagel, Totnes, Exeter, Bath and Dorchester. But the work also contained themes which, to our modern eyes, are simply fantastic, notably the prophecies of Merlin and the deeds of king Arthur and his circle. Geoffrey came from Norman-Welsh society on the marches, though much of his career was in Oxford. He said that a major source was an "ancient book written in the British language", and he mentioned also his use of the earlier writers Gildas and Bede. Historians have established that he knew the ninth-century Welsh writer later known as Nennius (who wrote a *History of the Britons*) as well as the *Welsh Annals*. His own origins, as well as his *History*, thus reflected the traditions of the Celtic-speaking world, particularly Wales. Whether he intended his work as a "history", or as an entertaining story, is much debated. He was criticised by later twelfth-century monastic chroniclers, who felt parts of his narrative to be fictional. In the later twelfth century, however, the traditions of the pan-Celtic world, from which Geoffrey's narrative sprang, were also taken up in the literature of courtly love which flourished in the Angevin empire and in which Breton traditions were very important. For example, Marie de France's tale of the Breton knight, Eliduc, relates an adventure in Devon and Brittany in which the hero serves British kings in both areas. Regular passage between the two territories occurs, and Totnes was the Devon port of entry. One of the warring British kings who figures in the narrative was based in Exeter. It is tempting to imagine that details of the world shared with south west Britain in the early middle ages had survived for centuries in the Breton memory. More likely, if more mundane, is the explanation that vaguer recollections of common history were now overlain with details familiar to the twelfth-century world in which these stories were written down. Cross-channel connections, at political, economic and family levels were everyday features of Norman and Angevin times. Exeter was then a port with international connections whose trade with northern France had begun before the Norman Conquest. It was from the circumstances of this period that Totnes would seem a suitable historic connecting port: but in the Dumnonian period (let alone in Brutus's "time") it had not even existed. We dismiss the materials of the "Arthurian" world because they do not meet the standards of modern academic enquiry for reconstructing the past. Thus they occupy no part in this book. We should beware, however, the danger of historical arrogance. The alternative view of the early middle ages represented by the "legends" of the French- and Celtic-speaking worlds was enormously influential for many centuries. It spawned a flow of creative literature and art down to the nineteenth century and, in certain respects, has been as influential upon popular notions of the period as has the "real" past created by historians.

Preface

This book grew out of a project of smaller proportions as my interest in its subject-matter developed. It is aimed at non-specialist readers who wish to understand something of how the county of Devon emerged and what its early history was like. But, despite being aimed at a general audience, this has not been an easy book to write. It has presented me particularly with the challenges of correlating disparate types of data from various academic disciplines and of finding a balance between Devonian detail and the wider English context. Though familiar with some Anglo-Saxon phrases, I cannot read Old English and am not an Anglo-Saxon specialist. I have written this book as an enthusiastic amateur: I hope it will appeal to others of like mind. Although it may irritate the professional reader, there are few academic references within the text (though there are in the Notes on Sources and in the Appendix on Crediton, which are of a more technical nature and are intended to illustrate something of the technicalities which lie behind the study of the period). For my anticipated audience, I thought it more appropriate to provide a list of sources and further reading at the end of each chapter, linked by author-name to a Bibliography. I wanted to get away from the all-too-common (and – to my eye – ugly) appearance of book pages, in which the flow of the text is constantly interrupted by authors' names and publication dates, and often by whole groups of such data, as well as frequent references to illustrations, all in parentheses. Instead, relevant illustrations are referred to *en bloc* at the start of each chapter sub-section. Then, within the text itself, I have referred by name to some authors, as a guide to their influential literature, in acknowledgement of their work and as a link to some of the items listed after each chapter. For convenience, author-date references are generally cited in the captions to illustrations to indicate sources of images reproduced. Although new maps have been compiled and photographs taken or acquired, other illustrations come from earlier publications and thus provide some quality of "historiography" to the subject. The chapters have sub-sections as a guide to the themes discussed, but they are not wholly self-contained and there is much interconnection. This is really a book to read for an overview of its subject rather than one to consult for the discovery of specific data.

To a degree, my interest has been stimulated by the recent and ongoing debates, in the political arena, about what it means to be British or English. These notions have differed from one era to another: the period covered by this book was crucial in their evolution. One might think that, given Britain's long experience of invasions from outside and turbulence from within, it would be easy to make parallels between one sequence of events and another. But this is not so. The Roman conquest, the English immigration and eventual supremacy, the viking incursions and the Norman conquests in England, Wales, Scotland and Ireland were all significantly different from each other in motive, scale and impact. In later times, the plantations in Ireland, the highland clearances in Scotland and the creation of world-wide British colonies presented circumstances in which conquest, social domination and economic exploitation figured side by side. But, though occasional comparisons with the early middle ages may be made, the pursuit of such analogy is of limited value. Every historical situation must be understood primarily in its own context.

Writing this book has been an exercise in synthesising the results of other people's work, supplemented with forays of my own into the primary source material. In general, I have depended upon the interpretations of the numerous specialists whose publications I have consulted, but I have tried to give the text some originality by adding my own ideas where I thought them helpful. I hope the book also has some distinctive quality in its chosen coverage. Other books on the period and region have been mainly about the whole south west, rather than Devon in particular. They have also dwelt more on the early post-Roman centuries than on the pre-Norman period as a whole. Some originality, perhaps, arises from the task of bringing a lot of disparate material together and injecting it with a mix of my own and other writers' views.

Although written with non-specialist readers in mind, I have (I hope) avoided dumbing-down or over-simplification, a process which would be disrespectful both to the subject and its audience. I have expected the reader

Preface

to make an effort, too. There is plenty of hard information here, and words and phrases are sometimes quoted in Latin or Old English in order to convey better their contemporary significance. The book, however, makes no claim to be comprehensive. Where categories of historical or archaeological data are met, every possible example is not necessarily listed; certain aspects of the book are, therefore, impressionistic. In order to illuminate the character of early Devon, I have often made comparisons with developments in other southern shires: contrasts with the experiences of Cornwall are especially frequent. At times, in order to explain Devonian history, it has been necessary to give a wider overview of England. Although some internal cross-references within and between chapters are used, the reader will also note some repetitions of material from one chapter to another as well as sometimes from one chapter sub-section to another. While repetition is not an ideal device, the same material can be very important in more than one context and these overlaps are deliberate: again, with a largely amateur readership in mind, enabling chapters and their sub-sections to be free-standing to a certain degree.

It is tempting to be overly concerned with "new" data and "the latest" ideas. I have tried to be as up-to-date as I can, with respect both to Devonian information and its wider English context, but it is also appropriate to acknowledge that some aspects of the study of pre-Norman Devon have a long ancestry and that anyone now studying the subject owes a debt to much earlier scholars. The archaeological dimensions of the subject in this region are mainly the product of the last fifty years, and often very much less than that, with a few exceptions: the pre-Norman structure beneath the medieval chancel of Sidbury church, for example, was recognised at the end of the nineteenth century. An important achievement was the recognition by Ethel Lega-Weekes and Alan Everett, in 1942–3, of the surviving late Saxon masonry of St. George's church, Exeter, which had been demolished in 1843. Everett's drawing of these remains, revealed by bomb-damage in 1942, was developed in Aileen Fox's publication of her later excavation of this site. Historical dimensions of Devonian study in this period have deeper roots. Much basic primary source material, for England as a whole, had been made available in published editions by the later nineteenth century. Notable early exponents of Devonian studies in the early medieval period included J.B. Davidson (1824–85), F. Rose-Troup (1859–1942) and O.J. Reichel (1840–1923). In the twentieth century, it is hard to dissociate studies of early Devon from the names of H.P.R. Finberg and W.G. Hoskins, who between them not only revealed an enormous amount but also laid out so much of the agenda for later work. The length of this book's *Bibliography* (not comprehensive) is testimony to the numbers who have contributed to our knowledge of early Devon.

This is not the place for a full analysis of the history of publication in this field, nor has it been possible, within the book generally, to do justice to the efforts of all who have written about early historic Devon, especially in the south-western academic journals from the later nineteenth century onwards. But, in order to illustrate the group of early exponents, I would like to pay tribute to a scholar whose work it is now easy to overlook in assessing Devon's medieval historiography. John James Alexander's publications on the early medieval period (he researched and wrote more widely) were the product of much personal enthusiasm and commitment on top of academic employment. He was the subject of an informative feature published on 26 May, 1938, in *The Paignton Observer*. From this, we learn that he was born, of ultimately Scottish ancestry, in Co. Donegal in 1865. He began his education in the north of Ireland, and pursued it further at the Royal University of Dublin and finally at Cambridge University, from which he took an MA. His principal university pursuit had been in mathematics. In 1895, he became headmaster of Tavistock Grammar School, where he remained until he retired in 1928, when he moved to Paignton. He was very active in various spheres of public life. Amongst many other responsibilities, he was a JP from 1912; chairman of Tavistock Urban District Council 1906-08; chairman of the Headmasters' Association for Devon and Cornwall in 1915, 1916 and 1921; and he spent ten years as a governor of the University College of the South West. During his Tavistock years and his retirement he pursued serious local historical interests, publishing numerous articles and notes in the local academic journals; he was accordingly elected a Fellow of the Royal Historical Society. He was President of the Exeter Branch of the Historical Association: his presidential address in 1924 was upon king Aethelstan. He was also sometime editor for the Devonshire Association, and its President in 1932: his presidential address, published in the *Transactions* for that year, was upon the Saxon conquest and settlement of the county. He contributed data for *The Place-Names of Devon*, published in two volumes in 1931–32. He was chairman of the archaeological and geological section of Torquay Natural History Society from 1933–35.

Some of the ideas he expressed on the early medieval period may now seem dated, and he worked in what was, for this period in this region, a pre-archaeological academic culture. But in other respects his writings have a very recognisably modern tone. He acknowledged that the Saxon "conquest" involved a complex series of developments stretching over many years. He knew the complementary nature of different sorts of data from chronicle, charter and place-name sources and made some observations whose full significance may not have been fully appreciated at the time. He noted in his article about Lifton (1931) that the hidation of the four Devonian *burhs* of Alfred's time was greater than Domesday Book's hidation for Devon and concluded that support for the Devonian *burhs* had come also from eastern Cornwall. This acute observation takes us part way towards recent views of how these four fortified centres were supported by the full hidation of both Cornwall and Devon. In his article about king Aethlelstan (1916), he analysed William of Malmesbury's treatment of his reign, giving a judicious account of the relative contributions of Aethelstan and Egbert, his predecessor of a century earlier, to the absorption of west Devon and Cornwall into the West Saxon kingdom. He also noted that William was probably well-disposed to Aethelstan because in the twelfth century it was believed (as recorded by the chronicler John of Worcester) that Aethelstan had been buried at Malmesbury following his death at Gloucester in 940.

Turning from past efforts to current ones, as I was completing this text in 2006-2007, important publications appeared, on a number of themes relevant to this book, from which I benefitted. These included: Sam Turner's *Making a Christian Landscape*; Roger Kain's volume in the *England's Landscapes* series; the south-western volume of Rosemary Cramp's *Corpus of Anglo-Saxon Stone Sculpture*; Barbara Yorke's *The Conversion of Britain, 600–800*; Howard Williams's *Death and Memory in Early Medieval Britain;* some new palaeoenvironmental studies by Stephen Rippon and others; some new metallurgical studies by Gill Juleff and others. Important field projects also occurred in 2006. An Exeter Archaeology excavation found not only medieval building foundations within Exeter castle but also part of a late Saxon cemetery beneath. Howard Williams (Exeter University) was exploring the evolution of Stokenham, in south Devon, whose church may have evolved from a Saxon minster. It stood beside a large oval enclosure, whose origin remains to be established. In 2007, a new research project, beginning with geophysical survey, was launched by Paul Rainbird, Derek Gore and others at the puzzling early medieval site of Oldaport in south Devon. On a wider front, in 2006 the Dorset County Boundary Research Group was established, by Katherine Barker and others, under the *aegis* of the Dorset Natural History and Archaeological Society. It has pursued pilot studies on its Devon, Somerset and Wiltshire borders, and its on-going work is refining knowledge (historical, archaeological and ecological) of the form and antiquity of these most fundamental of English landscape components.

In the summer-autumn of 2007, some relevant new books appeared, but too late for me to take full account of them. Roger White's *Britannia Prima* (Stroud, Tempus) discusses the special character of western Britain in general. Sam Turner's *Ancient Country: the Historic Character of Rural Devon* (Devon County Council and Devon Archaeological Society) covers a long period in which the pre-Norman centuries were very significant. Nicholas Higham's (edited) volume of essays, *Britons in Anglo-Saxon England* (Woodbridge. Boydell Press) arose from an important conference and several of its published themes are directly relevant to the content of this book: in particular, the linguistic evidence for the British and English proportions in early medieval populations (by Peter Schrijver, Duncan Probert, Richard Coates, Oliver Padel) and the evidence of Ine's law-code for British-English relations (by Martin Grimmer). Oliver Padel generously allowed me access to his place-name chapter, prior to its publication, so I was able to benefit from his latest views. Important post-Roman evidence from Burlescombe – on wood-working, flax-processing, woodland management and agricultural environment – was published by Jo Best and Tim Gent (*Archaeological Journal*, 164) in 2008, too late for me to include.

In my title, and generally in my text and illustrations, I have used the name "Devon" because that is what most people now say. But, by the ninth century at the latest, the name used by the English was "Devonshire" and by this fuller name was it also known to the Normans, as Domesday Book reveals. In modern parlance, though we normally talk (in the singular) of "the county" (a word derived from Norman-French use), we still tend to talk (in the plural) of "the shires". Historians rightly emphasise the crucial role played by the shires in English history, from their Anglo-Saxon origins to modern times. Although they have suffered changes in recent years, they were for many centuries well-defined geographical places with administrative functions and, crucially, their own social identity. Though I am not a Devonian, I have lived in Devon – or Devonshire - for many years and feel great affection for it. I hope that this book will contribute something to an understanding of its past. But, especially in the earlier periods, there is still a lot to be discovered, as well as much that is known to be illuminated afresh. New discoveries, especially in archaeology, can rapidly alter our views. The early historical sources are not plentiful and are often difficult to interpret. Much in what follows necessarily remains tentative in nature.

1

Prologue
Dumnonian and Saxon Foundations

Eadward cynge gret Leofric biscop, Harold eorl, Wada, alle mine thegenas on Defenascire freondlice ....

King Edward sends friendly greetings to bishop Leofric and earl Harald and Wada and all my thegns in Devonshire. And I inform you that I have granted to Ealdred, the deacon of Archbishop Ealdred, the minster of Axminster ... .as a pious benefaction for St Peter's minster at York.

(F.E. Harmer, *Anglo-Saxon Writs*, p. 419)

This writ of Edward the Confessor, issued at York between 1060 and 1066, was an instrument of royal government whose content reflected many centuries of historical development. The king was of the West Saxon line but had a Norman mother: the circumstances of his reign were to result in the Norman Conquest. Those to whom the writ was addressed comprised the shire court. The bishop, Leofric, was an appointee of the king who had amalgamated the dioceses of Devon and Cornwall in 1050. The earl, Harold, was from an English (Sussex) family elevated to the ranks of the earls by the Danish king, Cnut. Harold's mother, Gytha, was Danish. His hereditary earldom included all of southern England. In 1066 he was to become the last pre-Norman king. Wada was the king's sheriff, an appointed man with responsibility for military, judicial and tax matters in Devon. His name was Saxon and he was probably a thegn. The thegns were a landed gentry, descendants of Saxon landlords who had moved south westwards as well as of earlier British landlords who had successfully become part of English society. The shire of Devon, probably in existence since the eighth century and certainly in the ninth, was a sub-division of the western portion of the West Saxon kingdom and had been created out of an earlier, Dumnonian kingdom. Archbishop Ealdred had earlier been abbot of Tavistock, so already had a Devonshire connection. Though the clerics had English names, the church they governed had in centuries past also absorbed British traditions of Christianity. Axminster was a royal property in the centre of a hundred, an administrative sub-division of the shire. Edward the Elder held a royal council there in 901. Its church existed by the late eighth century at the latest: Cyneheard, a member of the royal house of Wessex, had been buried there in 786. Its minster church, which influenced its place-name, was typical of the Old English period. Originally, its priests had served a wide rural area. A later tradition asserted that king Aethelstan re-founded it with seven priests in the tenth century. But the granting of the church by Edward the Confessor to the clergy of York suggests that, by 1060, its former status had declined. By this date, throughout England, the fragmentation of minster territories into what would later become local parishes was in progress. In Domesday Book, compiled in 1086, the church was described as part of the manor of Axminster and no group of priests was mentioned. Much history, reflecting political, social and ecclesiastical developments, lies behind the content of this writ and the people it named. That it was written in English, not in Latin, reveals an important and distinctive feature of Anglo-Saxon culture.

The Devonian subjects of this kingdom were "English" in name and in allegiance to the state created in the tenth century. But the pre-English population here had (according to current ways of thinking about the period, though no accurate data can be reconstructed) out-numbered the "Saxon" immigrants and, initially separate, they later integrated. Though by now unidentifiable, and their Celtic language lost, Devonian descendants of the old Dumnonians were still there in significant numbers (in Cornwall, Celtic-speaking people survived for much longer). Social interaction had a long history between these supposedly distinct cultures, including their royal dynasties. Two early "West Saxon" kings, Cerdic and Ceawlin, had British names. The name of another, Caedwalla, was a borrowed British name (Cadwallon). The name of yet another, Cenwalh, ended in an element meaning "Welsh" or "foreigner". Nevertheless, it was to their English origins that royal dynasties looked, whatever this early use of British

Prologue: Dumnonian and Saxon Foundations

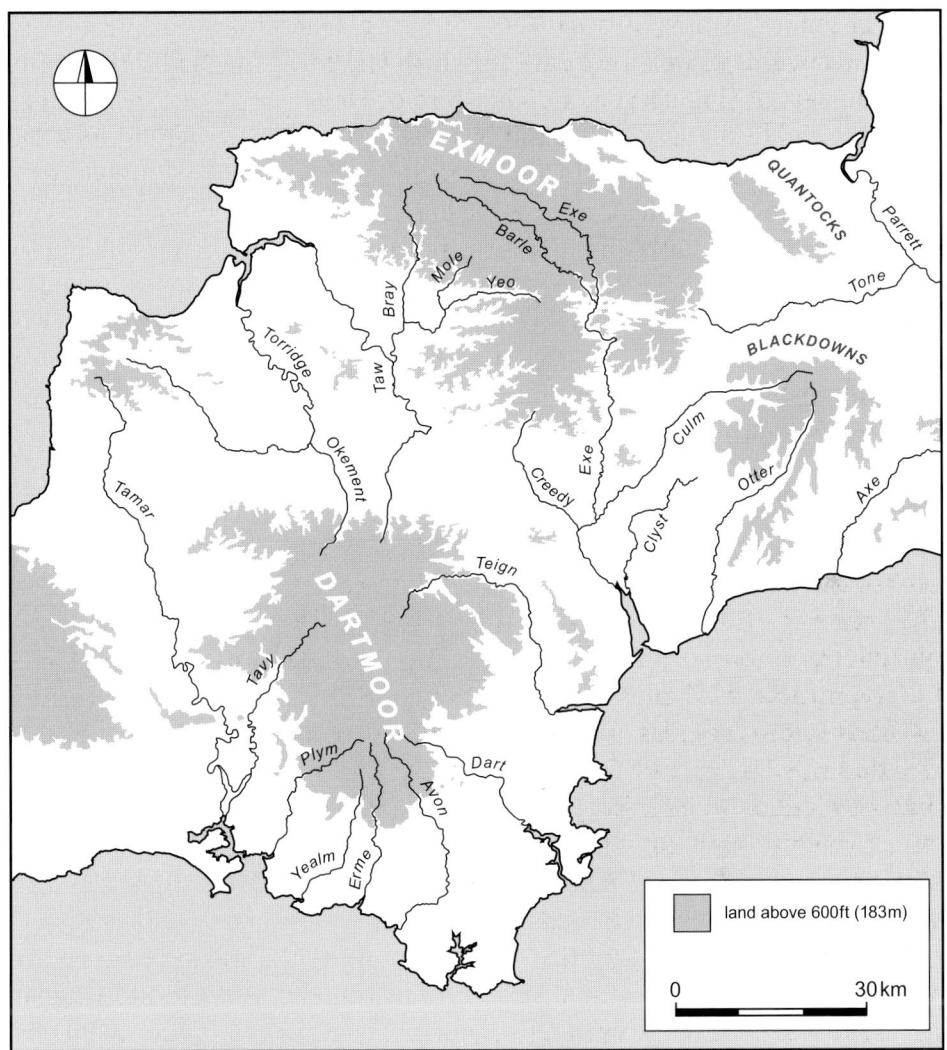

1.1: The physical framework: coasts, main rivers and higher land. The map extends eastwards to the rivers Axe and Parrett, the former limits of Dumnonia.
Map by Mike Rouillard.

names represented: perhaps symbolic of alliances, or perhaps arising from occasional marriage to high-born British women. The notion of "English" appeared clearly in the law-code of king Ine of Wessex at the end of the seventh century and, famously, in the monk Bede's *Ecclesiastical History* in the eighth. In the later ninth century, King Alfred created an enhanced idea of "Englishness" based in a part-historic, part-mythical Germanic past, to bolster West Saxon resistance to the Vikings. Later still, a sense of "Celticness" was stimulated in Cornwall, again partly from reality and partly from artifice, in the renewed veneration of western saints and promotion of ancient lore. In the nineteenth and twentieth centuries, Cornwall has also been caught up in the modern Celtic revival. Thus, notions of a dual past came to characterise the region, but neither fully reflected the true story of the post-Roman centuries. Another layer masking the past was created by the nineteenth- and twentieth-century emphasis on a narrative dominated by invasion, conquest and new settlement: very much a cultural product of Europe's imperial world experience. Thus, in addition to frequent paucity of contemporary evidence, various barriers lie between us and the early middle ages. In our time, as various historians have noted, we have the cultural baggage of the post-imperial age, as well as multi-culturalism, European integration and British political devolution, all of which can affect our attitudes to the early middle ages, also an era of cultural flux, of immigration and emigration and of political re-structuring.

This book might have been entitled *Dumnonians and Saxons in Early Devon*. But whereas the general public (at whom it is aimed) might now have an idea who the Saxons were, the Dumnonians (by name) have disappeared from the view of anyone not already acquainted with the period. But they bulked large in south-western populations, and some of their descendants must still survive here. "Anglo-Saxon Devon" is a problematic phrase in that it apparently suppresses the underlying Dumnonian contribution. But in another sense it is an apt label: everyone in the shire which emerged eventually regarded themselves as English, and the politically and linguistically dominant group within the shire had West Saxon origins. But the Dumnonians also survive within the phrase "Anglo-Saxon Devon" because their territory provided the name "Devon" when transformed into the Old English language. The Old English forms (*Defena* – men of Devon, *Defenascir* – Devonshire) may well reflect the pronunciation of the British word (which the Saxons presumably borrowed and adapted) for the Latin *Dumnonia*.

The British kingdom of Dumnonia originally embraced not only Cornwall and Devon but also part of what became west Somerset (see Chapter Two). Devon's absorption by a Saxon kingdom based in Hampshire and Wiltshire means that in order to make sense of "the Saxons and Devon" frequent reference to events and places immediately outside the modern county, in both the eastward and westward directions, is necessary. Further, because not everything which was happening in Devon is documented directly by

Prologue: Dumnonian and Saxon Foundations

"Devonian" sources, it is also necessary sometimes to extrapolate from trends of events occurring elsewhere in England. In the later seventh and eighth centuries Devon was to some extent a "frontier territory", but the paucity of documentation makes its nature difficult to observe in detail. In a better-documented period of time, its study might have contributed to the recently-flourishing field of enquiry into border societies, occupying the interface between cultures and peoples, for example in medieval Wales and Ireland. The loss of part of eastern Dumnonia to Somerset has had both historic and also academic consequences, from which the present book admittedly suffers. The shire boundary cuts through the Exmoor area, a zone with topographical and settlement integrity which should really, as in Hazel Riley's and Robert Wilson North's survey, be studied as a region regardless of the county division. Exmoor is a classic example of where "county-based study" does not always do justice to history or archaeology, despite the enormous cultural and administrative importance which the shires have had.

The two regions within Dumnonia, later known as Devon and Cornwall, represented an ancient division: it is not clear how culturally unified Dumnonia had been, despite having a common royal dynasty in the immediate post-Roman centuries. As Charles Thomas, in his studies of the inscribed memorial stones, has pointed out, once Devon had become English, "Cornishness" in the extreme south west aimed to preserve some independence there, not to restore an ancient and larger Dumnonia. The two Dumnonian regions had different experiences in becoming "English". The slow nature of the area's incorporation meant that Devon had a longer experience as a West Saxon shire than did Cornwall, which had not long been part of Wessex before Wessex itself became part of England. This difference was to influence south-western history and attitudes for centuries, indeed down to modern times. Moreover, the West Saxon kingdom was an evolving institution throughout its own life. It was at a crucial stage of internal development around 700 when the absorption of Devon was under way. It was a changed Wessex which defeated the Cornish (though not finally) around 800. It was a Wessex further changed which had successfully resisted the vikings by around 900. Wessex had changed further still by around 1000, when it was part of an English state resisting more Scandinavian pressure.

Similarly, we must not imagine that the westward-shrinking British area retained an unaltered, monolithic culture throughout these centuries. Indeed, as its population was progressively absorbed within the new society of a growing Wessex, it is likely that internal change within the ever-smaller independent area to the west was also stimulated. Thus, by the Norman Conquest, the south west was not simply the product of a defeat of a Celtic-speaking people by a Germanic-speaking people. It was rather the product of a pattern of evolution over many centuries. Several authors have treated the early part of the period as one of conquest: most famously, W.G. Hoskins in *The Westward Expansion of Wessex* (1960); also H.M. Porter, *The Saxon Conquest of Somerset and Devon* (1967), and recently M. Lambert, *The West Saxon Conquest of Devon and Somerset* (privately published:1999). But such a process is very difficult to reconstruct in reliable detail, and in any case hardly does justice to complex developments stretched out through time. An important theme of this book is that the Dumnonian population must have survived in Devon to a great extent even though it eventually became historically "invisible". In contrast, the story of English "conquest", in so far as it can be reconstructed, was the story remembered by, and thus the history created by, "the winners". Occasionally, in the Welsh sources of later date we find reference to Dumnonian matters, but with little comment, and earlier Gildas wrote from a British viewpoint. We depend, however, upon the *Anglo-Saxon Chronicle* for most of the recorded "events": and these came from the folk memory and earlier records of what, by the ninth century, was the dominant culture.

In a very important respect, an account of the early middle ages in Devon disappoints. The settlement archaeology and mundane artefactual data are so thin, that a description of "everyday life" in terms of material culture cannot be offered as it can for more easterly areas, richer in excavated sites and in the grave-goods of pagan Germanic religion. When the West Saxons came to Dumnonia they were already nominally Christian, as were the Dumnonians themselves. Beneficial though Christianity may have been to those concerned, its adoption means we cannot portray these people, adorned in costume jewellery and surrounded by household objects, as we can elsewhere. Indeed, we might ask whether, if we had only the physical evidence, we would suspect a West Saxon "conquest" of the south west at all, since specifically "English" data, such as coins and sculpture, do not occur until quite late in the period. In order to see what is lacking, the reader should consult, for example, M. Welch's *Anglo-Saxon England* (1992), or S. Glaswell's *The Earliest English* (2002) or K. Leahy's *Anglo-Saxon Crafts* (2003). Judicious use of artefact data has been excellently discussed on a wider front in D. Hinton's *Gold and Gilt, Pots and Pins: Possessions and People in Medieval Britain* (2005), which explores material culture as a source for the reconstruction both of social life and of senses of social identity. Sadly, such an exercise is impossible for early medieval Devon, though neighbouring Cornwall has a more varied surviving record in its larger numbers of inscribed stone memorials, and its native post-Roman production of pottery and stone artefacts: here, social identity in material culture may have been more apparent (see Quinnell 1993). But, to judge from surviving (or, rather, non-surviving) evidence, early Devonians of both British and English descent seem not to have enjoyed a conspicuous material culture. Caution is, however, required: it would be unwarranted to assume that early Devonians were therefore impoverished. Wealth and status can be held in control of land, livestock and people; fine wooden and leather artefacts can perform the functions of more archaeologically-stable pottery and metal items. And intellectual life, however rich, can remain quite invisible if not written down.

It is all too easy to study the past without actually picturing its people in one's mind. Good treatments of early medieval costume are to be found in C.R. Dodwell's *Anglo-Saxon Art* (1982) and in G.R. Owen-Crocker's *Dress in Anglo-Saxon England* (1986; revised edition 2004). There was much conservatism in dress over many centuries, revealed in evidence from England generally: from burials of the pagan period, from brief written references and from sculptural and manuscript art. The common use of brooches of various designs makes women's graves the more revealing. They wore a sleeved undergarment, a sleeved or sleeveless gown, girdled at the waist, with a cloak on top. Men wore a shirt, tunic, cloak and trousers (or leggings) with a buckled belt. Materials used were wool, linen, animal furs and leather (for belts and shoes). Status was shown in degrees of elaboration on these items, rather than in different types of garment: imported silk and embroidery were available to the wealthier people. Clerical vestments and some royal robes were more specialised. The repertoire of Dumnonian dress cannot have been much different, though the choice of brooches to hold garments in place was influenced by culture: in the Celtic-speaking areas of Britain ring-headed pins and penannular brooches were common. In the fifth and sixth centuries, differences between the British and English may have been clear in their clothing, hairstyles and costume jewellery. But by the later seventh century, when West Saxons were settling in eastern Dumnonia, such differences were probably far less obvious: by this time the art-styles of Britain's various cultural groups were being fused and visible differences between them probably becoming less clear. Within a Devonian context at this time, perhaps "Briton" and "Saxon" of comparable social standing did not look too different from each other.

The vast bulk of the population inhabiting the south-west peninsula in these centuries were illiterate. Until quite late in the period it is most unlikely that anyone not connected with the Church could read. At the beginning of the period, some legacy of the secular education available in the late Roman world was still available, as is revealed by Gildas's Latin-educated background and his expectation of an audience who would respond to him. Thereafter, the world of learning was essentially an ecclesiastical one. Even from the late ninth century onwards, when education had been spread more widely through king Alfred's initiatives, secular literacy would have been limited: restricted to the noble class and the local land-owners, the shire administrators in royal service and the moneyers in the towns (whose coins, with mint-names and moneyers' names, as well as kings' names, imply some degree of secular literacy in society). Historians cannot agree, however, on just how "literate" late Anglo-Saxon society was, though it is clear that written documents were important in many spheres of life. Many people could probably write their name or recognise a name, for example in a charter or its witness-list. But fewer could read more generally and even fewer could write at length. In contrast, it has been suggested that some slaves were literate, providing a service for their owners. In Appendix 3, I have listed the names of some influential people in pre-Norman Devon. They were all members of the literate class and are known to us because they occur in certain sorts of written sources. Compilation of a much wider range of named people, many of them illiterate, remains a task (for someone) at some future date.

It is a paradox that, in writing a history of this period, it is so difficult to know what ordinary people knew of their own history at this time. The issue of how English memories of the English-British confrontation were eventually included in the *Anglo-Saxon Chronicle,* in Alfred's reign, is touched on in Chapter 2. But for how long was knowledge of the rich and powerful Dumnonians, whose inscribed memorial stones still survive, retained in popular culture? To what extent did Dumnonians, even when becoming "English", preserve their heritage in family or wider circles: distinguishing for a time, perhaps, their public from their private lives? Indeed, we may ask exactly how much mundane detail of their own personal part-immigrant past (as opposed to their memories of past leaders and victories) was known by the ordinary West Saxons who settled in Dumnonia from the later seventh century? St Boniface, however, who was born in Devon, seems to have been conscious of his family's Germanic past, or at least of the general link between the English and the continent: he devoted his life to mission work in Germany (see Appendix 1). From today's perspective, we see the period and its society as one eventually (and successfully) blended from different elements. But we should also try to discard this familiar view, which is based on knowledge of the end-product, in order to appreciate the complexities of the situation which went before.

There is another area where an apparently familiar world must be discarded: we must beware the danger inherent in the continuously-evolving world of Christianity which is still with us. To say that a society was Christian in the early middle ages does not imply it practised religion, or held beliefs in quite the manner familiar to us today, or even the manner of the later middle ages. Very early in the period, it may well have been an elitist culture and the Christianity of many in rural society was perhaps fairly nominal. Throughout the whole period, most of the population could not read the Bible for themselves. Up to the eleventh century, when local churches were slowly emerging and ordinary people might have easier access to a church, rural populations depended partly on some old churches surviving from the Dumnonian period and also on the ministry of priests operating from English minster churches whose territories could be extensive. Itinerant royal and noble households had regular access to minster churches. But for most of society, for baptisms and burials, a sometimes lengthy journey was necessary. At other times, they depended on the visits of minster priests for their religious observance. In a recent assessment of church history-writing (Rowan Williams, *Why Study the Past? The Quest for the Historical Church.* 2005), the Archbishop of Canterbury has argued that in order to understand the past, we must first make it unfamiliar: abandon the assumptions we hold because they will be a barrier to understanding. This is good advice for historical study in general. But, despite the various obstacles to our journey, the "other country" which the early medieval past of Devon represents is a fascinating place to visit. Though, while it has left us an important legacy, it was a very different world from our own.

This book is interdisciplinary, with written or physical data leading the way as evidence dictates, but with neither theoretically dominant. This has always been my view of how the middle ages should be studied. Although sometimes complementary, historical and archaeological evidence reveal different sorts of past, neither of which (if we are honest) is always wholly convincing: there is an inevitable compromise between the understanding for which we settle and the reality of the past which, our instinct tells us, lies somewhere beyond and just out of grasp. Bearing in mind the intended non-specialist readership (to whom I am, in consequence, grateful in this respect) this book steers clear of the more theoretical ways of treating archaeological data and, broadly, an overall "historical" narrative and analysis is attempted. I have tried, as far as possible, to write about a past which early Devonians – were they somehow to be miraculously transported into the twenty-first century and confronted with it – might actually recognise in outline: even if, with benefit of hindsight, we can see trends and patterns which were less obvious, even invisible, to those whom we study. Thus I have tried to avoid writing about a past which is simply a modern intellectual construction, the product of academic navel-gazing. We should remember, however, that in attempting to re-create even a simple version of the past, we also create it. Our Dumnonian and Saxon ancestors would have understood that well, for that is what they did, from time to time, in making their "histories": for example, as new narratives of "remembered" events or as new records of "remembered" royal land grants.

The history "created" in this book is, broadly, a sketch of how various cultural groupings – the less-Romanised Britons, the more-Romanised Britons, a post-Roman Dumnonian society which emerged from them both, and a more Germanic-rooted group which moved into the south west – eventually merged to produce a unified society occupying a shire created out of part of old Dumnonia. This society, which regarded itself as "English", was first part of a West Saxon kingdom, and later part of an English one. The creation of this English society involved the progressive suppression of things "British". Various processes contributed to this, some being thrust upon Dumnonia from outside but others working from within it. Military victories, the advancement of new landowners and clerics from Wessex, the acceptability only of the Old English language in matters of church and state – these were the obvious signs of West Saxon "conquest". But alongside these processes, we can also see that the Dumnonians themselves must eventually have acquiesced in their own cultural disappearance: so as not to remain second-class citizens in a Saxon-dominated culture, they changed their language and their names and became "English". We may envisage a paradox in the seventh and early eighth centuries: the noble and land-owning Dumnonian class, upon whom military resistance depended, were also the people who, by making concessions, might preserve their traditional influence in local society. Thus we can imagine a situation in which not only was Devonian "Britishness" despised and suppressed by the English, but perhaps eventually also by the Devonian British themselves. To set this issue in a domestic context, we may suppose that, early on, Dumnonian families encouraged their children to speak British as a sign of pride and defiance. But later on, perhaps they discouraged or forbade it, knowing its use would impede their children's prospects in the new society which was now emerging.

When these societies began to interact, the Dumnonian and West Saxon groups to be found in various parts of Devon were politically, linguistically and culturally distinct (and had only recently lost a religious difference). Two centuries later, these distinctions had been subsumed by a sense of common (English) political and cultural allegiance. But there is also another way to define people: that is biologically, by their DNA. Research in this area (where I have no competence) has led to diverse ideas about the early middle ages: emphasising greater or lesser degrees of immigration from the continent. DNA evidence can confound long-held assumptions about origins. The message seems to be that the groupings created by people for themselves, on linguistic and other grounds, cut across biological lines. In this book, I have followed a traditional path: arguing that it is who people *think* they are (as well as who they are *thought* to be, by others) and who people *choose* to be that matters, both now and in the past: it is this which influences people's thoughts, words and deeds. In the particular matter of Germanic immigration, the issue is in any case less critical in the south west: by the time of its absorption in Wessex, the West Saxons themselves may have been a very hybrid British-Germanic population.

Had I lived in Devon in the fifth, sixth or early seventh centuries, I would have been an ultra-conservative Dumnonian, deeply disapproving of developments taking place further east where people with Germanic, or part-Germanic roots held increasing power. Had I lived here in the later seventh or eighth centuries, as Briton or Saxon, I would have been loyal to my own culture but open to interaction: if British, particularly aware of the advantage, and increasingly the necessity, of learning and speaking English. Had I lived here in the ninth to early eleventh centuries, regardless of my ancestry (if I knew it) I would have defended "English" Christian society against Scandinavians who were often pagans, heartily subscribing to the strengthened notion of English nationhood fostered by king Alfred and his successors. Had I lived here in the eleventh century, as a member of this early nation-state, I would have supported the anti-Norman rebellion of 1067–69, loyal to a strong sense of English local community focussed on the shire and on the city of Exeter. My hypothetical ancestor's evolving attitudes would, I think, in these ways have been a microcosm of Devonian social origins.

2

People and Place

Social groups, language and culture (*Figs 1.1, 2.1, 2.2, 2.3, 2.4*)

Early English kingdoms had populations with two components: first, descendants of the indigenous Romano-British people; second, descendants of the Germanic immigrants who came from north-west Europe to Britain in the fourth, fifth and sixth centuries. These kingdoms, described in the eighth century by Bede, the Northumbrian monk, included those of the South, East and West Saxons, with the various Anglian kingdoms to their north. From his northern view-point, Bede established an important precedent in the title of his famous work, *The Ecclesiastical History of the English People*, which in a very important sense marked the first stage in the creation of an English nation (though the notion of being "English" already existed – see below, on king Ine's law-code). But only in the tenth century did the second stage occur, on the emergence from Aethelstan's reign onwards of a single kingdom of "England", with a name derived from the Anglian regions but with a dynasty derived from the West Saxons. This second stage, however, had an important precursor, as described by Sarah Foot: facing the major threat of the vikings who had conquered the northern and eastern territories, Alfred had developed a binding sense of Englishness amongst unconquered West Saxons and western Mercians by promoting a common written language – a West-Saxon-based *Englisc* – in education, in translation of Latin works into the vernacular and in the compilation of the *Anglo-Saxon Chronicle*. Upon this foundation, there was to be a marked expansion of written Old English, for many purposes both secular and ecclesiastical, alongside Latin.

The Celtic-speaking neighbours of the English referred to them as Saxons

– *Saesneg* (viewed from the far west) and *Sassenach* (viewed from the far north). For those north of the old Roman frontier, the "English" employed the tribal name of *Scotti* (who had originally emigrated from Ireland). The Britons in the unconquered far west, as well as those still within the English kingdoms, were called (in the plural) *Walas* or *Wealas*, Old English words (singular: *Walh, Wealh*) with a general sense of "foreigner" but probably, to start with, labelling the Latin- and Celtic-speakers of the old Roman provinces who did not speak English. Thus emerged Wales and the Welsh in English terminology: a mixture of geographical description and somewhat disparaging comment. Ironically, English useage has become widely employed in Wales, but to themselves the Welsh were, and are, *y Cymry*, which has the much more positive sense of "fellow countrymen", and their language is *Cymraeg*. In discussing the early middle ages in south west England, the adjective "Celtic" is best used only to indicate the language use of northern and western Britain generally and not to invite debate on wider issues about what "Celtic-ness" might have meant. Bede said that five languages were spoken in his day: English, Latin, Irish (that is, Scottic), Pictish and British. Who, apart from the English, these people actually were, in wider ethnic and cultural terms is part of a pan-European Celtic problem, which stretches back into prehistory, explored in a fascinating manner by many scholars. The collection of essays edited by Miranda Green, and the more personalised treatment by John Collis are especially helpful. Throughout this book on Devon, the earlier inhabitants of the region are referred to as Celtic- or British-speaking, British or Dumnonian, according to context. The new arrivals are referred to specifically as (West) Saxon, but sometimes as Anglo-Saxon or simply English. Eventually, everyone became "English" regardless of origins.

"Englishness" – in its linguistic, cultural and political forms – was not imported from northern Europe, but made in southern Britain. The Anglo-Saxon kingdoms did not represent pre-existing units of power: they were created within Britain and later given their own foundation mythologies. The immigrants' language soon diverged from its continental source: Old English developed *in situ* and also developed regional dialects as the various kingdoms emerged. But, and very significantly for future developments, Old English was wholly Germanic in character and was not a hybrid tongue extensively embracing the vocabulary of the contemporary native British tongue, that is, the immediate ancestor of the Welsh, Cornish, Cumbric (in today's north-west England and south-west Scotland) and (across the sea) Breton tongues. This post-Roman British language is usually referred to as Brittonic, to distinguish it from the earlier Celtic language of late prehistoric and Roman times. As Thomas Charles-Edwards has clearly demonstrated, language and perceptions of social status were closely related. While the indigenous population may have felt themselves superior on grounds of precedent and their Christianity, the newcomers thought the British language socially inferior to their own and did not learn it (though their patterns of common speech may have been influenced by it – see below). Written Old English borrowed vocabulary from the Latin used in Britain, because that was seen as a suitably high-status language; but it borrowed hardly any vocabulary from British, which was seen as a lowly language. Correspondingly, a sense of "Britishness" in the shrinking western territories was sharpened as the Anglo-Saxons extended their power. At first, the native population was conscious of preserving a Latin-based Christian culture in the face of a Germanic-based pagan one. Later, while "Welshness" was still looked down upon by the English, it became the sole symbol of British independence in southern Britain until the final conquest of north Wales by king Edward I in the late thirteenth century. By that time, the Anglo-Saxon period had itself come to be seen as the origin of important principles of "English liberty", variously construed in personal, legal, ecclesiastical and constitutional terms right down to the nineteenth century. Julia Crick has shown how these ideas were really manipulations of the past: the essential idea of Anglo-Saxon *libertas* had been quite narrow, relating to freedom of land, granted by royal charter, from most of its traditional obligations to the kings (see below, Chapter 4).

An important dimension to the confrontation of British and English, that is the religious dimension, had (with our benefit of hindsight) a tragic element from the British point of view. It appears that both societies abandoned paganism without too much trouble (though Bede recorded reversions in the English areas). Rather like modern consumers faced with the hard-sell of domestic utilities, English and British, at different times and from different sources of influence, succumbed to the appeal of a single god who could provide all their needs: more effective than relying on numerous deities for individual provision of particular services. Christianity was ultimately a binding force crucial to the welding of all elements of the population, of whatever origin, into an English state. In the early stages, however, the tension between British and English churches was very great and must have posed some barrier to social integration even if their common Christianity meant there was no general "culture clash" as there was later with pagan vikings. But there were different practices, including styles of tonsures and calculation of Easter dates, as well as a resentment on the part of the English, voiced by Bede, that the indigenous Christians of southern Britain had not evangelised the English (unlike the Irish, northern British, and the Roman missions, which had). Keeping their Christianity to themselves may originally have been important to preserving the southern British sense of superiority over the pagan English. Had they been more pro-active in converting the English to Christianity, it is possible that the British might have secured a more influential role at an early date in the new political and social order which emerged in England. In contrast, in light of the second-class status which the English thrust upon the British, we may wonder how much "preaching" from the southern British the English would have tolerated. But, as Barbara Yorke has pointed out, Bede's attitude to the conversion was unbalanced: he was much better informed about eastern than western England and, for all we know, Christian occupants of what are now east Devon, Somerset and Dorset may have given some new religious encouragement to their English neighbours.

In what we might call its "political" dimension, Anglo-Saxon power gradually extended westwards, reaching the Severn estuary as a result of events which, much later, were remembered in the *Anglo-Saxon Chronicle* as the victory at Dyrham in 577: the place now called Dyrham lies north of Bath. It has often been said that, from this time, when Gloucester, Cirencester and Bath came under English control, "the free Welsh" became divided into two groups: the south-west peninsula occupied by the "west Welsh" and the land we now call Wales occupied by the "north Welsh". This is true in geographical terms, but it is important not to assume a previously continuous zone of British territory under some sort of unified leadership. As is clear from the account of Gildas, who described five tyrannical kings whose individual authorities were dispersed from Devon and Cornwall, up the (later) Welsh border, and into various parts of Wales, the western areas in British control were already politically fragmented by his time (variously suggested to have been the later-fifth or mid-sixth century). Nicholas Higham has, however, suggested that Gildas reveals Maglocunus (the king in Anglesey and north-west Wales) having overlordship over the other kings. The "west Welsh" of Dumnonia gradually disappeared as a visible culture as the kingdom of the West Saxons slowly absorbed them, but the "north Welsh" enjoyed degrees of independence from England for many centuries. Kenneth Jackson argued that the separate linguistic development of south-western British (later Cornish) and "Welsh" British

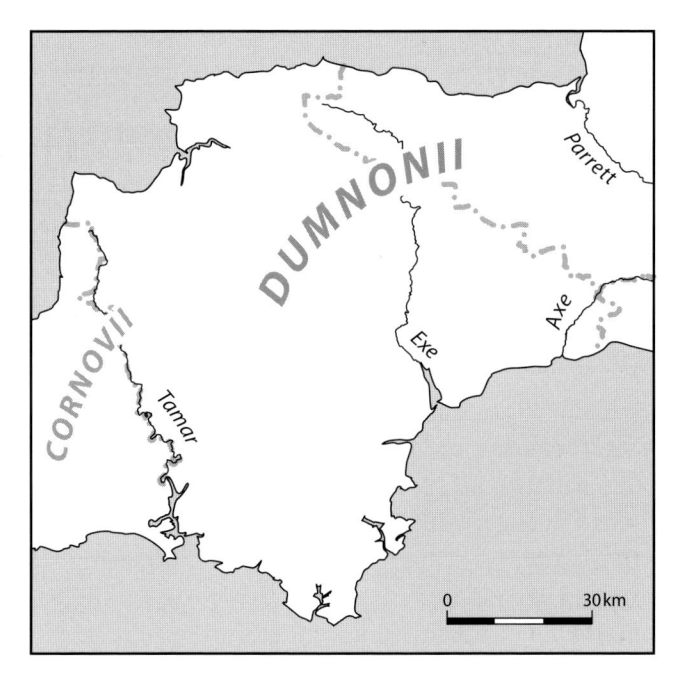

2.1: Central and eastern Dumnonia. The modern county boundaries are imposed. Map by Mike Rouillard.

accelerated around this time, though the two regions may already have had some differences of dialect.

By the Norman Conquest, the south west contained two shires, Devon and Cornwall. These shire names derived from much earlier terms of British origin. The south-western tribe of the pre-Roman and Roman periods had been the *Dumnonii*, whose territory occupied the whole south-western region: its eastern boundary is not known exactly, but it occupied a zone bounded by the rivers Parrett (in the north) and Axe (in the south) and the higher land, Quantocks and Blackdowns respectively, to their west. East of this region, the tribes known as the *Durotriges* and *Dobunni* had been coin-producing before the Roman conquest, which the *Dumnonii* had not. The Lizard peninsula was called the Dumnonian Promontory in Ptolemy's second-century *Geography* (which also named the rivers Exe – *Isca,* and Tamar – *Tamarus*). The region's tribal name is recorded on two inscriptions (*Civitas Dumni* and *Civitas Dumnon*) from Hadrian's Wall, arising from its contribution of resources to the re-furbishing of the northern frontier. Its centre, known to us as Exeter, was named from the British name of the river on which it stood and was thus called *Isca Dumnoniorum*. The succeeding

2.2: Two inscriptions from Hadrian's Wall, recording work by men from the *Civitas Dumnoniorum*. Drawn by R.P. Wright in Fox 1952.

British kingdom here was called *Damnonia* by Gildas (perhaps, as suggested by Nicholas Higham, intending an insulting pun based on *damnum*, in view of his moral castigation of its king, Constantine). Nicholas Higham has also argued that Gildas wrote from a base not far away in Wiltshire or Dorset, an area under English overlordship: close enough to be familiar with Dumnonian events, but distant enough not to fear its king's authority. In a letter from Aldhelm, abbot of Malmesbury, to the Dumnonian king Geraint, written around 700, it was spelt *Domnonia*. In his late ninth-century *Life* of king Alfred, Asser used the Latin *Domnania* for Devon alone. In later Welsh, Devon was known as *Dyfneint*, which also had the Dumnonian root. In modern historical writing it is customary to call the south-western kingdom *Dumnonia*, following the earlier form of *Dumnonii* from the Romano-British period. In formal Latin, *Dumnonia* continued to mean "Devon" for several centuries – as late as twelfth-century writers such as William of Malmesbury. Eventually, however, English forms took precedence in speech and writing. They had early origins: in reference to the events of 825, 851 and 893 described in the *Anglo-Saxon Chronicle,* we find Old English labels derived from the Latin root, supplemented with Old English *scir*: the men of Devon were *Defne* or *Defene* and the shire was *Defnescir* or *Defenascir*.

Cornwall eventually took its name from the occupants of a Dumnonian sub-territory, who were known as the *Cornovii*. Their name was compounded by the English with the *Walas* element of their own language, which reveals much about how they regarded this area. In modern usage, and somewhat paradoxically, Cornwall thus has a half-English name, whereas Devon's (when shorn of its Old English "shire" suffix) is British-based. In a poem of c. 700, also written by Aldhelm when he visited the region, a distinction was made in Latin between Devon (*Dumnonia)* and

Cornwall (*Cornubia*, perhaps also a name of earlier origin) both of which were described in unflattering terms. Though their boundary at this time is not known, the Tamar seems the most obvious possibility. The names were also to influence the administrative geography of Brittany as a result of emigration (see below). In his *Life* of king Alfred, Asser talked of the jurisdiction of Exeter's church (which he received from that king) being in both Saxon lands and in Cornwall (*in Saxonia et in Cornubia*). Interestingly, as late as the mid-eleventh century, there is evidence of ancient English attitudes to Cornwall: in an endorsement of Exeter Cathedral's "foundation charter" (see Chapter 3), the Devonian and Cornish bishoprics (which were now amalgamated) were referred to (in Old English) as *on defenan* and *on wealan*. The twelfth-century writer William of Malmesbury described how the tenth-century West Saxon king Aethelstan fixed the Tamar as the shire boundary when he expelled the remaining British population from the city of Exeter and forcibly moved them to the far west. He may simply have been restoring an ancient Dumnonian boundary, now as a feature of English administration. Aethelstan, according to William, also fixed the English border with the "north Welsh" at the river Wye.

When the West Saxons first extended their authority south-westwards, in the seventh century, they found an indigenous population who were descendants of the Romano-British inhabitants. These people spoke a Celtic language whose closest British living parallel is Welsh (and revived Cornish). Some historians of language now argue that in lowland Roman Britain the British language had become heavily Latinised and that westward movement of Britons in the fifth-sixth centuries accounts for the borrowings from Latin which we find in later Cornish and Welsh. For example, some Cornish place-names, like Welsh ones, contain *martyrium* and *ecclesia* elements: *merther/eglos* in Cornish and *merthyr/eglwys* in Welsh. But the early history of language use is a notoriously complex subject: whether Latin in Roman Britain was an essentially official language, or was adopted in more ordinary use, remains controversial. The post-Roman south-western population was at least partly Christian and Latin was certainly used by its educated clerical class. Figures of high status, both clerical and secular, were commemorated in stone memorials, inscribed in Latin and also sometimes in an Irish script known as *Ogam,* derived either directly from immigrants or indirectly from Irish settlers in Wales. Brought to post-Roman western Britain by the Irish, it was used by their leaders to show, on their stone memorials, an equal social standing with the Latin-using local rich. Inscribed memorials are plentiful in Wales,

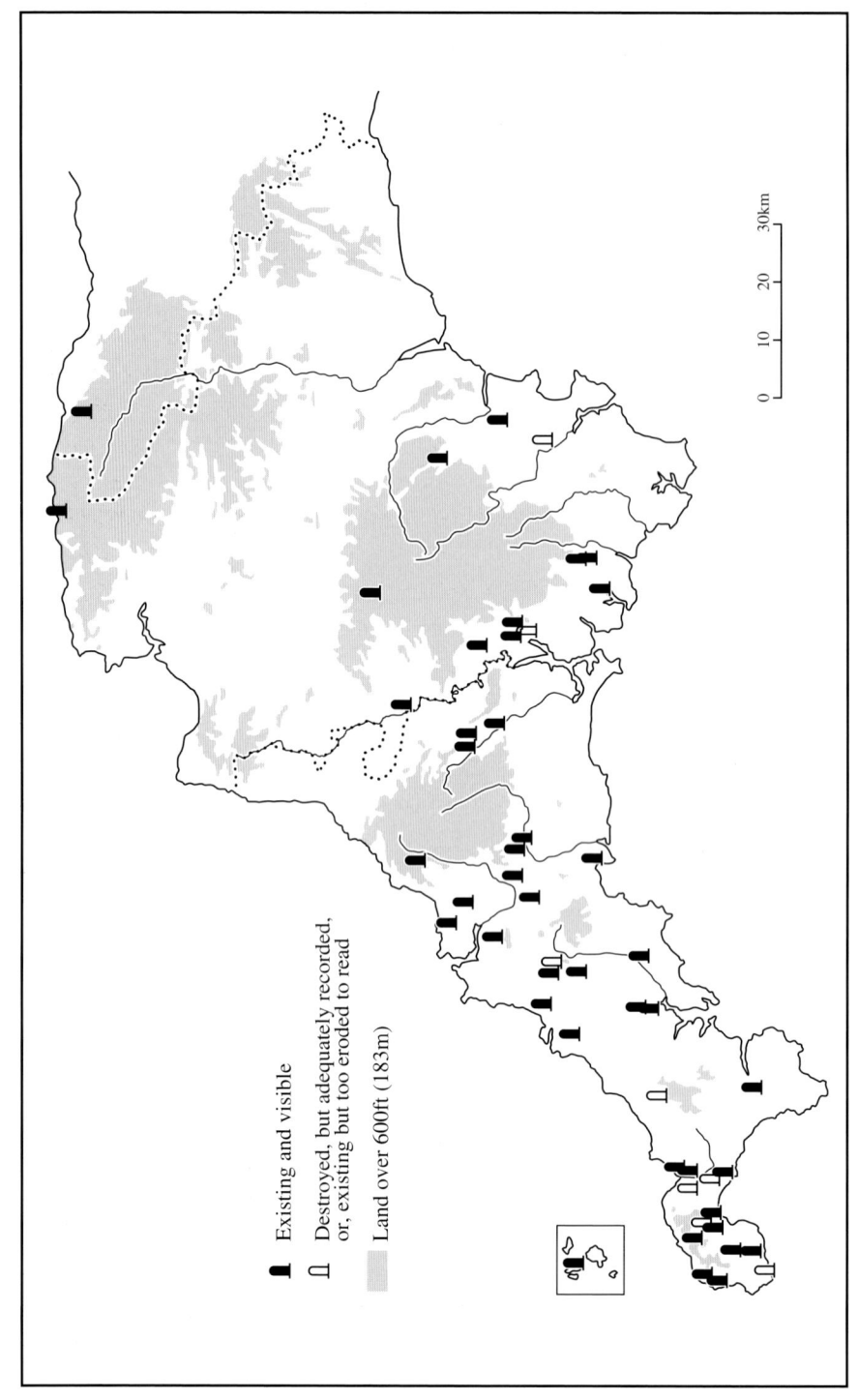

2.3: Inscribed memorial stones in Dumnonia, by Charles Thomas in Kain & Ravenhill (eds) 1999 (two additions in north Devon/Somerset). Positions of some "lost" stones, eg. Parracombe in north Devon, not shown. By permission of the author, University of Exeter Press and Roger Kain.

People and Place

and in south west England the majority of the surviving examples are in Cornwall. As in much of the western and northern British Isles, the Devon memorials (fewer than twenty in number) are in the form of upright, unworked pillar-stones with their texts arranged vertically (two examples on Lundy Island represent an alternative tradition, with horizontal texts). Their inspiration has been controversial, though their shape was surely modelled on the Roman milestones which would have been a familiar sight. Some have argued their origin in late Roman times, others only in the later fifth century resulting from influences in Wales and Gaul. Good arguments have recently been put forward, however, by Malcolm Todd and others, for a continuity of inscription practice from Roman to post-Roman times in the western and northern British areas which were not at first affected by Germanic culture: the inscriptions reflect, in archaeological terms, the on-going use of Latin in these areas – at least in the higher social circles – which is attested by documentary sources, and which is assumed in the audience to which an educated British writer such as Gildas appealed.

The names found on these memorials in the south west are a mixture of Latin, British and Irish, which well reflects the social interactions of Dumnonian society. Their aristocratic context is revealed occasionally by title and also by emphasis on genealogy: a common form reads "(the memorial) of *X* the son of *Y*". Much effort has gone into attempting dated sequences within these memorials, based on epigraphic (letter form) and phonological (language content and pronunciation) analyses, and much specialist literature has emerged which is too complex to describe here. But one recent analysis, by Charles Thomas, has proposed that they were introduced here by immigrants from south Wales, and that the earlier intrusive examples can be distinguished from the subsequent native ones. But, as the *corpus* of evidence compiled by Elizabeth Okasha shows, specific and independent dating is elusive and none is certainly in its original location (and some are known to have been moved in modern times). In the north of the territory, one example stands at Winsford Hill (now north-west Somerset, but originally in Dumnonia), one at Lynton and four in Lundy. Another was at Parracombe but has been lost since the 18th century. The Winsford Hill stone bears the British name *Caratacus*, and one of the Lundy stones bears the name *Tigernus*, again British. At Lynton, we encounter *Cauudus, son of Civilis* – the former British, the latter Roman. The remaining Devonian examples are in the south west of the county. They include several at Tavistock: *Nepranus, son of Conbevus* – the former a Roman name, the latter British; *Dobunnus the smith, son*

Making Anglo-Saxon Devon

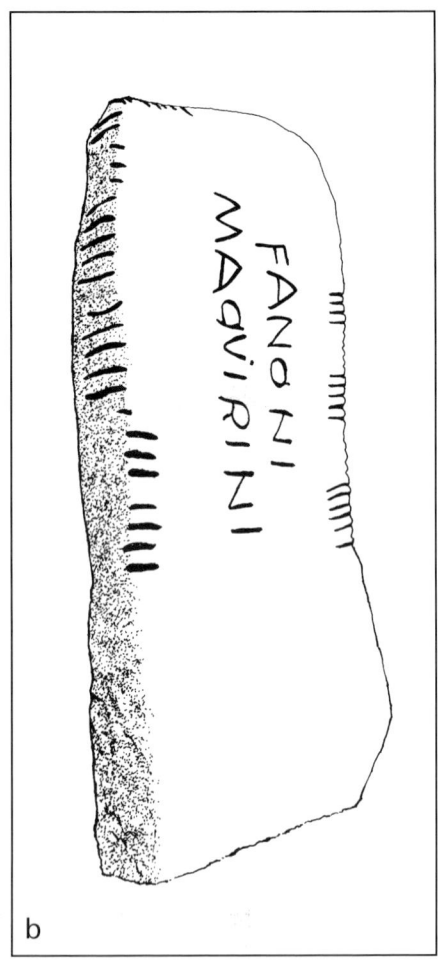

2.4: (a) Inscribed pillar-stone originally at Buckland Monachorum but moved to Tavistock vicarage garden in 1831. For discussion, see Okasha 1993, 274-277 (item Tavistock II). The Latin inscription, arranged in two vertical rows of capitals, reads: *SABINI FILI MACCODECHETI*, meaning "[the stone] of Sabinus, son of Maccodechetus".
The first name is British, the second Irish, but there is no *Ogam*.
Photograph: Royal Albert Memorial Museum and Art Gallery, Exeter.

(b) inscription (drawn from photograph in Okasha 1993) in Latin and *Ogam*, on one side of the memorial stone from Fardel, now in the British Museum. The vertical Latin inscription reads *FANONI MAQUIRINI*, meaning "[the stone] of Fanonus, son of Rinus"; the *Ogam* equivalent (with errors) is inscribed on the stone's edges. On its other side, the stone bears an inscription, in Latin, of an Irish name, Sagranus.
For discussion, see Thomas 1994, 267-8; Okasha 1993, 103-108.

of Enabarrus – the former British, the latter Irish, accompanied by an inscription in ogam; and *Sabinus son of Maccodechetus* – a British-named son of an Irish-named father, but with no ogam. At Lustleigh the inscription perhaps reads *Datuidoc, son of Conhino* – both British. At Sourton the stone commemorates a man who was *princeps*, a prince, and has a Chi-Rho symbol (the Greek letters representing "Christ"). The stone originally at Fardel, in Cornwood near Ivybridge, now in the British Museum, has texts in Latin and *Ogam*, commemorating people of Irish descent; at Yealmpton, an incomplete text includes the British name *Goreus*.

It is fascinating, if somewhat paradoxical, that since so little in general is known of Dumnonian society, these memorials present us with the specific data of named individuals. They are assumed to date from before the period of significant English influence or control in the eighth century. In contrast, a small group surviving in Wareham (Dorset) seems to represent a later-surviving British Christian community within an English-dominated society. Overall interpretation of the region's memorials is, however, bedevilled by the common issues of archaeological survival and distribution. If such memorials were always of stone, and their current distribution is meaningful, then (in the south west) they were essentially a Cornovian tradition which extended into west Devon (with odd outliers further east). If, on the other hand, there had also been wooden, carved equivalents (especially in areas with less suitable surface-available stone) the distribution may have been more widely Dumnonian. A potentially larger number would reflect perhaps the whole land-owning class. But a smaller number would seem to reflect only the highest nobility and royalty. The religious aspects of these problems are discussed below (see Chapter 3). A further aspect is the motivation for immigration of the Irish-speakers whose names and *Ogam* script occur on some memorials. It has been suggested that their movement may not have been a spontaneous element of the migration period as a whole, but rather the result of invitation from western British kings: thus the Irish were originally military supporters, rewarded with land. In Wales, at least one early medieval dynasty was of Irish origin. In both matters, there are parallels with earlier Roman invitations to Germanic settlers in more easterly areas, as well as with their unforeseen consequences.

In the late eleventh century, we can determine from exactly which places in northern France came the Norman and other conquerors: family-names, place-names and other links can often be matched with places in Normandy, Britanny and Flanders. But our view of "English" origins is more general. Bede ascribed the continental homelands to areas we know as northern Germany, Jutland and the Low Countries, and archaeological study broadly supports this. These Germanic newcomers, the "Anglo-Saxons", though sharing with their Celtic-speaking Christian neighbours a reliance on agriculture, were different from them in their language and, initially, in their practice of pagan religion. The peoples named by Bede as Angles, Saxons and Jutes originally worshipped a wide variety of gods in a religion based partly in the countryside and partly in shrines, but, as far as we know, having no organised "institutions" comparable with those of the Christian tradition. They were converted to Christianity from two main sources: missions from the continental Roman church; missions from the northern British church and its Irish antecedents. Also relevant, despite the lack of official southern British evangelisation, must have been a process of acculturation accompanying their spread westwards and the incorporation into their kingdoms of a significant British Christian population. Christianity also brought literacy to the Anglo-Saxons, though at first confined to the clerical class and, even later, limited in society at large. Like the contemporary Irish, they applied literacy to their vernacular language and not simply to the Latin used by clerics: literacy was eventually an important tool in government as well as in the Church. Ecclesiastical writing remained mainly in Latin, as did the opening texts of charters. But royal law-codes, charter boundaries, wills and, famously, the *Anglo-Saxon Chronicle*, were written in the vernacular. In addition, the creative Anglo-Saxon literature of *Beowulf* and other compositions became a distinctive cultural feature. Written Old English borrowed the Latin alphabet, supplemented with some new letters based on Germanic runes to cater for non-Latin sounds. But it is notable that, because Germanic influence was heaviest in those parts of Britain which had also been most Romanised (that is, the south and east), no Latin-influenced romance vernacular language emerged here, as happened in many continental former Roman provinces.

This new language evolved into what we call "Old English" and supplanted the British tongue. It had Northumbrian, Anglian and Saxon dialects reflecting regional variations in speech in the north, midlands and south. We cannot know how long the disappearance of the British language took. Presumably the Germanic language of the dominant Anglo-Saxons became a necessary and socially-desirable habit for the indigenous communities: bi-lingualism, as Kenneth Jackson proposed, was thus largely a British practice rather than an English one. The British learning of English was a process assisted by social necessity, by inter-marriage at all levels of society, as well as by the service of the British in English society at various levels. We may imagine, as Thomas Charles-Edwards has suggested, that the earliest English spoken by the British was very imperfect, but later becoming more pure. But whereas British survived in some river- and place-names, and influenced some English ones, it did not affect Old English vocabulary or the formal, written forms of the Old English language, except for a very modest number of words which were adopted. In a collection of essays by Markku Filppula and others it has, however, been suggested that the British language affected everyday Anglo-Saxon modes of speech. This influence on forms of speech (though far less, apparently, on sound) can be seen centuries later, it is argued, when Middle English emerged with features not known in written Old English but paralleled in medieval Welsh. Scholars of linguistics explain this by a process of "language shift". Here, one population group learns a new language from a neighbouring or inter-mixed society, thoroughly at the lexical level (that is, vocabulary) but less than perfectly at the structural level (that is, syntax and grammar). The result is the new language continues to be partly governed by the rules of the old one, even though the latter language effectively disappears. It has been suggested that, from the early contact of two languages to the point where one goes out of use, except in this residually influential way, a period of about three generations passes by. The extent to which spoken British affected spoken English remains, however, the subject of debate.

These observations are potentially very illuminating about the inter-action of "English" and "British" people. They also provide possible enlightenment of how Dumnonian people adopted English, how long this may have taken and how their original language continued to affect the way they spoke their newly-adopted one. Middle English emerged in the thirteenth century primarily from midland Anglian rather than from southern West Saxon. Even so, it is possible, according to the line of argument described above, that some south-western dialect features (for example, transposition of subjective and objective personal pronouns – we/us, she/her and so on) had their roots in the common Old English spoken in this region in the earlier middle ages. Is it perhaps also possible (if the phrase does not extend the historian's traditional caution to ridiculous lengths) that some south-western features owed their origin ultimately to British language influence? In lowland Britain, where Romanization amongst the ordinary population had been heaviest, the British language had also been influenced by Latin, so that here there was a double influence on everyday Old English. But in Dumnonia, where the ordinary rural population had been less touched by a Latin culture, this extra effect was probably less relevant: did this leave more scope for British language influence?

Place-name equivalents may have been in contemporary use for a long period. A south-western example is Creechbarrow (Somerset), described in a charter of the West Saxon king Centwine, in 682, as "*Cructan* in the British language, *Crycbeorh* in ours". It has been suggested that the place-names Clovelly and Dunchideock, in Devon, preserved not only Celtic forms (fairly unusual in Devon) but also original pronunciation, whose emphasis on the second syllable, in English useage, had been an earlier British feature. In Cornwall, where the place-names remained overwhelmingly Celtic, the native language evolved over the centuries, withdrawing progressively westwards as a spoken vernacular, finally dying out in the region circa 1800. Stages in its retraction may be seen in the pronunciation and spelling of a common place-name element, *coed* (wood): eventually fossilised as *cut* in the east of the county but evolving to *cus* in its west. Knowledge of British names was still current in the late ninth century: Asser noted that Selwood Forest, on the Wiltshire-Somerset border, was known in British as *Coit Mawr*, the Great Wood. The phraseology of some Anglo-Saxon charters in Devon seems to refer, indirectly, to late knowledge of the British language. Thus king Edgar's grant of an estate to the thegn Aelfhere, in 974, refers to land "in the place which is called in common parlance *Nymet*". King Eadwig's grant to Eadheah, in 958, referred to "land which is called by the English Ashford and Boehill" (in Sampford Peverell): this could be interpreted to mean that others still knew these places by different, presumably British, names. Nevertheless, despite residual speaking habits, eventually the British language disappeared in Devon. But traditions of the earlier Latin terminology for the region were long-lived. A charter of 833, by king Egbert of Wessex to three sisters relating to lands in Dorset and Devon, referred to Dartington (*Derentuneham*) as being *in Domnomiam*, using the Latin kingdom name as a Devon synonym. In a charter of 944 to a nobleman, Aethelstan, relating to Brampford Speke, king Edmund was described as not only king of the English but also as "ruler of this province of the Britons" – referring presumably to adjacent Cornwall.

Kingdoms and Conflict (*Figs 2.5, 2.6, 2.7, 2.8, 2.9, 2.10, 2.11*)

Anglo-Saxon rulers created kingdoms whose numbers shifted and evolved over time. Kingship initially emphasised authority over people rather than territory, but kings were nevertheless ambitious for new conquests at the expense of each other and their Celtic-speaking neighbours. Warfare was a necessary part of early medieval politics. Only through battle and conquest could plunder and land be acquired to reward followers, keep their loyalty and increase agricultural estates for the support of itinerant kings who had not yet settled down into "capital" centres. It has been suggested by Barbara Yorke that the process of Anglo-Saxon "conquest" of neighbouring lands probably had two phases. First, overlordship was established over existing rulers and populations, with regular tribute exacted. Later, territory was fully annexed, its political independence destroyed, and new forms of administration and exactions (initially food-rents, and later on, taxation in coinage) applied. Such a two-fold sequence could well have applied to Devon. It is misleading, however, to see this process as a simple Germanic *versus* British one because Roman Britain itself had had regionally-diverse societies and economies. Thus, in the south west, a relatively un-Romanised Dumnonian province was faced with a West Saxon one which had been created out of a much more Romanised area: so there was not just one layer of difference between the two territories, but two.

The people named by Bede as the West Saxons were originally known as the *Gewisse*. The British retained this name as a label, reflecting memories of the early days of confrontation: in the late ninth century, Asser noted its continued usage by the Welsh. The West Saxon kingdom had its origins in the upper Thames valley, but by the seventh century its heartland lay in Hampshire and Wiltshire and it was expanding into Somerset and Dorset. Its interest in south-westward colonization probably arose from ambitions in other directions being thwarted by powerful Germanic competitors, especially the Mercians to its north. Up to the eighth century, West Saxon kings were frequently subject to overlords who were Mercian or Northumbrian kings. We must remember the opportunistic nature of these developments and avoid the temptation of assuming an inevitable process of "expansion" to natural frontiers: notably, despite intermittent warfare with the British of Wales, the English of Mercia eventually decided that their conquest was either impossible or not necessary (and Offa's Dyke, built along the Mercian-Powys border, reflects that attitude). We must also remember that in "expanding" westwards, the English encountered different forms of British authority, and this must have affected the process of political absorption. When confronting Dumnonia from the mid-seventh century onwards, the West Saxons were faced with a kingdom, successor to that described a century previously by Gildas. But earlier, when confronting Wiltshire, Dorset and (east) Somerset, other British political structures had been faced whose character is (now) less certain: perhaps led by successors to the councils in the old Romano-British tribal territories.

Neither must we forget the evolving nature of English political organisation during this period. Although significant inroads into the south west were made by the end of Ine's reign (see below), in these early centuries the West Saxons had been a fairly insignificant group in the wider English framework. It was only later that they eventually emerged, under king Egbert (802–839), as a major influence in Anglo-Saxon history. Egbert and his successors were also from a different branch of the West Saxon royal house from that of earlier kings. They extended their influence northwards into Mercia with a victory at Ellendun in Wiltshire (825), followed by further conquest in Mercia and the annexation of Sussex and Kent. A campaign in Cornwall in 815 was followed by an engagement between the men of Devon (now obviously West Saxon in loyalty) and the British at Galford (near Lydford) in 825 (see also Appendix 2). Egbert himself defeated a combined force of vikings and Cornish in 838 at Hingston Down, near Callington in Cornwall. To what extent the victory in 838 stamped West Saxon authority, or simply overlordship, on the westernmost remains of the old Dumnonian kingdom remains unclear (see below). It was nevertheless one of the successes which laid the foundation for the future of Wessex, its resistance to the vikings and its role in the creation of an English kingdom.

Sadly, the chronology and character of the earlier stages of West Saxon "expansion" into the south west can be viewed but dimly, despite the efforts made by many commentators to illuminate them. We may reasonably assume that the pursuit of military campaigns involved the two main branches of the Roman road system into Devon (from Dorset to the east and from Somerset to the north-east) as well as the road running west of Exeter. An early West Saxon victory over the British was won in 614 at *Beandune*, variously identified as Bindon in Dorset or Bindon in south-east Devon. The region was further exposed to West Saxon influence with Cenwealh's victory in 658 at *Peonnan*, as a result of which, the *Anglo-Saxon Chronicle* tells us, the British were put to flight as far as the river Parret. Since this river is usually regarded as the limit of old Dumnonia, perhaps a British army had been campaigning in territory further east. But the battle site has been variously identified as Penselwood, on the Wiltshire-Somerset border, or Penn near Yeovil, or even Pinhoe near Exeter, making interpretation of the incident problematic. Cenwealh engaged the British again, in 661, at *Posentesburh*, perhaps Posbury, north-west of Exeter (see below), in which case the English were now campaigning within Dumnonia. But in

People and Place

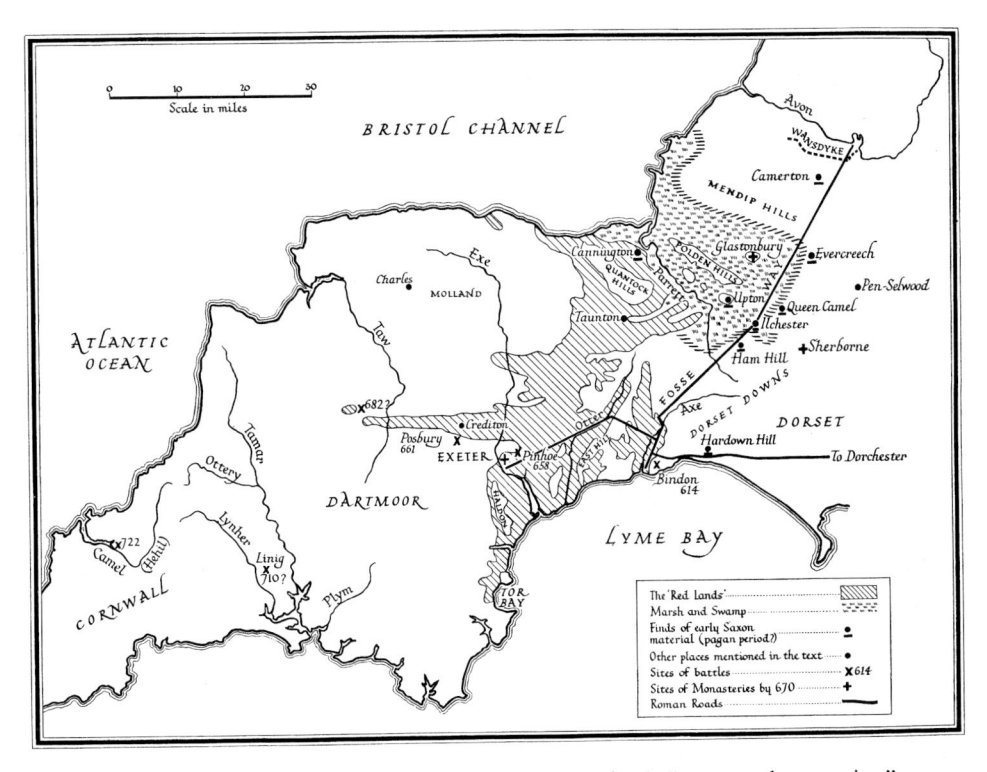

2.5: Map from Hoskins 1960, illustrating the author's "westward expansion" theme; a visualisation mainly in "narrative" terms, of recorded events in a geographical framework.

682 Centwine, a later West Saxon king, inflicted a defeat at an unspecified location and thus "drove the Britons in flight as far as the sea", perhaps to the south Devon coast, or to the Bristol Channel, or perhaps right through mid-Devon to the Atlantic. In 710 Ine defeated Geraint, the last known king of Dumnonia (as opposed to a reduced Cornish kingdom) and thereafter Saxon influence probably extended westwards at a steady rate: it is reasonable to assume that major territorial concessions would follow such a defeat. The battle was probably near the river Lynher, just west of the Tamar, since Ine granted land at *Linig* soon after (see below). Ine founded Taunton, in Somerset, as a fortified place at some point before 722, just inside the presumed eastern border of old Dumnonia. A tenth-century poetic Welsh tradition recorded that Geraint led the men of Dyfneint against the Saxons in battle at *Longborth*, perhaps Langport on the river Parret, where he was killed. If this identification is correct, it is notable that this encounter took place at the eastern extremity of old Dumnonia,

perhaps indicating that it was a crucial event. Moreover, Oliver Padel has suggested that king Geraint was later remembered as the saint Gerent who occurs in a tenth-century list of saints and who gave his name to the Cornish parish of Gerrans. King Cuthred later fought with the British, in 753, so not all problems had been resolved; in the *Anglo-Saxon Chronicle*'s account (for 757) of a West Saxon dynastic dispute we are told that king Cynewulf had "often fought great battles against the Britons". A charter of 766, recording a grant of land in Somerset by Cynewulf to the church at Wells, stated that the king's motive was partly expiation of his cruel treatment of the Cornish (*gens Cornubiorum*). On the whole, those events which eventually found written record told a story of English success, but this was not always so: the Welsh Annals later recorded that in 722 the British were victorious at *Hehil* (whose name in Cornish – *heyl* – meant simply estuary). This has been identified variously: by Sir Frank Stenton as Hayle, on the river Hayle, in west Cornwall, and by W.G. Hoskins as Egloshayle on the river Camel. Towards the end of his *Ecclesiastical History,* completed in 731, Bede wrote, of Britain generally, that "although [the British] are partly their own masters, yet they have also been brought partly under the rule of the English". This was a fair reflection of the south-western situation at this time.

It would be futile to create a chronological "history of conquest" on the basis of the sparse details which eventually found their way into later English and Welsh sources: we cannot know by what process some events and people were recorded whereas others were forgotten. Selectivity in collective memory may have been at work even in the south west, where the English-British confrontation was much later than in more easterly regions. But the situation for the south west is better than it might have been: whereas the fifth-sixth century content of the *Anglo-Saxon Chronicle* is thought largely to be a later invention, the West Saxons were probably maintaining contemporary annals from the seventh century onwards, that is, from the period in which confrontation with Dumnonia began. Inevitably, it was victories and defeats that were remembered because they were in tune with the ethos of heroic societies. The less dramatic and more peaceful aspects of this period, which would be of such great interest to us, faded into oblivion. Sarah Foot has usefully discussed the process by which oral tradition and early written tradition were turned into more permanent recorded form. Various processes of "memory" may have been at work: through important individuals and their families; through social groups; through the church; through royal circles. Crucial were the stages at which

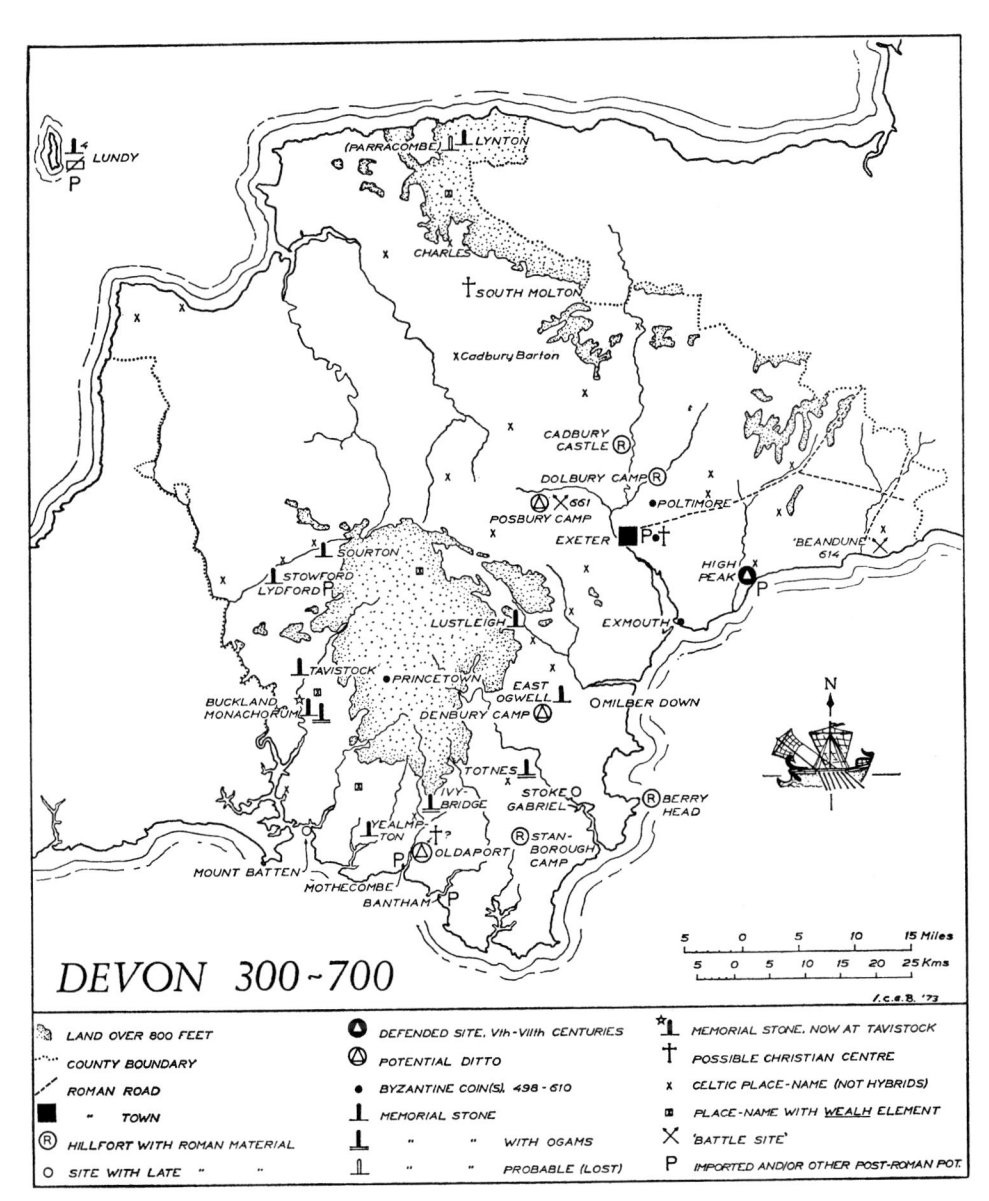

2.6: Map from Burrow 1973, illustrating a variety of evidence from around 300–700; a visualisation mainly in terms of "processes", indicated by various categories of evidence. By permission of the author.

"memory" was turned into "commemoration": at these points, selectivity reflecting the outlook of those concerned created a fixed story which was subsequently repeated. We see the final stage in this process, in relation to early Anglo-Saxon history, in Alfred's reign. His bolstering of the English image against the viking threat, as well as his promotion of the written vernacular English language amongst the unconquered, produced, *inter alia*, the *Anglo-Saxon Chronicle* in which this narrative of the past was fixed. By such processes was "history" made.

Despite the apparent thinness of the record which in this way was preserved, it is presumably safe to infer that, whatever had not been remembered, the events of which we read had been important enough (from an English viewpoint) to enter the commemorated culture. The likely two-stage process outlined above – overlordship and annexation – is not illuminated by the record of individual battles, which could have related to either stage. We are thus left with a broad period, in the second half of the seventh and first half of the eighth centuries, in which Wessex took over what was to be Devonshire. There is an impression that by the 680s British power had been weakened as far as the Exe valley, certainly enough for an English abbot to be ruling Exeter's monastery (see Chapter 3). By the end of Ine's reign, in 726, much of Devon was probably in West Saxon royal control, at least nominally. According to Glastonbury's later monastic records, king Aethelheard granted land in the Torridge valley to the church at Glastonbury in 729, and according to a surviving eleventh-century charter he granted land in the Creedy valley to the church at Sherborne in 739: clear evidence of West Saxon influence by this period (see Chapter 3). Quite possibly, important river valleys marked progressive stages in the process. Just as the Tamar was later to be a significant boundary, perhaps the Exe and then the Taw or Torridge valleys had been so during the later seventh and eighth centuries. In one sense, these events marked the political growth of a Germanic kingdom at the expense of a Dumnonian one; but in another, the process was rather one of competition for land. And we have no way of knowing, in some cases, where "borders" lay in relation to the sites of battles (which may have been fought well within one territory or another). A narrative is well-nigh impossible. Equally difficult is knowing what sorts of particular circumstances led to the battles themselves, but there are various possibilities. West Saxon or Dumnonian kings may, from time to time, have deliberately attempted to change the boundaries of power, with successive English take-overs of land occasionally provoking British reactions. Another possibility, given the impression (at least from surviving sources) of steady westward extension of English control, is that military confrontations arose from refusals by Dumnonian kings to pay the tribute which West Saxon kings demanded. Thus, an unworkable semi-independence may have led to full conquest. Whatever happened in detail,

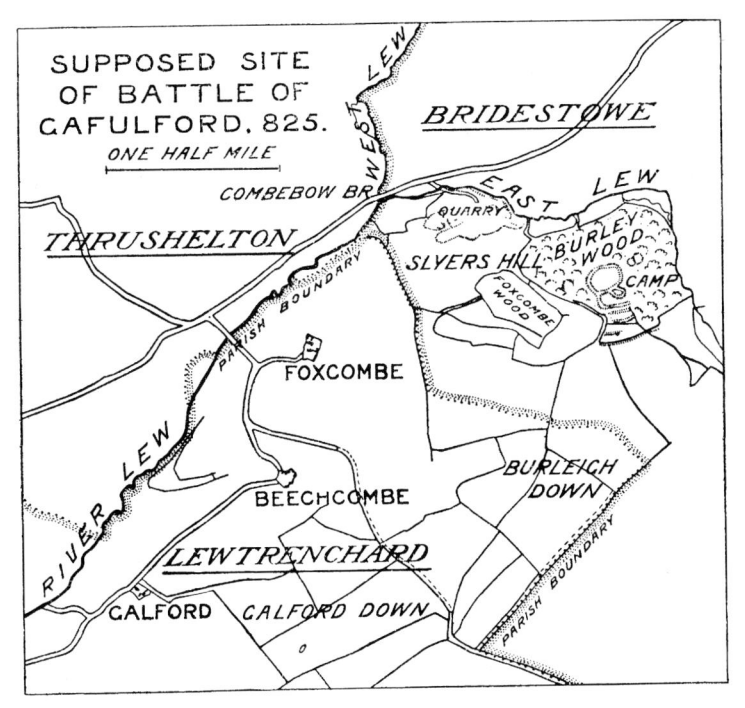

2.7: Map from Alexander 1922, showing the area around Galford, probable site of the battle fought in 825 between the Devonian English and the British of Cornwall. For location, see 2.11. By permission of the Devonshire Association.

it seems reasonable to assume that the victors in battle would be able to demand territorial concessions.

Relevant to these processes may be the site of the engagement with the British at Galford, in 825, noted in the *Anglo-Saxon Chronicle*. The Old English meaning of this place-name – *Gafol-ford* – is "tax/tribute ford", as explicitly stated in Michael Swanton's edition of the *Chronicle*. The site of this battle, on the river Lew in west Devon (in Lew Trenchard parish, where the name still applies to a farm as well as to Galford Down), may not have been fortuitous. It could have been a meeting-place for representatives of the West Saxon and Cornish kings at which tribute was exacted in the period when the far west was under English overlordship but not yet territorially annexed. Or it could have been a place where tolls on trade between the two territories were levied. The place lies not far from Lydford (on whose pre-*burh* history, see Chapters 3 & 4) and also not far from a complex of earthworks at Burley Wood, some of which are Norman but some of which are earlier, though undated. The possibility that this site may have had some early medieval use should not be discounted. The *Anglo-Saxon Chronicle* does not actually mention Egbert's presence in 825, and the men of Devon may have been led by their ealdorman. The outcome of the battle is not stated. But even after Egbert's victory in 838 at Hingston Down, client status remained for a time in Cornwall: the last clearly identifiable Cornish king, Dumgarth, did not die, according to the Welsh Annals, until 875. It was possibly his name which was recorded as *Doniert* on a stone memorial set up near St. Cleer.

While Dumnonian culture was now disappearing, in its earlier history it had certainly not been impoverished, though the coinage and pottery of the Roman period had gone out of use. Pottery imported from western France and the Mediterranean between the fifth and eighth centuries, including amphorae (for olive oil or wine) and fine table wares, had been prized by the rich parts of society, as also in other parts of the western British Isles. These various sorts of vessels have been subject to much debate and publication which it is not appropriate to detail here. They have been found at several south-western coastal sites, the best known of which is Tintagel in Cornwall. At High Peak in south-east Devon, an enclosed site whose area has been much reduced by coastal erosion, such amphorae sherds were excavated as long ago as 1871 by P.O. Hutchinson. The first recovered in the

2.8: Aerial photograph of High Peak, a high-status enclosed site in post-Roman Dumnonia. For location, see 2.6. Photograph: Frances Griffith (29/10/83), copyright Devon County Council.

People and Place

2.9: Aerial photograph of Bantham Ham, a site of trade and exchange in post-Roman Dumnonia. For location, see 2.6.
Photograph: Frances Griffith (6/3/86), copyright Devon County Council.

British Isles, though not recognised as such until much later, these sherds and their original drawings are displayed at the Royal Albert Memorial Museum, Exeter. Material of this period has also been found at trading sites at Bantham (at the Avon's mouth) and Mothecombe (near the Erme's mouth). At Bantham, a site examined at various times by Aileen Fox, Robert Silvester and, most recently, Frances Griffith, not only amphorae sherds were found but also occupation scientifically dated to around the seventh century, suggesting a settlement at least seasonally-occupied and exploiting a variety of maritime resources. Dumnonians controlled valuable commodities, such as tin and slaves, and perhaps wool, which attracted foreign traders. Bede noted that Britain's supplies of copper, iron, lead and silver were significant. The seventh century *Life* of John the Almsgiver related how a ship of Mediterranean origin was blown off course and reached Britain (presumably Dumnonia), where its crew traded their cargo of corn for tin. It was suggested by Aileen Fox that tin ingots found in the sea near the mouth of the Erme, in south Devon, may be a relic of this trading activity. Tin ingots have also been found at Praa Sands, Cornwall, in a context of perhaps the seventh century, but the ingots themselves could be much older (other Romano-British examples are known from Cornwall).

2.10: Amphora (type Bii) imported from the Mediterranean, found at Bantham. Photograph: Royal Albert Memorial Museum and Art Gallery, Exeter.

The resources of the west were also attractive to the Saxons, with whom there was contact in trade and gift-exchange: thus "Germanic" metalwork is found in Somerset and "Celtic" hanging-bowls are found in eastern England. It is important to recognise that the Dumnonians belonged to a British, continental and Mediterranean world, not a remote or peripheral culture.

The Dumnonian kings, like other western British kings of the period, comprised a dynasty which emerged from the native aristocracy of the late Roman period. How such families achieved power we do not know, and the internal workings of these kingdoms are obscure. Few kings of Dumnonia can be reliably identified: Constantine, in the late fifth or sixth century (depending on one's dating of Gildas, whose contemporary he was); Geraint, circa 700; the sixth-century Conomorus may be commemorated on an inscribed memorial stone near Fowey, Cornwall. The (possibly) seventh-century *Life* of St Sampson described how, arriving from Wales (in the sixth century) Sampson met a local ruler (*comes*), in Trigg (NE Cornwall), called Guedianus. Some hillforts were apparently occupied in this period, though, on present evidence, less so than in Somerset. A smaller proportion of Devon's hillforts have been excavated than in neighbouring Somerset, making comparisons potentially misleading, but Nicholas Grant has suggested that a similar range of military, religious and status motives inspired their use or re-use in Devon. A post-Roman phase has been identified in excavation at the hillfort on Raddon Hill. Late Roman finds (often, in Somerset, an indicator of post-Roman occupation) have come from Cadbury fort, in the form of a votive offerings in a well. "Cadbury" names also occur in Somerset: perhaps the Cada who was commemorated in them had been an early figure with a wide reputation. If the identification of "Posent's fort" (*Posentesburh* in the Anglo-Saxon Chronicle, where king Cenwalh fought the British in 661) with Posbury (the earthworks at Posbury Camp, near Crediton) is correct, then this too may have been a Dumnonian stronghold, as suggested by Andrew Breeze. Posent is not a Saxon name, but could well derive from the Latin name Pascentius (which produced, in Welsh, Pascen and Pasgen). The same author has also argued that a British personal name underlies the name *Arx Cynuit*, by which Asser referred (in Latin) to the fort in north Devon at Countisbury, where Danes and English fought in 878. Traditionally seen as combining the British element *cunet* (hill) with the Old English element *burh* (fort) to make "Countisbury", the British name Cynuit may well rather be based on the British *cuno* (hound), known to have been used as a personal name, thus preserving the memory of its builder or of an important occupant. The name of Denbury, in south Devon, means "*burh* (fortification) of the men of Devon" and has long been cited as a probable centre of post-Roman power. It is likely that hillfort occupation, however common, represented not simply opportunistic defensive needs but rather the importance of the British estates at whose centres they probably now lay, whether they were re-used, pre-Roman forts or newly-built ones. It was the lords of such estates who presumably provided, under the leadership of their kings, the opposition to West Saxon expansion as well as the normal framework of social and economic control within Dumnonia.

Perhaps some other Dumnonian estates were still centred on (by then unoccupied) rural "villas" of the Roman period, though such sites seem to have been rare in the south west outside south-east Devon (see Chapter 5). But it is possible that early estates retained their shape even though their focal settlement was abandoned. There are dangers in leaping across the centuries and making (possibly spurious) connections, but it is notable that, in south-east Devon, the Holcombe villa site lay in a territory later defined by a charter as an Anglo-Saxon estate at Uplyme, a territory which Harold Fox demonstrated was coincident with the later manor and parish. The Cornish place-name element *lis*, meaning a court, may reflect high status estate centres of the Dumnonian landed class: one such name survives in north Devon, at Charles. The Giant's Hedge in south Cornwall is a linear earthwork in the tradition of the Wansdykes in Somerset and Wiltshire, though its exact date and function is unknown. There seems to have been no single "royal capital". With itinerant kings, and quite possibly sub-kings in smaller regions, political power was diffuse. The headland at

Tintagel, on the north Cornish coast, was one centre of secular and possibly royal power, as well as an important access point for foreign traders, which inspired many later traditions. Tintagel has plentiful excavated evidence to show its date and character. Although there is no excavated evidence here, the earthworks at Wind Hill, Countisbury on the north Devon coast are also worthy of consideration for an economic role in the post-Roman period: this defended site overlooks Lynmouth, an important point of access from the Bristol Channel. The fort was said by Asser (who called it *Arx Cynuit* – see above) to possess ramparts built "in our fashion". Asser's own British (that is, Welsh) background reveals perhaps some memory of a Dumnonian origin (or re-use) of this place. Exeter, the Romano-British regional capital, was perhaps for a time one amongst a number of centres of post-Roman political organisation. As the administrative centre for the influential Dumnonian land-owning class, it was presumably not abandoned immediately, though its location was not central to the whole territory. There is, however, no direct evidence for secular occupation in Exeter in this period. But the development of a Christian cemetery in the fifth century, within the ruins of the Roman public buildings, may indirectly reveal a continuing secular authority here (see Chapters 3 & 4).

The Dumnonian land-owners were presumably descendants of the equivalent influential class of Romano-British times. Archaeological evidence suggests the latter's society had been less Romanised than that of their more easterly neighbours, which may have given Dumnonian society a distinctive and unsophisticated character. But it would be wrong to envisage a simplistic "reversion" to a pre-Roman culture. The Dumnonian territory of Romano-British times was probably created from amalgamation of smaller tribal septs. There had been no single pre-Roman tribal centre for the whole region: Exeter had no predecessor. And Christianity had since arrived: the western British territories referred to by Gildas, which included Dumnonia, had kings, bishops, priests and abbots. Michael Lapidge has shown that Gildas's Latin style reveals a man educated in the late Roman secular manner (though much later in life he became a monk). That such an education was still available (though presumably only to the upper classes) in Britain in the late fifth or early sixth century is itself a useful caution against under-estimating its culture. From amongst the land-owning British classes, royal dynasties had emerged. Gildas denigrated these kings for their evil ways, as well as the clergy for their low standards: he depicted Constantine of Dumnonia as a tyrant, murderer, adulterer and purveyor of sacrilege. But his attacks on British leadership, secular and ecclesiastical, were part of his exhortations towards better standards and resistance to the English: it would be wrong to assume that western society as a whole was lawless and disorganised. A framework of public order, inherited from Roman provincial government and augmented by native tradition, presumably existed, and it is a mistake to imagine that the long period of (geographically-contracting) Dumnonian independence did not see its own internal political and social developments.

In the seventh century, English kings (including Aethelberht and Wihtred of Kent, and Ine of Wessex) began to write down the laws which applied in their kingdoms. There is no reason why law-books may not have been written down for Dumnonian and other early British kings by their own clerics. There is certainly some evidence for lingering traditions of Roman property law in the Celtic-speaking areas, seen in surviving charters granting lands to the church (below, Chapters 3 & 4). Gildas referred not only to British kings, but also to judges (though not specifically in Dumnonia, and it has been suggested that these wielded power further east where Gildas himself was probably writing). From his condemnatory remarks about royal failings we can see that the kings were expected not only to be rich and powerful war leaders but also protectors of church and people. The royal link with Christian clerics, even the possibility of anointed kings, revealed by Gildas, shows that British traditions of kingship had characteristically medieval features before those of the English kingdoms, which were Christianised only from around 600 onwards. It has also been pointed out by several authors, including Ken Dark, that the "post-Roman" experience of western Britain in general, including Dumnonia, was now in some senses more "Roman" than it had been in Romano-British times. While no longer part of an imperial province, and no longer administered by the council which is presumed to have sat at Exeter, Dumnonia nevertheless displayed features which linked it securely with the Mediterranean world. These included its Christian, Latin-writing culture; its adoption of a Roman-derived practice of inscribed memorial stones; and its trade links which brought distant merchants to its shores. To these points may be added the current view that the rural settlement pattern of the Romano-British period also continued with little or no change until it began to be succeeded by the surviving historic landscape from the seventh and eighth centuries (see Chapter 5). There appears to have been a deliberate cultural choice to maintain much of the old world, and, from around 400 to 700, this second "Roman" period was virtually as long as that which preceded it.

It seems likely that progressive English "conquest" of the south west,

Dumnonia -- British/English Conflict

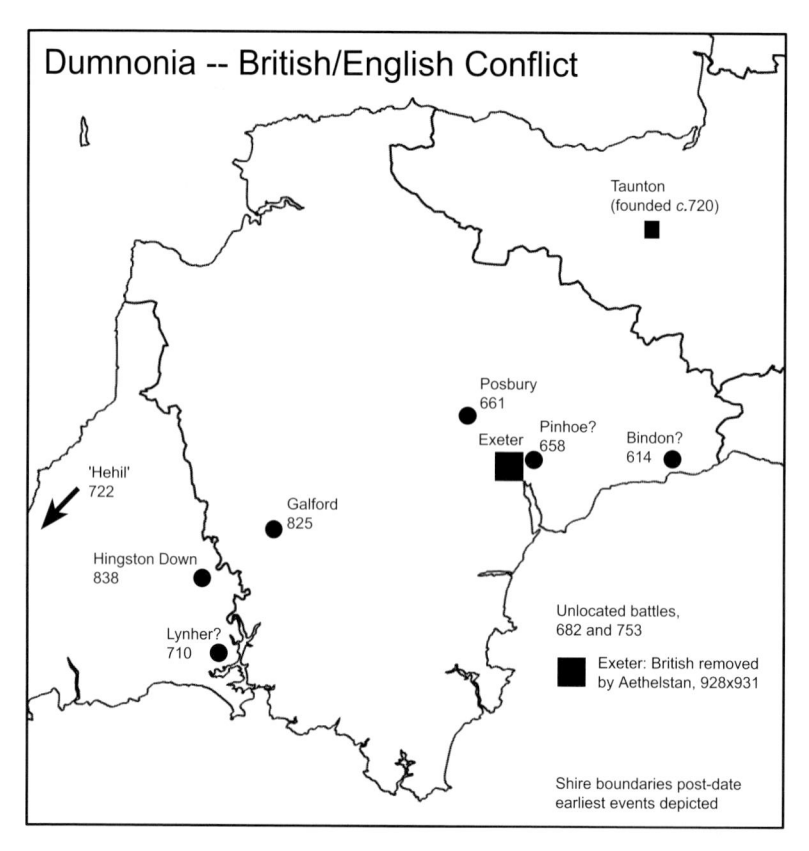

- Taunton (founded c.720)
- Posbury 661
- Exeter
- Pinhoe? 658
- Bindon? 614
- 'Hehil' 722
- Galford 825
- Hingston Down 838
- Lynher? 710

Unlocated battles, 682 and 753

■ Exeter: British removed by Aethelstan, 928x931

Shire boundaries post-date earliest events depicted

2.11: Recorded British-English conflicts in Dumnonia (with later shire boundaries). Map by Robert Higham & Oliver Creighton.

following significant military victories, involved the taking over of the estates of the Dumnonian kings and land-owners, rather than immediately re-shaping them. Some of these estates may have stayed intact for many centuries, whereas others were gradually broken up as West Saxon kings endowed both their church and their secular followers. It is, however, a mistake to think of the absorption of Dumnonia only as a process of conquest: it must also have involved a process of acculturation. It is tempting, because of the documented record of battles, to assume constant hatred between the two peoples. But for all we know, some English settlement in the area may have been achieved peacefully: despite differences and resentments between their churches (above, and Chapter 3) there was no Christian-pagan divide to complicate the situation. Dumnonia already contained a Christian society and the West Saxons were increasingly Christian from the 630s onwards. We find no pagan Germanic burials, accompanied by grave-goods, in Cornwall and Devon and a mere handful in Somerset and Dorset. Peaceful integration of Christian families from both cultures may have occurred alongside the heroic battles later recorded in chronicles. Though the British church at first no doubt resisted institutional encroachment, in 705 a new see was established at Sherborne (Dorset) in replacement of an earlier British Christian centre nearby called *Lanprobus*. By this date, presumably significant territories to its west were available for integration into the English church. As H.P.R. Finberg clearly demonstrated, the "expansion" of West Saxon political power was intimately connected with westerly endowment of the major churches of Dorset and Somerset, that is Sherborne and Glastonbury. Charters (or later monastic records of grants for which no charters survived) describing grants of royal lands to the church indicate the spread of ecclesiastical influence. King Ine granted lands at *Linig*, by the Tamar, to Glastonbury abbey as early as 712, probably following a victory in this area in 710 (see above). Later kings granted lands to the West Saxon church in the Torridge valley (729), in the Creedy valley (739), at Culmstock and Culm Davey (c.760) and at Uplyme (774). But even this process was not all one-way: king Geraint of Dumnonia had granted land at Maker, by the Tamar, to Sherborne in c. 705, perhaps as part of a diplomatic negotiation with the West Saxons or to calm friction between the British and English churches. Barbara Yorke has suggested, in extension of Finberg's theme, that taken in conjunction with Aldhelm's interventions with Geraint (see above, and Chapter 3), this reveals growing West Saxon church influence in the south west prior to formal political annexations: as though an extension of church influence was paving the way for kings to extend political control.

Alongside political and ecclesiastical processes of absorption and integration there must also have been more mundane sorts of social change. First, we cannot assume that all Dumnonians resisted English power all the time. Some, particularly in east Devon – already close to English-controlled territory – may not have been too concerned whether their overlord was English or British. It is also possible that, as English influence spread westwards, some Dumnonian landowners voluntarily transferred their allegiance in order to secure continued ownership of their estates. Second, acquisition of lands by West Saxon rulers – whether by negotiation or by force – led to the arrival of new landowners and settlers whose loyalty was now rewarded with territory. These men and women spoke Old English and, as their communities grew, they effected another sort of "conquest", from inside rather than from outside. Although this process of social change went wholly undocumented, in some ways it is the most fascinating part of the story. The society into which new landlords and settlers moved had developed continuously in the region for many centuries. Life probably went on much as before for the bulk of the rural population who had been the tenants of the old landed classes of Dumnonia. The latter were partly displaced by newcomers and partly succeeded by their own kind who "became English". The Roman city of Exeter was crumbling, though perhaps retaining some occupation alongside its early burial ground (and presumed church). Its location near the eastern end of its tribal territory may mean it had not been of equal interest to all of the Romano-British landed class and, with administrative functions now gone, its marginal situation would have been enhanced. Nevertheless, since major river valleys may have marked important stages in the extension of English domination (see above), English control of Exeter, at the head of the Exe estuary, must have been a significant step. This was certainly achieved by the late seventh century, when there was an English monastery here (see Chapter 3).

Significant also in this context must have been northward communications up the east side of the Exe valley. A road is presumed to have run from Exeter to the Roman fort at Bolham, near Tiverton. This was eventually succeeded by the medieval road from Exeter over Stoke Hill and through Stoke Canon, Rewe, Silverton, Butterleigh, Tiverton (and on to Bampton, near the Somerset border), all of which places existed by the late Saxon period. Routes across the Exe, at fordable places, also emerged: the eleventh-century charter (purporting to be of earlier date) for Stoke Canon (see Chapter 6) reveals such a road – *herepath* – running east to west across the river Culm (at *langanforda*) and across the Exe (at s*ulforda*). While Exeter had a Roman (and presumably late Saxon – see Chapter 4) bridge over the Exe, the bridges further north were of later date: those at Stoke Canon (over the Culm) and Cowley (over the Exe) existed before 1300; but the bridge at Bickleigh, further up the Exe, was not built until the early seventeenth century (leading to development of a new route northwards, up the west bank of the river, which is still the main road).

Emigration and Immigration

Related to these processes of immigration and integration is the intriguing evidence for earlier emigration from the south west of Britain to north-west Gaul. Much has been written about this subject and many and varied views have been expressed on the nature, impact, extent and chronology of

British settlement in Armorica, of which various accounts (in English) have been given by Kenneth Jackson, Nora Chadwick, Malcolm Todd, Patrick Galliou and Michael Jones. Emigration of British people was mentioned by British and continental writers, both contemporary and much later, of whom the earliest and most reliable were the British writer, Gildas, and the sixth century Byzantine writer, Procopios. Even they, however, have their limitations: neither says the emigrants were specifically from the south west; Gildas does not mention the destination of the British emigrants; Procopios says the emigrants were not only British but also English, and his knowledge of Britain contains much garbled information. But, on their testimony, some movement of British people had occurred in the late fifth and sixth centuries, and Procopios names their destination as a different "Britannia" from their homeland. Bede's statement, written in the eighth century, that the British of Britain had immigrated *from* Armorica, was perhaps a confused back-projection of the common name used for both areas by his (later) day. There are, in fact, good reasons (below) to believe that a significant part of the British emigration to Armorica was from south-west Britain: it was not, at this early date, therefore a direct response to growing West Saxon influence within the region. Kenneth Jackson thought that the English victory in 577 (see above) may have encouraged some emigration in anticipation of further English advances. But the motives may have been more general: stimulated perhaps by internal political, economic or social problems, or by the prospect of military service or fortune-seeking abroad, it was another facet of the wider British and European migration period. Some early commentators created an impression, from an argument based on an assumption of massive emigration from Dumnonia, of general south-western emptiness on the eve of "Saxon settlement", but this is no longer credited. The whole history of the Dumnonian centuries suggests a great deal of continuity of life throughout this period. We may conclude that some emigration took place but its extent cannot be measured, nor do we know whether it affected the south west generally or specific areas within it. But it may have had some effect on the distribution and density of population in the various parts of the region into which Saxon landlords and others eventually moved.

Under the influence of British immigrants, the Gaulish province of Armorica became known as *Britannia* (Brittany to us) no later than Procopios's time, though its British character was more obvious in the west, its eastern portion remaining more Gallo-Roman. It is hard to escape the conclusion that south west Britain was a major source of these emigrants, and not simply because it was closest to Brittany. The *Breton* language was closely related to the British of old Dumnonia: Kenneth Jackson argued that it remained very similar to the Cornish language (but not to "Welsh") down to the tenth century. Western Brittany had districts known (in the north) as *Dumnonia* and (in the south) as *Cornouaille*: a recurrence of south-western British names presumably indicating influence from both parts of Dumnonia (though whether *Cornouialle* was named as early as *Dumnonia* has been challenged because "Cornwall" as a name in England appears only later, "Cornubia" being the initial form). There was a common Christian culture in the two areas at a time when the English were still pagan: Brittany had some saints' traditions in common with those of south west Britain and Wales. It also had similar place-name elements to those surviving in Cornwall and Wales: all had variants of, for example, *tre* (farm), *lis* (court or hall) and *coed* (wood), as well as *lan* (whose interpretation has given rise to much discussion – see Chapter 3). The most recent survey of this part of Brittany's history and archaeology, by Pierre-Roland Giot and others, has concluded (rather like Kenneth Jackson, half a century earlier) that the main Dumnonian connections, including the language parallel, stemmed from a second phase of south-western British contact, after AD 500, when the movement of clerical figures and their followers, influential in both areas, was crucial. But, it is argued, this had been preceded by an earlier phase, stretching back into Roman times, in which people from a wider area of southern Britain had moved to Armorica in military service: it was their descendants who provided the foundations of a changed society. This longer-term view of "Breton" origins helps explain the significant common traditions in the two areas without resorting to notions of mass migration from, and extensive de-population in, south-west Britain.

Another development which may have affected the localised distribution and density of population in the south west was the recurrence of plagues. Plagues recorded in the Mediterranean and Europe in the 540s reached western Britain and Ireland soon after: the trade links between the two areas must have facilitated its spread. A century later, outbreaks hit England, recorded by Bede and other early English writers who noted their devastating effects between the 660s and 680s. This was, of course, at just the time when the West Saxons were first annexing Dumnonian territories to their west. There is no specific evidence as to their impact on the south west, in either century, but it is unlikely that the region's British or English populations escaped wholly untouched. Also relevant to general living conditions was the earlier climatic down-turn, identified through dendrochronological data (for example, in Ireland) and documentary references in Europe, dating from the 530s. This change, perhaps prompted by a series of volcanic eruptions or a meteor collision, led initially to many years of cold weather, relative darkness and poor agricultural yields, and in the longer term to a significant climatic low period whose reversal came only from the tenth century onwards.

A century ago, it was common to suppose that the "conquering" Angles and Saxons annihilated most of the British population, drove the remnants progressively westwards, destroyed Roman places and created new and very different settlements. This interpretation was influenced by the impression of Britain's destruction given by Gildas, but his purpose was religious and political and his account was not objective by modern standards. Our view of this period is now much changed. First, we may question a reliance on totally separate ethnic identities. While early immigrants were indeed Germanic and the indigenous people indeed British, from the days of the first settlers in the east, during the late Roman period, intermarriage and other forms of cultural interaction must have occurred. As time went on, this process surely developed further. Thus, when "Saxons" began to settle in the south west in the seventh century, many of them would not have had purely Germanic blood in their veins. Second, while we must not rule out the possibility of localised episodes of "ethnic cleansing" as part of the process of conquest, perhaps following significant military victories (on either side) there is no evidence of widespread extermination or enforced migration. Third, we must beware the temptation to see conflict in this period in terms of warfare between modern nation states. By the ninth century, when Alfred's Wessex resisted the vikings, there were shire levies who defended territories under local leaders on behalf of kings. But when the West Saxons first created their kingdom and extended it westwards, warfare was conducted by kings and their warbands not by societies or nations. And we must assume the same was true of the Dumnonian kings who from time to time engaged the Saxons in battle. Gildas wrote not only of the tryanny of western British kings, but also of "their military companions, bloody, proud and murderous men".

It is tempting to make generalizations about "conquest" which mask a process which probably had many layers. As a result of significant military victories, West Saxon kings would take over the lands belonging to Dumnonian kings and land-owners in a specific territory. Thus, a political "border" may gradually have moved westwards over several generations. But the indigenous population of territory annexed in this way would have been left *in situ*, presumably with some newly-arrived English landlords and the officials needed to administer the new royal estates. When eighth-century West Saxon kings granted Devonian lands to the church the implication is clearly that such lands lay in territory within royal English control. But alongside this process, there was probably a less structured one of "settler movement" or "land-grabbing". This is implied by conditions described in king Ine's law-code (below), but we do not know whether it applied only to territories already annexed politically through royal intervention, or whether settlers also had freedom to move beyond any "official frontier" and make their own, personal acquisitions of land. Such acquisitions may not always have been resisted or won through violence: enlargement of existing settlements, or creation of new ones in less used environments may have played a part.

It is sometimes argued, in historical and archaeological study, that relatively small numbers of immigrants can bring about change when they achieve positions of social and political dominance: the Norman Conquest provides the classic example. The current view of Romano-British landscapes suggests that they were generally well-occupied, with a population of perhaps three millions. The current view of the following period is that landscapes suffered a down-turn of population in the fifth-sixth centuries, which made some immigration easier to absorb, and thereafter there was a gradual growth in population to the levels recorded in Domesday Book in the eleventh century. Although scholarly views about the proportion of Germanic immigrants within the total population vary wildly (it being impossible to calculate figures with any certainty) there has been a debate in recent years, argued by Nicholas Higham and others, which has resulted in a playing down of the likely numbers of primary immigrants from Europe. In the fluid political conditions which followed the removal of Roman authority in the early fifth century, these newcomers in eastern and south-eastern Britain, however numerous they may or may not have been, gained the upper hand over native leaders who had inherited Roman power. It was thus a Germanic stamp which characterised the culture of succeeding centuries. But the earlier population did not disappear within the new kingdoms, and it is generally agreed that, as the creation of these kingdoms progressed westwards and northwards over the next three centuries, native society figured more prominently within their populations. The British were actually identified separately as the *Wealas* – that is, internal foreigners – in the law-code of Ine of Wessex written c. 690, when West Saxon influence was spreading into the south west, and their occurrence in this context has been helpfully discussed by Louis Alexander, Thomas Charles-Edwards and others. We know of Ine's code because king Alfred later appended it to his own: they survive in a tenth-century manuscript. Athough legally inferior to people of Germanic descent, in the value of *wergilds* and the status of oaths in court, the British described here still had their own social ranks, but described in English terms: from slaves (inferior even to English ones), through landless men, through rent-payers, through ordinary men with half a hide or one hide of land, and on up to noble land-owners with five hides (though even these were less high-ranking than their English counterparts; on "the hide" in general, see Chapter Four). We may safely assume that these people – the *Wealas* – were of indigenous descent and spoke primarily the British tongue.

It has been argued that despite inferior status, British legal freedom was recorded and preserved at this time because indigenous society was essential to the maintenance of the agrarian landscape and its political loyalty was also needed. The recognition of native ranks of status is certainly a corrective to an easily-made assumption about the "enslavement" of the British. Some may well have been enslaved, especially those captured in warfare, which is perhaps why *Wealas* came eventually to mean "slave" as well as "of native British origin". But the existing rural population would have been necessary to the working of rural estates. Ine's code also protected West Saxon estates from the neglect which might be caused by enthusiastic settlers moving westwards: an English landowner (*gesith*) had to leave six tenths of his land fully functioning and could take only a reeve, smith and children's nurse with his migrating family. This detail reveals an expectation of finding western lands already settled with an agricultural population, as well as the fact that West Saxon manpower itself was not unlimited.

The British whom Aethelstan expelled from Exeter in the tenth century were said (by the twelfth-century chronicler William of Malmesbury) to have lived there on an equal footing with the English. Whether this phrase was loosely meant, or specifically indicated that the urban British were of higher status than the *Wealas* of the countryside, we do not know. Nor do we know whether this community was of continuous survival from sub-Roman Exeter, or composed of later immigrants from the countryside when Exeter became a *burh* in Alfred's reign. Alfred's own law-code did not mention the *Wealas,* but the attachment of Ine's code to it as an appendix presumably shows its content was still applicable in the late ninth century. The British may still have been recognisable throughout Wessex at this time, or (more likely) the conditions laid down in Ine's code with reference perhaps especially to Dorset, Somerset and east Devon still applied to the British of Cornwall. But in Devon, as further east, the English-British distinction eventually disappeared and Anglo-Saxon society became undifferentiated. The new rulers soon found their control was better served by suppression of cultural differences, by absorption of existing populations and the forging of a common political allegiance. Being English thus became not an ethnic issue but an institutional one. As Barbara Yorke has recently and perceptively observed, eventually "to be Anglo-Saxon was not to be necessarily of Germanic descent, but an indication of political and cultural allegiance". By this process, what had originally been (to use modern terms) a multi-cultural society became a mono-cultural one. One explanation, explored by various commentators, is that the identification of the *Wealas* in Ine's code was intended not only to emphasise the different legal status of British and English (who were referred to here, at this early date, specifically as *Englisc*) but to provide the incentive for the British to learn English and lose their old identity. Avoiding perpetual definition as second-class citizens would have been an inducement to those still clinging to memory of British descent to "become English". By joining the dominant culture and abandoning the old language, together with its personal names, the status and prospects of the old Dumnonians became equal to those of everyone else. In a similar fashion, the Franks had also created second-class citizenship, defined in legal status, for their Gallo-Roman subjects. The British experience was part of a wider pattern.

At the risk of sounding flippant about what was, to those concerned, a matter of great issue, we may also wonder (though some have dismissed this) whether what was partly at play was a linguistic adeptness of the Celtic-speakers, and an equivalent uselessness of the English, at learning other peoples' languages! In any event, the indigenous population already had a dual (British/Latin) linguistic background, so that adopting a third, English, element may not have been too difficult a cultural choice to make (though, probably, with imperfect results, as explained above). This notion of British people voluntarily giving up their identity and "becoming English" in order to avoid perpetual second-class status, however it worked in practice, has been usefully explored by Thomas Charles-Edwards, Bryan Ward-Perkins and others. It may explain how substantial British elements of the population "disappeared" in Britain. Given the date of Ine's law-code in relation to West Saxon "expansion" into Dumnonia, and the presumption that the native population of the far south west would have out-numbered the newcomers, it is also a particularly helpful way to consider how early Devonian society may have developed.

Language and Place-Names (*see Figs 1.1, 2.12, 2.13, 2.14*)

By the time of Domesday Book in the eleventh century, the land-owning class in Cornwall appears as "English", whether through the replacement of Cornish landlords or through their adoption of English personal names. The tenth- and eleventh-century records of manumissions of slaves, preserved in the Bodmin Gospels and other sources, give us, however, the names of some lowly Cornish men and women. The charters of the same period, recording grants of land in Cornwall by English kings, refer mainly to the church or to thegns and nobles with English names, and their boundary clauses (where surviving) are in Latin or Old English (though they sometimes refer obliquely to living Cornish by describing a Cornish place-name as used "by the country folk": for example, Tregony and Trerice, granted in 1049 by Edward the Confessor to Eadulf). The charters nevertheless contain Cornish words: about fifty recur, relating to settlements, plants and animals, and natural and man-made landscape features. In them we can also occasionally glimpse the older, native land-holding Cornish class. Lands in Cornwall were granted by king Edgar to Aelfheah Geraint and his wife, Moruurei, as well as to Wulfnoth Rumuncant. Oliver Padel has noted that the adoption of these "double" names, part- British and part-English, may reflect the assumption of Englishness by the Cornish land-holding class in the tenth century. A later tenth-century bishop of St German's was the similarly "double-named" Wulfsige Cemoyre. Although we have no direct evidence, a process of acculturation through similar "double" personal name development could well have been a feature of Devonian life in the eighth century, as a stage in the disappearance there of British names.

Oliver Padel has also drawn attention to an interesting tenth-century Latin charter, dating from Aethelstan's reign, whose text relates that a Cornish land-holder named Maenchi and with the title *comes* (count) granted land at Lanlawren (in Lanteglos) to a church dedicated to St Heldanus (now St Ildiern in Llansallos). This charter was drawn up "in the land of the Saxons at the island of Athelney" before an abbot who also had a Cornish name (Seigno). This influential Cornishman, whose title of *comes* (whatever it may have meant in a Cornish context) suggests he was significant in local administration, travelled to an English monastery to have his charter drawn up. Perhaps he did so because he thought it would have more authority in an increasingly English-dominated Cornwall, or even because, as a result of Aethelstan's campaign in the region, English authorization for such a grant was now required. Perhaps he also knew the abbot, and perhaps he also had to travel to "England" on other official business: in all events, the episode

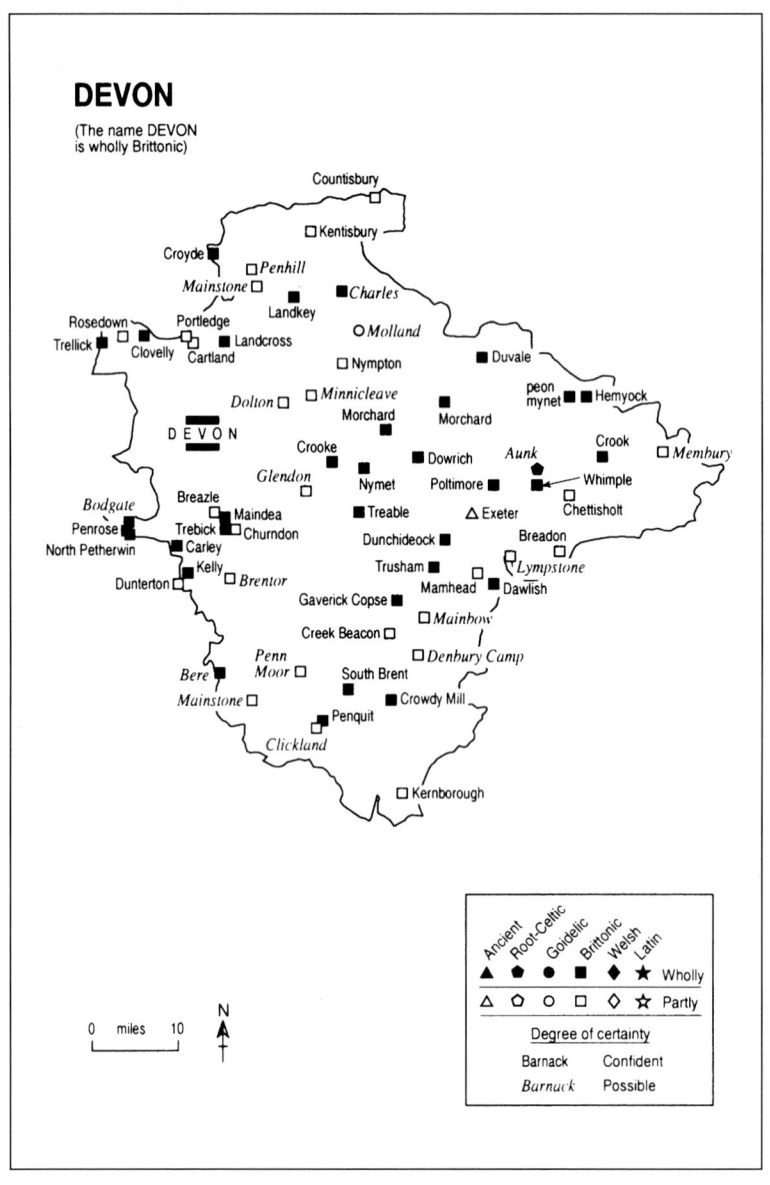

2.12: Map of Brittonic place-names in Devon, from
Coates, Breeze & Horowitz 2000.
By permission of Richard Coates and of Shaun Tyas, Stamford.

reflects the progressive absorption of Cornwall, indirectly revealing the sorts of process which had probably applied in Devon two hundred years earlier. This is the sole surviving example of a charter text of the period which actually records a grant by a Cornishman (as opposed to an English king granting land in Cornwall) and belongs to a wider tradition of charters from the Celtic-speaking areas (see Chapter 4). Though written in Latin, Oliver Padel also noted that this revealed some underlying British influence on its terminology.

Finally, a fascinating illumination of on-going cultural and linguistic prejudice comes from a charter of the English king Eadred, granted in 949 to a thegn called Wulfric. It recorded an exchange of land, made presumably at Wulfric's request, involving Pendavy in Egloshayle. Wulfric received land "in that place where long since the inhabitants of this region established the name Welford [Berkshire] in exchange for another estate which is reported to be situated in Cornwall (*in Cornubio*) where the country folk of that district call it by the barbaric name Pendavy (*Pendyfig*)". Wulfric was a thegn much favoured by king Eadred, who granted him several estates in Berkshire as well others in Dorset, Wiltshire and Gloucestershire. He was presumably seeking to "lose" a far-flung property in Cornwall which his family already held by grant from an earlier king (possibly Aethelstan?). Perhaps it was inconvenient to administer or perhaps, as the reference to the Cornish language implies, he regarded its environment as alien.

It seems clear that language, as well as senses of cultural and political affinity, became far more powerfully-defining features for society than distinctions of ethnicity in the biological sense. The latter must have become increasingly blurred as the generations passed. We must thus envisage the creation of "Anglo-Saxon Devon" not simply as a process of conquest and replacement (though both mechanisms played their part) but perhaps primarily as one of integration and absorption. And these processes were drawn out over a long period in the seventh and eighth centuries (extending to the ninth and tenth in Cornwall). Although we know the names of many individual places from pre-Norman sources, it is only from Domesday Book (1086) that we have an overall view of the region, recorded centuries later. On the reconstructed Domesday "map", Devon appears "English" because its settlement (habitative) names are overwhelmingly Germanic: the editors of the *Place-Names of Devon* estimated that only about one per cent of Devon's settlement names were of British origin. Their data on British names has since been refined by Coates, Breeze and Horovitz, but the overall pattern still remains thin. The county contains a scattering of names in which British and English elements are combined, such as Breazle, Dolton, Kentisbury and Mamhead. Some examples of purely British derivation include, in west Devon: Carley, Dunterton, Kelly, Maindea and Trebick. In mid-Devon they include Crooke, Treable, Trusham, Morchard, Dunchideock. In north Devon they include Charles, Landkey, Landcross and Trellick. In east Devon, they include Whimple, Crook, Hemyock and also Aunk (which is of an earlier Celtic form). But, despite the relatively late date of Dumnonia's absorption into Wessex, Devon's settlement place-name pattern is not a general hybrid of British and Old English traditions. It is predominantly Old English, with some British survivals, as is the case in shires further east. On the place-name map, Devon looks heavily "English", despite the thin record of specifically "Anglo-Saxon" archaeological data (see below).

Place-name scholars and historians have differed in their views of what level of English immigration led to Devon's English place-name pattern. Clearly, the overwhelmingly English character of Devon's place-names does not necessarily mean that all these places were Saxon in origin (though some were). It may also mean that a socially-dominant class had been naming and re-naming the landscape in its own language before these names were first written down. Cornwall's overwhelmingly Celtic place-names, in contrast, may have been written down in their original language before (at a considerably later date) Saxon administration dominated the area, and were thus preserved in both English documentation and Cornish everyday use. This appreciation of a source-based distinction between the place-name evidence of the two counties, largely promoted by Oliver Padel, gradually replaced older ideas of a mass English immigration into a landscape made empty by equally mass British emigration to Brittany. Even so, grasping the reality of early Devonian history through its place-names remains difficult: Oliver Padel's most recent published view (see Preface to this book) re-iterates a fairly traditional approach, stressing the much more "English" experience of Devon in comparison with that of Cornwall, and insisting on significant rural immigration as an explanation of English place-name formation for so many small settlements. Place-name scholars in general find it difficult to explain the "Englishness" of place-names (throughout England) except by reference to extensive and new "English" residents. The eventual English imprint even on Cornwall is demonstrated by Domesday Book, which reveals through personal names the English character of the (secular) land-owning class on the eve of the Norman Conquest. The places whose lords these people were had British names, and

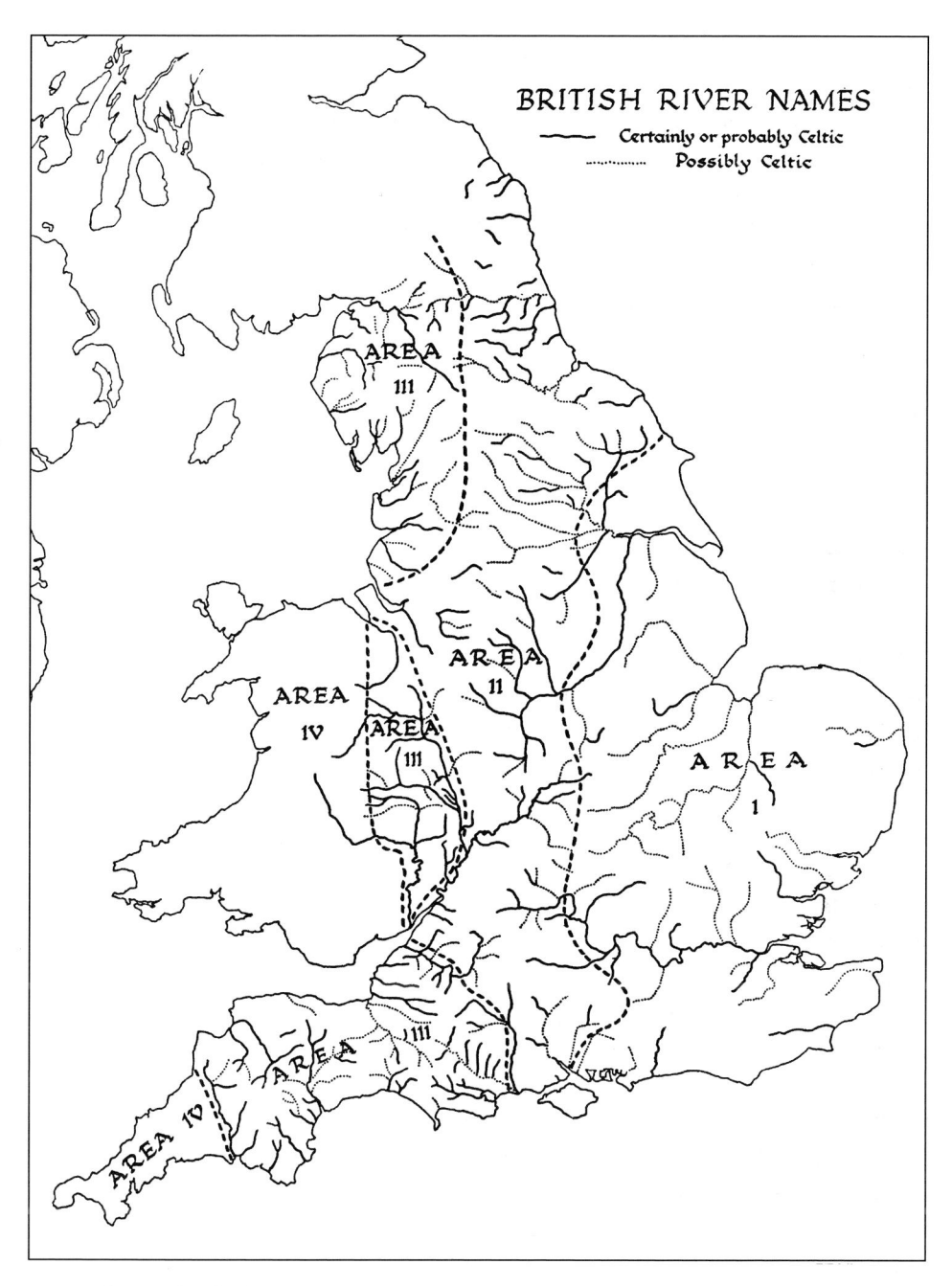

2.13: Distribution map of surviving British river-names, from Jackson 1953. By permission of Four Courts Press, Dublin.

their inhabitants were no doubt Cornish, but their lords had English names, whatever their ultimate ancestry (which, by now, may have been mixed). This is interesting because, were we simply to have the place-name evidence but no knowledge of the wider history, we might conclude that Cornwall had remained an independent region, like Wales, to a much later date than was the case. An underlying problem is knowing when place-names were actually created: we do not see most of them until recorded in Domesday Book, and we cannot easily distinguish those created fairly early from those created later when large estates were being broken up (see Chapter 4).

Topographical names, which commonly show more conservatism than habitative place-names, reveal a complimentary picture. Kenneth Jackson's famous map of British river-names, first published in 1953 in his *Language and History in Early Britain*, illustrates four areas in which the survival of British names increases from east to west. Cornwall's river-names, in the westernmost area, are British. Devon's river-names, in the adjacent area which stretches into central Wessex, were an English and British mix, whilst those in the two areas to the east were mainly English in character. The editors of *Place-Names of Devon* concluded that approximately one quarter of Devon's river and stream names are of known or likely British origin, including many of the larger ones: Avon, Axe, Clyst, Creedy, Culm, Dawlish [water], Dart, Exe, Kenn, Okement, Taw, Teign, Torridge and the Cornish border river of Tamar. Not all specialists, however, agree upon the original meaning of these British names, nor on whether they had originally applied only to the rivers themselves. Some have argued that what we know as British river-names had originally also been the names of the territories adjacent to rivers. Through various studies, Margaret Gelling has shown that the creation of Old English topographical names was just as important in the Anglo-Saxon "naming" of the landscape as was the creation of habitative names for settlements. She has argued that in most of England there was common application of a wide variety of Old English words for different types of valley, hill, wood and so on, and that these words were often applied before the habitative names emerged. However, in the far west, especially Devon, where the Old English language arrived relatively late, this consistency of useage had begun to break down.

Place-name evidence can sometimes illuminate other circumstances of English-British relations. Names containing a *-walh* element may refer to places with a definably British population which were recorded (in English) in this way because they still had landlords and inhabitants of British descent, whose families had survived centuries of change and maintained a separate, non-English-speaking, identity. On the other hand, because the British often slid down the social ladder in this period, the English use of "Welsh" was often synonymous with "slave", so that another way to interpret these places is as settlements characterised by very lowly people. Such –*walh* place-names are less common in southern England than further north, and few occur in Devon, though the element can occur in topographical or stream names, such as Walla Brook (a tributary of the Dart). Settlement names of this sort include Walland (Milton Damarel), Walreddon (Whitchurch, near Tavistock) and Wallover (Challacombe). Englebourne, near Harberton, shows labelling the other way around: it signifies "bourne (stream) of the English" and must have been formed when a significant indigenous population here had Germanic-speaking neighbours. As in other counties, some place-names emerged as hybrid forms: Old English *burh* (enclosed place) occurs, for example with British elements in Countisbury, Kentisbury and Membury. But making cultural distinctions on the basis of place-names may sometimes be misleading. It has been argued, for England generally, by Richard Coates, Andrew Breeze and David Horovitz, that deciding whether a name-element is British or English may not be as simple as supposed. Because an element is not obviously Germanic does not automatically mean it is British: when examined closely, some such elements do not fit into known Celtic language structure and may well be remnants of pre-Celtic language (referred to as Old European). The same authors have also argued that, while the proportion of British place-names in England (outside Cornwall) is indeed very small, their number may have been under-estimated because names posing difficulties of interpretation have been traditionally regarded as English where in fact they could be British. A north Devon example of this is Croyde, formerly explained as English but equally plausibly explicable as British (containing the element similar to Welsh *crud*, meaning cradle or valley).

A good illustration of the complexity of these issues is the area around Cheriton Bishop. Charter bounds, purporting to relate to the landed endowment around Crediton made by king Aethelheard in 739, make a significant detour to avoid this territory on the Dartmoor fringe. The excluded area coincides closely, however, with that bounded by a charter of 976 (of king Edward the Martyr to a thegn, Aelfsige) for an estate there described as "Hyple's old land". It was argued by H.P.R. Finberg, and subsequently by W.G. Hoskins, that *Ebel* was a British personal name, here rendered in Old English as "Hyple". The name was recorded, compounded

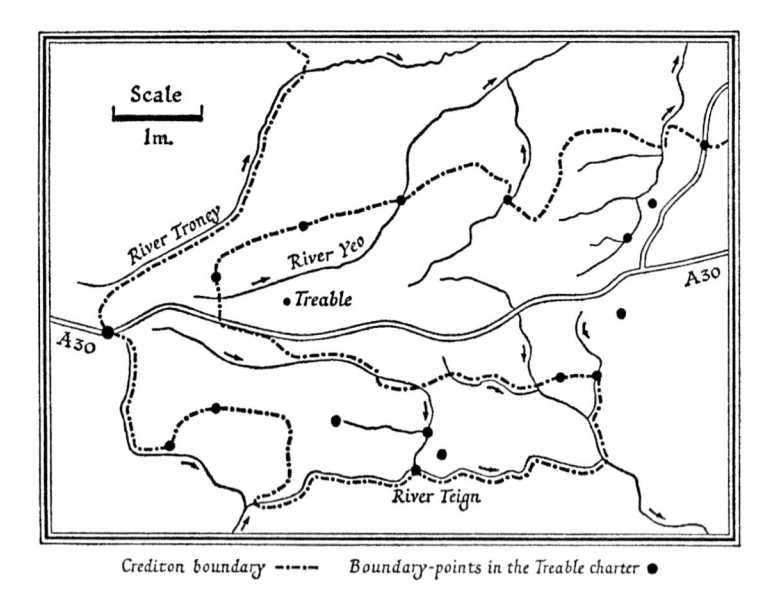

2.14: H.P.R. Finberg's map of charter bounds in the vicinity of Treable, first published in Finberg 1953.

with British *tref* (farm, hamlet, estate), as *Trefebel* in the thirteenth century, and survived as a farm name (Treable) into the modern landscape. It was suggested that this estate had still been in British ownership within living memory of 976, revealing why in the eighth century it had been outside Saxon royal control and thus excluded from the Crediton estate. Could this explain the handful (about three) of *tre* names in Devon? Perhaps they were still in British ownership at a late date when it had become common for names to be recorded, and (very tentatively) perhaps their owners were dispossessed by Aethelstan when he moved the British of Exeter to beyond the Tamar? Interpretation of the Crediton/Treable case is, however, burdened by the late date (eleventh century) of the Crediton boundary clause and the likelihood that the eighth-century estate had been smaller (see Appendix 2). The case also illustrates how fraught with problems the interpretation of individual place-names can be, since Andrew Breeze has since challenged the identification of the British personal name *Ebel*, emphasising how difficult it is to find convincing parallels for it. He has suggested, instead, the element *ebil*, a British word for a tool such as an auger or gimlet. This, it is proposed, applied to the nearby river – later known in English as the Yeo: rivers named after tools or weapons are known in Wales. If this is the correct interpretation, then the estate was named from a natural feature and not from an owner: the survival of its name in the tenth century is thus perhaps evidence for some late-surviving British-speaking rural population rather than for a land-owning family of consciously British descent.

Place-name evidence, illuminated by Oliver Padel, Margaret Gelling and others, also gives us broader insights into cultural zones, relatively free from the issues surrounding the interpretration of individual and unusual names. Amongst the topographical elements, *cumb* (valley) was popular amongst Devonians. Also popular was the element *hiwisc* (producing "huish") which perhaps meant a one-hide unit. Domesday Book reveals that of the common Old English elements, *tun* was that most frequently found in Devon manor (and later parish) names. In north Devon, the element *cott* was also much favoured. A great variety of Old English personal names also contributed to place-name formation. The list of these in the *Place-Names of Devon* runs to several pages, and is itself a most valuable reflection of early Devonian social history. There are, however, only a dozen examples of British personal names incorporated in place-names, including Branoc (Branscombe), Brioc (Brixham), Cadoc (Kigbeare), and Gall (Galsworthy). Richard Coates has suggested that Clovelly contains the British personal name *Felec*, the overall meaning being "the earthworks of Felec" (in reference to Clovelly Dykes), and that this personal name was compounded with *tre*, in nearby Hartland, to produce Trellick.

Shire Bounds (*Figs 2.1, 2.15, 2.16*)

The overall distribution of place-name elements, as studied by Oliver Padel, suggests that what became north-eastern "Cornwall", east of the river Ottery, had originally been part of "Devonshire" in terms of predominant English influence: an originally English administrative centre at Stratton (which also occurs in king Alfred's will – see Chapter 4) has been postulated on the basis of the English names of this area. More generally, the eventual shire boundary along the river Tamar cut through a zone of mixed place-name traditions. While British elements such as *tre* and *bod* are essentially Cornish in distribution, Germanic elements in Devon, such as *tun*, *worthig* and *cot*, also occur in some numbers in east Cornwall, suggesting considerable Saxon influence there at a date contemporary with Saxon influence in west Devon. Perhaps in order to create a boundary which was beyond dispute, that is the river Tamar, Aethelstan conceded this part of the far south west, which had become "English", to the new Cornish

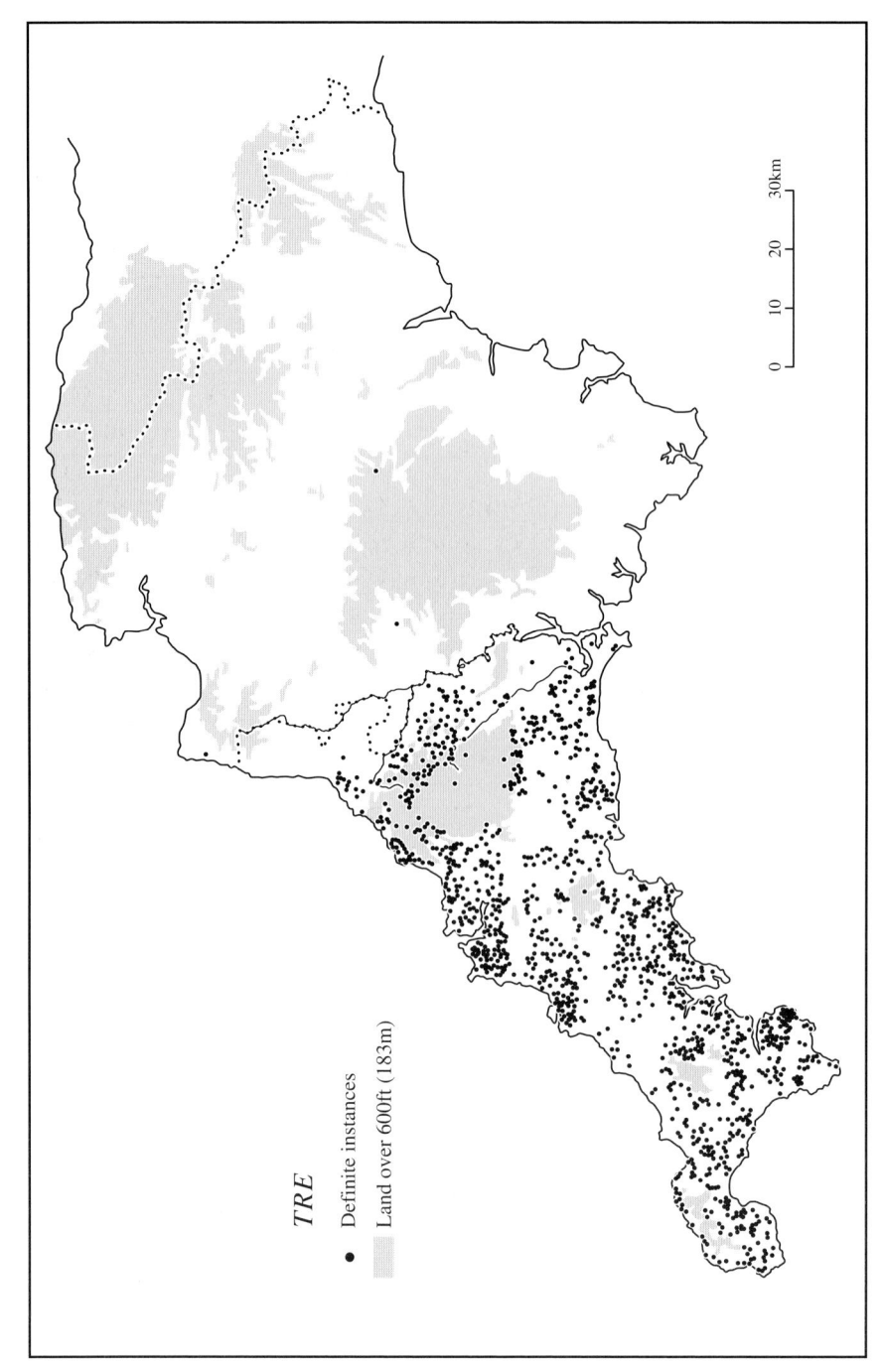

2.15: Distribution of the habitative place-name element *tre*, almost wholly in Cornwall, mapped by Oliver Padel in Kain & Ravenhill (eds) 1999. By permission of the author, University of Exeter Press and Roger Kain

shire. He may also have been restoring an ancient Dumnonian-Cornovian border.

A parallel example of non-conformity of shire and cultural boundaries occurs at the eastern end of the region. It is generally accepted that Dumnonia originally occupied the whole south-western peninsula, its most likely eastern borders being around the river Parrett in the north and the river Axe in the south. But that border did not become Devon's eastern limit as fixed by the West Saxons. Indeed, the processes by which Anglo-Saxon shire boundaries were created remain obscure, and perhaps different influences were at work: inheritance of pre-English lines in some cases, adoption of lines determined by a new pattern of land-holding in others, and perhaps also a deliberate creation of some new lines in order to destroy old territorial loyalties. In the south west, whatever applied, there were changes. First, Devon was to include land beyond the Axe, with its Dorset border east of that river, even though we might assume that the lower Axe valley would have made an obvious distinction for the new shires. Second, Somerset was to extend far to the west of the Parret. What the shape of Somerset may reveal is that, whatever the significance of battles commemorated in later sources (see above), permanent West Saxon cultural influence and political control was first established in the north-east part of Dumnonia. Thus, when the shire boundaries were laid down, the Brendon-Exmoor area, the first to be absorbed in Wessex, became part not of Devon, with the rest of Dumnonian territory, but part of Somerset. It has been suggested that west Somerset's Dumnonian origins lingered on for many centuries, sometimes leading to its settlements being erroneously described as "Devonian" by early antiquaries. When subjected to analysis by F.T. Elworthy in the nineteenth century, the dialect of west Somerset had more in common with that of Devon, with the river Parret suggested as a linguistic boundary, than it did with the dialect of east Somerset. This suggests that basic cultural features had been established before the shire boundaries were drawn up. In the twelfth century, William of Malmesbury preserved a tradition that, in 601, a Dumnonian king granted land in Somerset at *Inesuuitrin* to a monastery at Glastonbury. This has led to much speculation as to whether West Saxon Glastonbury succeeded an earlier British institution: the record of this grant, whose text William preserved and which was said to be witnessed by a bishop (Mauuron) and an abbot (Worgret), referred to the "old church". Most historians are inclined to dismiss these details as a later, and confused, fabrication: partly because this supposedly British gift of land was expressed in English hides.

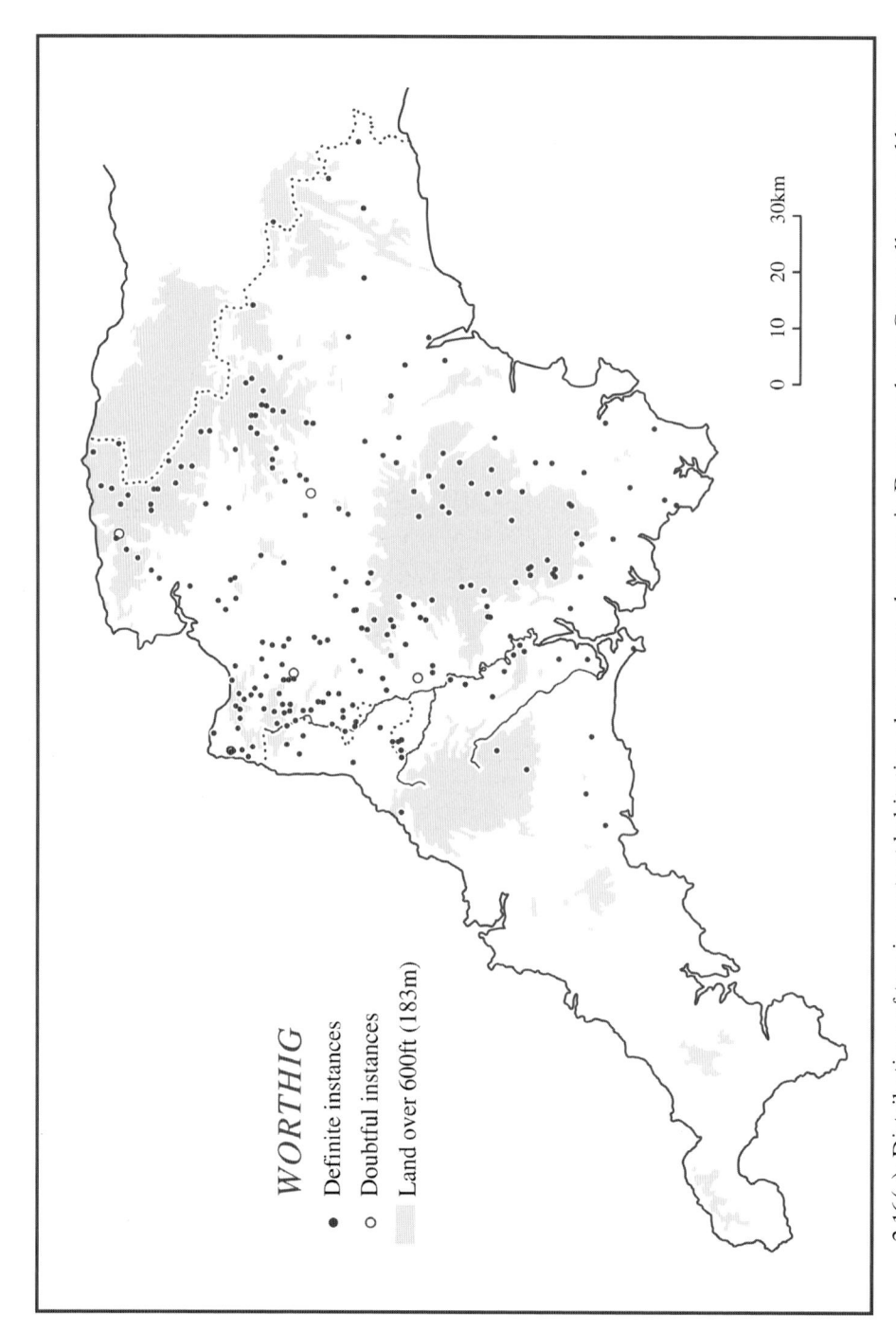

WORTHIG
- • Definite instances
- ○ Doubtful instances
- Land over 600ft (183m)

2.16(a): Distributions of two important habitative place-name elements in Devon and east Cornwall, mapped by Oliver Padel in Kain & Ravenhill (eds) 1999. By permission of the author, University of Exeter Press and Roger Kain.

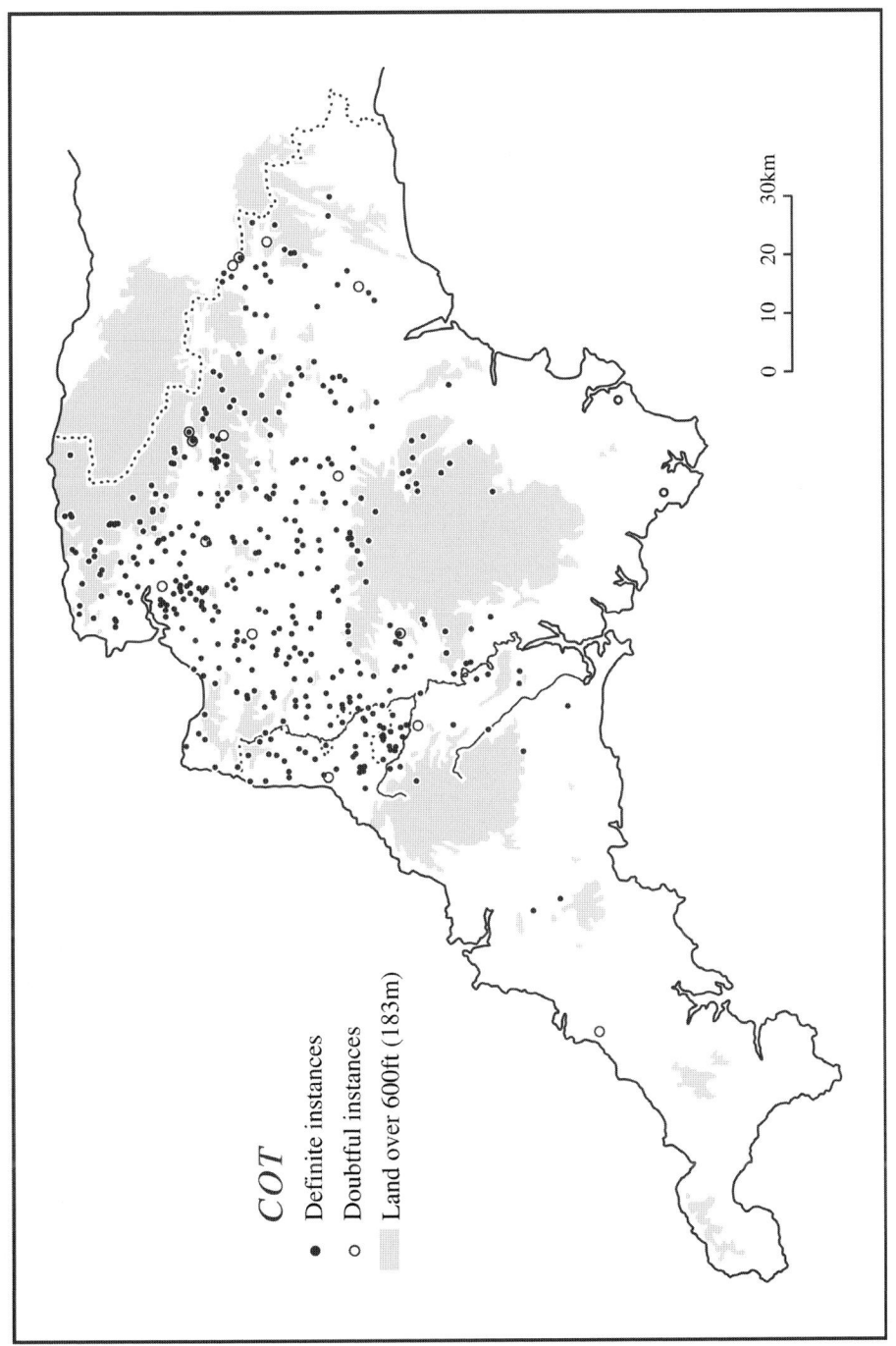

2.16(b): Note that the distribution of these elements, especially *cot*, complements the absence of *tre* names in N.E. Cornwall (see Fig. 2.15).

Fabrication though it may be, it is nevertheless of interest. It reveals that an early grant of land by a king of Dumnonia, made in what became Somerset, was felt to have been possible: had this not been the case, there would have been no point in making a pretence.

Several West Saxon shires existed by the later eighth century, when there must have been boundaries of some sort (see Chapter 4). But whether these were fixed from the start, or evolved before settling down into the forms known to us, we cannot tell. Sometimes, we can see from the descriptions included in Anglo-Saxon charters that estates already had boundaries partly coincident with that of the shire, providing a date by which such lines were recognised: this occurs in tenth-century charter bounds for Uplyme (against the Dorset border) and Culmstock (against the Somerset border). In the later middle ages, however, Devon was not exactly as it appears on the map today, as W.G. Hoskins explained in his well-known and influential book, *Devon*. The boundaries of Devon had included several anomalies. Stockland (originally a property of Milton Abbey) and Dalwood belonged to Dorset but were "within" Devon until 1842. Thorncombe (originally part of the royal estate of Axminster) belonged to Devon but was "within" Dorset until 1842. Chardstock and Hawkchurch were moved in 1896 from Dorset to Devon, when also Churchstanton was moved from Devon to Somerset. These outlying portions in adjacent shires may have reflected tenurial arrangements which pre-dated the defining of the shire boundaries: perhaps it was felt appropriate to include all the lands of an individual or institution in the same shire, even though these lands might not all be contiguous (for a similar issue relating to hundred boundaries, see Chapter 4).

At the opposite end of Devon, we find other anomalies besides those inferred from the place-name elements discussed above. Up until 1844, when it was transferred to Cornwall, the territory of Maker, just west of the Tamar, was part of Devon. This area had easterly connections from an early date: king Geraint granted land there to Sherborne around 705, and about a century later Egbert granted lands at Kilkhampton, Maker and Roseland to Sherborne. Whereas Kilkhampton (despite its location where English place-names are common) was to become part of Cornwall, Maker remained part of Devon even when the Tamar had become the shire boundary. It has been suggested that Edward the Elder had already insisted on this arrangement, early in the tenth century, so that he controlled both sides of the Tamar estuary in a critical period of defence against the vikings: he also acquired Plympton, on the east side, at this time (see Chapters 3 & 4). Finally, the loop of the Devon boundary which extended (for many centuries) west of the Tamar (to encompass the Petherwin/Werrington area) was an alteration of the early Norman period, whose creation was explored by H.P.R. Finberg: before 1066, when the Tamar was simply the boundary, this area had been in Cornwall (which accounts for some inconsistency in the way Devon's western boundary is depicted on various published maps relating to the medieval period). Even allowing for these various border complexities, the shire of Devon which emerged from the Anglo-Saxon period was amongst England's largest, surpassed only by Yorkshire and Lincolnshire.

Scandinavian influences (Figs 2.17, 2.18)

In considering people and place in the early middle ages, there is a final contribution to be considered: that of the vikings from Denmark and Norway, recently reviewed for Devon by Derek Gore. In the British Isles as a whole, these raiders, traders and settlers had a great impact from the ninth century onwards. But this impact was not uniform, and the south west of England was one of the least affected English areas. Eastern and northern England, having been subjected to a period of violent raiding, saw permanent viking settlement, the creation of an Anglo-Scandinavian culture in the countryside and towns, and the establishment of a whole viking-dominated territory known as the Danelaw. The south west, in contrast, in common with the rest of Wessex, experienced the primary phase of military confrontation revealed in the *Anglo-Saxon Chronicle* and in Asser's *Life* of king Alfred, but did not become part of the Anglo-Scandinavian zone because the West Saxons successfully resisted viking conquest.

Because the "viking period" so vividly brings into view the issue of maritime contacts, it is easy to overlook the importance which coastal traffic and travel must always have had along Devon's long coastlines. Frances Griffith and Eileen Wilkes have illustrated how a number of Old English settlement and topographical names around Bigbury Bay make best sense as descriptive names – relating to landed forms and resources – first created from the viewpoint of those moving at sea, but then transferred to features and estates on the land. A classic example is Thurlestone, a parish named from the off-shore Thurlestone Rock, whose original Old English name meant "pierced rock" (it still has arched form) and which occurs as a boundary point in king Aethelwulf's famous charter (847) relating to the South Hams. Although the development of roads and lanes (some of which

Making Anglo-Saxon Devon

Viking Conflict around Anglo-Saxon Devon

- (From Ireland) Sons of King Harold 1069
- Countisbury 878
- Porlock 1052 (Earl Harold from Ireland)
- Watchet 997
- Carhampton 836, 843
- R. Parret 848
- Pilton? 893
- Exeter 876, 893, 1001, 1003
- Pinhoe 1001
- Lydford 997
- Tavistock 997
- (Kings)teignton 1001
- Hingston Down 838
- Weekaborough? 851

2.17: Recorded English-Viking conflicts in and around Devon. Map by Robert Higham and Oliver Creighton.

are referred to in charter boundaries) was crucial to the emergence of the historic landscape (see Chapter 5), coastal movement, of both people and goods, was without doubt an everyday feature of early Devonian life which has left less obvious evidence.

The period of viking raids and military campaigns, nevertheless, had a considerable impact. In 836, a viking force attacked the royal estate at Carhampton, near the north Somerset coast and defeated Egbert's army. In 838, vikings allied with the Cornish (itself a reflection of Cornwall's partial absorption in Wessex at this time) but were defeated by Egbert at Hingston Down, near Callington. Three engagements followed in the reign of Aethelwulf, Egbert's son. At Carhampton again, in 843, the West Saxons were defeated. In 848, the vikings were defeated near the mouth of the river Parrett. In 851, Ceorl, the ealdorman of Devon, defeated a viking force at *Wicganbeorg* (perhaps Weekaborough, near Torbay, though other possibilities have been suggested including Wigborough in Somerset). Such events must have reverberated through south-western society, causing considerable apprehension, but local events were to become even more dramatic in king Alfred's reign. Between 865 and 875, the kingdoms of Northumbria, East Anglia and Mercia fell to viking conquest. In 875, the conquerors turned to Wessex, bringing an army overland to Wareham, in Dorset, and sending a fleet of ships around the coast to Poole harbour. In 876, having escaped Alfred's blockade at Wareham, the vikings moved south-westwards and occupied Exeter before the West Saxons could catch them. The fleet which left Poole, presumably heading for the Exe estuary, was broken up in a storm. Alfred blockaded the army occupying Exeter, but in 877, when a peace was negotiated, the vikings departed for Gloucester. Less than a year later, however, Wessex was on the defensive. Early in 878 the royal vill at Chippenham in Wiltshire was attacked, and at about the same time a viking fleet from south Wales attacked the north Devon coast at *Cynuit* (Countisbury: see above). Although the Devonian army, led by the ealdorman Odda, defeated these invaders, Alfred himself retreated to Athelney, in the Somerset Levels, to re-organise West Saxon resistance. His emergence, later in 878, and his victory at Edington in Wiltshire, led to an agreement with the vikings: from now on they consolidated their hold in the Danelaw. Nevertheless, in 893 the vikings attacked a fort on the north Devon coast and in the same year again came to Exeter. On this occasion, however, the city resisted: its assailants left when Alfred arrived with a relieving army.

Although these events must have caused great alarm, there had been no viking settlement of the region. But Alfred's reaction to the threat did bring about a development of enormous importance in Devonian history. Throughout Wessex, he created a series of fortified *burhs* to act as centres of military organisation and resistance to the vikings. A mixture of re-furbished Roman towns, newly-founded English ones and smaller forts, these places were not only crucial to the survival of Wessex but contributed greatly to the longer-term emergence of urban life. In Devon, *burhs* were established at Exeter, at Halwell, at Barnstaple and at Lydford. The re-development of Exeter, sometime after 877, must have been crucial to its successful defence in 893, and the north Devon fort attacked in 893 might well have been Pilton-Barnstaple. The significance of these *burhs*, stimulated by the viking threat, is discussed further elsewhere (see Chapter 4). The south west also contributed man-power to the large royal army raised by king Alfred in 893, after the relief of Exeter, for his widespread

Making Anglo-Saxon Devon

campaign against the vikings. The *Anglo-Saxon Chronicle* tells us that men came from Wessex "both east and west of Selwood", as well as from other regions.

In the late tenth century, however, Scandinavian raiding began again. In 981, the coasts of Devon and Cornwall were attacked and the monastery at Padstow in Cornwall sacked. Between 995 and 997, first the north Devon coast, and then the south coast were attacked. A fleet having entered the river Tamar, the vikings came up the Tavy valley. Their army sacked Tavistock abbey before moving on to Lydford. Here, however, the *burh* was successfully defended by the English. In 1001, ships came to the Teign estuary. Here the vikings sacked Kingsteignton, a royal vill, and then moved to the Exe estuary. The attack on Exeter was repulsed, though the vikings defeated an English army nearby, at Pinhoe. The entry in the *Anglo-Saxon Chronicle* for 1001 reveals that this English army had been raised, perhaps in a hurry, from Devon and Somerset. In 1003 the vikings returned, successfully entered the city and plundered it. The disaster was long remembered in Exeter's traditions. The Scandinavian threat remained throughout the reign of Aethelred II, culminating in the conquest of England by the Danish king Svein. Again, in Devon, this unsettled period is reflected in further development of the *burhs* (see Chapter 4). Excavation

2.18: Eleventh-century Scandinavian armlet, of twisted gold wire, from Goodrington on the south Devon coast. Published in Sykes-Balls 1978–79.
Copyright of and by permission of Torquay Museum.

66

has shown that Lydford's original earth and timber defences received a stone wall. During the tenth century, Halwell had already been replaced by Totnes. Recent scientific dating suggests that the fortification at Oldaport, near Modbury, was added to by Aethelred II in order to strengthen the defence of the south Devon coast. Excavation has revealed a significant re-fortification at this time of the prehistoric and post-Roman hillfort at South Cadbury, in Somerset. Other works of the period could await discovery in Devon. Perhaps to this period belongs the item published by Henry Sykes-Balls: an armlet made of twisted gold wire, from Goodrington Beach in south Devon. This high quality object, found by chance in 1978 and subsequently purchased by the British Museum, is closely paralleled by a similar armlet from Gotland, Sweden, found in association with a coin hoard of *circa* 1050. We can only guess at what personal circumstances led to the loss of this undoubtedly valued possession.

After Svein's victory, the kingdoms of England and Denmark were combined. The reign of king Cnut, his son, saw much change in England. Evidence of Scandinavian cultural influence in the south west is, however, rather thin. Like other important points of landing and navigation in western Britain, the island lying between Devon and south Wales received a Scandinavian name: the name Lundy means "Puffin Island" (*lund* – puffin; *ey* – island). A handful of place-names in south Devon combine Scandinavian personal names (*Grimr, Gripr, Ulfr*) with the English – *tun* element, to produce Grimston, Gripstone and Oldstone. Some coins minted in the Devonian *burhs* bear the Scandinavian names of their moneyers. In Cornwall, some stone crosses were carved in styles showing the influence of Scandinavian art, but none survive in Devon, if it ever had any. The most obvious place where a community of viking origin was to be found was Exeter. Here, some of the moneyers with Scandinavian names were to be found: Cytel, Carla and Thurgod. And here a church was dedicated to St. Olaf, the Norwegian king who Christianised his people and died in 1030. Between 1057 and 1065, St. Olave's church (in Fore St) was endowed with lands in Devon at Kenbury and Sherford by king Edward the Confessor and by Gytha (perhaps the church's founder –she was the Danish wife of earl Godwin of Wessex and mother of king Harold). It is quite likely that the foundation of this church marked the growth of a small but significant trading community of Scandinavians, centred on an urban property belonging to the Godwin family (see Chapter 4). These men and women represented the final contribution to Devon's cultural make-up before England was overwhelmed by the Norman Conquest. William the

2.19: Examples of pottery from late Saxon contexts in Devon. (a) imports from northern France, found in Exeter (b) Exeter's wheel-thrown Saxo-Norman products, found in Bedford Street (c) hand-made products of a rural industry in east Devon and Somerset (origin identified by the geology of the fabric's tempering). Photographs: Royal Albert Memorial Museum and Art Gallery, Exeter.

Conqueror, who besieged Exeter early in 1068 and subsequently replaced Devon's landed class with men from Normandy, Brittany and Flanders, was himself, of course, from a family of Scandinavian descent: the ducal dynasty of Normandy had its origins in the viking settlement of northern France.

Conclusion: "Englishness" and the archaeological record
(Figs 2.19, 2.20, 2.21)

In conclusion to this broad discussion of early south-western cultural development, it is salutary to note how little diagnostically "Anglo-Saxon" evidence has remained in the archaeological record of artefacts. This was emphasised in the Prologue (Chapter 1), where it was pointed up as a contrast with the plentiful data from grave-goods from pagan burials in more easterly parts of England (though even this is thin in neighbouring Somerset and Dorset). But the issue is not confined to the early centuries: throughout the pre-Norman centuries, the "English" are not very visible in Devon from traditionally-identifiable traits of material culture. Elsewhere (see Chapter 3), the limited evidence for Anglo-Saxon church architecture is described, together with a handful of stone sculptures decorated in styles attributable to this period. From circa 900 onwards, we have the evidence of coins minted in Devon, with stylised portraits of kings, mint-marks and moneyers' names (see Chapter 4). The latter represent the first appearance, in any quantity, of named and fairly ordinary, secular people: hitherto, "real" people emerging from our written sources were either ecclesiastical or of high secular status (see Appendix 3). "Real" British and English people, though anonymous, are also encountered in the succession of Christian cemeteries, in use from the fifth to eleventh centuries, excavated outside Exeter cathedral (see Chapter 3). Many were laid in simple graves, but some (in the later phases) were laid on a bed of charcoal in a manner also identified at other English urban cemeteries of this period, including Winchester, Hereford, Gloucester and Lincoln. The Devonians (and the occupants of west Somerset) produced their own pottery only from the tenth century onwards. They had built the defences and streets of the defensive *burhs* in the late ninth and tenth centuries, and we can still see parts of these today (see Chapter 4). They also produced elements of the rural landscapes which still survive, though these are often more difficult to date precisely (see Chapter 5).

Yet, despite their centuries of endeavour, the English of Devon left not much of their everyday possessions behind for us to find. Moreover, the

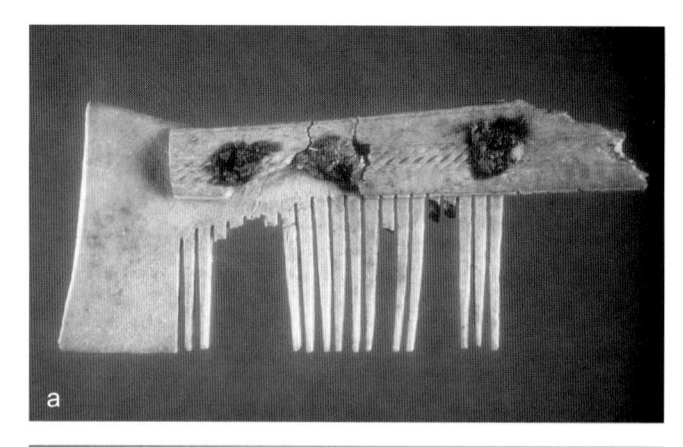

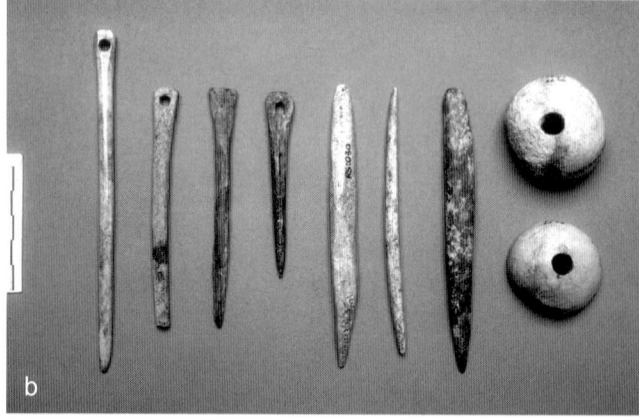

2.20: Examples of late Saxon bonework from Exeter, including
(a) comb with iron rivets (b) spindle whorls and needles.
Photographs: Royal Albert Memorial Museum and
Art Gallery, Exeter.

Dumnonian population which was absorbed within them soon became totally invisible in this respect: once their practices of inscribing stone memorials and of importing exotic pottery had ceased, the old British disappeared (artefactually) from view. In 1906, the *Victoria County History of Devon* listed only one item under "Anglo-Saxon Remains": found beneath a house in South St, Exeter, a bronze sword quillion decorated in Anglo-Scandinavian style, with an inscription reading "Leofric me fecit – Leofric had me made", identifying either its smith or its owner. A century later, the situation is more informative, but the number of known items is still small. A variety of wooden and bone objects (the former including an oak spade blade and barrel staves; the latter including flutes, combs, spindle

People and Place

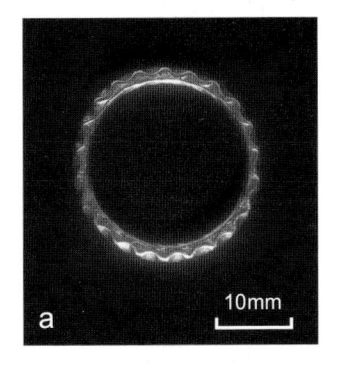

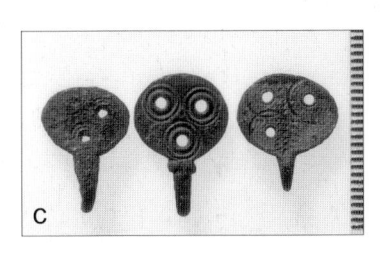

2.21: Examples of metalwork from Devon. (a) mid-Saxon gold finger-ring from a burial in Exeter Cathedral Close cemetery (photograph: Exeter Archaeology) (b) three late Saxon bronze stirrup-mounts from a total of six found by metal detectorists at Poltimore, Clyst Honiton, Cullompton and Kingsbridge (photograph: Royal Albert Memorial Museum and Art Gallery, Exeter) (c) three late Saxon bronze hooked fasteners from the Guildhall Shopping Centre, Exeter (photograph: Royal Albert Memorial Museum and Art Gallery, Exeter).

whorls and needles) have been excavated in Exeter from levels which are either very late Saxon or early Norman, and are displayed at the Royal Albert Memorial Museum, Exeter. At the same museum, pre-Norman metalwork displayed includes: a ninth-century strap-end from Poltimore; a late Saxon copper-alloy finger-ring from High St, Exeter; some late Saxon garment-fasteners from behind the Guildhall, Exeter; a gold finger-ring (over-glove size) from a mid-Saxon grave near the cathedral; some copper-alloy late Saxon stirrup-mounts from Kingsbridge, Cullompton, Clyst Honiton and Poltimore. Interesting though these items are, they hardly represent a compelling material impression of several centuries of English-dominated culture: an understanding of early Devon has to be approached on a wider front.

SOURCES USED AND FURTHER READING

Alexander 1916; Alexander 1919–22; Alexander 1932; Alexander 1995; Baugh & Cable 1993; Biek *et alii* 1994; Birch 1885–1899; Breeze 2005; Burrow 1973; Cameron 1979–80; Campbell 1962; Chadwick 1969; Charles-Edwards 1995; Charles-Edwards 2004; Coates, Breeze & Horovitz 2000; Colgrave & Mynors (eds) 1969; Collis 2003; Cramp 2006; Crick 2004; Dark 1994; Ekwall 1960; Elworthy 1875/1877; Elworthy 1886; Filppula *et alii* 2002; Finberg 1953; Finberg 1964; Finberg 1964(a); Finberg 1964(b); Foot 1996; Foot 1999; Fox 1970; Fox 1973; Fox 1995; Galliou & Jones 1991; Gelling 1978; Gelling 1993; Gelling & Cole 2000; Giot *et alii* 2003; Gore 2001; Gore 2004; Gover *et alii* 1931–32; Grant 1995; Green (ed) 1995; Griffith 1986; Griffith & Wilkes 2006; Gunn (ed) 2000; Handley 2001; Higham 1991; Higham 1992; Higham 1994; Hill 1981; Hills 2003; Hooke 1994; Hooke 1999; Hoskins 1954; Hoskins 1960; Jackson 1994; Kain & Ravenhill (eds) 1999; Keynes & Lapidge (eds) 1983; Lapidge 1984; Maddicot 1997; Morris 1973; Morris 1980; Okasha 1993; Orme 1991; Padel 1978; Padel 1985; Padel 1988; Padel 1999; Padel 2005; Pearce 1978; Pearce 2004; Pelteret 1995; Quinnell 1993; Riley and Wilson-North 2001; Rose-Troup 1937; Sheldon 1928; Snyder 2003; Stenton 1947; Swanton 1996; Sykes-Balls 1978–79; Thomas 1994; Thomas 1999; Todd 1987; Todd 1999(a); Todd 1999(b); Wade-Evans 1959; Ward-Perkins 2000; Watts (ed) 2004; Whitelock (ed) 1955; Winterbottom (ed) 1978; Yorke 1995; Yorke 1997; Yorke 1999; Yorke 2006; Yorke forthcoming.

3

Church and Society

Christianity was adopted in Dumnonia in the post-Roman period, and had perhaps been practised there in the late Roman period. The West Saxons were converted to Christianity in the seventh century. For the English, the conversion process was generally top-down, starting with kings, affecting higher social groups before whole populations. Whether a similar mechanism had applied in the earlier British adoption of Christianity is not known, but is quite possible. How far down British society Christianity reached in the immediately post-Roman period remains controversial. Nevertheless, a legacy of paganism survived in rural life and folk-lore amongst both English- and Celtic-speaking groups. Church writers railed against it from time to time, and the suppression of popular paganism was still an issue towards the end of our period, though by then it had been complicated in eastern and northern England by the arrival of Scandinavian settlers who were at first pagan. A law-code of Aethelstan's condemned witchcraft and sorcery; and one of Cnut's addressed the worship of idols, heathen gods, wells and trees. C.E. Stevens has shown that an extensive pagan sacred wood in the upper Taw area of mid-Devon survived long enough in folk-memory to influence the written place-name tradition: about a dozen Nymet or Nympton names here, in Domesday or modern form, are based on Latin *nemus*, meaning a sacred grove. Malcolm Todd has suggested that the tribal name of the *Dumnonii* was derived from the name of a pagan god – *Domnu* or *Domnunu* – whose worship had at some point been a common feature in the region. Similarly, the *Corn* element of the name *Cornovii* may reveal the worship of a (horned) god in the farthest south west. As everywhere else in the Mediterranean, Europe and British Isles, the success of Christianization in south west Britain, amongst people of all cultures, would have involved some adaptation of pagan practices, festivals and shrines to the new religion. Thus, an under-current of the older world survived, perhaps sometimes still reflected in folk-lore recorded in modern times, though this remains controversial. But the story of religion which we can study in this period, through history and archaeology, is essentially a Christian one. Although he was aware of a pre-Christian, pagan past, Gildas was concerned to castigate failings in British Christian leadership; if there was any surviving popular paganism in the west it was not an issue relevant to his critical theme. Devon's best-known early churchman was St. Boniface. He became famous, however, not from his English career but from his continental one, as well as from his later "re-discovery" in Devon (see Appendix 1).

Dumnonia (*see Figs. 3.1,3.2, 3.3, 3.4, 3.5*)

It is tempting to see a reflection of Christianity practised in Exeter from a late Roman pottery sherd, found near the forum site, inscribed with a Chi-Rho symbol (the Greek letters representing the word *Christ*). It has been generally assumed that any late Roman Christianity in Dumnonia would have been confined to Exeter, but it has been recently argued by Malcolm Todd that the octagonal building at Holcombe villa, hitherto interpreted

3.1: A late-Roman sherd from Exeter, marked with a Chi-Rho symbol.
Photograph: Royal Albert Memorial Museum and Art Gallery, Exeter.

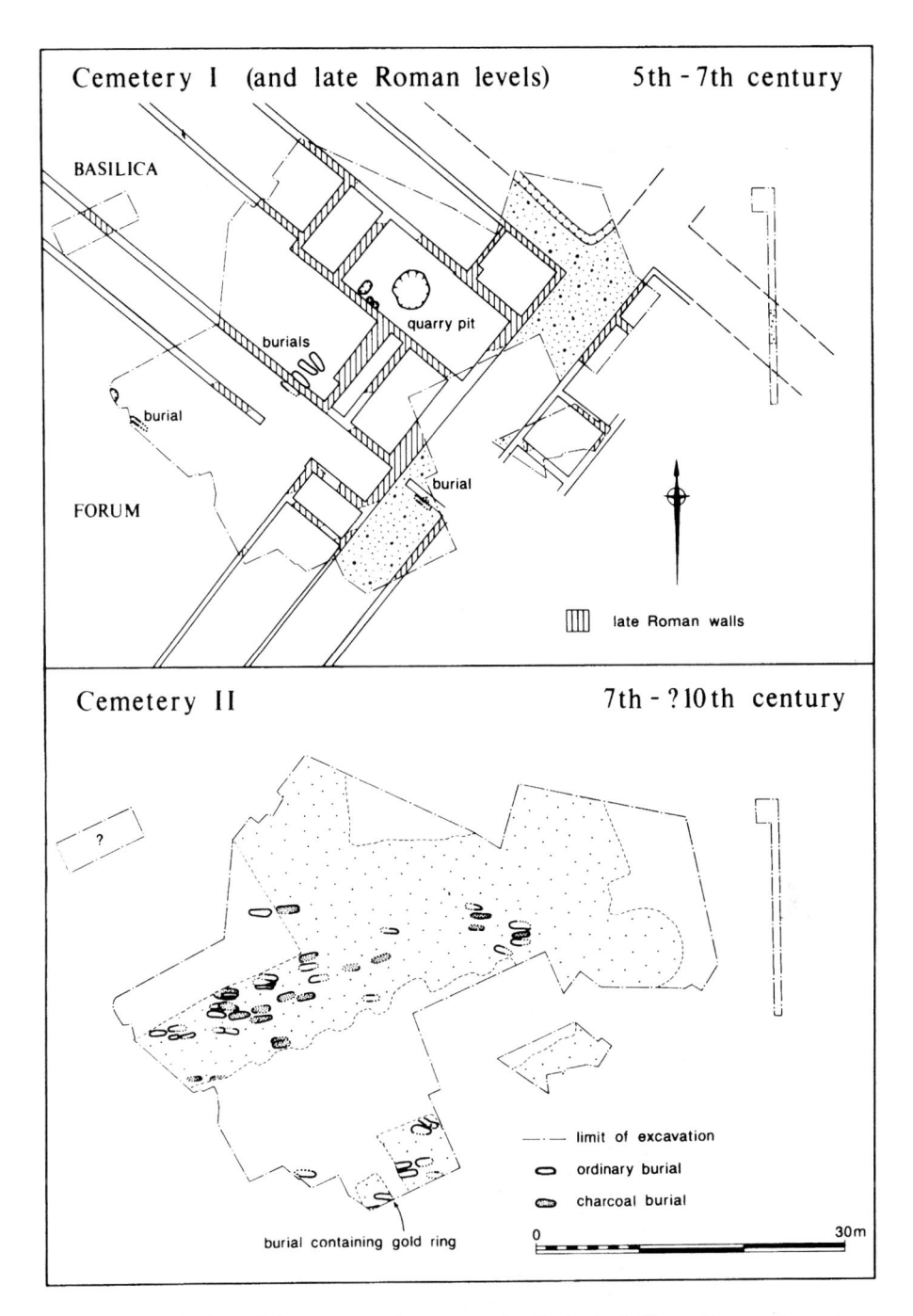

3.2: The evolution of the excavated cemetery in Cathedral Close, Exeter, from the fifth to tenth centuries, from Allan, Henderson & Higham in Haslam (ed) 1984. By permission of Jeremy Haslam.

3.3: (a) Sub-Roman burials and (b) a late Saxon burial (laid on a bed of charcoal) in the cemetery illustrated in 3.2. Photographs: Exeter Archaeology.

as a bath, was in fact a baptistery (similar structures are known at some Somerset and Gloucestershire villas). If this is true, there may also have been a rural strand to early Christianity in the region: even so, the high social status and east Devon location of this site are notable. Dumnonia as a whole became more widely Christian only during the fifth century, perhaps with some survival of practice from the Roman period, but probably also as a result of influence from Wales and possibly Gaul. In the western British society described by Gildas, writing in the later fifth- or mid- sixth century, there were monks, bishops, priests and deacons. Perhaps Exeter had been the centre of a British diocese for a time, with bishops established in the fourth century, as at London, York and Lincoln. Perhaps some lands owned by such a diocese could have survived through the Dumnonian and early Saxon periods into the documented church estates of later centuries? This is, however, purely speculative.

In the centre of Exeter, an early graveyard developed from the fifth century onwards, considered Christian from its intra-mural position and its lack of grave-goods. The earliest graves, up to the seventh century, followed the alignment of the demolished Roman forum basilica. A contemporary fifth-sixth century church, its patrons perhaps the Dumnonian kings, or another authority surviving within the city, may await discovery. Subsequent phases of this cemetery's development (over a hundred graves were discovered here) followed the alignment of the Saxon minster, part of whose tenth- and eleventh-century plan has also been excavated. Thus Exeter already had a minster church when king Alfred re-furbished the city as a *burh*. It had been there since the late seventh century, when St Boniface received his early education there (see Appendix 1) under an English-named abbot. The establishment of English abbots in Exeter must have been an important symbol of English influence and control in east Devon and the Exe valley.

The only relevant rural evidence from Devon at this time is a presumably Christian cemetery (with at least a hundred graves, mostly aligned east-west, with wooden coffins but without grave-goods) excavated by Peter Wedell at Kenn, a few miles from Exeter, and in use from the fifth to eighth centuries. It belonged to the period before Christian burial grounds were automatically attached to churches, a period much longer than we, from a modern perspective, might imagine. For a long time, except at minster churches, burial grounds seem to have stayed associated with rural settlements, only focussing on local churches as these became more numerous in the late Saxon period (see below). Roman material found here

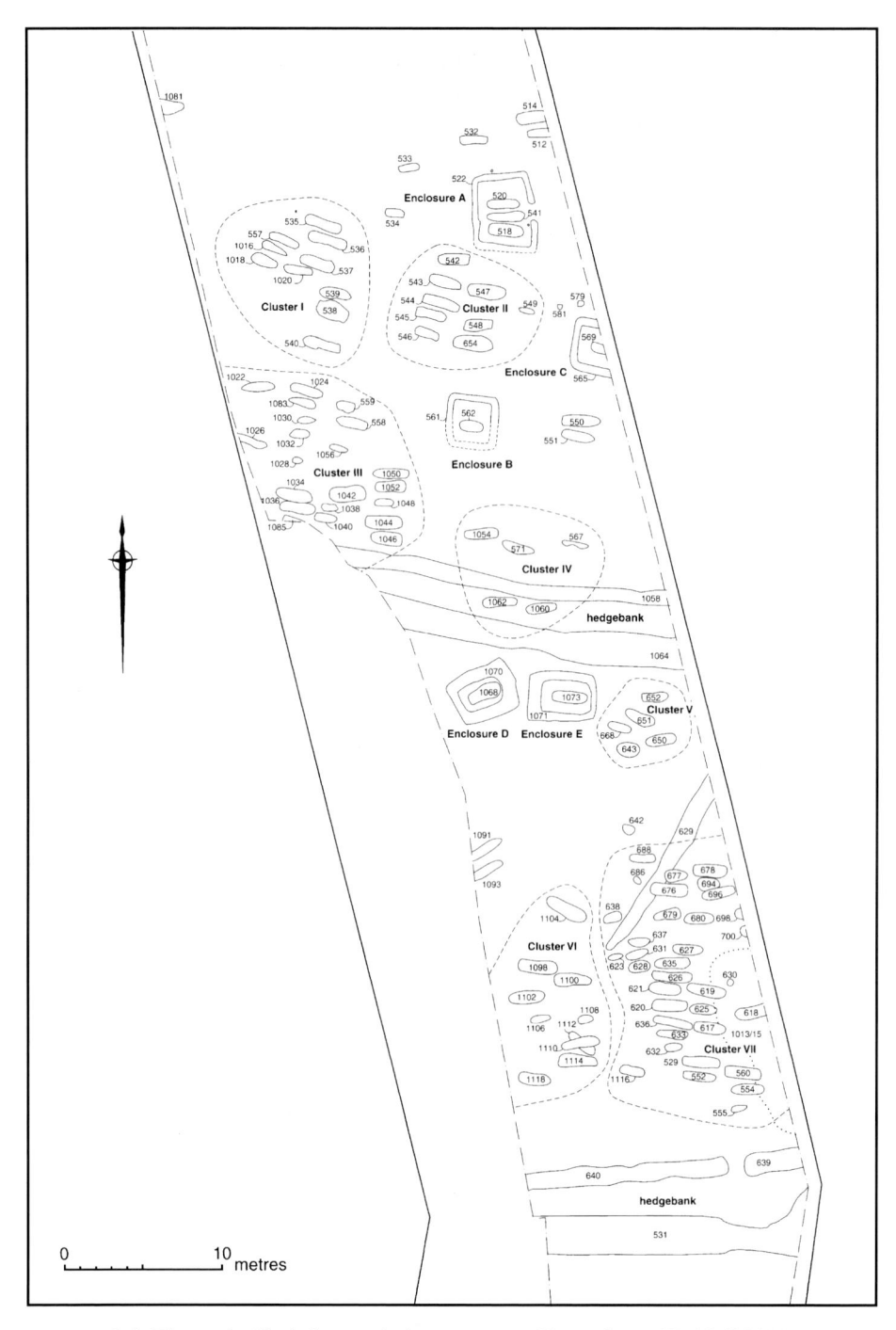

3.4: The early Christian period cemetery at Kenn, from Weddell 2000.
By permission of the author and Devon Archaeological Society.

may mean the cemetery at Kenn had earlier origins. The field-name here, "Long Stone Field", could even reflect an inscribed memorial, no longer surviving, to a Dumnonian of noble birth. Some of the graves, within ditched enclosures, perhaps represented people of higher status (the fourth-eighth century cemetery at Cannington, Somerset, seems to have evolved around some important individual graves).

The organisation of Christian institutions and practice varied in detail in the northern British, Welsh, Irish and Dumnonian territories, and there was never such a thing as "the Celtic Church". Power was wielded over specific areas by bishops and abbots: there was no over-arching authority. Just because the Dumnonian church was eventually subsumed in the West Saxon, we should not under-estimate the ecclesiastical culture which it may have produced. In the eighth century, Bede recorded the struggle in which English churchmen still engaged to persuade British priests and bishops to adopt English customs, and told how Aldhelm, as abbot of Malmesbury (he was later bishop of Sherborne), wrote a tract criticising British practices. This was the background to the letter written around 700 to "king Geraint and all the priests of God in Dumnonia", in which Aldhelm encouraged the observance of English liturgical customs. That he felt Geraint could effect this presumably reveals that, like its West Saxon counterpart, the Dumnonian church was under royal patronage. But that he wrote with some expectation of co-operation also suggests Geraint had already accepted some degree of English church influence in his territories.

Much later, in the mid-ninth century, Kenstec, a Cornish bishop based at a monastic see called *Dinnurrin*, finally agreed to the supremacy of Canterbury over his territory in the far south west. *Dinnurrin* may have been near Bodmin, though it is not certain whether the see was territorial (ie. a predecessor of that established in 931 at St German's by king Aethelstan) or whether Kenstec's authority was more personal in nature. Monastic communities in Cornwall, much illuminated by Lynette Olson, were flourishing in the later Anglo-Saxon period, notably at Padstow, Bodmin and St Germans. Although monastic life clearly did exist in earlier times, its full extent and nature is difficult to assess, though more is known about Cornwall than about Devon. But we must beware of uncritically back-projecting impressions from a later age. With the exception of St Docco, who appears in the (possibly) early *Life* of Samson, our earliest general view of south-western "saints" with British names is a list compiled only in the tenth century.

In south-east Wales, Gloucestershire, Somerset and Dorset the proximity of some early monasteries to Roman villa sites has been noted, perhaps indicating monasteries founded by the land-owning class on their own estates, which had remained intact. The thin distribution of known villas in Devon and their virtual absence in Cornwall makes testing this hypothesis in Dumnonia impossible, though it should be borne in mind for Devon. But there clearly was some monasticism at an early date, as in his castigation of the Dumnonian king Constantine, Gildas makes reference to an abbot (un-named) and also implies that Constantine himself became an abbot (in this, he was not alone: other British and English kings did the same). Our perception of Dumnonian Christianity is clouded by traditions of the "age of saints" – a mainly retrospective creation of later centuries. The first *Life* of St. Samson, perhaps written in seventh-century Brittany (some commentators believe it to be of later composition), is the only example of possibly early origin which relates to the south west: it reveals that monasticism existed in Cornwall in the sixth century. But the creation of later traditions means that church sites may be ancient, but not necessarily founded by those with whom they were later associated. Imbalance in our knowledge also derives from the slow process of English absorption of Dumnonia. By the time Cornwall was annexed its Christian institutions had enjoyed several centuries of development. In Devon, British Christianity disappeared from historical view in an earlier, less well-documented period: its institutions were either swept away or adopted by West Saxon kings, bishops and abbots. So we do not know for certain whether Devon enjoyed the same level of early Christian culture as appears in Cornwall from its better evidence, or whether developments in Devon had been more limited. Only the north of the county (also true of north Somerset) bears the clear mark of early "Celtic saints": Brannoc (at Braunton), Nectan (at Hartland), Kea (at Landkey). Other associations in Devon may be later back-projections, though certainty is impossible and published views vary on the extent to which we may assume early connections of saints and church sites based on dedications known from later sources: some commentators have been more inclined to trust the associations than have others. The case of St Petroc, Cornwall's best-known saint (though of Welsh origin) illustrates the difficulties, as revealed by Karen Jankulak's study of his cult. He lived in the sixth century, but the sources for his career, including a *Life* and *Miracles*, are creations of the eleventh and twelfth. His original cult site was at Padstow, where an eighth-ninth-century cemetery has been excavated by Pru Manning and Peter Stead, but it moved to Bodmin around 1000. Eventually, Devon had more churches dedicated to this saint than did Cornwall, but the bulk of the Devonian dedications are known only in later medieval sources. None (in Devon) is demonstrably of pre-Saxon origin, so great caution is needed in interpreting the significance of churches dedicated to St Petroc in, say, Exeter and Lydford. The Petroc dedications at Newton and Hollacombe are probably pre-Norman in origin, since Bodmin held both places. Petrockstow, a property of Buckfast Abbey, was a pre-Norman Petroc cult centre. But the "influence" of this saint on the region's churches was largely a product of his enhanced popularity after his promotion at Bodmin from the eleventh century onwards.

Devon inherited from early times another feature shared not only with Cornwall but with many other parts of the British Isles, namely a reverence for rural holy well sites, studied extensively in England by James Rattue. These were however, a popular feature for centuries, continuing to be created throughout the middle ages. Since most of them are not documented until later times it is normally very difficult to know when, individually, they originated. Overall, Devon had fewer in relation to its area than did the other south-western shires. Devonian examples included dedications shared with England and Wales generally (such as St Peter and St Thomas) as well as dedications with a more south-western or Welsh character (such as St Petroc and St David). Wells in Cornwall, like the churches there, had a high incidence of association with local saints. Since the worship of wells also figured in late Anglo-Saxon anti-pagan regulations, it is possible that some wells with Christian associations had much earlier origins associated with the pagan past, being "adopted" during the conversion process, perhaps as baptism sites in some circumstances. But, in Devon, distinguishing between pre-Christian, Dumnonian and Saxon creations seems an impossible task. And when we find, as is often the case, a holy well not far from a parish church, it is possible that the location of an early well influenced the later church site or equally that the well was created later during the church's life. In Exeter, recent archaeological investigation has shown the "holy well" previously thought to be the focus of the minster/cathedral site to be illusory. Another Exeter well, called St Martin's Well, still survives in Cathedral Yard beneath the (appropriately-named) Well House public house, but its interpretation presents a classic problem: is it a very early holy site from which St Martin's church, standing only a few yards away, was named in the eleventh century ? Or is it so named simply because it lay in the small urban parish of St Martin which emerged after the church's foundation?

The two counties also shared a tradition of inscribed memorial stones, now surviving mainly in Cornwall but including some in Devon (though more are known to have existed here). Such memorials occur also in Wales, Ireland and parts of northern Britain. The origins and dating of these memorials, which have been much studied in the south west by Charles Thomas, Elizabeth Okasha and others, have given rise to much debate (see Chapter 2 and illustrations there). Some have argued for beginnings in the late Roman period, inheriting the tradition of Roman tombstones; others have argued for later origins, more towards circa 500. They represent high society, mainly men but occasionally women, and names and titles are often specifically noble: x son of y is a common form. These stone memorials, in western Britain generally, are crucial evidence not only for social and religious practice, but also for contemporary spellings (in Latin and Irish *ogam*) of personal names. Some are clearly Christian, as they commemorate priests or bear a chi-rho symbol (the Devonian chi-rho example is at Sourton, where the Latin-named Audetus was designated a prince – *princeps*). The "here lies . . ." phrase (*hic iacit*) found on some (a few occur in Cornwall) may derive from Christian continental practice. In Britain generally, the latter obviously marked burials, but other examples (inscribed *memoria*) were memorials of a less specific nature. A Christian context is normally assumed for these monuments as a whole, though this need not be true for any which may be of late Roman date. From antiquarian records and place-names we know that many examples, scattered through all regions, were destroyed in antiquity. Whether the current distribution, including that in Devon, is also distorted by the disappearance of wooden equivalents, perhaps memorials to people of lower social status, or used where suitable stone was not available, is not known. The surviving Devon examples are (now) associated with graveyard and church sites as well as with trackways and boundaries, but many now at churches have been moved there and their original location is unknown. It is also interesting to speculate whether their survival reflects places where estates remained longest in Dumnonian ownership, others having been destroyed by West Saxon landlords to eradicate memory of those they supplanted. Their predominantly western survival within Devon may give some support to this idea. The popularity of these memorials may also have arisen partly from the conscious statement of British Christianity which they helped to make at a time when areas to the east were subject to increasing English (and at first, pagan) influence. Howard Williams has rightly emphasised that monuments to the dead are much more than funerary memorials. They make strong statements about a group's identity, linking past, present and future in a way which helps social cohesion. But fascinating questions about the Dumnonian memorials remain unanswered, including (as with many forms of funerary monuments) such basic issues of why people were buried where they were and whether burial and memorial monument were necessarily at the same place. Burial might, for example, be where someone was born, where they mainly lived, where they owned their main estate, or simply where they happened to die. Burial and separate memorial might, equally, occupy any two of those possibilities.

These Dumnonian memorial stones also present a paradox: they contain very specific information, yet challenges in their dating and evolution remain. A case has been made by Charles Thomas for their introduction to Dumnonia from Wales, whose stones have similar content. It was probably also from Irish settlements in Wales that the users of *Ogam* script came to Devon. According to this interpretation, early examples were erected by settlers, whereas later ones, distinguished by the style of their inscriptions, were native Dumnonian. An intriguing possibility is that the small number of inscribed stones found in Brittany may have been the work of Dumnonian emigrants. Emphasis on Dumnonia's connections with Wales raises the possibility that Christianity and Latin literacy largely came to the Dumnonian countryside through this Welsh link (allowing also for any residual Roman Christianity). Traditions gave Welsh origins to saints such as Samson and Nectan, and an early Christian cemetery with inscribed stones is known on Lundy Island, between Wales and Dumnonia. By the later Dumnonian period, of course, Devon was open to influence from the Christian kingdom of Wessex to its east: thus its Christian culture probably had more than one source of inspiration. The practice of erecting inscribed stones is thought to have died out in the eighth century, as West Saxon influence became stronger, but specific dating evidence is again elusive.

Another Dumnonian feature was the occurrence of embanked graveyards, often signified by the Celtic place-name element *lann*, for which Old English *stow* seems to have been an equivalent (at least in the south west). The former survives frequently in Cornish place-names, but there are two north Devonian place-name examples (Landcross and Landkey). Jacobstowe, Instow and Stowford (which also has an inscribed stone) are Devonian examples of the *stow* element, which is concentrated in north-east Cornwall and north-west Devon, where the subject has been explored by Susan Pearce. She has suggested that, in Devon, *stow* was the name applied by the English to pre-existing graveyards of British origin, which they adopted. The Old English place-name element *stoc* is also relevant

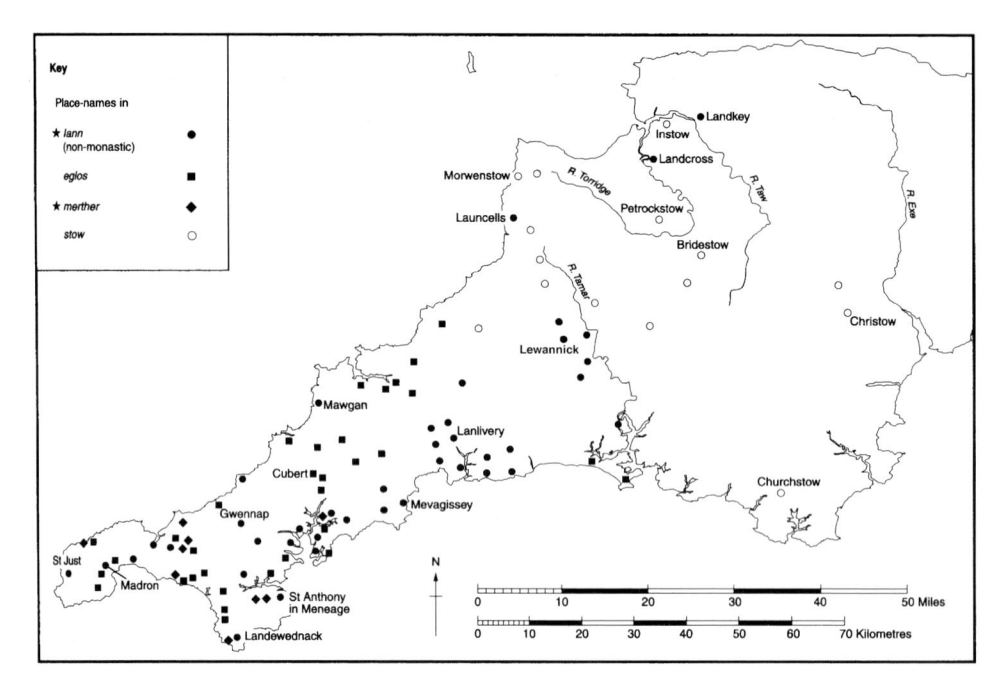

3.5: The distribution of *lann, eglos, stow* and *merthyr* names, from Pearce 2004. By permission of the author and Leicester University/Continuum Press.

since in some cases it was associated with an eventual religious site: Devon examples are Tavistock (compounded with a river name) and Halstock ("holy place", near Okehampton, where there was a medieval chapel). But *stoc* also occurs in places with no particular religious connection, and it cannot be used as a general indicator of early church sites. Even Tavistock may simply mean the *stoc* (outlying place) associated with two nearby River Tavy settlements (Peter and Mary).

Some embanked graveyards are known without these place-name elements, and *vice-versa*. Devonian examples surviving in the field include Lustleigh (which has an inscribed memorial stone) and Lydford. In one sense, such graveyards were the ecclesiastical equivalent of the "rounds" and other enclosures which characterised secular rural settlement in the immediately post-Roman period (see Chapter 5), and some (in Cornwall) seem to represent secondary use of "rounds". Independent dating of the origins of these graveyards (deliberately so-called because it is not certain that churches were originally associated with them) is difficult. Early dates are commonly suggested where there is an associated inscribed memorial stone (as at Lustleigh), or with a later tradition of a Celtic saint. But neither assumption can be demonstrated. The *lann* and other name elements are often documented only later in the first millenium, and inscribed stones may have been moved to "suitable" locations in the middle ages just as they were in the nineteenth century. Association with saints was an on-going process, not one confined to the early period. Recent work by Ann Preston-Jones and others has tended to warn against making unwarranted assumptions of early date for these graveyards. Indeed, recently there has been debate as to whether the *lann* element refers only to graveyards at all. Even if originally having that meaning, it may well have become a place-name element which refers to the entire settlement or estate around a church or graveyard (a meaning which it seems to have had in Brittany). Where a personal name is compounded with it, there is the possibility that it belonged to the secular Dumnonian patron who founded the site, not necessarily to its principal holy man. Such debates illustrate how difficult is the clear illumination of the details of this enigmatic period.

Despite such uncertainties, it is possible that some of these places originated as Christian burial grounds on estates of the Dumnonian landed class (even of royal dynasties) whose names we find on the inscribed memorials. The "longer history" of Dumnonia in Cornwall than in Devon accords with the distribution of the data. Sometimes old names survived, but elsewhere they changed as estates were taken over by Saxons or inherited by Dumnonians who adopted the English language. These places have also been used to suggest social continuity of another sort, because these embanked graveyards often (but not always) became the churchyards of parish churches in later centuries. Since it is recognised throughout England that parishes were commonly formed from secular estates (see below), these estate-parishes, developing from the very late Anglo-Saxon period, may sometimes have been successors to estates of pre-English origin, preserving earlier boundaries of great antiquity. But caution is needed in making such arguments. It is tempting to link the name on a memorial with the establishment of a graveyard (even a church) in a putative estate which later emerges as a known parish, especially if the existence of an Anglo-Saxon church can be demonstrated or inferred in the intervening period. Where connections of this sort have been suggested, as for example at Yealmpton, they may reveal one important line of Devonian church evolution which occurred more frequently than available evidence reveals. But they cannot be taken as a general explanation of the subject throughout the county: church origins were diverse.

Establishing the sites of specifically Dumnonian churches in Devon is notoriously difficult because developments in the Saxon period heavily masked the preceding centuries. Like most of southern Britain, Devon lacks the *eccles* place-name element (found mainly in the midlands and north) which indicates late Roman and early post-Roman Christian churches or communities. The "Celtic saint" dedications found in the south west are not necessarily evidence of pre-English origin for a church because of their on-going popularity throughout the early middle ages. Some have argued that where an inscribed memorial lies in or near a churchyard, we may very tentatively suggest an early Christian site despite the absence of a Celtic saint dedication: there are some half dozen such examples in Devon, including East Ogwell. As often in early history and archaeology, there may have been more continuity of site use than can ever be demonstrated. Exeter's English monastery may have succeeded a British one associated with the adjacent earlier cemetery, and at Hartland and Braunton, both in north Devon, continuity of place has been convincingly argued by Susan Pearce. Both were Saxon royal estates (Harton and Brannocminster) and had minster churches (see below) retaining strong associations with prominent Celtic saints (Nectan and Brannoc respectively). It is possible that the Saxon minsters here were successors to British monasteries and that the royal estates were the same as the earlier ones with which the original monasteries had been endowed by Dumnonian kings. Continuity between Dumnonian and Saxon periods may well have occurred at other places where no evidence survives to suggest this story to us. Parallels may be found in West Saxon shires to the east. The churches at Sherborne and Wareham, in Dorset, succeeded British institutions: revealed by name (*Lanprobus*) and by a group of inscribed Christian memorials, respectively. The pre-Sherborne *Lanprobus* name is useful in revealing an early formation of a *lann* name, a long way east of Cornwall where such names largely survive. It must have been formed before Sherborne was founded in 705.

English Minsters (*Figs. 3.6, 3.7*)

From the earliest conversions of the English by Augustine and his followers, from around 600, a mutually beneficial alliance between kings and clerics emerged. Kings granted lands for church foundation and support. The church needed protection and in turn it contributed structure and literacy to royal government. The West Saxons were converted from the 630s onwards and enjoyed this same profitable relationship, the results of which we observe when their influence extended to the south west. The spread of West Saxon church influence south-westwards, later in the seventh century, was not simply a matter of extending an English clerical culture at the expense of a British one. It was also part of the wider process of English conquest and colonization, a mechanism of ultimately royal control brought about by the promotion of new abbots and bishops and the granting of lands in newly-annexed territory to new or re-founded churches within the region, as well as to older West Saxon ones further east (see Chapter 2). The growth of the Anglo-Saxon church in this way also cemented a relationship between territoriality and Christianity which was to be a fundamental feature of the medieval world. The later seventh-century West Saxon "expansion" into Dumnonia coincided with the period in which a truly "English" church emerged, led and staffed by English people as opposed to, so often in the earlier period, by personnel from abroad. By the end of the seventh century, we can also see some familiar features of early medieval Christian society in the law-code of king Ine of Wessex, though whether the theory described always matched the practice achieved we cannot be certain. At least nominally, however, children were to be baptised within thirty days of birth, on pain of a fine; the tax called church-scot, payable to the church (annually, by Martinmas) was already established; and criminals could claim sanctuary in a church of minster status. Whether similar regulations existed within the Dumnonian church at this time (and earlier) we do not know because no written record has survived: but the British church of the far south west can hardly have existed without conventions supported by secular authority; its corresponding liturgical ones were much-criticised by the English.

The classic English "minsters" – important churches with groups of priests – have been much illuminated by the work of John Blair and others. When they emerge individually in record, it is no surprise to find the location and distribution of these churches connected with the framework of royal estates and with royal urban sites. The minster churches (sometimes referred to in modern literature also as mother churches or superior churches) were commonly situated in or near the eventual hundred manors (on which see Chapter 4) and sometimes influenced their names: as at Exminster, Axminster and Brannocminster (as Braunton was originally known). Axminster is mentioned by this name in the *Anglo-Saxon Chronicle* as the burial place of a West Saxon prince in 786, and its church is mentioned in Domesday Book. Exminster was mentioned by this name in king Alfred's will, and a priest here figures in Domesday Book. Since several of the

Devon estates mentioned in Alfred's will (see Chapter 4) had known minsters (that is, Exminster, Hartland, Cullompton) it is quite likely that the others mentioned in that source also had churches of some sort, thus increasing the likelihood of early churches at or near Tiverton, Branscombe and Lifton (on the latter two see below; Axmouth may have been covered by Axminster). Other known, probable or possible examples of churches in or near hundred manors were at: Crediton (see below and Appendix 2); Cullompton, whose church is mentioned in Domesday and which is not far from the hundred centre of Silverton; South Molton, where Domesday Book reveals four priests holding land of the king; and Plympton, whose *monasterium* and estate was acquired by Edward the Elder from the bishop of Sherborne in exchange for three estates in Somerset (it was mentioned as St Peter's, in the Geld Inquest, which also mentions St Mary *de Alentuna* in Plympton Hundred). At Tavistock and Buckfast (not hundred centres) it is likely that earlier minsters pre-dated the abbeys founded in the late tenth and early eleventh centuries respectively. The Geld Inquest conducted in the south west at about the time of Domesday also reveals other pertinent information. This survey, related to the collection of a tax in about 1084–85, was conducted within the framework of the hundreds. In Devon, groups of priests are referred to in the hundreds of Exminster, Hartland, Braunton and South Molton, confirming the activity of minster churches there.

Devon's first-known English minster or *monasterium* (see below for a discussion of the terminology) was in Exeter in the late seventh century, probably a foundation of king Cenwalh of Wessex (died 674). In his discussion of Boniface's early monastic career Christopher Holdsworth concluded that the life led here was probably a variant of the Benedictine rule. King Cenwalh was also the founder of Sherborne and Glastonbury. At Sherborne, in granting 100 hides at *Lanprobus*, he was certainly re-founding an older British institution. Opinion remains divided as to whether English Glastonbury also had a British predecessor. There is no evidence that Exeter was a daughter-foundation of either of the others. The general circumstances, together with the archaeological evidence from the adjacent cemetery (see above), suggest that Exeter may also have been a re-founded house of British origin. All three were established within the diocese of Winchester. There is no early tradition that Cenwalh endowed Exeter's minster with estates, though it is quite possible that he did so: his reign was still remembered as a period of endowment when charters were being "re-created" in the mid-eleventh century (see below). Alternatively, he may have confirmed the minster in possession of adjacent land associated with a

British predecessor, land which perhaps had been the extra-mural territory of the Romano-British city (see below and Chapter 4). Apart from Exeter, however, Devon's early churches of English foundation, or Dumnonian ones of English re-foundation, originated in the context of the new diocese for western Wessex founded in 705 and based on Sherborne itself, situated near the border of territories which were to become the shires of Somerset and Dorset.

In 739, king Aethelheard granted a (now unknowable) quantity of land in the Creedy valley to the church at Sherborne, for the building of a minster. This is recorded in a surviving charter of eleventh-century date, by which time the estate had been enlarged to some twenty hides (see also Appendix 2). Patrick Hase has emphasised that West Saxon kings granted "bookland" (see Chapter 4) in this way only to churches of high status: Winchester, Malmesbury and Abingdon in the centre of Wessex; Glastonbury and Muchelney in Somerset; Sherborne in Dorset. At various dates, from the reign of king Ine onwards, both Sherborne and Glastonbury received lands in Devon in addition to endowments in Dorset and Somerset. Although only the Crediton grant survives to reveal a specific intention of church foundation, there are reasons to believe that Sherborne was connected with other churches in Devon (see below). The founding of a minster at Crediton, which extended Sherborne's influence, was a serious step, reflecting a significant strengthening of English influence west of the river Exe (as had Aethelheard's grant of land in the Torridge valley to Glastonbury in 729, referred to in its later monastic records). It has been suggested by Rosamond Faith that when king Aethelwulf granted land to himself in the South Hams in 847, even though the charter does not say so, he may have set up a minster church in the royal estate of West Alvington, which lay within this territory: in the later middle ages, the church here is known to have had dependent chapelries, a useful indicator of earlier minster status, and it also had Sherborne connections (see below).

Though many minsters were associated with royal estate centres, they also came to serve the populations of larger rural areas. Minster status may have existed at other churches in royal hundred manors, in addition to those mentioned above: for example at: Tiverton, whose church was served in later times by a group of priests; Colyton, where king Edmund held a royal council around 945 and whose cruciform church has a fine Saxon cross shaft; and Hemyock, whose church was also originally of cruciform plan. We may wonder whether an early church may also have existed at Ottery (St Mary), the head manor of a small hundred, though no mention of it was made in the charter recording its granting in 1061, by Edward the Confessor, to St. Mary's church in Rouen. We might expect that Heavitree church, outside Exeter and at the centre of the royal estate of Wonford, had origins as a minster, but there is no specific evidence for this. It is notable that some of the known or likely minster sites had later medieval churches with a crossing tower and cruciform plan – a form generally uncommon in Devon. Examples include Crediton, Axminster and Colyton. Perhaps, as Ralegh Radford suggested, where this plan occurs at a later date in a parish church, more important origins may be inferred? But some known or potential minster sites had later medieval plans of simpler form, as at Exminster, so there was clearly no general rule.

Whether every hundred had a minster church at some time cannot be shown, but this may have been the intention. In Cornwall, where the hundreds were different (fewer, larger) and minster churches of the English pattern were late to emerge, the only minster with a large territory seems to have been St Stephen's, near later Launceston. For Devon, as elsewhere, there is a danger in assuming that the pattern of minsters and hundreds, seen clearly only in the later pre-Norman period, had been regularly planned from the start. The hundreds themselves emerged in final form only in the tenth century, and early in their history the minster territories may also have been less well defined: the situation in England generally is far from clear, and it has been argued that what is visible at the end of the Anglo-Saxon period was largely a product of re-organisation in the ninth and tenth centuries. Demonstrating that all minsters eventually identifiable by the tenth century had been operating two centuries earlier is difficult. In their earlier days, it is also possible that some minster territories related to the administrative *regiones* into which the early English kingdoms and shires were sub-divided and which may have influenced the hundreds which eventually emerged. In the south west, with its pre-English Christian history, some minsters may have taken over the territories of the Dumnonian churches, or possibly Dumnonian administrative areas. The landscape of Anglo-Saxon churches was probably not as neat and tidy as we might like it to be, and there were probably many regional variations in practice.

Sometimes, the larger territories served by minster churches can be tentatively reconstructed by identifying the parishes into which they were divided at a later date. W.G. Hoskins explored this theme in his influential essay "The Making of the Agrarian Landscape", and Nicholas Orme has discussed it in the context of wider Devonian church history. These territories were sometimes whole hundreds, for example at Hartland,

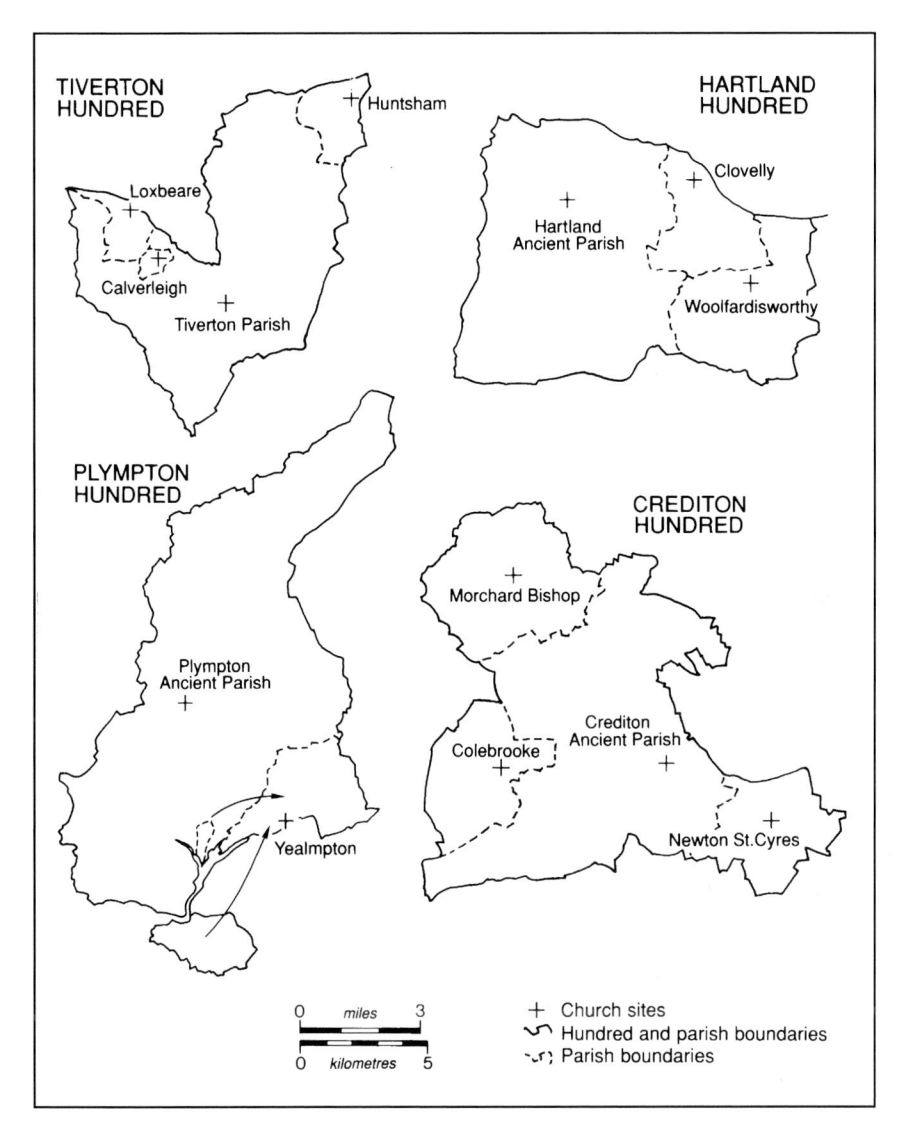

3.6: Reconstructions of some early minster territories/hundreds, from Orme 1991.
By permission of the author and University of Exeter Press.

Braunton, Tiverton, Plympton and Crediton. Susan Pearce made this argument in detail for Hartland, where Cheristow, Welcombe and Harton were dependent on Stoke St Nectan, in her study of the early church in north Devon. Long ago, O.J. Reichel noted how the original dependent chapelry status of some eventual parishes was a clue to early minster territories coincident with hundreds. He drew attention, for example, to

Plympton (on whose church Plymstock, Wembury, Brixton and Shaugh had been dependent), and to West Alvington (on whose church South Milton, Marlborough, Salcombe and South Huish had been dependent, comprising Stanborough hundred). Not far away, Stokenham, with dependencies at Sherford and Chivelstone, was probably the minster church for the large royal estate centred on Chillington. Its name contains the element *–stoc,* one of whose meanings can be a holy place (see above). In his study of the South Hams region, Terry Slater has suggested that early churches may also have existed at Harberton (within which the Alfredian *burh* at Halwell was situated) and at Diptford, the centre of the hundred known as Diptford or Stanborough: the churches at North Huish, Woodleigh and Churchstow were all dedicated to St Mary, like Diptford itself.

We are unlikely ever to be able to reconstruct all the minster territories which at some time existed, but wherever or however they may have been defined, we know that in Bede's world the minster clergy were supposed to travel to rural communities and offer pastoral care and the sacraments. The minster churches also provided baptism and burial services for their territories, but their role as burial places for the general population seems to have been a late development: earlier this role had been preserved for those of royal or noble status and more lowly burial grounds were settlement-related. In return for pastoral provision, the rural population paid an annual render of grain to the church: this was the church-scot mentioned in Ine's law-code of c. 690. Nevertheless, despite this overall picture, historians are divided in their opinions as to whether a "minster system" was ever fully developed and whether minsters were the sole source of pastoral care for the countryside. An interesting national debate has been conducted, involving particularly the authors Blair, Cambridge and Rollason. We must remember that in Bede's world and later, bishops and their priests also had important pastoral functions within their dioceses and it is easy to under-estimate their importance. Eventually, the growth of local churches made the situation more complex (see below), as had (in the south west) the survival of some Dumnonian churches.

Another approach to identifying sites of possibly early churches is through association with Devonian estates specifically owned by the bishops of Sherborne, whose see was created in 705. At two such places, the associations are well-known. First, Sherborne received land in 739 at Crediton for the building of a minster (see above). Second, Edward the Elder exchanged lands in Somerset (between 899 and 909) with Sherborne in order to acquire Sherborne's estate and minster at Plympton. For how long Sherborne had held Plympton is not known: it may have been an eighth-century acquisition (like Crediton but with no surviving charter) but according to another theory it had only recently been acquired, originating in a gift from king Alfred to Asser. If this was the case, then its church may not have been very ancient. The wider pattern of early Sherborne holdings in Devon is masked because of the creation of the Crediton diocese in 909 and its own subsequent land-holding evolution. Fortunately, there survive, among the Sherborne sources published by Mary Ann O'Donovan, two fourteenth-century lists of pre-909 Sherborne properties revealing estates scattered across the south-western shires. Some of the place-names in these lists are difficult to identify on the map (there being several possible candidates in more than one shire). But Tawstock (in north Devon) and Culmstock (in east Devon) seem to be reliable identifications. Together with Plympton (in the south) and Crediton (in the centre) they might represent locations deliberately chosen, in different areas of Devon, as a framework of episcopal influence and perhaps as bases for visits: if so, churches at these places might be expected. Perhaps also relevant is the later medieval form of Tawstock church: a cruciform plan with crossing tower, associated with minster origins in some cases (see above). The later medieval bishops (by then of Exeter) had a residence nearby at Bishop's Tawton.

Yet another route into early minster origins comes from identifying Devon churches whose benefices' patronage lay with Salisbury (originally at Old Sarum) which replaced Sherborne as the see in 1075. Since it seems highly unlikely that Sherborne would have acquired Devonian interests after the creation of Crediton diocese in 909, Devon churches with Salisbury connections are also good candidates for having been created by Sherborne in Devon before 909. Churches noted in this category by various early commentators, such as Frances Rose-Troup and O.J. Reichel, include West Alvington, Kenton, Kingsteignton, Harberton and Yealmpton. A church at Kingsteignton, in a royal estate controlling the bridge over the Teign, would be not surprising. Yealmpton and West Alvington (on which, see above) were also royal estates, and Domesday Book specifically mentions priests at Yealmpton. Not all early churches, however, may have been full minsters: Kenton seems too close to Exminster for each to have a sizeable "minster territory" so perhaps Kenton was a sub-minster of Sherborne ? It is interesting, however, that in its later medieval form, Kenton was a much more impressive church than Exminster, so perhaps it had become the more important of the two at some point?

Various writers, including Ralegh Radford, John Blair, Nicholas Orme,

Christopher Holdsworth, Susan Pearce, Della Hooke and Sam Turner have produced (slightly different) lists or maps of known or likely Devon minsters. Several can certainly be identified on one or more of various grounds discussed above: direct reference in Anglo-Saxon sources; mentions of church, groups of priests or significant land-holding in Domesday Book or later sources; situated in large parishes with dependent chapels; connections with hundred centres or other royal estates. In addition to those already mentioned, others fitting one or more of these criteria have been suggested with varying degrees of certainty at: Hollacombe, Newton St Petrock, Kingskerswell, Modbury and Stokenham. Several of these were royal manors before 1066. Domesday specifically mentions the church at Kingskerswell. The Geld Inquest mentions St Mary's church at Modbury. The sizeable church at Stokenham, though not documented until around 1200, served a very large territory based on a royal manor at Chillington (by which name the hundred of Coleridge was first known). It is very likely to be of early origin (and see below, on its dedication). Hollacombe and Newton St Petrock present difficulties. Domesday Book mentions groups of priests: these were priests of St Petroc's in Bodmin, which is said by Domesday to have held land at both places, but there was no specific Domesday mention of churches. On the other hand, the Geld Inquest refers to priests at both these places as though they were resident here, in which case presumably there were also churches. In his commentary on *Exon Domesday*, R. Welldon Finn argued that priests would only be relevant to the Geld Inquest if they were holding land in the particular hundred where they are mentioned. If there were early churches at Hollacombe and Newton, they were perhaps sub-minsters of Bodmin.

It has also been suggested that minsters may have existed at or very near the places where slaves were freed, because the records commonly refer to the presence of priests at the ceremony: for example, the tenth-century manumissions for ealdorman Ordgar (who died in 971) at Bradstone, in Lifton hundred, make such reference, including priests named as Cynsie, Goda and Aelfric. While these priests may have come from a pre-abbey minster at Tavistock, their presence also raises the possibility of a minster at Lifton itself, which lay much closer to Bradstone (an issue also relevant to interpretation of the *burh* church at Lydford – see below). Ralegh Radford, on the other hand, speculated whether an early church of minster status in Lifton hundred, from which these priests came, may be reflected in the *stow* name at either Bridestowe or Marystow. A groups of priests, but whose names were not specified, was also present at a manumission at

Okehampton, raising the possibility that its eventual parish church also had earlier, and different origins. But interpreting this aspect of manumissions is made complicated by our ignorance of how far away from a minster priests may have travelled to be present at the ceremonies: travel within a territory was, after all, part of their normal function.

But whatever the number of Devon minsters suggested by currently available evidence, these churches cannot have provided easy access for this large shire's scattered population: there seem not to have been enough. Nearly half of Devon's eventual hundreds had no (at least known to us) known minster of full status. This may mean that minsters did not develop in Devon to the extent found in some other English shires. It should, however, be noted that minsters did not appear with similar densities in all parts of England: eastern Mercia and parts of the north had fewer than Wessex and western Mercia. Even in Wessex, different shires had different "minster histories" as studies by Patrick Hase and Teresa Hall have illustrated. Alternatively, it may mean that some places later known as parish churches had an earlier existence which has left no direct evidence: either as English minsters, or as churches surviving from the Dumnonian period. With its pre-Saxon Christian origins, however, Devon may simply have been less dominated by English-style minsters than were some shires to its east. Just as some Devon minsters may have developed from Dumnonian churches, it may be that other Dumnonian foundations had a continuous existence as lesser churches, later emerging, in different guise, as parish churches. The challenge of "hunting the minster" – fascinating exercise though it may be – is not the sole key to understanding church organization in Saxon Devon. And thus, a methodological paradox is inescapable. For while, as argued earlier, proving (from direct evidence) early dates for churches at specific sites is often impossible, it is also possible to argue on more general grounds that more of Devon's rural churches may have had a Dumnonian origin than we can now demonstrate in detail. In this respect, Devon's experience may have been more like that of Cornwall and Wales though in some other respects (see below) Devon's experience was to become more "English".

While the number of full minsters does look rather thin for Devon, the total of churches at the end of the eleventh century is great deal larger when other types are taken on board: possible sub-minsters, possible Dumnonian survivals and local churches (see below). The accompanying map, which illustrates all the categories, gives a more convincing impression of a Christian shire by the eleventh century. It is interesting to note that, while the issue of minster development is still a topical one early in the

Some Churches in Early Devon

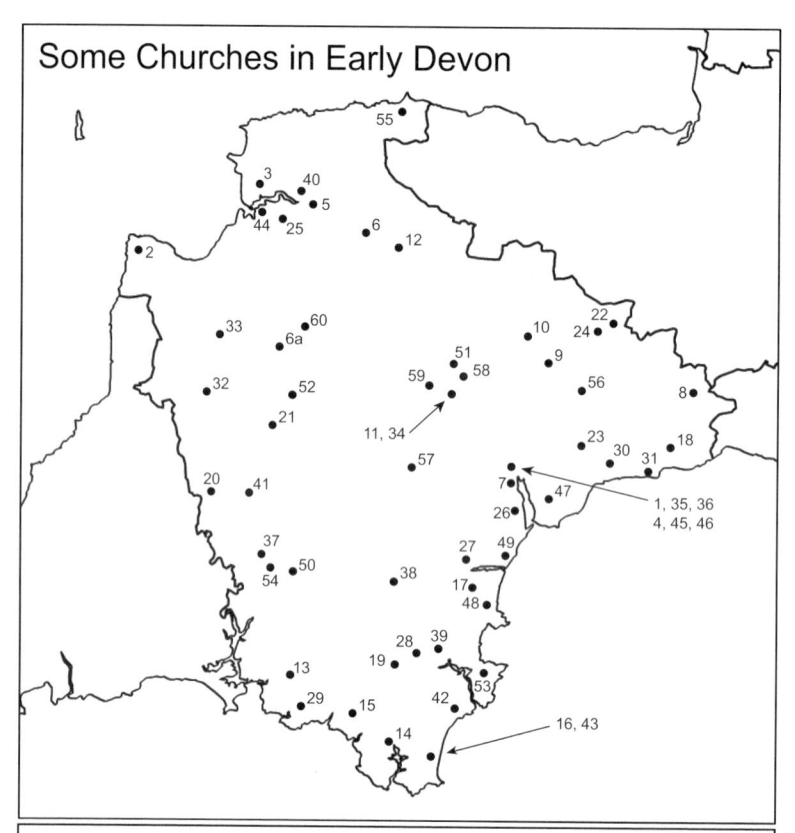

A. Major Dumnonian churches transformed into English minsters
1. Exeter?
2. Hartland (Nectan)
3. Braunton (Brannoc)

B. Other churches of Dumnonian origin (also possibly 32, 33, 41)
4. Exeter (Sitfolla?)
5. Landkey (Kea)
6. Chittlehampton (Urith)
6a. Petrockstowe

C. English rural minsters (also Groups A, D; and 37? 38?)
7. Exminster
8. Axminster
9. Cullompton
10. Tiverton
11. Crediton
12. South Molton
13. Plympton
14. West Alvington
15. Modbury
16. Stokenham
17. Kingskerswell
18. Colyton*
19. Diptford?
20. Lifton?
21. Okehampton?
22. Hemyock?
23. Ottery St Mary?

D. Possible Sherborne minster/sub-minster foundations (and 11, 13, 14)
24. Culmstock
25. Tawstock
26. Kenton
27. Kingsteignton
28. Harberton
29. Yealmpton

E. Possible sub-minsters of Exeter
30. Sidbury*
31. Branscombe

F. Possible sub-minsters of Bodmin
32. Hollacombe (Petrock)
33. Newton St Petrock

F. Cathedrals
34. Crediton
35. Exeter

H. 10th- to 11th-century reformed monasteries
36. Exeter*
37. Tavistock
38. Buckfast

I. Burh minsters/sub-minsters (also 1/35/36)
39. Totnes
40. Barnstaple
41. Lydford

J. Dedications to local Old English saints
42. Stoke Fleming (Earmund)
43. Stokenham (Hunberht)
44. Instow (John?)

K. 11th-century references or indicative place-names
45. Pinhoe
46. Heavitree (St James)
47. Woodbury
48. Marychurch
49. Teignmouth
50. Walkhampton?
51. Poughill
52. Honeychurch
53. Churston (Ferrers)
54. Whitchurch
55. Cheriton (Brendon)
56. Cheriton (Payhembury)
57. Cheriton (Bishop)
58. Cheriton (Fitzpaine)

L. Additional crosses
59. Copplestone
60. Dolton

twenty-first century, the history of this debate in Devon goes back almost a hundred years, when it was pursued by W. Page (who had been editor of Devon's *Victoria County History*) and O.J. Reichel (who had prepared the Domesday text translation and commentary for the Devon *VCH*). They disagreed (though Reichel's view was published only posthumously) about the extent to which early churches related in a systematic way to the hundreds: Page favoured an essentially hundred-based royal system of foundations; Reichel favoured a more varied situation with churches of diverse character and origin.

It can be difficult to distinguish in record between minster churches and monasteries (in the classic sense of enclosed communities of monks), not least because the Old English word *mynster* was derived from Latin *monasterium*. As late as Ethelred II's law-code of 1008, *mynster* was still used for both enclosed monasteries and churches with groups of clergy. Increasingly, historians use the word minster for all these institutions, to avoid misleading assumptions based on the enclosed Benedictine monasticism of the tenth and later centuries. English minsters, defined in this overall way, could be staffed variously by monks, priests and nuns, in various combinations. But in Devon, nunneries never seem to have developed in the pre-Norman period, or at least not to an extent which has left any record. William of Malmesbury thought that the monks established at Exeter by king Edgar in 968 were accompanied by a group of nuns, expelled by bishop Leofric. His view has generally been dismissed

3.7: Some churches in early Devon. Map by Robert Higham and Oliver Creighton.
Notes
(i) Churches of Dumnonian origin in groups A & B are probably under-represented; others could underlie sites listed elsewhere, especially group C.
(ii) The map does not indicate possibly early church sites based on *lann* or *stow* names (for which see fig. 3.5).
(iii) Some churches dedicated to St Petrock occur here because there is reason to regard them as of pre-Norman origin (eg. 32, 33, 41). But examples of this dedication are generally omitted because many are likely to be of later date (see discussion in Chapter 3). Petrockstowe is listed under group B (as an extra item, 6a), since its early date has been generally accepted.
(iv) For local churches within the city of Exeter, see fig. 3.9.
(v) Some churches appear as separate numbers in different groups. Thus, in Exeter, nos. 1, 35, 36 are the same church in different stages of its evolution; as also Crediton, nos. 11, 34; as also Stokenham, nos. 16, 43.
(vi) The early Christian history of Lundy is not illustrated.
Places marked * also had an associated stone cross

because nothing in the circumstances of Leofric's move of the see from Crediton to Exeter in 1050 suggests this. But there is a reference to an abbess, Eadgyfu, who made an agreement with another Leofric (abbot of Exeter's minster, 973-993) about the occupancy of Stoke Canon. So, it is possible that – assuming Eadgyfu was an abbess in Devon – a community of nuns had existed briefly at Exeter, and, like Edgar's monks, had long disappeared by Leofric's day: this issue has been fully explored by Sarah Foot. Devon's minster history was, however, essentially one of monks and priests. The latter distinction was important not only institutionally, but also in practice: only ordained priests could administer the sacraments necessary for pastoral care in rural communities. Some churches changed their character, in relation to staffing by monks or priests, during this long period. Minsters of whatever sort, in England generally, shared high status: they were founded by kings, nobles, bishops and abbots, and their abbots and priests often came from high social ranks, including the royal families. For a long time they were regarded, in effect, as the property of their founders and their descendants.

In Devon, minster churches were dedicated to English or international saints, and their related place-names were largely topographical or habitative (even if occasionally incorporating the *–minster* element). In Cornwall, churches commonly had Celtic saint dedications, which in turn often influenced the place-name: the experience of the two shires was different. Devon, in this respect, shared the practice of Wessex, whereas Cornwall, whose practices were well-established before significant English influence developed, shared that of Wales. In Devon, starting with Exeter's church, minsters and their estates were established from the late seventh century onwards. Alongside this process, some Dumnonian churches survived, while by replacement, demotion or removal, other Dumnonian churches disappeared, together with their (presumed) Celtic dedications. But in Cornwall, which was not exposed to full West Saxon influence until Egbert's reign, and later Aethelstan's reign, the Dumnonian churches survived in greater numbers and the tradition of Celtic saint dedication was on-going. There is no reason to suppose that, in general, Dumnonian Devon had originally possessed fewer churches than Cornwall, but the character of the two counties was to become very different. Few dedications were to survive in Devon in conjunction with saints' resting places, as genuine reminders of the pre-English era: St. Rumon at Tavistock abbey (but this Cornish saint's relics were removed here only in the tenth century); St. Nectan, at Hartland; St Brannoc at Braunton; St Urith at Chittlehampton.

In addition, Landkey preserves the name of St Kea, whose main centre was near Truro. Finally, at St. Sidwell's church, outside the walls of Exeter, the relics of a virgin martyr were venerated not later than the eleventh century, when her cult site occurs in a list of saints' resting-places in England. The documented tradition is to an English woman born in Exeter, but her name may actually be a transformation of the sixth-century Cornish saint, Sitofolla, who appears in a ninth-century source. There are, of course, other churches dedicated to Celtic saints in Devon, some twenty-odd in total, including Petroc (by far the most common – see above), Bridget, David, Nectan (not only at Hartland) and Kerrian. But the antiquity of these dedications is not known, and is perhaps too easily assumed. It has been suggested that, in the tenth century, when the Cornish church was finally absorbed into the English framework, Celtic saints may have enjoyed some renewed popularity in neighbouring Devon. It has been argued by Barbara Yorke that in Devon some early Celtic saint dedications had existed side by side with those to Anglo-Saxon saints favoured by the seventh-eighth century West Saxon dynasty. But this earlier pattern in Wessex generally was masked in the ninth and tenth centuries by the later West Saxon dynasty's preference for other English or international saints, and it was these which endured.

The subject of church dedications in the south west has been explored to great effect by Nicholas Orme. Despite the general English popularity of dedications to local Anglo-Saxon saints (as opposed to major English clerical figures), very few churches in Devon were dedicated in this tradition, surviving as a mere handful of eventual parish churches: St. Earmund at Stoke Fleming (where the dedication was later changed to St Peter); possibly St John at Instow (the place-name means "the *stow* of John", though this could be St John the Baptist rather than the local martyr referred to in later sources, the *Life* of Nectan and the writings of John Leland); and St Hunberht at Stokenham (where this Old English name is suggested as more likely than the twelfth-century international saint Humbert). In what circumstances, and at exactly what date, these churches had been given these dedications, is not known, but dedication to local English saints seems unlikely to have occurred after the Norman Conquest, so these, too, may be reflective of churches established during the eleventh century at the latest. In tenth-century Cornwall, some of the numerous early churches dedicated to Celtic, and often very local, saints, now became minsters along English lines (sometimes retaining traditions of endowment by king Aethelstan) and many of the others became local churches (parish churches, as they would eventually be known). Reduction to "parish status" was also the fate of some of Devon's minsters, whose territories and jurisdictions were encroached upon (see below). An institutional change of character was another fate of some old rural minsters: Plympton and Hartland were re-founded by Norman bishops in the twelfth century as houses of Augustinian canons.

Urban Minsters *(see Fig. 3.7, and also illustrations in Chapter 4)*

In addition to Exeter's ancient minster, churches of this rank also appeared when new *burhs* were developed, from Alfred's reign onwards, to serve royal interests and urban populations (see Chapter 4). Terry Slater suggested that the Alfredian *burh* at Halwell was served from a mother church at Harberton, of which parish Halwell was originally a chapelry. At Totnes (which succeeded Halwell) and Barnstaple, churches seem to have been founded specifically for the *burhs*. At Totnes, the church of St. Mary was re-founded at the end of the eleventh century as a Benedictine priory, though the townsfolk continued to use it. In the thirteenth century, the priory built its own church, immediately adjacent, and the earlier one became an urban parish church. In the fifteenth century, the latter was re-built on a larger scale; a century later, the priory church was demolished. There is a local tradition that one of king Edgar's Totnes-minted pennies bore, in addition to its Totnes mint-mark, the legend "Sancta M". Though this coin is currently difficult to trace, if the tradition is true then it must be a tenth-century reference to St Mary's'church. Domesday Book records that Judhel, the Breton lord of Totnes, gave land to St. Mary's, also indicative of the dedication's pre-Norman origin. At Barnstaple, St. Peter's church represents the site of the *burh*'s minster (and perhaps its cruciform plan reflects that of its predecessor?). The early twelfth-century Cluniac priory here was not a minster re-foundation, but was on a new site outside the town defences. But excavation by Trevor Miles of the Norman castle rampart revealed an earlier cemetery, whose role in the town's history is problematic since it is distant from St Peter's and no other early church is known. Perhaps it represents a primary burghal church site of the Alfredian period, with St Peter's a secondary church site belonging to the town's tenth-century development?

St. Petrock's at Lydford presents difficulties because other than its location in a *burh* there is no specific indication of its minster status and it is possible that the church and its embanked churchyard (a *lann*?) pre-date the *burh*. This argument does not rely solely on its Celtic dedication, which could as easily be tenth-century or later (see above, for discussion of Petroc dedications), but also on a sherd of post-Roman pottery (an import from the Mediterranean) which was found nearby in excavation. According to one theory of Lydford's settlement evolution, the *burh* was in any case fashioned out of a pre-Roman defended site, so it may have had post-Roman occupation in the manner of a few other "hillforts" (see Chapter 2). The church, with its Petroc dedication, first appears in record in the thirteenth century: in 1237, when the tithe and herbage of Dartmoor were allocated to its chaplain's support. In 1267, Richard, earl of Cornwall, received a yearly fair on the vigil, feast and morrow of St Petrock. In 1272, John de Furbur became rector of both Lifton and Lydford (presented by the bishop of Exeter to Lifton and by the earl of Cornwall to Lydford) and Adam de Bremelle was appointed chaplain at Lydford. This reveals the strong possibility that, in the late Saxon period, Lydford's church had been not a *burh* minster of full status but a subsidiary to a superior church at Lifton, the royal estate and hundred centre (which was also mentioned in Alfred's will). In this case the hundred of Lifton may have had at least two minsters, since it is often assumed that Tavistock was a minster before its establishment as a monastery. This raises the possibility that there occurred in Devon a category of sub-minsters, whose existence is also known in other parts of Wessex (and see below on Sidbury and Branscombe). By the thirteenth century, however, Dartmoor had become Lydford's (enormous) ecclesiastical parish (as it was to be for many centuries) – hence its relevance to its chaplain. Perhaps the small size of the *burh* at Lydford and its specialised functions in relation to Dartmoor (see Chapter 4) meant that a full minster foundation here was not appropriate in the tenth century – the large area of its moorland territory relating not to a large population but to its hunting and tin resources. Lifton's own possible possession of a minster may also be reflected in the manumissions of slaves recorded at places in its hundred (see above).

While these observations support a late Saxon existence for the church at Lydford, they do not, in themselves, solve the issue of its origins. It may have been a pre-English church, with an early dedication to Petroc, taken over as the *burh* was founded (when perhaps this dedication may have seemed appropriate to the largely Cornish territory which supported the *burh* – see Chapter 4). It may, however, have been a new foundation for the *burh*, with a Petroc dedication given in a period of renewed interest in this saint (see above). In the latter case, perhaps the story of a miracle performed on Dartmoor, recorded in his *Miracula* at Bodmin in the twelfth century, is relevant. Is it even possible that the *burh* church originally had had a traditional "English" choice of dedication (as in the other Devon *burhs*) and that Petroc was substituted only in the thirteenth century to strengthen the link with the earls of Cornwall, Lydford's new lords? Earl Richard's rebuilding of the castle at Lydford in the manner of a motte and *donjon*, certainly has symbolic overtones; he also built Tintagel castle, on the north Cornish coast, as a symbol of links with ancient Cornish kingship.

Originally, the walled areas of late Saxon towns had consisted of a number of large plots of land, referred to as *hagae*. The urban minster churches, as well as the earliest private and parish churches, were built within these frameworks, which deserve more analysis (see Chapter 4). A related issue is that of the urban minsters' original territories. We may assume these included the walled areas of their respective towns, but the later growth of parishes in the adjacent countryside may possibly mask original extra-mural areas under these minsters' jurisdictions. The history of urban religious guilds, which has been explored by Gervase Rosser, may offer some assistance with respect to Exeter. By the eleventh century, there had been a prayer guild within the city, meeting three times a year: it organised burials as well as masses at the minster for both its dead and living members. It is not wholly clear whether its membership was purely clerical or both clerical and lay. But there are also two hints of Exeter minster's early connections beyond the city itself. First, in the early Norman period, there is evidence for about fourteen rural prayer-guilds in the surrounding countryside (including Woodbury, Nutwell, Colyton, Sidmouth, Whitestone, Halsford, Exmouth, Clyst St George and Broadclyst). These were of pre-Norman origin and their distribution may represent some vestige of the extent of the minster's original (rural) pastoral responsibilities carried out by its priests (though complications arise in the case of Colyton, which probably had a minster anyway; and Woodbury had its own church by 1086). The guilds arranged burials and paid money to the minster in Exeter for masses to be said for their dead. Second, it is known from analysis by John Allan and Christopher Henderson that in the Norman period the extra-mural parishes of St David, St Sidwell and St Leonard belonged to the city: this could indicate that Exeter's immediate environs had originally been part of the minster's territory. It is not impossible that these lands were adapted for this purpose from earlier suburban estates of the Dumnonian, or even Roman periods. Since the lands from which these parishes were eventually created lay exclusively on the east side of the river Exe, this link was possibly created soon after the minster's foundation in the late seventh century, when perhaps the (then un-bridged?) river formed the westward limit of the West Saxon church's influence. If this was the case, we might expect an entrance into the minster precincts at this time to have been on the east side, though none has yet been identified archaeologically. In contrast, by the later Saxon period, the (known) entrance to the minster precincts was from the west, at the "Little Style" gate in South St, on a route from the crossing of the river Exe, which was probably bridged from Alfred's reign (see Chapter 4).

Reformed Monasteries (*see Fig. 3.7*)

In England generally, the ninth century saw a decline in the minsters' culture. They had fewer monks and more priests; kings and nobles sometimes re-claimed estates with which they had been endowed; and in some regions they suffered from depradation at the hands of the vikings. But king Alfred began re-vitalization of the church and this continued in following reigns. The later tenth century was a particular period of church reform, in which kings, especially Edgar, took a major role alongside influential clerics: new monasteries, following a stricter and enclosed Benedictine life, were created out of some of the older minsters. The south west, little affected by viking disruption, enjoyed more continuity than did some regions. Cornwall had no tenth-century monastic re-foundations (though it did see the emergence of a smaller number of English-style minsters). But in Devon, re-foundation of presumed earlier minsters occurred at Tavistock (very close to the Cornish border) and Buckfast (on the eastern edge of Dartmoor), both of which became Benedictine houses. Glastonbury is the likely source of monks for both new houses. Tavistock's history was much explored by H.P.R. Finberg and its foundation has also been richly illuminated by Christopher Holdsworth. Ordulf, a local noble who was son of the ealdorman Ordgar and also King Edgar's brother-in-law, endowed Tavistock, in Lifton hundred, with estates; in 981, the young king Aethelred II issued a charter to confirm these grants. After 981, Ordulf brought the relics of the Cornish saint Rumon to Tavistock, from their earlier resting-place at Ruan Lanihorne. Buckfast, in Diptford hundred, was re-founded in 1018 by the ealdorman Aethelweard, who was a member of the family descended from king Alfred's brother (king Aethelred I) which had also produced the late tenth-century chronicler, Aethelweard. He was an associate of king Cnut, though later removed from office by him. Tavistock had a richer endowment than Buckfast. One of its abbots, Ealdred, was archbishop of York in the eleventh century.

In Exeter, according to a twelfth-century tradition recorded by John of Worcester, the ancient minster was given a group of Benedictine monks by king Edgar in 968, with Sideman as its abbot (he was later bishop of Crediton). This community of monks seems not to have survived very long in this form, perhaps disrupted by the Danish sack of the city in Aethelred II's reign. Exeter had, of course, been monastic in an older sense when first established in the late seventh century – Boniface served here as a young monk under its abbot, Wulfheard – but it subsequently lost this character. It was enriched after 1050, when it became the centre of a new diocese (see below). As Nicholas Orme has shown, Domesday Book reveals that the majority of Devon's minsters, whatever their original endowments may have been, had modest lands, generally one or two hides, probably reflecting their long-standing dependence on association with a royal estate or hundred centre. But the minsters affected by the tenth-century monastic reform, while enjoying royal patronage, were more independent as institutions and were much wealthier – Tavistock (with 24 hides), Buckfast (with 16), and Exeter (with 17) – as was the earlier diocesan centre at Crediton minster (with about 15).

The Dioceses (*see Fig. 3.8*)

The dioceses in which the urban and rural churches lay had their own development, starting with the West Saxon diocese based at Winchester. In 705 king Ine created a new diocese based at Sherborne, reflecting a significant westward extension of English conquest and influence by that date. The *Anglo-Saxon Chronicle* described this territory as "west of the wood" (that is, Selwood Forest) on the death in 709 of Aldhelm, its first bishop. Sherborne was endowed during the eighth century with lands in Dorset, Wiltshire, Somerset and Devon. Soon after 705, King Geraint of Dumnonia endowed Sherborne with land in Maker, in Cornwall (a grant which Egbert of Wessex enlarged a century later). There seems already to have been a church at Sherborne, founded by king Cenwalh in replacement of an earlier British monastery in the vicinity, called *Lanprobus*, and this probably influenced the choice of Sherborne as the new see (Ilchester, a former Roman town, might otherwise have been chosen – as with Winchester, and its predecessor Dorchester-on-Thames). There was, of course, already a church in Exeter, within the West Saxon diocese of

Winchester. That Exeter was not at this time chosen by king Ine as the new diocesan centre must mean that early in the eighth century the Exe valley was still too near the western fringe of effective West Saxon power. Two centuries later, the situation had changed: in the 890s, king Alfred appointed his Welsh friend Asser as bishop for Devon and Cornwall, based in Exeter, an appointment most easily understood as a suffragan position under Sherborne (where later Asser became bishop). This presumably means that the minster in Exeter was sufficient to act as an episcopal centre: perhaps it underwent some re-invigoration with Alfred's establishment of the *burh* here (see Chapter 4). In 909, however, when Asser died, Edward the Elder created new dioceses for Somerset (at Wells) and for Devon and Cornwall (at Crediton). Crediton was chosen perhaps because the endowment for a minster there, dating from 739, was suitable for the support of bishops (see also Appendix 2). Perhaps Edward also wished to keep the *burh* at Exeter, crucial to the shire's security at the head of the Exe estuary, exclusively under royal influence (cf. his acquisition of Plympton, a Sherborne estate on another important estary – see above, and also Chapter 4). A subordinate Cornish diocese, at St. German's, was created by Aethelstan (its British-named bishop, Conan, was present at the royal council held at Lifton in 931) but was not fully independent until 994. When Crediton and Wells were established, Sherborne's lands (in Devon/Cornwall and Somerset respectively) were transferred to them and Sherborne's diocese became Dorset-centred. Sherborne was reformed as a Benedictine house in the later tenth century; the Normans subsequently moved the see to Old Sarum and Sherborne then remained as a priory under the bishop. In these successive events, we see not only the superimposition of English church organisation over a British predecessor, but also a reflection of the expanding nature of English government and culture in general. At least one bishop of Devon was buried in his see: the twelfth-century chronicler John of Worcester related that bishop Aelfwold was buried at Crediton in 972. The *Anglo-Saxon Chronicle* records that bishop Sideman died at a royal council in Oxfordshire in 977 and that, despite his wish to be buried in his see at Crediton, he was buried at Abingdon on the instruction of king Edward (the martyr) and archbishop Dunstan.

In 1050, however, Exeter became the central place in Devon's eccesiastical organisation. It had already become the major town of the south west, since its revival in Alfred's reign (see Chapter 4). Tradition maintained that Aethelstan had re-founded the minster in the tenth century, and Edgar later established monks there (see above). In 1019, its abbot Aethelwold acquired a charter from king Cnut restoring the minster from its damaged position following the viking sack of Exeter in 1003. In 1050 it also became the diocesan centre. Leofric (bishop of both Devon and Cornwall from 1046 – they had been held by one bishop since 1027) petitioned Pope Leo IX for permission to remove the see from Crediton to Exeter, arguing that the walled city was a more secure and prestigious location than a rural setting. The latter, of course, was true but the former was not: Crediton's cathedral had not been affected by the vikings in 1003 when Exeter was attacked. The request was granted and king Edward the Confessor was authorised to implement the move. In establishing the new see at Exeter, Edward exceeded the Pope's instructions, allowing Leofric to amalgamate the dioceses of Devon and Cornwall. This move was part of a general trend in the church at this time to enlarge sees and move rural ones to towns. Crediton and St Germans were left with some estates, to support the minster churches and priests remaining there, but their other lands were transferred to Exeter. The existing minster in Exeter was taken over (not

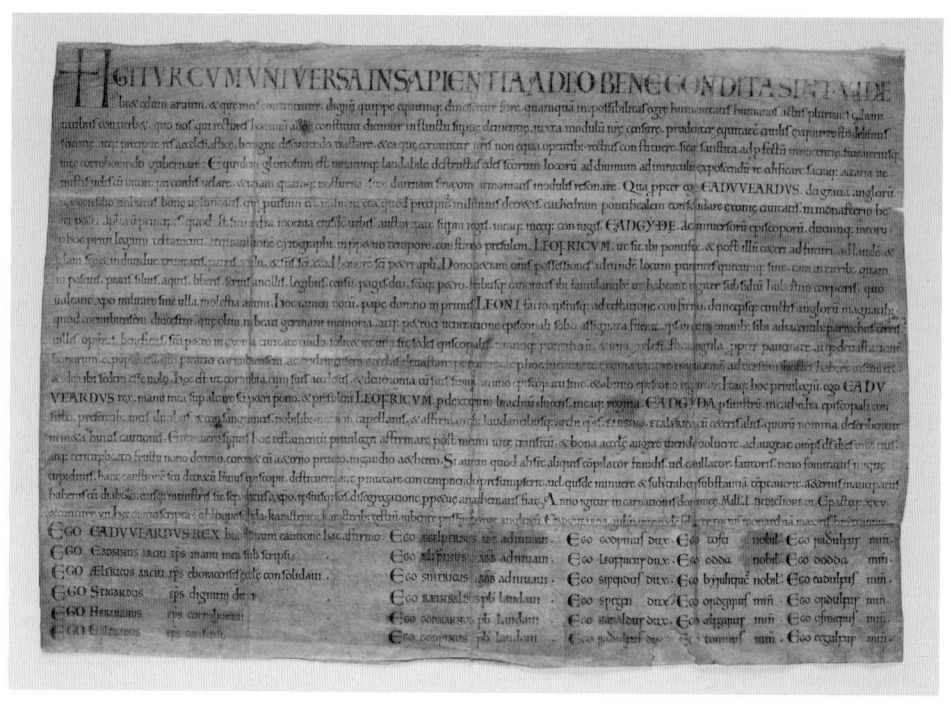

3.8: The foundation charter of Exeter cathedral. It records Edward the Confessor's establishment of the cathedral in 1050.
Photograph: Exeter Cathedral Archives, D. & C. 2072, by permission of the Dean and Chapter.

rebuilt), and an order of new canons was established, following the Rule of St Chrodegang (see below). Leofric was installed as bishop in a grand ceremony attended by the king, queen Edith and the many notables who made up the king's council. This probably took place on St Peter's day, 29th June. These events were recorded in an account of Leofric's career written shortly after his death and included in his Missal, as well as in a charter still at Exeter cathedral: the earliest one to survive for the foundation of a new cathedral anywhere in England. Oddly, the narrative in the Missal does not mention the union of the two dioceses into one, which the charter emphasises. The large collection of witness-names in the charter includes archbishops, bishops, earls and other nobles, abbots, priests and thegns. The charter was written as though by the king, but was probably created at Exeter, for Leofric, at some point subsequent to the actual event. Another version of it was also created at some time, slightly different in some of its detail (including some of the witnesses, though they are equally plausible). This survives (like some of Leofric's other manuscripts, including his copy of the Rule of St Chrodegang) at Corpus Christi College, Cambridge, in a thirteenth-century copy. The puzzling relationship between these two versions of the Exeter charter has been discussed by Pierre Chaplais and by Frank Barlow.

The diocesan situation at the Norman Conquest has been analysed by Christopher Holdsworth. As recorded in Domesday Book (and including some estates recovered by Leofric and other additions since 1066) the episcopal estate extended over some 100,000 acres, with an annual income of around £377. Two thirds of the manors lay in Devon, the others in Cornwall. Only the king, Robert of Mortain in Cornwall, and Baldwin, the royal sheriff of Devon, were wealthier. By now, Exeter was England's fourth largest diocese, but its episcopal estate ranked sixth in wealth, perhaps because the rural economy of the region was less strong than in some other dioceses. In the 1070s, movement of rural sees to towns continued: Lichfield to Chester; Selsey to Chichester; Sherborne to Old Sarum.

Local Rural Churches (*see Fig. 3.7; and also Fig. 5.8b*)

In the later Anglo-Saxon period another development was taking place which had an enormous long-term impact on ordinary people, that is the development of what would later be known as the parish and the parish church. The Old English word for a local church was *cirice*, and just as *mynster* became a place-name element, so too did *cirice* by the time of

Domesday Book. In a law-code of around 960, King Edgar distinguished the old minster churches from newer churches whose numbers had been growing in the countryside at the initiative of secular lords *(thegns)*. Some of these were stated, in Edgar's code, to have their own graveyards. Possession of a graveyard must have been a crucial stage in the development of tenants' allegiance to their local church as opposed to their minster church. The emergence of such churches meant it was now necessary to regulate the tithes (a payment of a tenth of produce, adopted earlier in the tenth century, in imitation of Carolingian practice, to supplement the traditional English payment of churchscot) and other payments due to both sorts of church, old and new. Such developments must also have encouraged definition of local church "territories", since it would have to be clear at which church local rural populations owed payments. Law-codes of Aethelred II and Cnut subsequently described a whole series of church types, from chief minsters down to field churches (which lacked graveyards). A treatise on social ranks, written in the early eleventh century and sometimes known as *People's Ranks and Laws,* listed a church amongst the features of *thegnly* status. While some private churches might be serviced by a priest from a minster, many had priests who were appointed by the *thegns.* Late Saxon wills often mentioned the bequeathing of a private church, which was called a *tunkirke* (in Scandinavian-influenced speech, because most of these wills are from eastern England). Manorial estates were increasingly provided by their lords with small churches for their own communities: it seems likely that it was for their benefit that graveyards were developed here and that the land-owning class itself continued for a time to prefer traditional burial at an ancient minster. In turn, the *thegns'* estates themselves became convenient units of ecclesiastical administration and thus the territories of the old minsters were gradually subdivided. These sub-divisions, centred on private churches, were to emerge as parishes during the twelfth and thirteenth centuries. Eventually there were more than 400 parishes in Devon and more than 200 in Cornwall: they are listed in 1291 in relation to a papal tax.

 A similar process developed in the late Anglo-Saxon towns, where the monopoly of the original minsters was gradually broken down by the foundation of small churches, which emerge as urban parish churches by the thirteenth century. In the towns, a number of processes seem to have been at work in England generally. Some urban parishes grew from the foundation of private churches on the urban properties attached to manors of rural land-holding *thegns.* Some grew from subsidiary churches founded by urban minsters and cathedrals. Some may have been established by like-minded groups of citizens as urban population and prosperity developed. Others may have been linked to the early devlopment of wards, the important units of urban organisation which emerge more clearly in later times. Fundamental features of English religious and social life, the parishes and parish churches in town and country, were thus in the making at the end of the Anglo-Saxon period. But the process continued through the twelfth century and, in many cases, parish boundaries, both rural and urban, were finally fixed only in the thirteenth.

Whether this process had much earlier beginnings and a slow development, or whether it occurred more rapidly from the tenth century, has been much debated. Also subject to some disagreement is whether the emergence of local churches necessarily marked a significant decline in the authority of minsters, at least to start with. The development of tithe payment at this time, as well as on-going patronage by kings and nobles, continued to support minsters. It has been suggested that some English minster churches which appear in tenth-century sources were not ancient institutions only now emerging into documentary light, though they were "old" as defined in Edgar's law-code in the sense that they pre-dated newer, local churches. Some minsters may actually have been quite recent creations: evidence of an on-going minster culture not as yet too threatened by the growth of local churches. And while (in England generally) most of these new local churches owed their foundation to the secular land-owning class, others were chapels created by the older minsters themselves. A chapel at Sutton, later to be part of Plymouth, belonging to the minster at Plympton is mentioned in the twelfth century. Creation by a nearby minster may be suspected when local churches never became parochial but remained dependent chapels, without burial or baptismal rights, or became parochial only very much later. The discussion of some minster territories (see above) is relevant to that issue. Other ties may hint at creations of local churches by minsters, as perhaps at Sidbury and Branscombe which may have been subsidiaries of Exeter (see below). But, whatever their various origins and processes, the establishing of local churches went on for a long time: it was very incomplete at the time of the Norman Conquest. We should call these churches "private" rather than "parish" until the twelfth century: only then did the development of canon law create parishes within each diocese and secular landlords surrendered much of their control over the local churches. Now, the "parish" was a fixed entity, where previously it had simply constituted the landlord's estate. Since these estates could change in their extent, with amalgamations and divisions, it is likely that some early private churches disappeared before formal parishes were created in the twelfth century. But great variety existed in the size of *thegnly* estates as well as in some surviving minster territories, and this was eventually reflected in the similarly great variety in parish sizes. The smallest were, of course, often the intra-mural urban parishes.

So in the generations immediately before the Norman Conquest, ecclesiastical landscapes and townscapes were undergoing a process of fragmentation: just as large rural estates were giving way to smaller ones in the hands of a more numerous *thegnly* class (see Chapter 4), so also large minster estates were giving way to smaller ones served by the private churches of the *thegns*. Some "snowball" effect was probably at work here. The more thegns established local churches, the more their immediate neighbours might feel it necessary to do likewise: otherwise their tenants might attend a neighbour's church, rather than an old minster, and thus divided loyalties might be created. Patrick Hase has suggested that, in Wessex, the process of local church foundation accelerated in the Norman period because the new landlords felt no allegiance to the older minsters. This is very likely and was probably also an influence on Devonian developments. In contrast, the creation of rural deaneries in the Norman period re-established wider territories of jurisdiction, rather like (though different in extent) those of the earlier minsters. Devon was to have three archdeaconries: Exeter, Totnes and Barnstaple. Each contained several rural deaneries (Exeter and Totnes, nine each; Barnstaple, six), and each rural deanery comprised a number of parishes. Some of the rural deaneries were centred on churches which had been minsters in the Saxon period, as at Exeter, Totnes and Barnstaple themselves, and Tiverton, Plympton and Hartland. But other rural deaneries were centred on places with no known significant pre-Norman history.

It is impossible to know exactly how many private churches existed by the mid-eleventh century because the earliest reference to such churches in any written source is often of the twelfth or even thirteenth century, even though their origin may have been earlier. There are also two variables at national level which need taking into account. First, available evidence suggests that the foundation of private churches proceeded more quickly in the east of England than it did in the west. Large parishes based on old mother churches remained for centuries in Lancashire and Cheshire, for example, and the process of fragmentation also seems to have been fairly slow in Somerset, Devon and Cornwall. Second, the prevailing settlement pattern must be taken into account. The largely dispersed nature of this in Devon (see Chapter 5) creates an interesting issue in understanding local church origins. In shires where nucleated villages came to predominate, parish churches were often part of the main settlement. Here it is easy to imagine the church's origin as a private establishment, convenient for manorial lord and tenants alike. But where settlement components are scattered through an estate, as in the south west, such associations are less clear. The likely choice of private church site would be near the demesne farm and, if there was one, the manorial residence. Thus, we now quite often find the parish church near the "barton" which is the successor to the medieval demesne farm. But this was not always so, and if some of the population occupied a nucleated hamlet elsewhere, that may have been a more appropriate location for the church, accessible to its main local community. A third influence on choice of local church site may have been the existence of an ancient holy place – a church with Dumnonian origins, or a holy well or other shrine – which still played a role in the community's religious observance.

There was, however, clearly a diversity of experience. At Dartington, for example, the pre-nineteenth-century parish church stood immediately adjacent to the manor house (now known, in its late medieval phase, as Dartington Hall), presumably succcessor to a conveniently-situated private chapel founded in the late Saxon or early Norman period. At Bickleigh, in contrast, the substantial and free-standing chapel of the Exe-valley manor house (now known, in its late medieval phase, as Bickleigh Castle) kept its private status, and remains as an unusual (for Devon) survival of a simple Romanesque church. Bickleigh's parish church lies across the river Exe, situated where the main rural community developed. In regions with dispersed settlement patterns, a case such as this reminds us that more local churches may have been founded than subsequently were needed as parish churches. Perhaps when we find substantial late medieval private chapels near manor houses they were not all new foundations of that period, but sometimes successors to earlier private churches? A possible example (deserving of further investigation) may be Fardel (Cornwood) in south Devon. Here the late medieval manor house has a large, free-standing chapel immediately adjacent. Although there is no specific evidence of a predecessor, could this late medieval chapel have succeeded an earlier private church associated with a manor house, keeping its role when the church at Cornwood – at the other end of a large rural territory – achieved parochial status? The choice of private church – and eventually parish church – sites in dispersed settlement patterns would be a very fruitful topic for further research, building on the revealing work carried out by Richard Morris on English churches in landscape contexts of many sorts. Settlement-related studies of local churches also need to accept the possibility that early church sites could be moved, in conjunction with settlement development, as the example of Shapwick in Somerset reveals (see Chapter 5).

Similar processes were at work on estates owned by the church, though whether late Saxon ecclesiastical landlords might have retained allegiances to old minsters longer than their secular counterparts is an interesting question. But when we see, for example at Paignton, a late medieval bishop's palace adjacent to a very substantial parish church, we are surely viewing a parallel situation with the pairing of secular manor house and local church. The fine Romanesque west doorway at Paignton church is evidence of considerable twelfth-century investment, perhaps suggesting the episcopal residence there had earlier origins.

The problem is compounded because Domesday Book, while providing much detailed information on the countryside, is relatively silent on local churches in England and appears to give very disparate data from one area to another. The interest shown by Domesday's compilers in local churches, of course, arose not from their ecclesiastical character but because they were private property. It has been estimated that, in England generally, despite the relative silence of written record, perhaps 75% of local churches (in both town and countryside) existed by around 1100, but this generalisation disguises considerable regional variation. In Kent, for example, documentation independent of Domesday reveals about 400 churches by the late eleventh century. Our view of Devon churches at this time, as in so many other shires, is certainly inadequate. It is further complicated by the church sites themselves, which even if having early origins, present themselves as later structures because of successive alterations or total re-buildings. Thus it is impossible to know how many such churches existed in Devon by the end of the Anglo-Saxon period. It is, however, possible that the creation of small rural churches was slower in areas of dispersed settlement pattern: with fewer obvious focal points being equally convenient for widely-scattered tenants, perhaps the traditional roles of minster churches, serving larger areas, continued longer. If this is true, the progressive westward reduction in Domesday's mention of churches in England may be genuinely revealing. Leofric, bishop of Exeter in the mid-eleventh century, was remembered as a founder of churches, but we cannot quantify his activities in any way.

The Devon churches revealed in Domesday either directly or indirectly, numbered about twenty. They have been usefully studied by Christopher Holdsworth and others. Some of these were known or probable minsters (see above) such as Axminster, Braunton, Colyton, Cullompton, Plympton, Hartland, Kingskerswell, South Molton, Yealmpton and St. Mary's in Totnes. Others named, of lesser status, were Pinhoe and Woodbury, both of which manors had belonged to the Godwin family in 1066 and in 1086 were in the Conqueror's hands. But he had granted the manorial church of Pinhoe to Battle Abbey (in Sussex) and that at Woodbury to the abbey of Mont St Michel (in Normandy). Domesday recorded that in 1066, Dotton and Stallenge (Thorne) had been held by priests, Doda and Alric respectively: so these places, too, may have had local churches at this time, though not certainly so. Two other churches are revealed by Domesday place-names: at St Jameschurch (Heavitree) and St. Marychurch (Torbay). In 1044, St Michael's church (Teignmouth – see below) occurred by name in the boundary clause of a charter relating to Dawlish, but it was not mentioned in Domesday Book.

An interesting example of the potentially misleading silence of Domesday Book concerns Poughill, in mid-Devon. Here there seem to have been two manors, one of whose lords in 1086 was the Breton, Ruald Adobed ("the dubbed" – that is, a knight). He later entered St Nicholas's priory, Exeter, to spend his final years there and granted to the priory, as a gift, land at Poughill together with its church. The date of the gift is not known but it is documented in a confirmation by Osbern (bishop, 1072-1103) preserved amongst the records relating to the priory published in the nineteenth century, with Devon's other monastic sources, by George Oliver. While it is possible that Ruald founded this church on one of his rural properties after 1086, it is also possible that it already existed and had been built either by himself or by one of his English predecessors: perhaps Edmer, who was lord of Poughill in 1066. This Edmer was also Ruald's antecessor at other manors, as well as antecessor at a number of manors held in 1086 by count Robert of Mortain, who held the other manor of Poughill in 1086. So Edmer was a man of some substance on the eve of the Norman conquest: the sort of man who might well found a local church. But we should also note that throughout the episodes here described, or at least postulated, this church was still a private one: it was as such that Ruald was able to give it to St. Nicholas priory. Its status as a "parish church" lay in the future. Even in the later form in which it now survives, it is still a very modest building with only one aisle. Its small nave could well represent the shape of the church of the eleventh century.

Occasionally, the process of creating local churches, and eventually parishes, may be illuminated by place-names as, for example around Sampford Courtenay. This was discussed by W.G. Hoskins, who argued that the original estate of Sampford was a large block of land between the rivers Taw and Okement in mid-Devon. Its size and natural boundaries suggest it was the sort of estate whose creation in many other examples is revealed in a surviving charter. By the late Saxon period, two small manors, Exbourne and Honeychurch, had been carved out of the northern end of the Sampford estate. All three units eventually became parishes with parish churches. The clue to this process lies in the place-name Honeychurch, containing the Old English word *cirice* – church. It was named *Honechercha* in the Exon Domesday and means "the church of Huna" – or of someone with a name similar to this: presumably the name of the church's founding Saxon thegn. This event took place at some point well before 1066: in that year the manorial lord had been one Alwin. The postulated "Huna" must have preceded this by sufficient time for his name not only to have been attached to the church but to have become, in turn, the manor name. The foundation of the church on this private estate may thus have been in the early eleventh or tenth century. Although there is no independent evidence for the origin of Exbourne's and Sampford Courtenay's churches, it is quite likely that they were of comparable date. But none of the three churches is mentioned in Domesday Book. The unaisled nave and simple chancel of the tiny twelfth-century building, which still stands at Honeychurch, may well reflect its original shape and size.

Other Devon place-names also contain the element *cirice*. The editors of *The Place-names of Devon* identified about a possible twenty, but not all have equally secure derivations. The most reliable group, as indicators of early local churches, are (like Honeychurch) those found in Domesday Book. Here we find Churston (Ferrers) and four instances of Cheriton (that is, *-tun* with a church): near Brendon, Payhembury, Crediton (Cheriton fitzpaine) and at Cheriton Bishop. In addition, Domesday names Whitchurch (near Tavistock) whose name presumably means "white church" in reference to the rendering of timber, cob or rough stone. Some other *cirice* names first appear only in thirteenth-century sources, so it leaves the date of origin unclear for the churches implied. Chercombe (near Ogwell) and Hawkchurch (at the Dorset border) could well have pre-Norman origins. At Churchstow (near Kingsbridge) and Cheristow (near

Hartland), *cirice* and *–stow* are compounded. Although neither appears by name before the thirteenth century, these too may well be of much earlier origin (indeed, Cheristow is relevant to minster territory reconstruction at Hartland, discussed above). The editors of *The Place-names of Devon* thought that the Domesday name *Chereforda* (Charford, near South Brent) contained *cirice*: the place-name literally meaning "church ford", indicating a church not far away. The charter recording the grant by King Cnut of land at Meavy, in 1031, included a boundary point called "the church way": Della Hooke has suggested this refers to a lane leading to a church, perhaps at Walkhampton or Sheepstor.

Many of the references to early churches in Devon relate to those associated with royal or church land-holding, or to the reformed monasteries, so perhaps the foundation of local churches by secular manorial lords was genuinely slow here. But we may suspect, also, a bias in the source material which does not reveal all the local churches which, by analogy with other regions, were surely emerging in the tenth and eleventh centuries. Equally, we know nothing of the priests appointed to serve the smaller local churches whose existence we may suspect. Where Domesday Book does refer to local churches (in England as a whole) it appears that they were often simply part of their manor and so the priest may have been a member of the peasant class: many of them were no doubt also involved in agriculture. How much clerical education they had, and where they received it, is an interesting question: perhaps at the minster church of their territory. It is probably safe to assume a fairly unsophisticated culture at local church level. But throughout England local estate priests became sufficiently numerous during the tenth century to be cited (in king Aethelstan's law-code issued at Grately) as appropriate witnesses (alongside the reeves and landlords) of rural trade transactions. In other cases (since they were listed in Domesday Book as tenants-in-chief) thegns seem to have become priests and perhaps they were members of nearby minster churches. For example, Swimbridge was held in 1066 by Brictferth and in 1086 by his nephew, Saewin; and in 1086, Algar held land in Braunton from the king. All were described as priests.

The editors of *The Place-Names of Devon* listed about twenty-five instances in which the Old English *preost* (priest) has been compounded with another Old English element – including *tun*, *cott* or *cumb* – to form place-names scattered around Devon such as Preston, Prestacott, Priestacott, Prescott, Priestland, Prescombe, Priestaford. These do not occur in written sources until the thirteenth century onwards, and some may be creations of this later period. But given the antiquity of the elements with which *preost* is combined in these names, it would be surprising if at least some of them were not of Anglo-Saxon creation. Applied to a piece of land, they may well reflect the endowments of priests serving at early local churches, or perhaps to properties belonging to older minsters.

Given the sparse documentation before the twelfth century, it is not surprising that we have fewer than twenty Devon churches (of all categories) whose dedications are known in the period up to Domesday Book. But from the twelfth to sixteenth centuries the majority of the churches' dedications are known and have been analysed by Nicholas Orme. This period seems not to have seen much alteration to dedications of Saxon date, but there was extensive re-dedication after the Reformation, sometimes involving attributions of misleadingly early character. Cornwall's parish church dedications suffered less alteration, and include a high proportion of Celtic saints. Dedications in Devon were more mixed, including Celtic ones such as Petroc and Nectan (sometimes original but sometimes of later, spurious creation). Mainly (as with the earlier minsters) Devon's parish church dedications drew from the traditions of indigenous figures (including Cuthbert and King Edward the Martyr) and international ones (including Andrew, Mary, Michael, Paul and Peter). In this respect, Devon's habits were English ones, and it is likely that some parish church dedications known only from the twelfth century and later were, like some churches themselves, of Saxon origin.

Local Churches in Exeter (*see Fig. 3.9*)

In Exeter, apart from the Cathedral, and the chapel of St Mary in the new Norman castle, only St. Olave's occurs by name in Domesday Book (by which time it was held by Battle Abbey) though two others (un-named) are also referred to: St. Lawrence's has been identified as the church belonging to Robert of Mortain and the church belonging to the bishop was identified by early commentators as St. Stephen's, which is later known to have been an episcopal possession. More recently, however, it has been argued by John Allan and others that the latter was only acquired in the twelfth century, and that the church referred to in 1086 must have been another: perhaps St. Sidwell's, the land around which was also the bishop's property. St. Olave's was founded sometime after the saint's death in 1030, and perhaps during the 1050s: it occurs in documentary record by around 1060 (when it was endowed with property by Edward the Confessor and Gytha, widow of earl

Church and Society

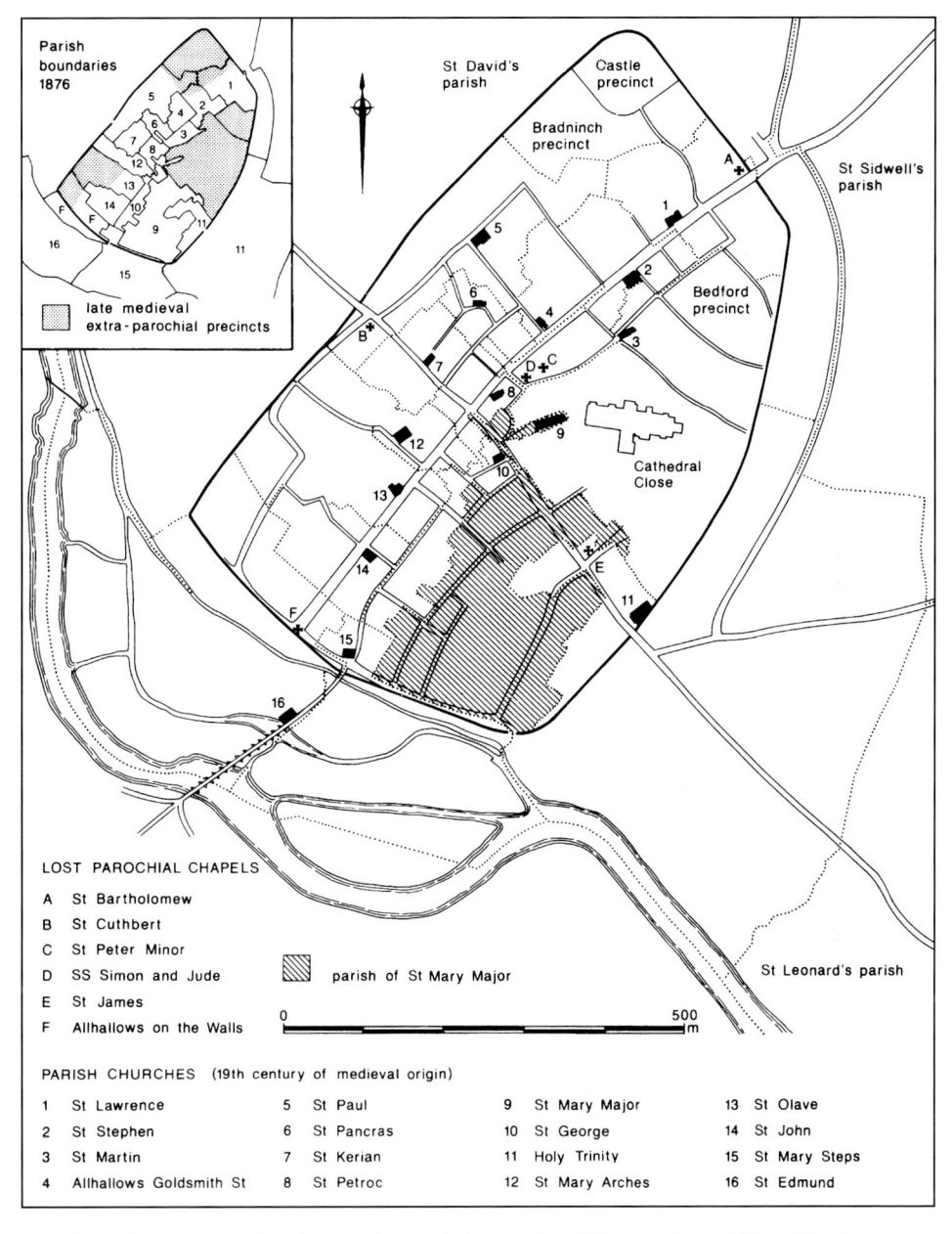

3.9: Parishes, local churches and chapels in medieval Exeter, from Allan, Henderson and Higham in Haslam (ed) 1984. By permission of Jeremy Haslam.

LOST PAROCHIAL CHAPELS

A St Bartholomew
B St Cuthbert
C St Peter Minor
D SS Simon and Jude
E St James
F Allhallows on the Walls

PARISH CHURCHES (19th century of medieval origin)

1	St Lawrence	5	St Paul	9	St Mary Major	13	St Olave
2	St Stephen	6	St Pancras	10	St George	14	St John
3	St Martin	7	St Kerian	11	Holy Trinity	15	St Mary Steps
4	Allhallows Goldsmith St	8	St Petroc	12	St Mary Arches	16	St Edmund

Godwin of Wessex). Its proximity to the area of the city originally known as Earlsbury (*Irlesbyri* – the earl's enclosure) may indicate its connection to a property first held by Godwin himself, or by his son, Harold. Other examples of this dedication in England were also mainly in towns, for example at Chester, perhaps reflecting small Scandinavian merchant communities.

The situation at Exeter, however, clearly reveals the limitations of Domesday Book, since we know of other churches of pre-Norman date which it did not mention. St. Martin's was dedicated in 1065 (the source is 15th century, but believed reliable). St. Kerrian's and St. Petroc's may also be of mid-eleventh century origin, and St. Sidwell's (outside the walls) already existed (whether the saint commemorated here was Celtic or English was discussed above). But in the context of Exeter's topography, another possibility deserves attention at St. Sidwell's and St. David's: both were situated near Roman cemeteries just outside the city and may thus have succeeded mausolea of the late Roman period. The cemetery evidence is, however, early Roman rather than late, and the earliest evidence for St. David's church is around 1200. A church dedicated to Edward, king and martyr (who died in 978), formerly stood near the cathedral, and is a good candidate for a late tenth-century foundation. Though lacking early documentation, the churches near the city gates may have early sites since this was a characteristic church location in some other English *burhs* (in Exeter these were: St. Mary Steps, Holy Trinity, and the chapel of St. Bartholomew). Whereas the positions of Exeter's churches generally reflect the late Saxon street pattern, the alignment of St. Pancras is at odds with the street alignments and so may be of earlier origin, though in what circumstances is unknown. Laid out after (or with) Exeter's streets, it is notable that many of the city's churches sit parallel to them, suggesting they were originally built in larger properties (*hagae*) before these were sub-divided into narrow tenements (see Chapter 4).

According to medieval traditions Exeter had twenty-nine churches in the Conqueror's day. Allowing for some possible exaggeration, and for some possibly new foundations during William's reign, there was clearly a large number by 1066, reflecting a populous and flourishing city at this time. Exeter eventually had sixteen parish churches and six parochial chapels, all carved out of a townscape which had earlier been served solely by the minster: accordingly, rights of burial within the walls remained with the cathedral and St Mary Major's church, successors to the old minster, for many centuries. The minster graveyard would have been the resting place not only of abbots, priests and the town's population, but also of some Devonian notables from elsewhere. The only such (secular) person known by name is the ealdorman Ordgar, whose burial here in 971 is mentioned by the twelfth-century writer John of Worcester. Ordgar was father of Alfthryth, king Edgar's second wife. The complex patterns of urban property-ownership which existed by around 1066, and further developed after the Norman Conquest, eventually gave rise to the multiplicity of urban parish churches which is so characteristic of the older English towns. In contrast, the "new towns" of the Norman and later periods, with a simpler tenurial pattern, tended to have but a single church. The distribution of parish churches within an older town or city may therefore reveal the approximate densities of population before around 1100. On this measure, for example, Exeter's "west quarter" was less occupied at this time than other parts of the city. This impression is supported by the evidence of excavation which has shown this area was not built up until the thirteenth century. The "west quarter" occupied much of the parish of St. Mary Major, successor to the Saxon minster (some of whose fabric was incorporated in the later church). When the minster was demoted to parochial status after the new cathedral's consecration in 1133, it was given as its own parish that part of the city's interior not already provided with parish churches. St Mary Major was thus a sort of "superior" parish church within the city.

In England generally, it is now felt that the bulk of urban church foundation took place from around 1000 onwards, continuing into the twelfth century. It was thus, like the corresponding emergence of local churches in the countryside, an Anglo-Norman process rather than a purely Anglo-Saxon one. The relationship of these new urban churches to the existing urban minsters took a long time to settle down: it was often not until the thirteenth century that urban parishes with fixed boundaries are documented. In Exeter, the boundaries as understood in 1222 survive in a fourteenth-century source. By the thirteenth century, the whole of Exeter's walled area was parochial apart from its cathedral close and the precincts of its castle, priory and two friaries. Two parishes (Holy Trinity and St Mary Steps) were partly extra-mural. How the shapes of the city's numerous parishes came to be defined is a subject worthy of much further study.

Early Church Fabric (*see Figs. 3.10, 3.11, 3.12, 3.13, 3.14*)

However thin the documentary record of Devon's local churches, the record of surviving church fabric, of any sorts of church in Saxon Devon, is even

3.10: The robbed-out foundations of the apsidal east end of Exeter's late Saxon minster church. Photograph: Exeter Archaeology.

more disappointing. The excavated part-plan of Exeter's apsidal minster church, as published by Christopher Henderson and Paul Bidwell probably in its tenth-eleventh-century phase, represents a building of undoubted high status. Excavation by Andrew Reynolds and Sam Turner has indicated that Buckfast abbey's original site was where the later parish church (dedicated to Holy Trinity) stood from the thirteenth century onwards: early building foundations as well as burials found here pre-date the twelfth-century shift to the medieval and later abbey site (when the original dedication to St Mary was also moved). Susan Pearce has suggested that the presumed early minster at Tavistock underlies not the late tenth-century monastic site but the nearby parish church.

Sufficient fabric survives in the churches of St. Martin's and St. Olave's, both in Exeter, to confirm that these are the buildings to which there is pre-Norman documentary record. At St Olave's "long and short" work (where the axes of individual stones are alternately vertical and horizontal) occurs high up in the north-west angle of the original nave (the church was subsequently extended northwards). St. Martin's has been the subject of re-assessment, by Stuart Blaylock and Keith Westcott. "Long and short"

3.11: St. Olave's church, Exeter, showing late Saxon triassic sandstone long-and-short quoins high up in the north-west angle of the nave.
Photograph: Exeter Archaeology.

work occurs in the south wall of its nave, together with remnants of a small window, all constructed with the volcanic trap and mortar mix also found in the Norman castle gatehouse (commenced in 1068). It appears that the church dedicated to St Martin in 1065 comprised the nave of the present building, the chancel and tower being added in the fifteenth century (when the west end of the original nave was also rebuilt). Also in Exeter, late Saxon fragments from St. George's church can be seen in South Street, where they were re-built in 1954. This, however, was not

Making Anglo-Saxon Devon

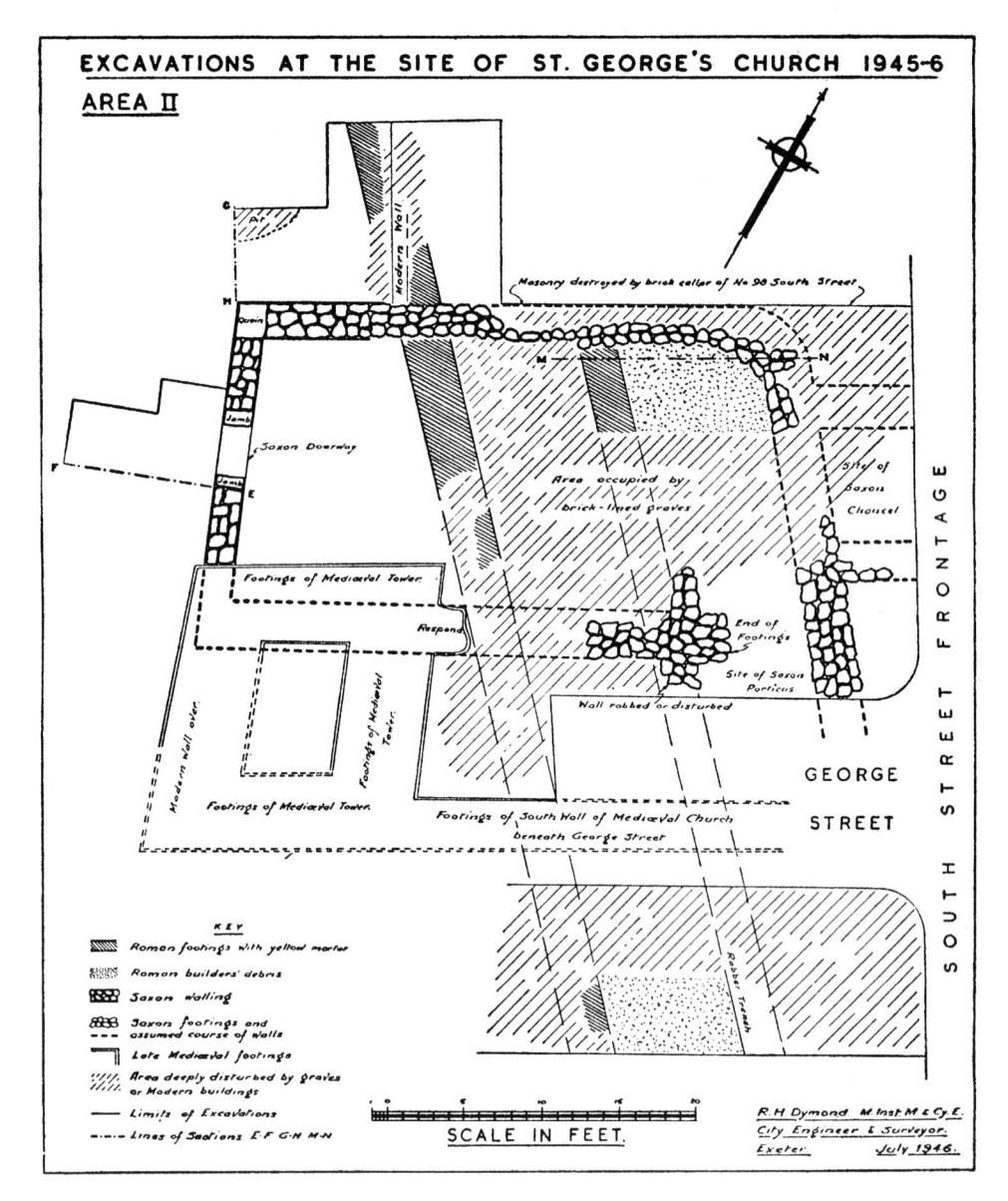

3.12: (a) Plan and (b; opposite) elevation of the remains of St George's church, South St, Exeter. From Fox 1952. Based on surveys by R.H. Dymond and A.W. Everett.

their original site, which was opposite, on the other side of the street. The church had been largely demolished in 1843, when a widening of the street removed its chancel. Its Saxon remains, with "long and short" quoins and re-used Roman materials, became visible in 1942, exposed by bombing, and were recorded in elevation by Alan Everett. The plan of the building was excavated by Aileen Fox after World War II. The Saxon church had walls two feet thick, with chancel, nave and perhaps one *porticus*. A south aisle and tower had been added in the later middle ages. In an unpublished dissertation by Jim Navin, it has been suggested that in the late Saxon and early Norman periods all of the city's local churches were simple, two-cell structures with square-ended chancels.

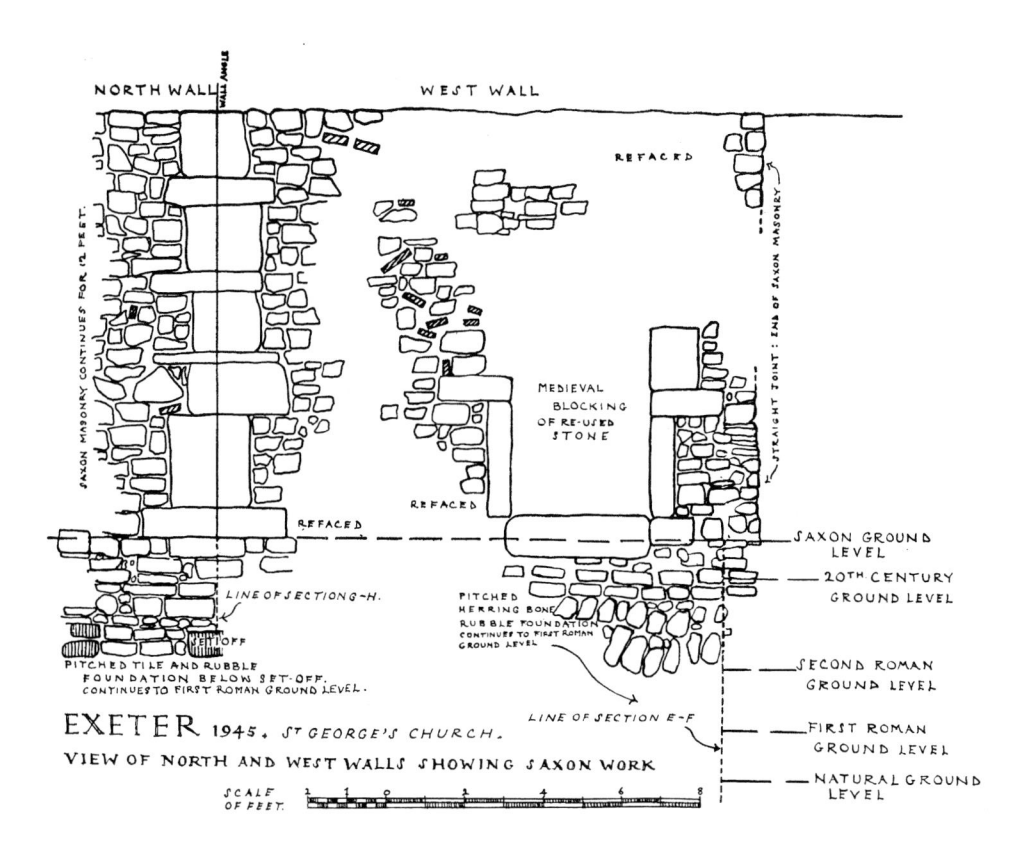

At Sidbury, a stone crypt or relic chamber sealed beneath the Norman chancel of the church is the most puzzling of Devon's early church fragments, studied by various commentators including Walter Cave, Ralegh Radford and Harold Taylor. Discovered and emptied during renovation work in 1898, this masonry structure is some twelve feet square. Only its lower parts survive, the upper having been destroyed when the structure was filled in during building of the first phase of the chancel above in the twelfth century (the chancel was later extended eastwards). A surviving fragment of "long-and-short" work in the steps leading down into it suggests a date of construction in the tenth or eleventh century. Opinions vary as to

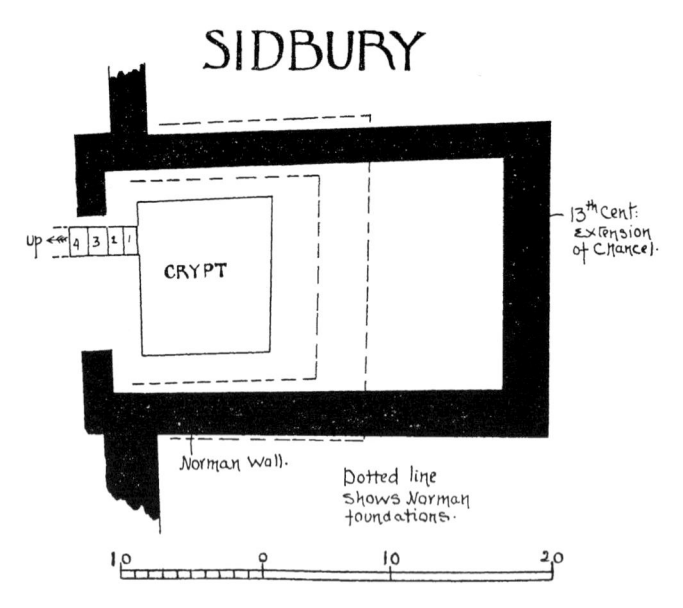

3.13: Plan of the crypt at Sidbury church, from Cave 1899.
By permission of the Royal Archaeological Institute.

what this structure represents. It could have been a mausoleum, part below and part above ground, existing independently and out of use before any church was built. It may be relevant that the structure's alignment and that of the church above it do not coincide exactly. The tenth-century cross of which a fragment still survives (below) is evidence of a Christian site and must have stood here or nearby. But no tradition of a saint associated with a holy place has survived. Alternatively, as suggested at the time of its discovery, the structure may have been part of the east end of a late Saxon church with chancel raised above a crypt whose ceiling was higher than the floor-level of the nave (as known in some Saxon churches elsewhere in England and in St Stephen's church in Exeter during the Norman period). This might explain why the down-steps into the structure are not central to it: the central position would have been occupied by the up-steps into the chancel. Thus, we may have another possible church with early origins. Sidbury was a large rural manor, rated at five hides in Domesday Book, which belonged to Exeter's minster church (the cathedral from 1050). The present church (St Michael, but St Giles from the eighteenth century) has, for Devon, an unusual amount of fine twelfth-century work, including a rib-vaulted ground floor in the western tower and excellent figure carving higher up the western tower, as well as a Romanesque-Gothic transitional style in the interior. It was clearly a church of above average status when it was re-developed and could well have been so earlier: original status as a sub-minster of Exeter is a strong possibility.

Though again lacking pre-Norman documentary reference, another candidate for origin as a sub-minster of Exeter is Branscombe, also in east Devon. Originally a royal estate (it figured in Alfred's will) it was granted by Aethelstan to Exeter's minster. In 1066 it was an episcopal manor, and Domesday Book states that it had a specific function of producing supplies for Exeter's canons. The present church is a very fine building, of cruciform plan, with much surviving Norman fabric. Some commentators have suggested traces of late Saxon work in the base of the circular stair turret of the twelfth-century central tower. Ronald Branscombe has tentatively suggested that this structure may be successor to an earlier one of the "nave-tower" type which occurs in various places in England at the very end of the Saxon period and early in the Norman period: here the tower was the main component of the church, to which a small chancel was attached. Comparisons have been made, with respect to this argument, between Branscombe and the church at Teignmouth. This church was demolished (in order to be replaced) in the early nineteenth century but is known from a sketch made earlier: it, too, had a central tower with circular stair-turret. The church was mentioned in a charter of 1044 (see above) and Ernest

3.14: St Michael's church, Teignmouth: an image based on a watercolour by John Swete of 1792 (from Fisher 1969, who also referred to a similar early picture of Bishopsteignton church), perhaps preserving parts of the eleventh-century structure, even a "tower-nave" church? By permission of David and Charles, Newton Abbot.

Fisher argued that some fabric of the church shown in the sketch may have survived from late Saxon times.

The remains of the tenth-eleventh-century minster in Exeter have been re-evaluated since their first publication. Initially, a modestly-sized church was postulated: it was a simple, apsidal structure some 35m long, about 8m in width and with a structure (perhaps a *porticus*, or side chapel) on its north side. Lead window cames excavated from the twelfth-century demolition levels (and displayed in the Royal Albert Memorial Museum, Exeter) reveal that it had glazed windows. It should be noted that, in additions made to The Exeter Book (see below) in the Norman period, which Frances Rose-Troup showed to be manumissions and other matters of a legal nature, there is also a record of bishop Osbern, Leofric's successor, consecrating a (presumably new) *porticus* dedicated to St. Mary. It is difficult to see this as being part of anything other than the minster, alerting us to the possible post-Conquest evolution of this simple building. However, the possibility of a much larger and more complex late Saxon church was later suggested by Christopher Henderson, and hypothetical plans published. Current opinion, however, has reverted to the original view, of a small, narrow building whose width followed that of the excavated remains of its apse. The seal dating from 1133, at the time of the later Norman cathedral's building, bears a depiction of a grand church, sometimes thought to be a depiction of the late Saxon minster: but this idea has been discounted and the non-real but symbolic nature of this depiction (as on other seals of the period) has been stressed.

Another issue relating to Exeter's excavated minster is whether it had been the only church of the Saxon period, to which the history of the site's dedications is relevant. It appears to have been St Peter's up to 968; St Mary's and St Peter's from 968 (when, according to the twelfth-century writer John of Worcester, monks were established); and (mainly) St Peter's again from 1050, when its new cathedral status was conferred (and the earlier group of monks had long disappeared). It has been suggested by John Blair and Nicholas Orme, however, that the double dedication related to the building of a second church nearby, and that this helps explain the modest size of the excavated church. According to this theory, which has much to commend it, the first church stood where the Norman cathedral was built (and was thus swept away without trace in the twelfth century) and its dedication to St Peter was transferred to the new building. The dedication to St Mary was preserved at the other church (which was of tenth-century origin only) and was transferred to the medieval parish church which succeeded it. Since the area for testing this idea lies underneath the present cathedral, the issue will probably remain unresolved. But it has raised an important question about Exeter's development and its possible similarity to other major English sites of the period, many of which had more than one church.

Two important features of Devonian culture conspire to give us such a thin physical record of early churches. First, a great deal of church fabric was transformed in later medieval re-buildings of the parish churches, so that survivals in detail from even the Norman period are not numerous compared with some other counties. Second, the widespread building technology of cob, clay-bonded rubble and timber which is found at vernacular level in the south west, may have been employed to produce considerable numbers of early rural churches whose fabric has left no trace at all, even within later re-buildings. These considerations must be set against a currently influential view of the surviving smaller English churches everywhere, proposed by Richard Gem. These modest stone structures, mainly dating from around 1000 onwards, are regarded as evidence of a general shift in the emphasis of local church-building from a vernacular base to an architectural one; that is, from timber and/or cob technology, which would need periodic replacement, to stone technology producing permanent structures. This process, which went on into the early twelfth century, paralleled the emergence of the "parish church" itself, and the permanence of the new buildings mirrored the progressive fixing of parishes as stable territorial units. From this point onwards, local churches of stone were rebuilt piecemeal by successive generations, resulting in the multi-period structures of which so many parish churches now consist. Surviving church fabric suggests that this process, sometimes called a "great re-building" with reference to the comparable process in vernacular secular building some centuries later, advanced at greater speed in eastern England than in the west. Thus, it may have had limited impact on Devon during the period when "Anglo-Saxon" architectural styles were current, making much more progress when Norman Romanesque was in vogue in the twelfth century. Up until around 1100, most of Devon's local rural churches (in whatever numbers they existed) may still have employed timber or cob construction in their initial construction and subsequent replacements: thus, in the twelfth century, architecturally-speaking they were replaced not by an "Anglo-Saxon" church but by a "Norman" one. These, in turn, were massively altered during the later fourteenth- to sixteenth-century rebuildings which Devon's prosperity then sustained.

The most common survivals from the Norman period in Devon's parish churches are fonts, of which more than a hundred survive. They were probably treasured, and retained by later generations, not only because they were central to a church's on-going functions, but because they were intimately associated with the church's development. The point at which a church acquired baptismal rights was crucial in its evolution from "local" status under a minster's authority to independent "parish" status within the diocese. Acquisition of fonts may therefore have been intimately connected with parochial community development in the twelfth century. However, the interpretation of the surviving early fonts in this way is complicated by the fact that few Anglo-Saxon stone fonts survive from England generally: earlier baptismal practice was different (see below).

Exploitation and Use of Stone (Figs. 3.15, 3.16, 3.17, 3.18)

Limited though the survival of early church fabric in Devon may be, it reveals a late Saxon quarrying industry for building stones, an industry that would otherwise be largely unknown to us. The foundations of Exeter's minster were of the volcanic "trap" drawn from the city's own surrounds and whose reddish/brown colour later gave the Norman castle its popular name "Rougemont". The ninth-tenth-eleventh-century fabric in the city wall in Northernhay (see Chapter 4) was triassic sandstone from the east side of the lower Exe estuary. St. George's church contained re-used Roman architectural fragments, local "trap" and stone from Salcombe, south Devon. The early fabric of St. Martin's church was principally local "trap". That at St Olave's included triassic sandstone. The castle gatehouse, built in 1068 under Norman direction but with English masons who employed indigeneous architectural features, was also constructed of local "trap", together with triassic sandstone. While this quarrying industry may not have produced many buildings in Devon at this time, there was willingness to transport stone, presumably by coast and estuary, over some distance for use in important structures, particularly in Exeter. This has implications for our view of their cost, as well as for the origin of related specialist activities, especially stone-carving.

In Cornwall, the carving of stone crosses flourished from the ninth to eleventh centuries, employing a mix of art-styles from Celtic, Anglo-Scandinavian and European backgrounds. Production of these distinctive items coincided (perhaps intentionally?) with increasing absorption of the Cornish church into the English sphere. There was no general Devonian equivalent, and the county's collection of Anglo-Saxon sculpture is thin, even allowing for the probable loss of some evidence (as known at

Church and Society

3.15: Left: tenth- or early eleventh-century cross-shaft from Exeter (head missing). Made of granite probably from southern Dartmoor (as 3.17). The side illustrated comprises panels of diagonal key patterns. Source of data: Cramp 2006. Photograph: Royal Albert Memorial Museum and Art Gallery, Exeter.

3.16: Right: early tenth-century cross-shaft (with reconstructed head) at Colyton church. Made of limestone (Corallian Group of the Osmington Oolite) from south- or mid-Dorset (as 3.18). The side illustrated has a background of plant motifs within which are set (below) a backward-reaching animal and (above) a backward-reaching bird. Source of data: Cramp 2006. Photograph: Ben Higham.

Winkleigh). West Somerset has virtually none at all, but east Somerset and Dorset are much better endowed. The Devonian examples have recently been published in detail by Rosemary Cramp, and a selection is illustrated here. The cross-carved upright slab at Belstone is difficult to date with certainty. Those pieces of certain Anglo-Saxon date are mainly parts of crosses, though at Braunton there is a grave-cover (and at Dolton a cross was later re-used to make a font). At Sidbury and Colyton, cross-fragments were later incorporated in the church walls: they have been recovered and restored in modern times. Crosses had various possible functions. Some may have been memorials to local church-founders or patrons; others probably marked places at which preaching or sacraments were delivered by priests from minster churches, before local churches existed. But the cross called *copelan stan* is mentioned in a charter boundary of 974, describing land at *Nymet*, later to become part of Down St Mary and Copplestone, neighbouring the large estate belonging to the minster at Crediton. It is still virtually *in situ*, having been moved only slightly in modern times, and its location must have had particular significance. Perhaps standing near the divergence of important routes (north to Barnstaple, west to Okehampton) was significant: ceremonies at which slaves were freed sometimes took place at cross-roads (see above, and below, Chapter 5). Or perhaps it perpetuated the site of an earlier burial ground from the era before local local churches and churchyards developed. In many cases, however (as with inscribed Dumnonian memorials), it can be difficult to know exactly where "Saxon" crosses originally stood. The original site of Exeter's cross is unknown, but association with the minster or a boundary of its urban territory in the tenth or eleventh century is a possibility. It was discovered built into the Exe bridge, so an original location near the river or west gate of the city has also been suggested. But since the bridge contained re-used material from St Nicholas Priory, which may have been built in a former late Saxon aristocratic *haga* (see above, and Chapter Four), the associated church of St Olave is an alternative possible site. At Sidbury and Colyton, where they were later built into church walls, the crosses must have been at or near the church sites at least by the time of their rebuilding.

At Dolton, on the other hand, another possibility emerges. W.G. Hoskins pointed out that the name Halsdon, at the west edge of the parish near the river Torridge, may reveal where the cross had originally stood. The name means "holy stone": the editors of the *Place-names of Devon* noted its occurrence here in the thirteenth century as *Halgheston*, and thought it to have derived from Old English *halig stan*, as Hoskins later argued. If this interesting idea is correct, then this cross first stood quite near a boundary. The occurrence of this fine piece of early ninth-century sculpture at Dolton, in western Devon, is itself an intriguing fact (though we should note that an apparently Anglo-Saxon dedication of the church, to St Edmund the Martyr, is known only from post-Reformation times). It

3.17: Late tenth-century cross-shaft at Copplestone (on modern base; head missing).
Made of granite from the Merrivale-Princeton area of Dartmoor (as 3.15).
The side illustrated comprises three panels: lowest (with plaited pattern);
middle (with pairs of ringed knots); upper (an inter-looping pattern).
Source of data: Cramp 2006. Photograph: Exeter Archaeology.

is tempting to speculate whether the area once belonged to an important church elsewhere. In 729 king Aethelheard of Wessex granted ten hides of land in the Torridge valley (*in Torric*) to Glastonbury abbey. In 802 king Egbert enlarged, or reduced, this estate by five hides, or granted a separate five-hide estate. H.P.R Finberg suggested that these grants, which survive not as actual charters but only as events recorded centuries later by Glastonbury's monks, may have related to Hatherleigh, Jacobstowe and Petrockstow: these were later properties of Tavistock and Buckfast abbeys (whose foundation he believed had benefitted from Glastonbury's support). But in her survey of Glastonbury's endowments, Lesley Abrams has emphasised there is no independent evidence for these identifications and the Glastonbury estate may have been somewhere else. If Dolton was within this territory, then perhaps the sculpture was put up as a Glastonbury showpiece in a far-flung part of its world, a remote part of Devon whose rural population surely remained essentially Dumnonian in origin? By 1066, however, Glastonbury had long since lost this Torridge estate, wherever it had been situated. Rosemary Cramp has noted that the Dolton cross shared some similarities with sculptures surviving at Ramsbury (Wiltshire), raising also the possibility of a connection with this West Saxon abbey site. On the other hand, the face with animals flowing from its nostrils is a particular Dolton feature: sculptural parallels may simply reveal the use of common sources of inspiration (in manuscripts) rather than actual institutional connections.

Place-name evidence may be helpful in providing some further context for the Dolton cross. The editors of the *Place-names of Devon* noted that the spellings in Domesday Book revealed that Dolton (*Duueltone*) shared the first element of its place-name (an element which may be British) with its neighbouring parish, Dowland (*Duuelande*). They suggested that both had once been part of the same, much larger estate. In the north-west part of Dolton parish, we also find a property called Buckland, which was listed as a separate manor (*Bocheland*) by Domesday Book. Such names derive from *bocland* and generally reveal that the estate to which they belonged had been "booked" at some time by royal charter (see Chapter 4). So perhaps, in the Anglo-Saxon period, Dolton had been part of an estate granted by a king to an important thegn or to a Devon minster church, or (as postulated above) to an important church elsewhere. And perhaps such a landlord was responsible for acquiring the fine early cross? Dolton itself is a large rural settlement by mid-Devon standards, though this may reveal more about its later development than about its early history. By 1066, however, this postulated Dolton estate had been split up into separate manorial units. Buckland was held by Goda; Dolton, apparently comprising two units, was held by Edric and by Ulf; Dowland was held by Alward. The total assessment of these elements was only a few hides, so, if the Dolton estate *had* earlier belonged to Glastonbury then it had only been part of the abbey's total endowment in the Torridge valley. It was perhaps during the process of estate fragmentation that the cross was brought from its original location to a new local church founded by a late Saxon thegn or an early Norman lord. The large number of twelfth-century fonts surviving in Devon's churches gives a good clue as to the period when this cross was probably broken up and put to new use. In the east of Dolton parish the farm-name Cherubeer may contain the *cirice* element, though the name is not documented until the thirteenth century. Perhaps this property had a particular link with the newly-built church.

3.18: Parts of an early ninth-century cross-shaft (later re-assembled as a font) at Dolton church. Made of limestone (Corallian Group of the Osmington Oolite) from south- or mid-Dorset (as 3.16). The side principally illustrated comprises (a) upper portion (upside-down) with human face and (b) lower portion with five rows of figure-of-eight knots.The human face has given rise to several interpretations, with either breath flowing from its nostrils or a long moustache: these features terminate in animal/reptile forms.
Source of data: Cramp 2006. Photograph: Stephen J. Price.

The cross shaft from Exeter (now in the Royal Albert Memorial Museum), and those at Copplestone and Plymstock are made of granite. But other pieces reveal a more varied use of building stone sources, with interesting implications for the transport of stone overland or by sea and estuary. Doulting stone from Somerset was used at Braunton; Bath stone was used at Sidbury and Porlock (the only west Somerset piece); limestone from Dorset was used at Dolton and Colyton. Devon's crosses reflect separate traditions from east and west of the shire. The use of granite and the construction of head and shaft from one piece (as at Plymstock) are in the Cornish style. The use of other types of stone and the jointing of head and shaft from separate pieces (as at Colyton) are in the West Saxon style. The range of artistic motifs employed, sometimes in conjunction, include: animal and bird designs (as at Dolton and Colyton); plant ornament designs (as at Colyton and Braunton); and figure carving (as at Dolton and Copplestone). Although the Dolton cross was later made into a font, the absence of early stone fonts in Devon is notable in comparison with the large numbers of examples surviving from the Norman period. It would appear that Anglo-Saxon baptismal rites may have been out of doors, making use of wells, springs or rivers. Or perhaps other sorts of water container, for example wooden tubs or lead tanks, were employed?

The dating of this sculpture lies within fairly broad limits and is sometimes tentative. The analogies are mainly between the artistic motifs employed and their occurrence in dated manuscripts from Wessex and elsewhere. These issues are discussed in relation to the Devon material in Rosemary Cramp's *corpus*. As a whole, the Devon items post-date the earlier tradition of Dumnonian inscribed memorial stones (see above and also Chapter 2). Devon's earliest "English" piece is the Dolton cross-shaft, belonging probably to the early ninth century. The cross at Colyton is of classic West Saxon fashion of the early tenth century. The remaining examples span the tenth and eleventh centuries. Two Devon pieces have (or had) inscriptions in Old English, almost certainly including personal names, of which a few letters survive: on the grave-cover at Braunton; and on the cross-shaft at Plymstock. At Sourton, a Dumnonian inscribed stone was re-carved into a simple cross, perhaps in the later Anglo-Saxon period. Were those responsible aware of its earlier significance? Later still, it became a road-marker, inscribed with directions to nearby towns: of practical use at least a thousand years after its creation.

Conclusion: church culture on the eve of the Norman Conquest
(see Fig. 3.19)

Finally, we may consider some wider aspects of ecclesiastical culture. An impressive achievement, of a very different sort from the sculptures, was the library of bishop Leofric of Exeter, which has been usefully discussed in its national context by Patrick Conner. Amongst this collection was the Exeter Book, containing some of our most famous Old English texts, including the poem *Widsith*. The oldest surviving manuscript of Anglo-Saxon poetry, this book dates from the later tenth century. Opinion is divided about whether it was written at Exeter or Crediton, as suggested by Patrick Conner, Bernard Muir and others, or written outside Devon (perhaps Glastonbury or Canterbury) as suggested by Richard Gameson, or even much further west at Tavistock, as cautiously suggested by H.P.R. Finberg. Its poems contain a mix of religious and secular themes, some originating deep in the Germanic past and transmitted orally for centuries before being written down. As well as poems, the book also contains a collection of riddles. Leofric's 67 manuscripts, in Latin or Old English, were outnumbered at this time only at Worcester (71), Salisbury (81) and, in a class of its own, Canterbury (221). Leofric's library, containing items acquired from elsewhere and items copied for him at Exeter, was bequeathed to the cathedral: hence the existence of a contemporary list of its contents. But the collection was later dispersed, though the Exeter Book has remained continuously at Exeter. The (poorly-titled) "Leofric Missal", published in the nineteenth century by F.E. Warren and more recently by Nicholas Orchard, contains three "layers" of content, the first two from the tenth century, probably compiled for an archbishop of Canterbury. Additions of the mid-eleventh century were made for Leofric.

Tavistock abbey's library contained some important items in the eleventh century, including manuscripts of Aelfric's *Homilies*. Their discovery here in the sixteenth century gave rise to a tradition, repeated by antiquaries down to the nineteenth century, that the study and teaching of Old English had been preserved at Tavistock as late as the Dissolution. This tradition, as H.P.R. Finberg showed in his his major study of the abbey, was based on a mistaken appreciation of these sources by Matthew Parker, archbishop of Canterbury in Elizabeth's reign. Still further west, in Cornwall, the Bodmin Gospels Book of about 900 provides further evidence of cultural accomplishment, and the important late-ninth century hoard from Trewhiddle (near St. Austell) contains silver ecclesiastical objects. There

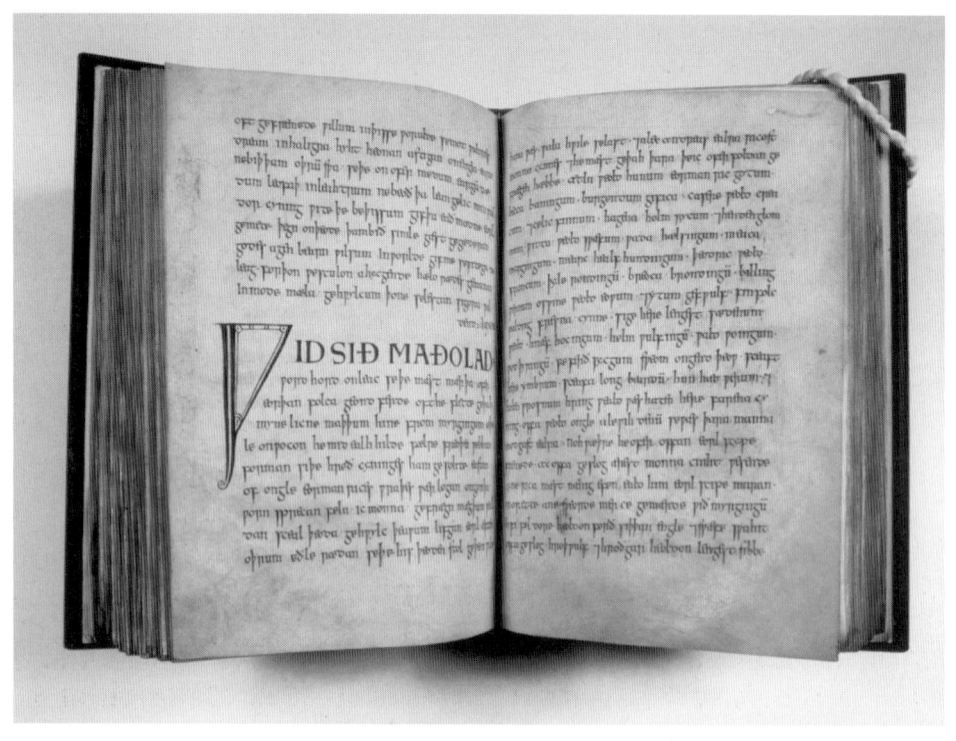

3.19: The late tenth-century Exeter Book of Poetry open at the beginning of the poem *Widsith*. The subject of the poem travels widely through the continental homelands of the Anglo-Saxons, long before they came to Britain.
Photograph: Exeter Cathedral Archives, by permission of the Dean and Chapter.

are some documentary hints of high quality objects, such as the vestments and liturgical books mentioned, alongside secular possessions, in the will of bishop Aelfwold of Crediton (died 1012), himself of the Devon land-holding class. But the south west was not characterised by great richness and none of its churches had a great reputation far outside the region. Although there were a few places in Devon associated with saints' resting-places (see earlier in this chapter), only two places (St Sidwell at Exeter; St Romanus at Tavistock) figured as such (and thus as cult centres) in an early eleventh-century English list (in which, however, several other shires also had as few). An eleventh-century Exeter relic list included items from Palestine and Europe which, it was maintained, had been donated by Aethelstan to the minster: this source, known as the "Aethelstan Donation", maintained that Aethelstan had re-founded the minster at Exeter, endowing it with many estates and many of his own holy relics.

Nevertheless, Leofric, whose career has been much illuminated by Audrey Erskine, Frank Barlow and David Blake, found St. Peter's minster at Exeter impoverished: in 1050 he had to build up its texts, vestments and liturgical equipment more or less from nothing. He was an erudite man, educated in Lotharingia according to William of Malmesbury, where he encountered the Rule of St. Chrodegang – in which secular canons followed a communal life – which he was to establish at Exeter. He returned to England with Edward the Confessor in 1041 and became an influential clerk at the king's court, before being made bishop in 1046. In the twelfth century, John of Worcester recorded that, while born to an English family, in his place of birth he had been "British", perhaps meaning Wales, south-west England or specifically Cornwall. David Blake has suggested that Edward the Confessor's early grant to Leofric, of land at Dawlish in 1044, could relate to the area of his birth or where his family had earlier held land. Whatever his origins, it is likely that his (thegnly) family had left England on the accession of king Cnut. Later in life, he seems not to have been politically active: no mention of him is made in narratives of the civil war of 1051-52 nor of the Norman conquest of Exeter in 1068. But he remained close to the king and attended major royal councils, for example that at Westminster for Christmas 1065.

Leofric seems to have struggled with a certain lack of sophistication amongst his Exeter staff: the charters he had drawn up, demonstrating title to his church's lands, contained many scribal errors. The documents whose "creation" he organised, to replace originals probably destroyed in the viking sack of Exeter in 1003 (the likelihood of this disaster to the minster's archive is strengthened by its mention in a charter of king Cnut) contained a confusion which reveals an interesting symmetry. These charters, relating, for example, to lands in Topsham, Stoke Canon, Culmstock and Monkton (Shobrooke), purported to record grants by king Aethelstan at the time of his re-foundation of the minster in the tenth century. But, in a curiously unscholarly (from a modern perspective) exercise, an impossibly early date of 670 was attributed to them. It is difficult to see why this date, as opposed to any other, would simply have been invented: its choice presumably reflected a tradition, continuously maintained in Exeter and its church's records, of the period when the first English minster had been established there, in the time of king Cenwalh of Wessex (died 674). Thus, Leofric's well-intentioned efforts "created" another version of Exeter's "history" founded on continuity with the past. Leofric's career also gave important contemporary continuity both to the diocese and to Exeter through the upheavals of the Norman Conquest. He remained in office until his death in 1072, and was buried in the crypt of the minster church which he had made his cathedral. His remains were later translated to the new cathedral which was built in the twelfth century.

SOURCES USED AND FURTHER READING

Abrams 1996; Allan *et alii* 1984; Baker & Holt 1998; Barlow 1963; Barlow *et alii* 1972; Barlow 1996; Birch 1885-1899; Blair 1985; Blair 1987; Blair (ed) 1988; Blair 1992(a); Blair 1992(b); Blair 1995; Blair 2002; Blair 2005; Blair & Orme 1995; Blake 1974; Blaylock & Westcott 1989; Boggis 1922; Branscombe 2004; Cambridge & Rollason 1995; Cave 1899; Chaplais 1966; Cherry & Pevsner 1989; Colgrave & Mynors 1969; Conner 1993; Cramp 2006; Darby & Welldon Finn 1967; Darlington & McGurk (eds) 1995; Davies 1992; Edwards & Lane 1992; Erskine *et alii* 1988; Faith 2004; Farmer 1992; Finberg 1951; Finberg 1953; Finberg 1964; Fisher 1962; Fisher 1969; Foot 2000; Fox 1952; Gameson 1996; Gem 1988; Hall 2000; Hall 2005; Handley 2001; Hase 1994; Henderson & Bidwell 1982; Henderson 1999; Holdsworth 1980; Holdsworth 1986(a); Holdsworth 1991; Holdsworth 1999; Holdsworth 2003; Hooke 1994; Hoskins 1954; Jankulak 2000; Kain & Ravenhill (eds) 1999; Lapidge 1984; Lepine & Orme 2003; Manning & Stead 2002–2003; Miles 1986; Morris 1989; Muir 1994; Okasha 1993; Oliver 1846; Olson 1989; Orchard 2002; Orme 1980; Orme 1986; Orme 1991(b); Orme 1995; Orme 1996; Orme & Henderson 1999; O'Donovan 1988; Padel 2002; Page 1915; Pearce 1982(a); Pearce 1982(b); Pearce 1985(a); Pearce 1978; Pearce 2004; Petts 2002; Pounds 2000; Preston-Jones 1992; Radford 1957; Radford 1975; Rattue 1995; Reichel 1939; Reynolds & Turner 2003; Rose-Troup 1929; Rose-Troup 1937; Rosser 1988; Rosser 1992; Slater 1991; Sims-Williams 1990; Stephan 1970; Stevens 1976; Swanton & Pearce 1982; Taylor & Taylor 1965; Thacker & Sharpe (eds) 2002; Thomas 1981; Thomas 1994; Thomas 1999; Thorne & Thorne 1985; Todd 1987; Todd 2005; Turner 2003; Turner 2006; Warren 1883; Wedell 1987; Wedell 2000; Welldon Finn 1964; Whitelock (ed) 1955; Williams 2006; Winterbottom (ed) 1978; Yorke 1995; Yorke 2006(a); Yorke 2006(b); Yorke forthcoming.

4

Government and Towns

This chapter combines two themes. They had been related in the Romano-British period, subsequently became largely separated, but eventually became inextricably connected. Although by the eleventh century Devon had fewer towns than did many other parts of southern England, those that existed were crucial to its defence, to its framework of royal administration, to its development of further economic activities, to the emergence of a new elite class, and, in with respect to Exeter, to a growing sense of shire community centred on a regional capital.

Shires and royal lands (*see Fig. 4.1*)

On the eve of the Norman Conquest, the south west was part of an English kingdom which many now believe enjoyed some of Europe's most sophisticated administration in government, taxation and coinage. Patrick Wormald has argued, in an overview of early legal history, that the effectiveness of Henry II's development of common law in the later twelfth century was made possible because there was such a strong foundation of royal law and authority going back to Anglo-Saxon times. We can discern in outline how this late Saxon situation had developed, though the picture is thin up until the ninth century. From the ninth century onwards, it is clear that the shire was the crucial building-block of this framework of royal government. Much earlier, there had been a tradition of sub-division in the early Germanic kingdoms, originally composed of *regiones* where we find "sub-kings" of particular territories, often relatives of the main dynasty. The system was helpful when neighbouring English kingdoms conquered each other or their British neighbours, new sub-kings being installed or defeated dynasties taking on their role. This may have applied as the West Saxons first extended their influence into eastern Dumnonia, during the seventh century. But annexations further west, in the eighth century, coincided with the demise of the era of sub-kings, who had a tendency to hereditary power-building, and we do not know for certain whether any West Saxons or co-operative Dumnonians had acted in this capacity in what became Devon.

The names of Dorset and Somerset are compounded from places (Dorchester; and Somerton, in which estate lay the town of Ilchester) and names of groupings of people – giving *Dornsaete* and *Somersaete* – which Sir Frank Stenton thought revealed their earlier character as *regiones*. The case of Devon is somewhat different, taking its name – *Defenascir* – from the Roman tribal name and the Dumnonian kingdom which succeeded it, not from Exeter nor from any particular West Saxon royal estate. In this respect, Devon is similar to shires such as Sussex, Essex and Kent: all named from formerly-independent early medieval kingdoms and among which Kent provides a Devonian analogy in that its name derives from the Roman tribal area. Whether sub-kings had ever ruled in Devon, based in Exeter or somewhere else, we do not know. Much later, after the nominal conquest of Cornwall by Egbert, we find native Cornish client kings occurring by name, such as Dumgarth (the last, who died in 875), perhaps reflecting a similar situation of earlier date in Devon which has left no direct trace. But there is also an interesting Devon-Cornwall contrast: when Cornwall was fully absorbed into Wessex by Aethelstan, the new shire was not provided with a new or re-furbished fortified place – a *burh* – as happened when the West Saxons conquered and "shired" the Danish-occupied midlands in the tenth century. The shire of Cornwall was named, from its peripheral position, after its British tribal origin (*Corn*- from *Cornovii*) and its "internally foreign" people (*Wealas* – an overwhelmingly British group). Looking at the region from its prehistoric and Romano-British roots, Henrietta Quinnell and others have questioned how unified Dumnonia had actually been. Though given this single name in Roman government, it may always have contained a significant cultural-administrative division which emerged later as two separate shires. These two areas were certainly known by different times not later than the time of Aldhelm (see Chapter 2). How the internal structure of the region (or the role of Exeter within it) affected its reaction to the message from the Emperor Honorius to the British *civitates*, in 410, that they must thereafter look to their own security, we do not know.

Turning to the end of our period, we find a description of royal land-

Late Saxon Royal Interests in Devon

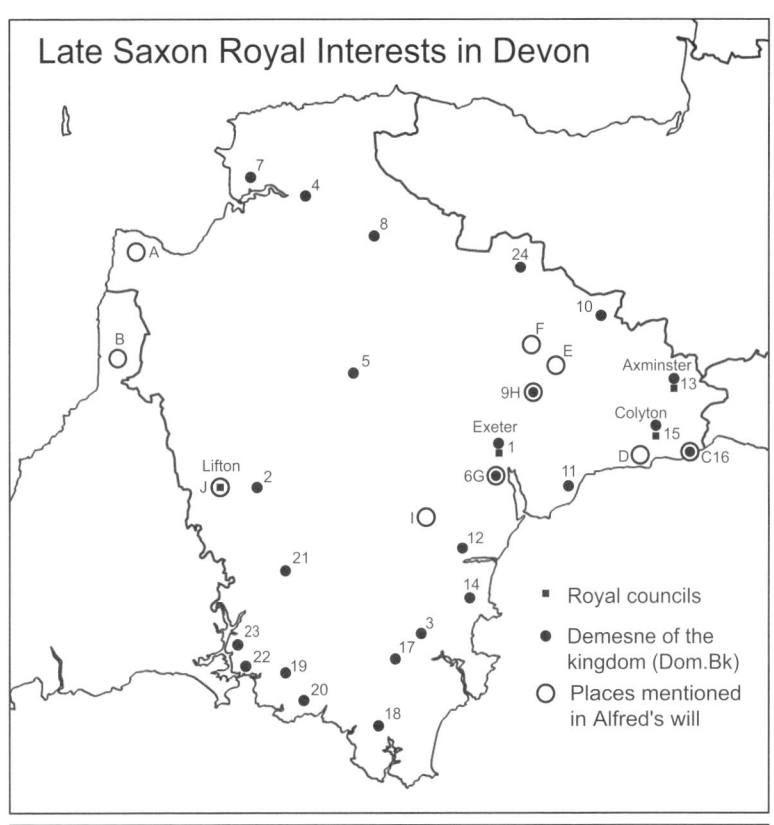

Royal Councils
- Axminster, 901
- Colyton, c.945
- Exeter, 924, 928, 935, 1050
- Lifton, 931

Ancient Royal Demesne (Domesday)
1. Exeter
2. Lydford
3. Totnes
4. Barnstaple
5. North Tawton
6. Exminster
7. Braunton
8. South Molton
9. Silverton
10. Hemyock
11. East Budleigh
12. (King's)Teignton
13. Axminster
14. (King's)Kerswell
15. Colyton
16. Axmouth
17. Diptford
18. West Alvington
19. Plympton
20. Yealmpton
21. Walkhampton
22. Sutton
23. (King's)Tamerton
24. Bampton

Places Mentioned in Alfred's Will
- A. Hartland
- B. Stratton (Cornwall)
- C. Axmouth
- D. Branscombe
- E. Cullompton
- F. Tiverton
- G. Exminster
- H. Silverton
- I. Lustleigh
- J. Lifton

4.1: Some late Saxon royal interests in Devon. Councils, royal demesne and places mentioned in Alfred's will. Map by Robert Higham and Oliver Creighton. In 904, Edward the Elder issued three charters in a council held at a hunting estate called Bickleigh: *in villa venatoria quae Saxonicae dicitur Bicanleag* (*BCS*, 604, 612, 613). If this was a Devon Bickleigh (perhaps near Plymouth) it could be added to the list.

holding in Devon in 1066 given by Domesday Book. For earlier centuries, it has to be pieced together from a variety of sources: narratives, charters and place-names, an important royal will (Alfred's), as well as from indicators such as royal council meeting-places, hundred centres and important churches. The West Saxon kings had acquired Devonian lands in two capacities. Their dynastic lands, probably combining Dumnonian royal estates with others won through conquest from Dumnonian nobles, passed from each king to his successor. These originally very extensive holdings were reduced, over the centuries, by grants of bookland to the church and secular classes (see below). But along the way, kings acquired other lands: personal estates which could also be disposed of as a king wished and which did not have to pass to his successor. After 1066, William the Conqueror acquired both categories – the ancient royal lands and the personal lands of king Edward the Confessor and king Harold Godwinson's family. From the *Exon* Domesday, we see that "the king's demesne belonging to the kingdom in Devonshire" had in 1066 included: one city (Exeter), three boroughs (Lydford, Totnes, Barnstaple) and about twenty rural estates. These were: (North) Tawton, Exminster, Braunton, South Molton, Silverton, Hemyock, (East) Budleigh, (King's) Teignton, Axminster (with dependent manors), (King's) Kerswell, Colyton, Axmouth, Diptford, (West) Alvington, Plympton, Yealmpton, Walkhampton, Sutton, (King's) Tamerton, and also Bampton (which the Conqueror disposed of). Many of these places coincide with hundred centres and minsters; place-names in *-tun* frequently occur at these places, as elsewhere in southern England. Domesday Book reveals that Silverton, Axminster, Axmouth and Bampton had never paid tax: they were presumably very ancient West Saxon royal estates (an idea which their location in the eastern part of the shire supports). Many of the others had very low hidations, reflecting their favoured status. These royal estate-centres represent an un-tapped source of potential archaeological data: we would expect them to have had buildings suitable for the housing of royal officials and, on some occasions, for visits of royal parties.

Our main point of comparison with the Domesday picture is the will of king Alfred, drawn up probably in the 880s (it is the earliest English royal will to survive), which reveals not the holdings of the West Saxon dynasty but the king's personal estates throughout the southern shires: lands which he designated as the inheritance of various members of his family. It has received helpful commentary (with a map) in Simon Keynes's and Michael Lapidge's edition of Alfred's works. It is not clear exactly how these southern lands had been acquired by Alfred's family: one theory is that they had formerly belonged to minster churches founded by the West Saxons, whose lands were reclaimed in the ninth century. Two of Alfred's family were to receive, amongst their shares, lands in Devon. Edward (his elder son) was bequeathed Hartland, as well as Stratton in Trigg (in Cornwall). Aethelweard, his younger son, received Axmouth, Branscombe, Cullompton, Tiverton, Exminster, two estates probably to be identified with Silverton and Lustleigh, and Lifton together with lands in Cornwall belonging to Lifton (except Trigg). It is interesting that Alfred's will included some lands (Silverton, Exminster, Axmouth) which by the eleventh century were regarded as royal demesne, blurring the traditional distinction of the two types of possession. It is also interesting that hundred centres (Lifton, Tiverton) and minster centres (Cullompton, Exminster) could emerge from within the personal royal estates and not simply within the ancient demesne. Nevertheless, despite such blurring, the distinction between dynastic and personal estates explains why a king might grant royal lands to himself in person: such booklands were free of (most) normal obligations and could be disposed of within his family at a later date. A Devon example is the charter of 847 recording the grant by king Aethelwulf, to himself, of land in the South Hams.

Devon's evolution, from a possible *regio* within Wessex to a shire, took place in the eighth century. It may have been king Ine who introduced important changes in government, bringing to an end the era of the sub-kings. Though it is not clear whether at this date the term referred to old-style *regiones* or to later-style shires, Ine's law-code of c. 690 referred to "shiremen", and by the mid-eighth century this rank had emerged as the *ealdorman* (known first in Latin as *princeps* or *praefectus*, later as *dux*). Seven such officials occur in royal charters issued in Cynewulf's reign, probably indicating that the West Saxon shires had now emerged. By this period, one of these would have been Devon. The witness-list of the charter recording king Aethelheard's grant of land at Crediton, in 739, to bishop Forthhere of Sherborne, contained the names of three *praefaecti* – Herefryth, Ecgfrith and Puttoc – one of whom may have been the shireman of Devon (perhaps the other two were for Somerset and Dorset?). Given the late date of the surviving version of this charter (see Appendix 2) we cannot be certain that such details had accurately survived the passage of time, though it is hard to imagine how such specific detail would have been invented centuries later and most commentators have accepted this witness list as having early origins. Although in everyday speech (as well as with reference to local government) we now refer to a "county" (adopting the

Norman-French *compté)* the Old English "shire" *(*from *scir* – meaning a portion of, or share of, the larger kingdom) survives in many modern county names. Hampshire, Berkshire, Wiltshire, Devon(shire), Somerset and Dorset (the latter two names formerly also had the –shire suffix) were probably eighth-century creations within Wessex, though often appearing by name in only the ninth century. Each shire was governed by one or more *ealdorman*, with major responsibilities including defence and justice. These men, of noble birth, were appointed by kings. Thus, Devon's absorption in Wessex coincided with a strengthening of the West Saxon kingdom, of which the extension of English church institutions south-westwards, under royal patronage and in association with newly-won royal estates, was another feature. Preservation of (admittedly second-class) British rights, seen in Ine's law-code, helped maintain the loyalty of conquered subjects and further welded this new "state" into a coherent whole (see Chapter 2). Thus, Devon became part of Wessex when the latter was undergoing considerable evolution. The *Anglo-Saxon Chronicle* tells us that in 851 an ealdorman named Ceorl led the men of Devon in victory against the vikings in a battle at *Wicganbeorg*. Though brief, this reference reveals Devon's military (and probably other) organisation as functioning and the ealdorman's role as fully established. Cornwall, however, was absorbed as a shire later, when this "new" Wessex had undergone a period of stabilization, and when the emergence of an English kingdom lay not far ahead. Thus, ancient east-west differences within the old Dumnonian territory were perpetuated by its drawn-out English conquest.

Hundreds, ealdormen and earls (see Fig. 4.2)

Another aspect of the east-west difference is the structure of the "hundreds", the shire's sub-divisions which had courts where law and taxation were administered (the equivalent name in the Danelaw was *wapentake*). English hundreds emerge (by that specific name) in record in the tenth century: so-called from their common correspondence to a hundred hides in the newly-organised lands of the re-conquered Danelaw. The mid-tenth-century Hundred Ordinance (it is not clear for precisely which king it was issued) described their basic organization: hundred courts were held every four weeks; the men of each hundred were divided into smaller groups, known as tithings, in relation to court business, the pursuit of criminals and other matters. But in Wessex, the hundreds had much earlier origins and grew, in a great variety of sizes, from sub-division of the ancient sub-kingdoms and newly-annexed territories. Asser's *Life* of Alfred refers to cases heard by ealdormen and reeves, very suggestive of the shire-hundred distinction. Edward the Elder's second law-code (924-925) refers to the *gerefa* who held a *gemot* every four weeks: it is hard to see what this was if not the precursor of the formally-named court of the later Hundred Ordinance.

The hundreds in Devon, as elsewhere in Wessex, often had a royal vill as their centre and sometimes (though not always: see Chapter 3) a church of minster status: it is fairly safe to assume that the proceeds of the hundred courts were paid to the king. Even before hundreds were formalised, these were the places where folk-moots convened and royal justice was available. We do not know exactly by what process the hundreds were formalised, nor exactly when, and evidence is sometimes ambiguous. The hundred of Plympton, for example, was perhaps known by name only after Edward the Elder acquired Plympton as a royal estate: but was the notion of the hundred fresh at this point, or had the district existed earlier but with a different centre? Eventually, Devon had more than thirty hundreds. In Cornwall there were originally only six, probably organised from earlier Dumnonian units, perhaps even survivals of *pagi*, sub-divisions of Romano-British origin (see Chapter 2). It has been noted by Oliver Padel that some of the eastern Cornish hundreds contained approximately 100 *tre* names, thus inviting analogy with English hundreds and with Welsh *cantrefs* which contained 100 *trefs*. One of the Cornish hundreds, *Trigg*, was mentioned in king Alfred's will. Knowledge of the hundredal names and territories in Devon comes from early Norman records, compiled long after their creation. *Exon* Domesday does not name the hundreds but names lands in a sequence following the hundreds. The hundreds occur in two lists and in the Geld Inquest, also from around the time of Domesday, enabling reconstruction of the hundreds through correlation with Domesday data. It would be an interesting challenge to see whether, by amalgamating groups of Devon hundreds, approximations of earlier and larger units, along Cornish lines, might be suggested. Fuller knowledge of Devon's hundreds comes from still later centuries, and their mapping is nineteenth century. Their reconstruction from the eleventh-century evidence reveals a contrasting pattern. Those in east Devon were relatively small, whereas the westernmost (Hartland, Torrington and Lifton) were very large – not wholly unlike their Cornish counterparts. This difference may reflect variety in the conditions and chronology of their creation, the eastern units presumably being of earlier origin. Variety in economic richness may also have been relevant – the population being thinner further west. It has

Hundred boundaries are shown as solid lines, except in four cases where dotted lines are employed
(a)   no. 22a, Axmouth, a Saxon royal manor-hundred later absorbed within no. 22 (Axminster)
(b)   no. 8, Tavistock, a post-Saxon creation
(c)   no. 32, Winkleigh, a post-Saxon creation
(d)   no. 27, West Budleigh, a post-Saxon creation
(e)   the dotted area within Axminster hundred was originally part of Dorset (an original part of Axminster hundred outlying within Dorset is not shown).

The remaining numbers on the map correspond to the names given below, in use in the eleventh century. The numbers are taken from Hoskins' (1954) map, but with extra data drawn from Thorn's publications (1985, 1991). Where two names are given, the first is that in use at that time, that in brackets being the name used in later centuries. Where the second name is indicated (*) it has been suggested by Frank Thorn that the later name reflects an original name, based on a "hundred meeting-place". By the Norman Conquest, Devon's hundred names had mainly become "manorial" in form. Thorn noted also that in the eleventh century, several discrete manors seem also (as originally was Axmouth) to have been small hundreds of a different sort. These are generally not distinguished on this map, though Ottery (shown) was such a unit, as was Uffculme (here depicted as the southerly portion of Bampton hundred). Crediton was an ecclesiastical hundred.

1.   Braunton
2.   Sherwill
3.   Fremington
4.   Merton (Shebbear)
5.   Hartland
6.   Torrington (Black Torrington)
7.   Lifton (Lifton & Tavistock – 8)
9.   Walkhampton (Roborough*)
10. Plympton
11. *Alleriga* (Ermington)
12. Diptford (Stanborough*)
13. Chillington (Coleridge*)
14. Kerswell (Haytor*)
15. Teignton (Teignbridge*)
16. Exminster
17. Wonford
18. Cliston

19. Budleigh (East Budleigh)
20. Ottery (St. Mary)
21. Colyton
22. Axminster
22a. Axmouth
23. Hemyock
24. Bampton / Uffculme
25. Halberton
26. Tiverton
27. West Budleigh
28. Silverton (Hayridge*)
29. Crediton
30. Witheridge
31. Tawton (North Tawton)
32. Winkleigh
33. South Molton

Outlying portions of hundreds are identified by the same serial number as the hundred itself. All commentators on Devon's hundreds, some of whom have depicted the data in map form, have noted how difficult it is to portray the original situation with accuracy. See Chapter 4 for discussion.

4.2: Map (opposite) and list (above) of Devon's hundreds, based on Hoskins 1954, Thorn & Thorn 1985, Thorn 1991. Map by Mike Rouillard.

further been suggested that the burdens of royal service were organised more leniently in the far west – that is, on bigger territories – because of its ongoing "frontier" challenges.

The pattern visible in Devon at the end of the eleventh century, helpfully analysed by Caroline and Frank Thorne in the Phillimore and Alecto editions of Domesday Book, may, however, have been significantly different

Government and Towns

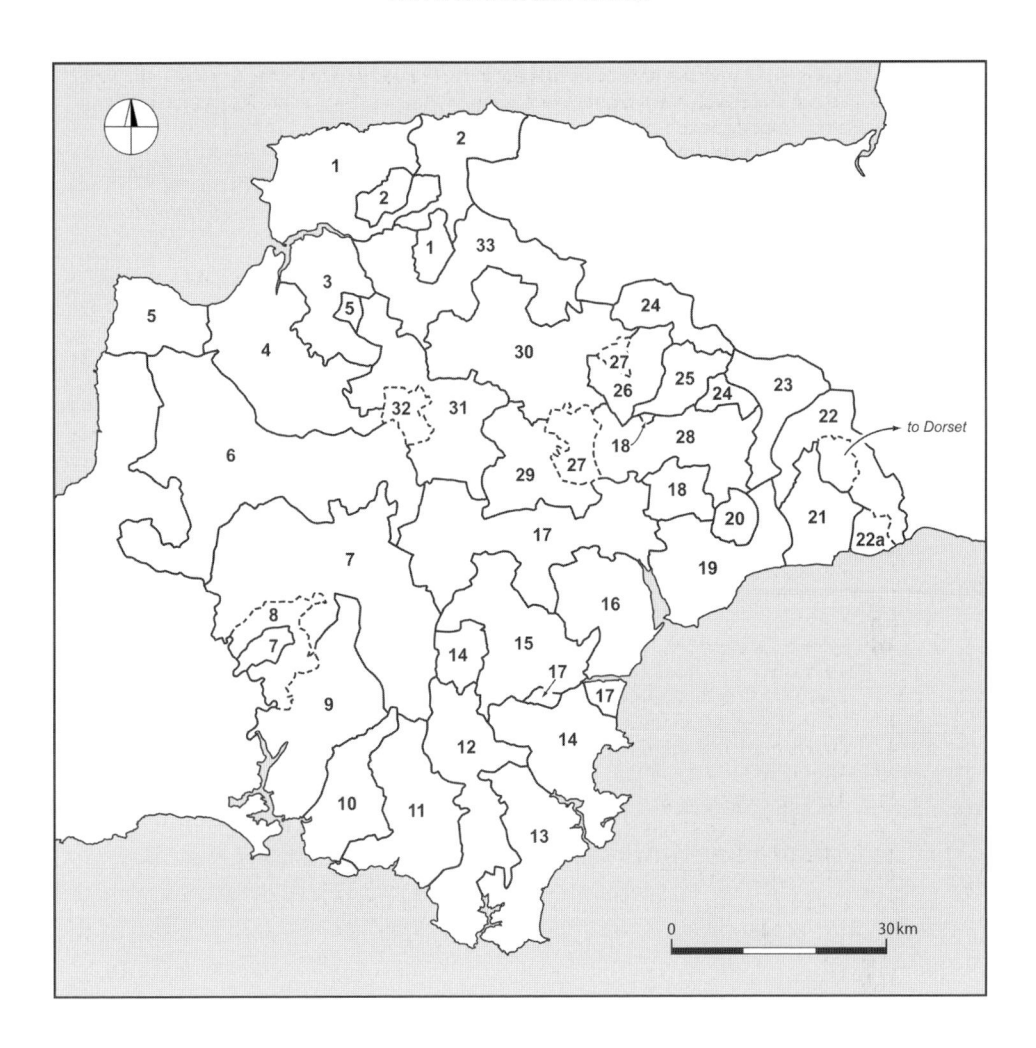

from that of earlier times. It is clear that hundreds sometimes underwent changes both in name and in extent, with amalgamations and divisions. The study of Kingsteignton published by Peter Weddell illustrates the complex task of reconstructing an early hundred: the hundredal pattern known in later times cannot simply be back-projected into the Anglo-Saxon period. Some later hundreds did not then exist. Colyton and Axmouth hundreds had been created before 1066, but their territories had probably once been part of Axminster hundred (as they were also later). Tiverton and Halberton may also originally have been a single, larger hundred (with implications for the minster church postulated at Tiverton: see Chapter 3). The existence of "outlying" portions of hundreds suggests that final hundred boundaries post-dated earlier tenurial patterns, whose integrity might be respected to keep their separated components within the same hundred. By the eleventh century, though the Devon hundreds varied greatly in size, most of them had a royal manor at their centre. These manor names, by which the hundreds were now known, had in some cases replaced an earlier name which had been the meeting-place of the hundred court. Modbury (which means -*moot burh*) was presumably an early meeting centre for what became Ermington hundred (Modbury was also the location of a minster church – see Chapter 3). Frances Griffith has suggested that the original hundred meeting-place, the site (*burh*) from which Modbury was ultimately named, may have been the hilltop enclosure surviving near the junction of Modbury and Bigbury parishes. Some later name changes reflected what had presumably been the original hundred meeting place: thus, the Domesday hundred of Silverton was called Hayridge in the later middle ages; Teignton was re-named Teignbridge; Kerswell became Haytor; Diptford became Stanborough; Chillington became Coleridge; Walkhampton became Roborough. It is possible that some of the meeting-places determined by landscape or by topographical features had been focal points in the *regiones* which preceded the emergence of the shire structure. It is not impossible that some of them were inherited from the framework of Dumnonian life.

Up to around 900, there was generally one *ealdorman* for each shire in Wessex. In Devon, we know the names of three such individuals, Ceorl, Odda and Aethelred. Ceorl figured in 851 (see above). Odda defeated the vikings in 878, at Countisbury: he was mentioned by Aethelweard I (himself ealdorman of western Wessex from 973) in his Latin version of the *Anglo-Saxon Chronicle*. Aethelred's death was mentioned in the *Anglo-Saxon Chronicle* in 899. But Edward the Elder and Aethelstan reduced the number of ealdormen to two: one for western Wessex (Cornwall, Devon, Dorset and Somerset) and one for the east (Hampshire, Wiltshire and Berkshire). This division was, in a sense, the secular equivalent of the old ecclesiastical division: the diocese of Sherborne had been created for the specifically western territory (though, in contrast, in Edward's reign, this diocese was sub-divided on a shire basis: see Chapter 3). These ealdormen came from the highest ranks of society. They were not only rich and politically powerful, but also benefactors of the church. Ordgar, ealdorman from 964, was father of Ordulf the founder of Tavistock abbey; Aethelweard II, ealdorman from 1014, was founder of Buckfast abbey. Aethelweard I reveals, in his Latin *Chronicle*, that his family were descended from king Aethelred I, king Alfred's brother. In 997, he witnessed a charter to the Old Minster, Winchester, as *dux* of the western provinces. The new system produced an hereditary tendency. Aethelweard I's son, Aethelmaer, who offered the surrender of his territory to the Danish king Swein at Bath in 1013, belonged to a family who held this office through three generations. His son and son-in-law (the ealdorman Aethelweard II) were killed or exiled around 1020 by Cnut, Swein's son, perhaps because he felt their descent from the West Saxon royal house posed a potential threat. But other descendants from the old ealdormanic families survived into the new era, for example Ordwulf, who was a holder of extensive lands in Devon in 1066, as Domesday Book later reveals.

Cnut, however, abolished the old system and grouped the shires together into new earldoms, with earls whose powers ranged over greater areas than even those of the tenth-century ealdormen. The earldom of Wessex comprised all of England south of the Thames and by 1020 its earl was Godwine, a Sussex thegn who married Gytha, Cnut's sister-in-law. His family, whose fortunes have been explored by Frank Barlow, built up massive personal estates in many areas, including Devon, and exerted much influence through their control of shire courts. These new earls were powerful (they controlled the shire-based armies); they were rich (they enjoyed a third of the royal revenues coming from the shire and borough courts); they were well-connected. Godwin's daughter, Edith, was the wife of Edward the Confessor, and his son, Harold, was the last pre-Norman king. When they challenged the king's power between 1049 and 1051, the west country was important to them, providing a direct sea-route to the Scandinavian community of Dublin. In the Godwinson family's own disputes, which contributed to this fractious period, Swegn (Godwin's son) treacherously abducted his Danish cousin, Beorn, at the family's estate at Bosham (Sussex) and, in 1049, brought him by sea to Dartmouth in Devon, where he was murdered and disposed of (though his body was later recovered and buried suitably at Winchester). When the family was in exile, king Edward gave the south-western shires of Godwin's earldom to Odda, usually known as "of Deerhurst", a thegn with west-country connections who retained the title of earl and died in 1056. Harold's raid near Porlock in 1052, launched from the family's Dublin refuge, was opposed by an army from Somerset and Devon, but at considerable cost. Much later, when the sons of Harold attempted a come-back after 1066, it was to the Bristol Channel and the coasts of Devon and Cornwall that their ships came.

There is a tradition that Gytha, Godwin's widow and Harold's mother, was in Exeter at the time of the Conqueror's siege in 1068 (she later went to Flanders). She had endowed St Olave's church in the city earlier in that decade, and there is no reason why she could not have been resident in Exeter. In 1066, the Godwinson family were bigger landholders in Devon than king Edward (by 1086, William the Conqueror was pre-eminent, controlling the estates of both). The Devon connections of the Godwinson family are also reflected in the provision made earlier for queen Edith, daughter of Godwin and Gytha, by her husband Edward the Confessor. Domesday reveals that two-thirds of Exeter's £18 annual render to the king had been apportioned to the queen before 1066. In 1086 the royal sheriff, Baldwin de Meules, had £6 (had the earls of Wessex earlier had this?) while a reeve named Colwin had £12 towards the administration of Edith's estates. Perhaps these connections added fuel to Exeter's rebellion against the Conqueror in 1068, but William treated Edith well: she kept her lands (in Devon at Lifton, Kenton, North Molton and, immediately adjacent to Exeter, Wonford) until her death in 1075, living mainly at Wilton and Winchester. Her estates, however, continued to be administered separately in the same way, even though they passed into the king's hands, as Domesday Book reveals.

Royal households and councils (see Fig 4.1)

In Anglo-Saxon England, the royal life-style was itinerant: the court was wherever the king was. Only towards the end of the period, when important royal centres emerged at Winchester, in the West Saxon heartland, and at Westminster, promoted as palace and abbey outside London by Edward the Confessor, was the notion of "capital" emerging. Thus, before the late Saxon period, when coinage was circulating in quantity and making taxation more flexible, the direct render of agricultural produce, for maintenance of the royal household and others in attendance, was crucial. Collecting such renders was presumably one function of the king's reeves in the estate centres of the manors which might figure in the royal itineraries. In earlier times, Ine's law-code specified the food-rent which was due to the king from a ten-hide estate in terms of vats of honey, loaves of bread, quantities of ale (in which Welsh ale and "clear" – English? – were distinguished), cattle, sheep, geese, hens, cheeses, butter, salmon and eels. Interestingly, a related feature of early rural organisation occurs in record at the very end of the period. Domesday Book preserved occasional remnants of the system by which royal properties were held by tenants for the "farm of one night" (*firma unius noctis*), that is for providing food and other renders to support the itinerant royal household for a day and night. Although this once-extensive system had been largely commuted to money payment by the eleventh century, it was still specifically referred to in particular instances: in Devon, three royal manors in the south of the shire – Walkhampton, King's Tamerton and Sutton (later in Plymouth). Such properties had traditionally been exempted from the hidation and geld systems, so that when we find other royal manors which Domesday recorded had never paid geld (see above) we may suspect the same origin.

Given their extensive territories and itinerant life-styles, it is not surprising that documented visits of West Saxon kings to Devon are not numerous. Ine (and his predecessors) campaigned against the Dumnonians, as later did Egbert and Aethelstan, and Alfred pursued the vikings there. Asser, Alfred's biographer, tells us that the king went hunting in Cornwall. Perhaps this involved the lands dependent on the royal estate at Lifton, mentioned in his will. Edward the Confessor and his queen were present at Leofric's installation as bishop of Exeter in 1050, with a gathering of a size that was effectively a royal council. Royal itineraries are indicated by those charters in which the place of issue is stated. By this means, we can see that, whereas up to around 900 royal itineraries reached only Somerset and Dorset, royal councils (assemblies of the *witan*) were also held in Devon in the tenth century: by Edward the Elder (901 in Axminster; 904 in Bickleigh?; 924 in Exeter); by Aethelstan (928 and 935 in Exeter; 931 at Lifton); by King Edmund (c. 945 at Colyton). Edward the Elder's second law-code emerged from the *witan* of 924 in Exeter; one of Aethelstan's law-codes was issued at one of his Exeter councils; Edmund's third law-code emerged from his Colyton council. In the tenth century, the size of these gatherings (and the verbal pomposity of the associated charters which the royal writing office produced) became greater, especially under Aethelstan. In the charter which he issued at Exeter in 928 relating to land in Hampshire, Aethelstan referred to the city grandly as a royal fortress (*arx regia*). The charter's witness list reveals the size of the assembly: two Welsh vassal-kings; the two archbishops; twelve bishops; three ealdormen; and seventeen thegns. The witness list for a charter issued at the council at Lifton in 931, relating to land in Wiltshire, was even longer, including: two Welsh vassal-kings; the two archbishops; seventeen bishops (including Eadulf of Crediton); fifteen ealdormen; five abbots; and fifty-nine thegns (including some from as far afield as the Danelaw). It is highly likely that a significant element of this council's business at Lifton was to ratify the Tamar as the Cornish boundary, as later mentioned by William of Malmesbury. Perhaps other Cornish matters were also attended to, as well as ratification of the new diocese at St German's (its recently-appointed bishop, Conan, figured in the witness list mentioned above). The nature of these councils also raises the interesting question of how they were housed. In Exeter, were the minster and its (presumed) associated buildings taken over, or was there a royal hall in the city? In a rural location, such as Lifton, was the gathering encamped in tents, with the council held outdoors? Or did royal manors at hundred centres have a large hall for such events, to which the hundred courts were eventually attracted away from their originally outdoor locations as folk-moots?

Military service

Despite land-giving to the church and nobility, kings retained many estates in the shire, and there was still much royal land in Devon in 1066. Centuries of royal grants, however, had created a local landed gentry, known as *thegns*, whose descendants were the landowners revealed in Domesday Book. The *thegns* commonly comprised men whose lands lay within one shire. Some were lords of only a single estate. The *ealdormen*, in contrast, and the earls who replaced them, held land in many shires. In Ine's time, around 700, all free men owed military service direct to the king. Although levies of ordinary men remained valuable (for example in the period of viking threat), provision of trained and equipped warriors increasingly fell to this *thegnly* class, with (at least in theory) every estate rated at five hides of land producing one warrior. The assessment of land in hides was also used for levying the *heregeld* (the army tax, to pay for royal mercenaries) in the eleventh century. Its imposition had started in the 990s, in Ethelred II's reign, and became effectively a general annual tax, though it was temporarily suspended by Edward the Confessor in 1051. A commonly-applied rate was two shillings' tax on each hide (note that this was not what became known as the Danegeld, tribute paid to the invading Danes in Ethelred II's reign, known at the time as *gafol* – tribute). The hide (which makes its first clear appearance in Ine's law-code) was originally, according to Bede (whose Latin word for it was *familia*), the land needed to support a freeman's family. But it was to have a longer history as a method of assessment for other purposes, essentially military and fiscal. Not all land was hidated: royal estates were often exempt as might others be by special concession. Total hidations of individual shires, as revealed in Domesday Book, varied greatly, reflecting not only variety in shire size but also the antiquity of their creation. Devon had about 1100, far more than Cornwall, which had only about 400. In contrast, Dorset had well above 2,000 and Somerset had nearly 3,000. The low hidations of the far south west have commonly been interpreted as evidence of the region's thinner population and "frontier" character over a long period: the difficulties encountered there by new land-owners and royal servants were compensated by assessments which placed lighter burdens on the land.

In England generally, when kings granted out land its recipient held all mundane rights over it as well as the right to dispose of it: such land held by secular lords often became hereditary within their families; land held by the church was passed down institutionally. Thus, some of the ancient "folkland" – belonging, in a sense, to the whole people but in the person of the king, became "bookland" – so called because from the late seventh century its granting was commonly recorded in a *boc* or charter. This was one of the major ways, together with the writing of law-codes, in which Christianity's introduction of literacy to the Anglo-Saxons affected royal government, and charters were first adopted in relation to lands granted to the church. But, despite alienation of rights over land through grants recorded in charters, kings reserved to themselves three major obligations on rural populations, acquitted through land-holding thegns, necessary for maintenance of royal power. These were: military service, work on fortifications, and work on associated bridges. This practice is known from the eighth century onwards, when it begins to occur in royal charters issued in Mercia, and became widely adopted. These conditions applied in Devon: its thegns contributed manpower to royal building works on fortifications and bridges, to royal armies, and to local forces raised by the *ealdormen* for defence against the vikings. For example, king Edgar's grant of land at *Nymed* to the *thegn* Aelfhere in 974, contained the phrase: *nisi tantum expeditione pontis arcisve constructione* ("except only for the army, fortification and bridge construction"). We tend to think of these details as being an Anglo-Saxon development because that is the context in which they appear. But Nicholas Higham has argued that arrangements of this sort may have been amongst the powers which English rulers took over from the post-Roman British leaders whom they had displaced. Similarly, it has been argued, the "English" system of hidation and tax (see above) may be an older arrangement now expressed in new language. If this is the case, it also has a bearing on the possible antiquity of the rural estates which we first see described in English charters (see below).

In their earlier senses, a *fyrd* was probably an organised force raised as part of official defence, whereas a *here* was often encountered in more aggressive, raiding contexts. But later in the Anglo-Saxon period, the usage of these "army" terms became blurred. The raising of a royal army in late Saxon England operated at various levels. It is probable that an ancient obligation upon all free men to fight in defence of their region still survived. This may have originated in the earliest days of the Germanic kingdoms in England, surviving the evolution of *regiones* into shires, and its spirit survived in much later centuries in the form of local militias. Historians sometimes refer to such a force as the "great *fyrd*". But when, in the period of the Danish wars, for example, the *Anglo-Saxon Chronicle* tells us that "the men of [a certain] shire" fought in battle led by an ealdorman, it is difficult to know whether the great *fyrd* is indicated, because the ealdormen and shires were also the basis of the "select *fyrd*". This is how some historians, including Warren Hollister, have referred to the royal army of trained and equipped warriors, and it is because contemporary sources do not make a distinction for us that historians have created the terminology: how real such distinctions were, in actual practice, we do not know. From Domesday Book and other sources it appears that, in England outside the Danelaw, one such warrior and the finance for his maintenance was produced by each rural estate rated at five hides. Estates with higher ratings would produce more; those with less would make a contribution. Such warriors could be expected to serve both on land and in the king's warships. This system emphasised service by the land-owning class of *thegns* and recent studies have underlined the high status character of this crucial core of military life. The system also had secondary application to towns: Exeter counted as a five-hide unit for this purpose (below). Finally, royal armies eventually contained also an important component of mercenaries, whose elite core just before the Norman Conquest were known as *huscarls* and who seem to have originated in Aethelred II's reign. They were supported by royal taxation – the *heregeld* of the late tenth and eleventh centuries. This was raised in the countryside also on the basis of hidation and might also fall on towns: Exeter again counted as five hides in this respect. Whether all these military arrangements always worked efficiently in practice, we do not know. But that such arrangements were in place at all is evidence of sophisticated government, and it was this military culture which William the Conqueror faced in 1066. The defence of the *burhs* – the fortified centres which grew in number and importance in the late Saxon period – had a similarly sophisticated system of support (see below), significant in the town-based rebellions which the Conqueror overcame from 1068 to 1070 (Exeter's being the first).

It is commonly held that communication between fortifications and armies was achieved by beacons: these have been identified in some areas, including Hampshire, Wiltshire and other parts of Wessex, through their mention in charter boundaries. It is a reasonable assumption that they existed in Devon, and their employment has been suggested by Terry Slater in his study of the South Hams region. In England generally, a road suitable for military use (and presumably under royal control) was called specifically an "army road" – *herepath:* these occur in charter boundaries. For example, one ran along the north edge of Brampford Speke and Stoke Canon, and another ran between Exeter and Topsham. In time, however, the word may simply have meant a good road or highway.

The *Anglo-Saxon Chronicle* entry for 893 recorded that king Alfred divided his army so that, apart from the men defending the *burhs*, half were serving in the field and half were at home. This military reform has become part of popular perceptions of his achievements, as also has his role in founding a royal navy. In 897, the *Anglo-Saxon Chronicle* recorded his introduction of "long ships", their development a reaction to the effectiveness of those used by the Danes. Alfred's ships have been helpfully discussed by Michael Swanton in the wider context of literary and archaeological evidence. The king's vessels had 60 or more oars and, we are told, were built to his own design rather than in imitation of Danish or Frisian patterns. It is easy to overlook the practicalities of this dimension of service to kings in areas near the coast. The early eleventh-century tract, *Rectitudines Singularum Personarum*, reminds us that the *thegn* with bookland owed not only service relating to the army, fortifications and bridges, but also, where appropriate, provision of ships and coastal guard. This must have been important in Devon, with its long coastlines and many estuaries. In the will of bishop Aelfwold of Crediton (who had died by 1012) we find ecclesiastical vestments and texts, gold and silver, disposable land and various items left to named individuals (including Ordulf, founder of Tavistock abbey). We also find, left to the king, his lord, a quantity of horses, shields, spears, helmets, mail coats and a 64-oared ship – that is, a ship whose manning required 64 armed men who would both row or sail the ship and then fight when engaged – such had been the vessels introduced by king Alfred's reform. The law-code of Aethelred II issued in 1008 required that ships were to be re-equipped after Easter each year. In the same year, the *Anglo-Saxon Chronicle* recorded that the king introduced renewed measures for provision of ships, with units of 310 hides (perhaps an error for 300) of land required to provide one warship. In a letter (preserved in Sherborne's records) written between 1002 and 1014, Aethelric, bishop of Sherborne, complained to Aethelmaer, ealdorman of western Wessex, that his ability to aquit his liability (known as *shipscot*) was threatened: he had lost some of his Dorset lands (and was in danger of losing more, including Holcombe in Devon) thus leaving him with less than the 300 hides which he and all other bishops were supposed to have for this purpose. Aelfwold's possession of a warship (above) presumably reveals that the Crediton episcopal estates had been drawn into the same system. It has been suggested that bishops were included in the framework of naval provision in the tenth-century church reform period, especially in Edgar's reign, which had enhanced their status and power. It has also been suggested that the 300 hide allocation (notionally three hundredal divisions within the shires) provided a ship's crew of 60 men through application of the five-hide principle. Kings also used the *heregeld* to support a personal navy: in 1050, Edward the Confessor's own fleet comprised fourteen ships, with warriors supported in this way: in that year, he paid off nine and retained five.

Estates and charters (see Figs. 4.3, 4.4)

The *thegnly* class, which developed as a permanent pattern of land-holding evolved, came to be what would later be called a country (and county) gentry. In the society described by Domesday Book for 1066 this local gentry was still entrenched, but in the record for 1086, it had been pushed down the social ladder by land-owners from Normandy and elsewhere. This social class of *thegns* had originated in the *gesiths,* the king's companions, who served him wherever required, often in a military capacity. As conquests developed, their support often merited reward with land. In the south west, as elsewhere, we find not only the church but also secular society receiving royal land, the grants recorded in *bocs* or charters. Because they survive in great quantity in their "English" form, it is easy to assume that Anglo-Saxon kings first employed these charters, but, since the Damnonian (and other British) kings would also have had the services of literate clerics, it is possible that the use of written records in the south west had started in earlier times. When king Geraint granted land in Maker, Cornwall, to the church at Sherborne, around 705, presumably some written record of the act was made. Wendy Davies has drawn attention to a distinct style of charter (mainly Latin, sometimes vernacular) found in early medieval Wales, Ireland and Brittany, recording grants to the church in these areas.

In the legal ideas and terminology used, they reflect traditions inherited from the late Roman world and probably originated with western British bishops. The tenth-century example from Cornwall recording a grant by landowner called Maenchi is a surviving Dumnonian example of this tradition from the Celtic-speaking regions (see Chapter 2). It may tell us, indirectly, that pre-English Dumnonia had more written administration than we know.

Although the granting of land by kings involved alienation of most (but not all – see above) rights over it, a link with the royal origins of such land was maintained in the practice of *heriot*, by which payment was made to the king on the succession to bookland of the deceased holder's inheritor. In the eleventh century, in Cnut's law-code, heriots were specifically graded, according to social rank of earls, king's thegns and lesser thegns. These *heriots* were expressed in different quantities of horses, coats of mail, spears, shields, swords and gold. They applied not only to laymen, but also to holders of bookland who were clerics: thus the bequest to the king made by bishop Aelfwold of Crediton (discussed above). Recent discussion of the late Anglo-Saxon *thegnly* class, by John Gillingham and others, has emphasised how much they had in common, as lords of a developing manorial society, with what we later call the county gentry. They were leisured, living on income derived from tenants as well as from direct exploitation of their lands (see Chapter 5); they provided royal service; they appeared at the shire courts; the Old English word for the ordinary amongst their ranks (that is, excluding major king's thegns) was *cniht* – which survived to become "knight" in later English. Within this rural class there was developing a sense of "community of the shire" which becomes more evident from later medieval sources. Its allegiance to a shire court held at Exeter, as well as *thegnly* property-holding interests there (see below), must also have helped form a more defined sense of "Devonian society" by the eleventh century.

The surviving Saxon land charters for Devon, extending from the eighth century to around the Norman Conquest, number some seventy in total, of which nearly thirty have clauses describing boundaries of the lands in question. Their boundaries have been described and mapped, alongside those of Cornwall, in a most helpful way by Della Hooke. They reflect (and there were many more grants than those whose record has survived) a process by which extensive royal territories were broken down: families crucial to the fabric of an extended West Saxon kingdom became embedded in the landscape. Thus the class of *gesiths* was transformed into a new class

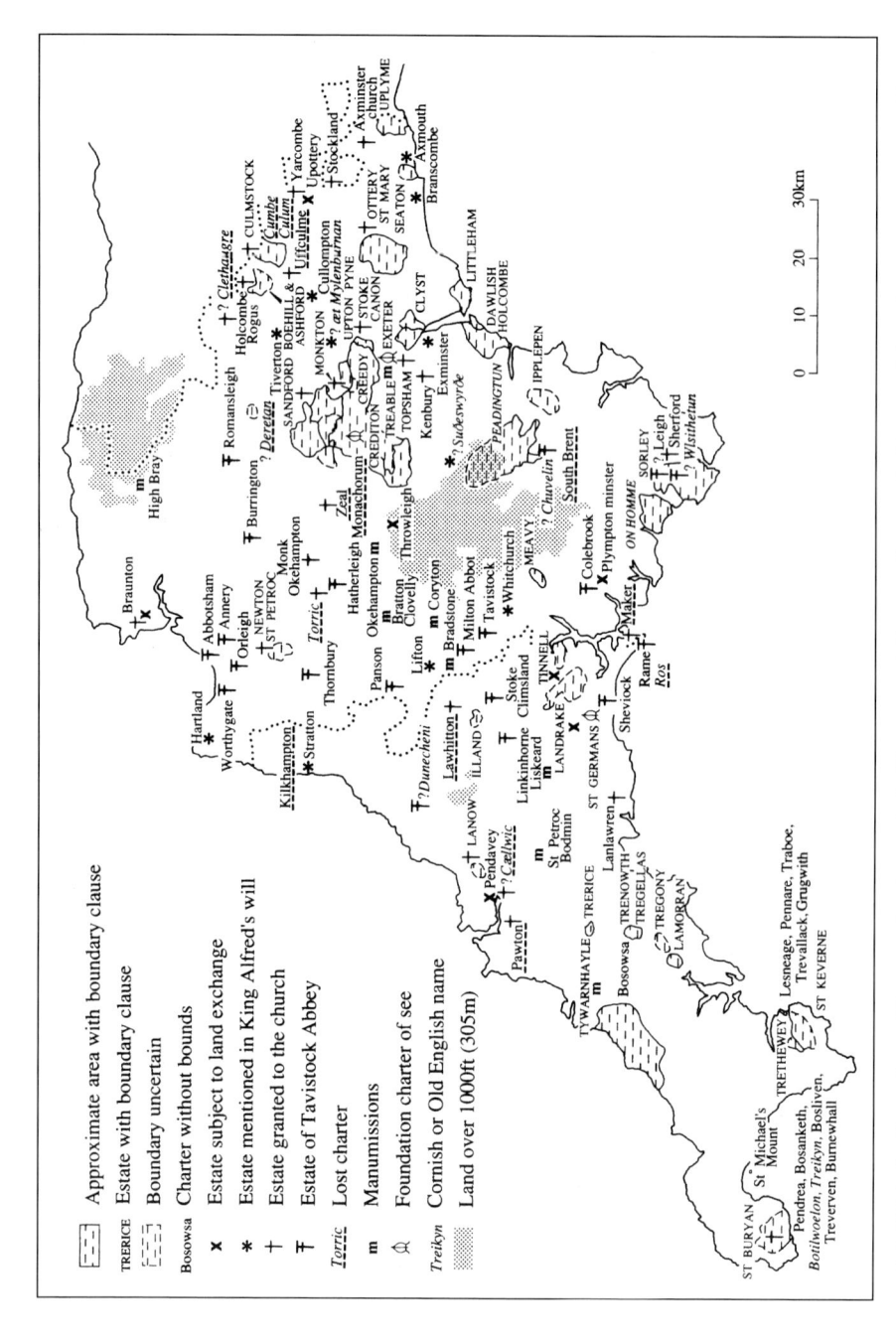

4.3: Distribution of pre-Norman land-grants in Devon and Cornwall recorded in surviving charters, as mapped by Della Hooke in Kain & Ravenhill (eds) 1999. By permission of the author, University of Exeter Press and Roger Kain.

of *thegns* (literally servants) with a significant landed base but retaining close ties with military and royal household service. It has been argued from case-studies elsewhere in Wessex, that many of the personal names within old English place-names belonged to these landlords, and originated in their endowments rather than in the earlier phases of Saxon conquest and settlement. It was perhaps in the context of these endowments that the older, British place-names in Devon disappeared from record. The names reflect a widespread fragmentation of the tenurial landscape, with which re-organisation of settlement and agriculture may have been associated (see below, and Chapter 5). Occasionally, this process of fragmentation may be reflected in place-names. The editors of the *Place-names of Devon* volumes commented that the name of Fardel, a manor in south Devon, derived from *feorthandael*, that is Old English for "a fourth part". It already had this name in the mid-eleventh century (*Ferdendel* in Domesday Book) and had presumably at some time been part of a much larger estate which became fragmented between several lords. It is tempting to conclude that the other parts of this earlier estate had been the three manors mentioned by Domesday Book (Cornwood, Dinnaton and Blatchford) which were also situated in the territory which by the thirteenth century had become the parish of Cornwood. If so, then the parish re-created, for ecclesiastical purposes, a larger territory of much earlier origin.

Well before the Norman Conquest, the management of estates by a sedentary local gentry had produced a manorial structure, parts of which had a long ancestry: Ine's law-code mentioned rents and labour services due from tenants. Tenth-century royal law-codes insisted that all men had lords. Rural society included not only free men: there were also unfree rural classes (see Chapter 5). Although we have no examples known in Devon, excavations elsewhere in England have identified large timber halls and other structures, sometimes within enclosures, which lay at the centre of estates, rather like the manor houses and castles of later centuries. An early eleventh-century compilation on social status, sometimes called *People's Ranks and Laws*, reveals possession of a "*burh*-gate" (and a five-hide estate) amongst the attributes of thegnhood: this implies enclosed, even defended homes. In this period began also the foundation of private churches which were later the churches of ecclesiastical parishes (see Chapter 3). Thus the medieval landscape and its landed gentry was emerging. Though "Saxon" in culture and name, however, this class of local landlords in the south west was not necessarily purely Germanic in the strict sense of ethnicity: native British society, though eventually invisible, presumably contributed to its evolution through intermarriage and through its gradual adoption of "English" status from the late seventh century onwards.

The charters which provide our evidence for these developments, in Devon as elsewhere, survive in manuscripts of various dates (some long after the grants to which they refer) and, while some are authentic records, others may contain spurious claims. Some were "forged" to demonstrate legitimate title to land for which no earlier written record actually existed. Others are lost and only known through reference to them in other, later sources. Anglo-Saxon charters are called by historians "evidentiary": that is, they recorded an act witnessed in ceremony and independently valid. The charters themselves seem often to have been drawn up by, or on behalf of, the beneficiaries, even though worded as though drawn up by royal clerks. The charter was simply a record of the event, rather than a necessary part of the event itself. (The documents which we call Anglo-Saxon wills have the same character, being evidence of an independently valid and witnessed arrangement for gifts to be made on death). But as subsequent proof that a grant had taken place, a charter was very valuable, especially to the ecclesiastical institutions whose emergence had added a new dimension to traditions of land tenure. Recipients of bookland, whose grant was recorded in such charters, may well have paid the king – a sort of compensation for the king's loss of rights over former folkland. Charters evolved in style and length during this period, eventually settling on the common form of a Latin "proem" explaining the grant itself, followed by a boundary clause, describing the land in question, written in Old English. The lists of witnesses vary in length, the longer ones revealing grants made in full royal councils, and are an important source for the names and life-spans of ecclesiastical and secular notables. But because those present with the king on any one occasion often came from several shires, it can be difficult to know which thegns came from the shire where the grant was made or from the shire where the land granted was situated: it is clear from those charters which name the place of issue that these were not necessarily the same.

The surviving Devon charters record grants by kings to various sorts of recipient, of which the following examples may be quoted. First, land might be granted for the establishment and endowment of churches. In 739, Aethelheard granted land at Crediton to the bishop of Sherborne for foundation of a new minster (see Chapter 3 and Appendix 2). Aethelred II supported the land grants in Devon and Cornwall made by his uncle, the local nobleman Ordulf, as founder of Tavistock abbey, in 981; Cnut granted Zeal (Monachorum) to Buckfast Abbey after 1018. Around 1060, St.

4.4: Charter recording a grant of land at Stoke Canon (text of grant in Latin; boundary of estate in Old English). Photograph: Exeter Cathedral Archives, D. & C. 2525, by permission of the Dean and Chapter. There are several charters relating to land with this boundary, mapped in 6.2 (a). The one illustrated here, generally regarded as an authentic document (perhaps produced at Crediton) was granted by king Cnut to Hunuwine, *minister* (thegn). Another was created later, in the time of bishop Leofric, as evidence of a much earlier grant by king Aethelstan to the minster church at Exeter, for which written testimony had perhaps been lost. Leofric's effort to recover a church estate lost by the early eleventh century was clearly successful: when it appeared in Domesday Book, Stoke was an episcopal manor.

Olave's in Exeter received Kenbury from Edward the Confessor, as well as Sherford from Gytha, earl Godwin's widow: the church may not have been very old, since king Olaf of Norway, to whom it was dedicated, died only in 1030. Second, grants by various kings added to the endowments of existing West Saxon churches further east. Glastonbury received lands in Devon, for example, in the Torridge valley in 729, at Culmstock in 760, and at Braunton around 850. Sherborne received land at Tawstock around 860, in addition to that at Crediton (above). Sometimes, kings arranged exchanges of lands which were also recorded in charters: Edgar gave land in Somerset to Glastonbury and took Braunton back; Edward the Elder gave lands in

Somerset to bishop Asser in exchange for Plympton. Third, the minster at Exeter had a group of charters purporting to record grants, including Stoke Canon, Topsham, Culmstock and Monkton, made by Athelstan. But these were actually "forged" in the time of bishop Leofric, to replace charters lost earlier, probably in the sack of Exeter by the Danes in 1003. Fourth, senior clerics might receive lands in their own right, as did bishop Aelfwold of Crediton who was granted land in Sandford by Aethelred II: the bishop bequeathed it, in his will, to the minster church at Crediton. Fifth, and reflecting the overall national trend, the grants to secular recipients occur later in the period rather than earlier. In 956, Eadwig granted land at Ipplepen, Dainton and Abbotskerswell to Aethelhild, described as a noble lady. Athelstan (938) and Edmund (944) granted lands at Uplyme and Upton Pyne/Brampford Speke respectively, to Aethelstan, described as an earl (*comes*). The wider class of rural landowners, each referred to in the charters as a *thegn* (or in Latin, *minister*), were well represented in tenth- and eleventh-century royal grants, including: Eadwig to Eadheah in 958 (in Sampford Peverell); Edgar to Aethelnoth in 961 (in Clyst St Mary and St George); Edgar to Wulfhelm in 963 (in Ottery St Mary); Edgar to Aelfhere in 974 (in Down St Mary); Edward to Aelfsige in 976 (in Cheriton Bishop); Aethelred II to Eadsige in 1005 (in Seaton); Cnut to Aethelric in 1031 (in Meavy); Cnut to Hunuwine in 1033 (in Stoke Canon); Edward the Confessor to Ordgar in 1042 (in Littleham). Broadly speaking, these grants reveal a progression from the creation of large (and commonly church) estates in the eighth and ninth centuries to that of more numerous and smaller (and commonly secular) ones in the tenth and eleventh. Many of the earlier grants related to estates rated at ten or more hides, but many of the later ones were rated at only one or two. Another aspect of this process of fragmentation was the foundation of more local churches and the breakdown of the earlier minster territories (see Chapter 3).

Sheriffs, laws and courts

Crucial to government of the society in which this pattern of land-holding developed was the *scir gerefa* (shire-reeve, sheriff). Occupants of this office managed royal business in the shires in the tenth and eleventh centuries when the ealdormen had been reduced in number. They were not lineal descendants of the ealdormanic class, but were subordinate to them, drawn from the ranks of royal reeves in general and sometimes from the lower *thegnly* class. Unlike earldormen, they were not generally witnesses to formal royal charters, at least not as specified by their office (though they could be within the groups of thegns who attested). In some royal writs, the sheriff was identified by office. But in others (including the Devon example quoted in our *Prologue*) the sheriff is identifiable simply by his position in the list of those at the shire court to whom the writ was addressed. The use of writs (literally, in Old English, something written) as an instrument of royal government in the eleventh century has been helpfully discussed by Florence Harmer and, more recently, by Richard Sharpe. A writ's authority related to the reign of a particular king, whereas a formal charter's authority was in perpetuity. The writ was probably acquired by the beneficiary, taken to the shire court where its reading gave it public validity, then returned to the beneficiary.

In origin, however, the office of sheriff went back further than this late period when shires had been amalgamated into earldoms. The first landing of vikings in Wessex, in Dorset in the 790s, had resulted in the murder of the king's *gerefa* from Dorchester. Alfred's laws mentioned a *gerefa* who managed royal properties, and administering royal estates continued to be crucial to the duties of sheriffs. Originally, the *shiremote* was supervised by the ealdorman, and the *folkmote* (probably synonymous with the hundred courts) by a *gerefa*. In the early Norman period, sheriffs in England were to be drawn from a higher social class than they had been in the late Anglo-Saxon period. Peter Clarke's analysis of the land-holding classes at the time of the Norman conquest illustrates this point well in the case of Devon. The sheriff in 1066, Wada, had held lands in Devon and Somerset worth about twenty pounds: a man of substance but not amongst the richest of the local thegns. Two other thegns, Osfrith and Siweard, whose properties were amongst those held by the new Norman sheriff, had held lands worth about forty pounds in Devon and Cornwall. This Norman sheriff, at the time of Domesday Book in 1086, was Baldwin, a kinsman of William the Conqueror; he was one of the south-west's richest men, holding numerous estates all over Devon. It is not surprising that in the Norman period the Latin term used for the sheriff was *vicecomes*: the man who acted in place of an earl.

Where shires were named from places of presumed early importance, such as Somerton (for Somerset) and Dorchester (for Dorset), we may suppose that in these places an ealdorman had convened the *shiremote*. In Devon, whose name was not derived from a specific place, the assembly's early location is more difficult to guess: it may have been at Exeter, or in some rural royal estate centre, perhaps in neighbouring Wonford. Indeed, although the existence of some West Saxon shires can be deduced in the eighth century, we do not know when their boundaries emerged and their names first occur mainly in the ninth century (see above and Chapter 2). The influence of earlier *regiones* may have lasted longer than we know for certain, and it was perhaps only in Alfred's reign that the later, more familiar, framework clearly emerged. His viking wars and the rise of *burghal* towns also brought a shift in emphasis because more *burhs* tended to emerge as shire centres: only from this point onwards does Exeter develop a clear importance beyond its existing possession of a minster church. In Aethelstan's laws a town-reeve was the king's representative in the *burhs*. In Edgar's laws a clear statement emerged about the twice-yearly meetings of the shire court alongside the *burh* court (three each year) and the hundred court (monthly). When the vikings defeated an English force at Pinhoe, near Exeter, in 1001, the sheriffs apparently carried out a military role more normally associated with the ealdormen. By comparing the different versions of the *Anglo-Saxon Chronicle* in which the event is related, we see that the English army was raised in Somerset and Devon and led by two royal reeves named Kola and Eadsige: presumably the sheriffs of the two shires. These men, we are told, led "what army they could gather", perhaps explaining why they, rather than the ealdorman of western Wessex, were in charge.

When king Cnut removed the ealdormen, the local role of sheriffs was enhanced, though their power was subject to the earls of the new earldoms which he created. In his shire, the sheriff handled a crucial blend of judicial, taxation and military business. Late Anglo-Saxon sheriffs' records, and the evidence of shire and hundred courts, must have been crucial to William the Conqueror's Domesday inquest, especially information held on hidation and geld liability for each manor. In the period leading up to the Norman Conquest (and beyond) sheriffs "farmed" their shires: they rendered fixed sums to the king, at Easter and Michaelmas, thus making profit as the "farm" was less than the sum they actually exacted. Domesday Book reveals another level of royal administration in the shires, through the class of people described as "the king's thegns". These provided local royal service in return for tenure of land. In Devon, Domesday lists about twenty whose fortunes had survived the Norman conquest and who were still in occupation of land in 1086: Aelfric, Aldred, Algar, Alnoth, Alsgot, Alric, Alward, Alwin, Andret, Ansgot, Colwin, Dunna, Edric, Edwin, Godric, Godwin, Leofric, Odo, Saewulf and Ulf. Three women also figured in this class: Alveva, Alfhilla and Godgifu (Brictric's widow). In 1066, the lands held by these people had either been held by themselves or by predecessors who had also been English. By 1086, they had been joined by a small group of Norman "serjeants" (that is, *servientes*, royal servants) also holding lands in Devon.

The royal laws administered in the courts had their roots in the pagan Saxon past, and perhaps in some adopted British practices. The literacy which came with Christianity meant they could now be written down, in English. Indeed, as with the emergence of written charters recording land grants, writing down of laws was probably stimulated in the first instance by the protection of church interests. Bede informs us that Aethelberht, king of Kent, who welcomed the Augustinian mission, had his laws written down in English. Many kings, between the seventh and eleventh centuries, had their law-codes committed to record and these became a symbol of royal authority. But it is not the royal records themselves which have survived. We are dependent for our knowledge on copies, made in late Anglo-Saxon and Norman monasteries, of the versions originally circulated to the shires for the use of ealdormen and eventually of sheriffs. Survival was also helped by the interest shown in pre-Norman law in twelfth-century England. The laws of Offa of Mercia do not survive, but the code of Alfred of Wessex made use of them, as also those of Aethlberht of Kent (which do survive independently). With this incorporation of material from different kingdoms, as well as his attachment to his own code of the laws of Ine of Wessex, it has been suggested by some that Alfred attempted to create a notion of "English" law, where laws had previously been kingdom-specific. But others have emphasised that the laws were also part of his wider literary output and that, in the preface to his own code, he called himself only king of the West Saxons. His repetition of Ine's laws has generally been regarded as accurate, though Patrick Wormald has argued that Ine's laws were actually an accumulation rather than a single code. Alfred's employment of them suggests that recognition of those of British descent, enjoying lower status within English society was still relevant (above, Chapter 2). We have no knowledge of Dumnonian law itself, though it presumably survived in independent or semi-independent Cornwall. The heirarchy of British social ranks preserved in Ine's law-code could, however, have been derived from Dumnonian practices, thus reflecting earlier conditions in Devon.

It is important to recognise that Anglo-Saxon law-codes, elements of which are quoted in various parts of this book, were not "legislation" in the modern sense. Much actual law, on important matters such as inheritance, was customary law and not fully written down. The codes did not create law, or even possibly dominate law in practice, but rather stated, clarified or modified existing practice, often, it has been suggested, to re-inforce laws which were not being fully observed or to make recent judgements in individual cases a precedent for future ones. Justice based on laws could be meted out in the king's own court to those of high status, and, as Asser's *Life* of Alfred reminds us, in cases where the judgements of ealdormen or reeves had been disputed. Asser also informs us that Alfred threatened to remove from office ealdormen and reeves who gave bad judgements based on ignorance: this was to encourage literacy amongst the administrative classes in the shires (as he also did within his court circles). It has been suggested Alfred was trying to introduce a more written basis for royal government in general, a situation which developed more fully in the tenth and eleventh centuries.

For most people, justice was encountered in the local courts – in folk-moots, in hundreds, in *burhs* and in shires. Folk-moots were originally open air occasions, and hundred courts long remained so, especially when still associated with meeting places with topographical names. But they may eventually have been attracted to a building in the royal hundred-manor. Though *burh* and shire courts may initially have been outdoors, by the end of the period they too were taking place indoors within the shire town: this tendency was consolidated in the Norman period when the royal castles in shire towns became the location of shire courts. Since, in the late Saxon period, shire courts were presided over by earls and bishops, their own urban properties are possible court locations. This duality of supervision is reflected in the mix of secular and ecclesiastical business with which the courts (and the royal law-codes) dealt. In criminal procedure, the accused had to appear, or suffer outlawry. Weight of accusation or defence rested on the status of oath-givers, rather than on presentation of evidence in the modern sense. Levels of compensation due also depended upon varying status, through the *wergild* attached to each social rank. Alfred's law-code reveals that prisons were provided on royal estates. A few crimes were punishable by death. Hanging sites and criminal burials seem to have been near the boundaries of hundreds, away from consecrated ground. This practice, discussed by Andrew Reynolds, must have emphasised the effectiveness of the law to those entering hundredal jurisdictions: such places emerge in some charter boundary descriptions and from recent burial-site excavations in various parts of England. Most offences, however, were punishable by fine, paid to the king. The idea of justice as a source of royal income was thus established at an early date. An accused could, in an attempt to prove innocence, choose to undergo the "ordeal" – by water (hot or cold) or by (hot) iron.

The shire court at Exeter is revealed in surviving documentation among the Sherborne records, published by Mary Ann O'Donovan, about a dispute over Holcombe (Rogus) in Devon, on-going since the reign of Aethelred II, between the church at Sherborne and the king. Around 1012, Sherborne agreed to lease Holcombe to the Aetheling Edmund, for his life. Edmund (as king Edmund Ironside) died in 1016. But instead of reverting to Sherborne, Holcombe was taken by king Cnut. Agreement was eventually reached in the shire court in 1045 or 1046. Bishop Aelfwold recognised the leasehold, for one further life, of a family apparently established there by king Cnut (family members had Scandinavian names – Care, Toki and Ulf). By 1066, Holcombe's tenants were Ulf and Siward, but Sherborne lost the manor completely thereafter: it was granted to Baldwin of Okehampton, and by him to his tenant Rogo, from whose family the name Holcombe Rogus was created. The court of 1045/6 was held before earl Godwin of Wessex, and its full composition is revealed by the witness list to the recorded agreement, copies of which were kept at Sherborne and Crediton. Whether these were kept there in addition to being kept at Exeter – not named as it was assumed – or instead of Exeter, is not wholly clear; if the latter, then an interesting question arises, since we might expect the shire town by this date to have a record depository for such items. The sheriff was not identified by office but presumably occurred within the list of thegns. The court was attended, in addition to earl Godwin, by Aelfwold (bishop of Sherborne), Lyfing (bishop of Crediton and St. German's), Aelfwine (abbot of Buckfast), Sihtric (abbot of Tavistock), Odda (of Deerhurst?) and Ordgar (both earls); about fifteen named thegns; and Godman, a priest. Godman also witnessed Edward the Confessor's "foundation charter" of Exeter cathedral in 1050 and was probably a priest in royal service: in 1066 he held land in mid-Devon, at Brampford Speke and Clannaborough, and so may also have had a connection with the minster/cathedral at Crediton (see also Chapters 3 and 5).

Exeter's re-emergence (Figs. 4.5, 4.6, 4.7, 4.8)

Royal administration thus eventually settled in the shire's most prominent place, Exeter. This had been the administrative centre of the Dumnonian tribal area, itself part of the western British province of *Britannia Prima* in the late Roman period. Following Alfred's re-furbishment of Exeter in

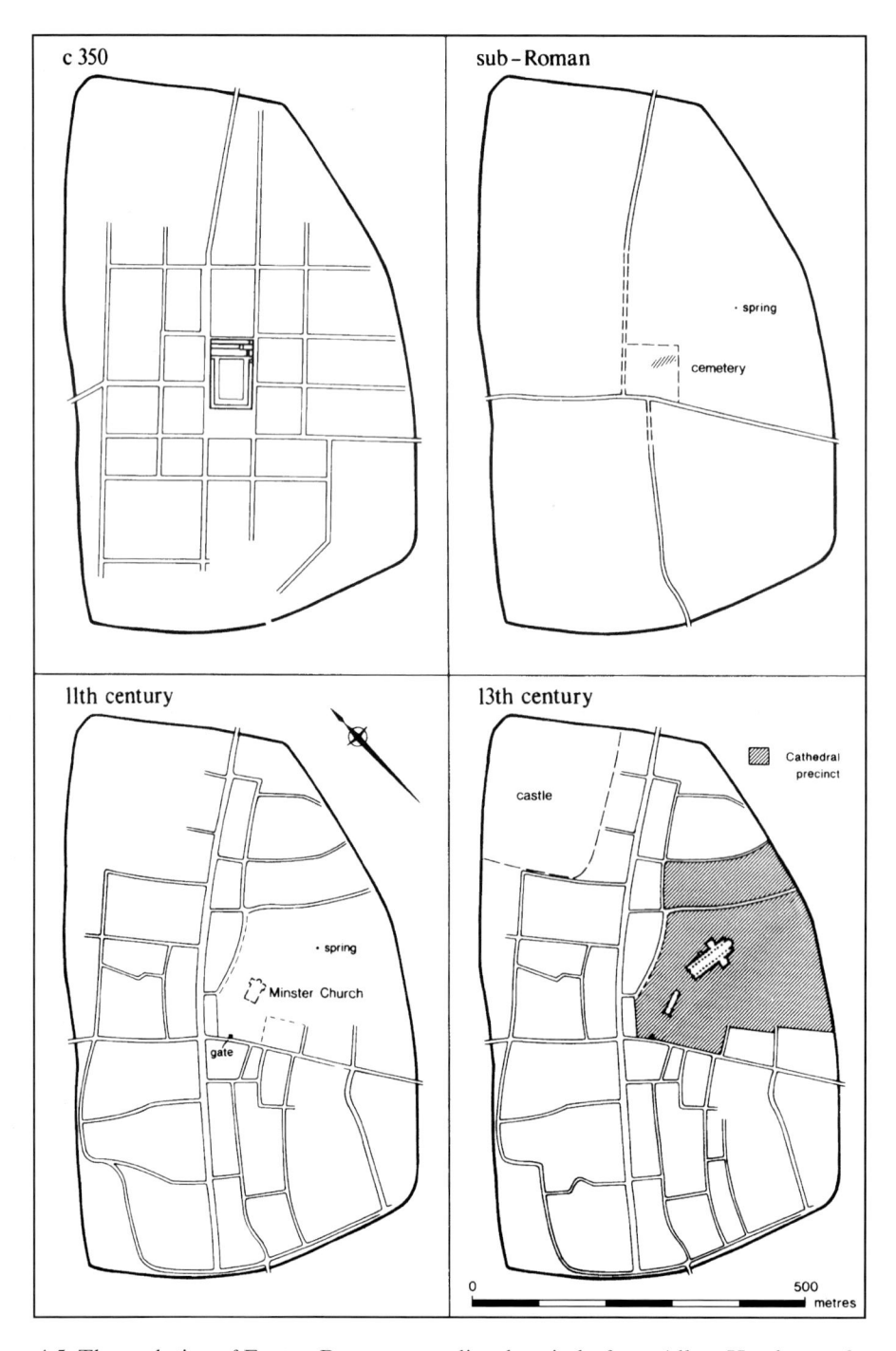

4.5: The evolution of Exeter, Roman to medieval periods, from Allan, Henderson & Higham in Haslam (ed) 1984. By permission of Jeremy Haslam.

the late ninth century, the city had become Devon's "shire town", which it has remained to this day. Its name derived ultimately from the British name (*Isca*) of the river at whose crossing-place it stood, and thence from its Roman title: *Isca Dumnoniorum*. The West Saxons then compounded the river-name with Old English *ceaster* (from Latin *castrum*) to produce *Escanceaster*, as seen in the Anglo-Saxon Chronicle and *Execestre* as recorded in Domesday Book. It was the likely centre of operations for the south-western circuit of Domesday commissioners and *Exon* Domesday may have been compiled there (it was kept at the Cathedral, where it still remains). Exeter's position by 1066 was remarkable in comparison with its circumstances five hundred years earlier, when, archaeological evidence suggests, occupation had been minimal. The Anglo-Norman chroniclers, Orderic Vitalis and William of Malmesbury, noted the city's prosperity and its foreign merchants. In later times, Exeter was to have jurisdiction over all the trading settlements of the Exe estuary. Domesday Book called Exeter a city (*civitas*) and recorded that it had paid the geld only when it was paid by London, Winchester and York. Study of the late Saxon coinage suggests that production of silver pennies at Exeter's mint, established by King Alfred, had at times approached that of Winchester. Up to 1066, the four highest mint outputs were, in descending order: London; York; Lincoln; Winchester. The fifth position was held, at various times, by Exeter, Chester, Norwich and Thetford. It is these points of comparison concerning geld and coinage which reveal Exeter's high national status, rather than its description as a *civitas* in 1086: Domesday Book's use of *civitas, burgus* and *villa* as terms for towns and cities in England was actually quite flexible.

No evidence has come to light to suggest a mid-Saxon trading settlement outside Exeter's walls (as found in relation to Roman London and York) or an estuarine trading emporium some way off (as found in Wessex at Hamwic, twenty miles from Winchester). It remains a strong probability, however, that Topsham's later medieval history as a port had much earlier origins. Occupation in the Roman period is attested by excavated evidence, both military and civilian. Andrew Jackson has argued convincingly that Topsham's documented trading activity of the twelfth and later centuries was not a recent departure, even though Domesday Book described it as a rural estate. In the tenth century Topsham had been a property of Exeter's minster, a gift attributed to king Aethelstan in a charter later written in bishop Leofric's time. But it was acquired by the Godwinson family: Harold held it in 1066. Moreover, the royal estate of Wonford, whose position east and south of Exeter joined the city up, so to speak with Topsham, had been

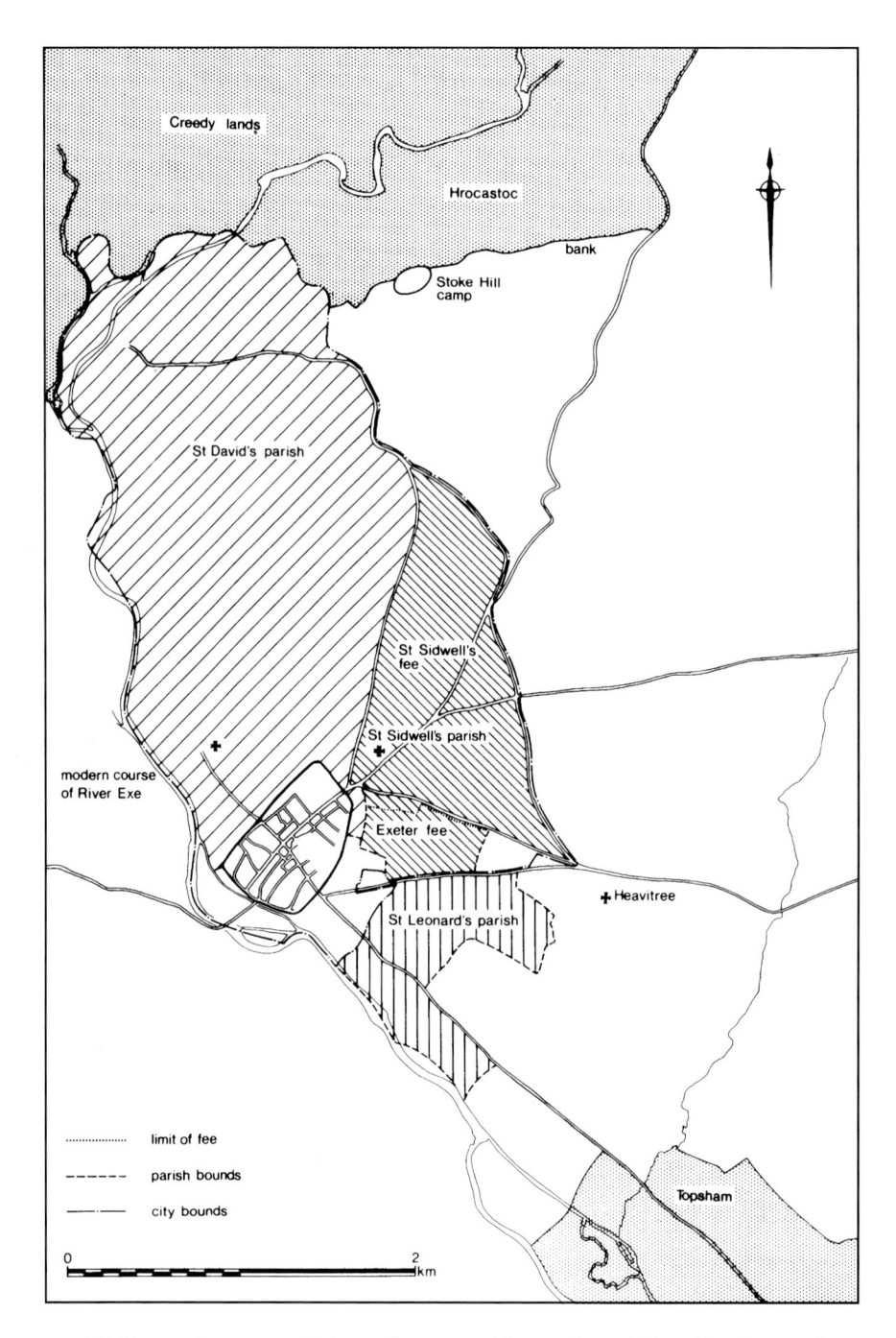

4.6: The environment of eleventh-century Exeter, from Allan, Henderson & Higham in Haslam (ed) 1984. By permission of Jeremy Haslam.

held before 1066 by queen Edith, Harold Godwinson's sister. It would appear that the importance of the estuary, and not just Exeter itself, had been recognised by this powerful family.

Exeter's street pattern developed on mainly different lines from the underlying Roman plan, reflecting a period of post-Roman disuse. Only the upper part of High Street coincided with the Roman line, though the Roman gate sites were also preserved. As well as the four main streets, there were some long lanes running out to the defences, as well as some development of back lanes. Parts of the present-day pattern have their origin in the late Saxon period, and not only in the four main streets: Martin's Lane and the way through Cathedral Close (to the "New Cut" in the city wall) follow a primary route to the defences of which other examples have disappeared. Unlike some other late Saxon towns in Wessex, however, Exeter does not seem to have had a continuous intra-mural street running behind its defences: but excavation has revealed a discontinuous and simpler pathway for this purpose in several places. The Roman gates were presumably repaired and replaced over time, and the walls were well kept up. Later developments have generally masked whatever was done at this time, but three areas have been illuminated by modern analysis.

First, studies by Christopher Henderson of the excavated and other evidence for the South Gate (brought to publication by Frances Griffith and several former colleagues) suggest various stages in the rebuilding of the Roman structure between the ninth and eleventh centuries. Second, the surviving late Saxon fabric in the city wall in Northernhay, first observed by Ian Burrow and later analysed intensively by Stuart Blaylock and Richard Parker, is almost unique in English towns in an important respect (some masonry in the city wall of Canterbury provides the closest parallel). Its details include in-filled crenellations, which now seem too low to have been defences: but this illusion arises from the raising of the ground level and the addition of more masonry to the wall-top when the adjacent castle was built by the Normans. William of Malmesbury wrote that Aethelstan had improved the defences: "he fortified [the city] with towers and surrounded it with a wall of squared stone". But we cannot determine whether these surviving and exceptional details at Exeter were the work of Alfred, Edward the Elder, Aethelstan or Aethelred II, in all of whose reigns a suitable military context could be suggested. Exeter's walls withstood the Danes in 1001, though two years later the city fell (reputedly through treachery from within). But when William the Conqueror besieged Exeter in 1068, he eventually negotiated its surrender on terms favourable to its

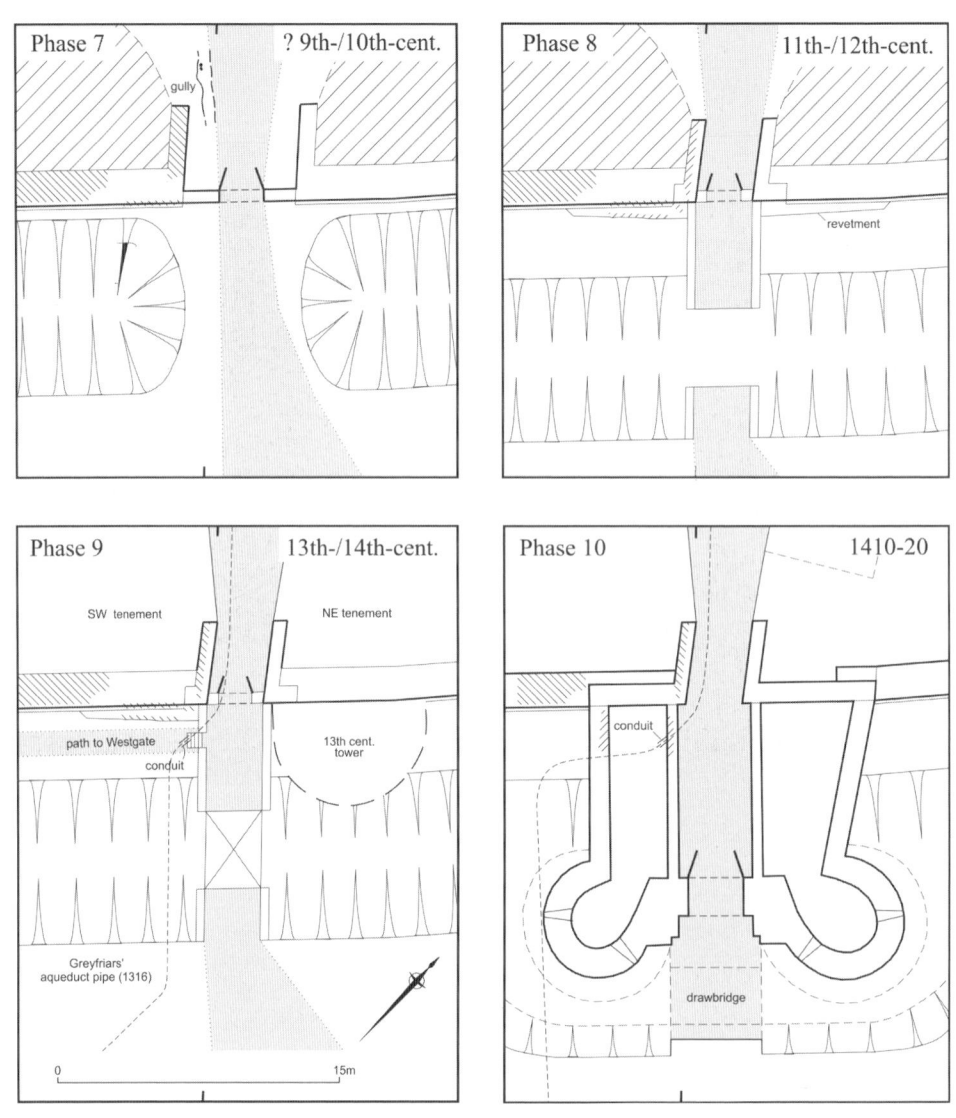

4.7: The evolution of Exeter's south gate, Anglo-Saxon to medieval, from Henderson 2001. By permission of Exeter Archaeology and Devon Archaeological Society.

citizens because he could not force entry: the walls, gates and their system of manning were clearly still very effective. Third, the medieval stone bridge over the Exe is not documented until around 1200, and it is not clear whether it replaced a ford or a series of earlier timber structures evolving since the ninth century. The latter seems most likely, since without a bridge Exeter's defensive role as a *burh* in relation to the river would not have

4.8: Late Saxon crenellations in Exeter's city wall (Northernhay gardens). These were in-filled when the wall was raised at the building of the Norman castle. Photograph: Exeter Archaeology.

been fully effective (and labour on bridges associated with fortified places was one of the obligations on land which kings carefully preserved). Other important estuaries certainly had bridges by the late Saxon period: that at Kingsbridge was mentioned in a charter (see below); that at Teignbridge is revealed by the place-name (see above). It was suggested by Christopher Henderson that since the alignment of Cowick St, west of the Exe, does not exactly match that of the thirteenth-century stone bridge, the Cowick St approach may reveal the location of earlier fords and/or bridges of Roman and post-Roman date, immediately downstream of the later bridge.

By 1066, Exeter had some private churches, built in stone, in addition to the old minster which had become the cathedral in 1050 (see Chapter 3 for discussion of urban churches). As well as listing nearly three hundred occupied royal house tenements, Domesday Book refers to almost a hundred and fifty town houses belonging to ecclesiastical and secular lords. Other houses had been wasted since the arrival of the Normans, perhaps in the building of Rougemont castle (though Domesday Book does not specifically reveal this), and nearly fifty such tenements were held by the king in addition to those in occupation. Domesday Book reveals that the customary annual payment to the king, for each house site (whether occupied by a house belonging to the king or to another lord) was a sum of eight pence: what we might now call a ground-rent. Modern estimates of the city's population at this time vary from a conservative 2,000 to a more generous 4,000, depending on whether the tenements listed accounted for the whole or whether there was a lower stratum of houses and occupants beneath a certain threshold of financial value. Exeter was certainly in the top rank of English towns in the eleventh century as well as Devon's political, economic and cultural centre. However, although excavations have produced fascinating artefactual and environmental evidence from the rubbish pits which Exeter's citizens created, as well as fragments of eleventh-century century structural timbers, no plan or part-plan of a late Saxon urban house has been recovered. This evidence has been masked by the continuous development of the house-plots over many subsequent centuries.

The Burhs of King Alfred and his successors (Fig. 4.9)

The roots of this urban revival at Exeter lay in Alfred's resistance to the vikings in the late ninth century and in the measures he took to provide defensible strongholds. Each was referred to in contemporary sources as a *burh*. The Old English word *burh* had a basic meaning of something "enclosed": it was used for a wide variety of settlement forms, including enclosures of farmsteads, of royal or noble residences, of temporary military works, of major fortifications and of urban defences. Exeter, as the region's only Roman city, with remnants of defences and a functioning monastery, was the obvious choice for Alfred's main investment. He re-furbished the city between 876, when it was occupied by a Danish force, and 893, when it successfully resisted a further attack (and when it was referred to by the *Anglo-Saxon Chronicle* as a *burh*). We also know, from the list called by historians the Burghal Hidage (see below), that Alfred had also created new centres at Lydford (in the west), at Barnstaple/Pilton (in the north) and at Halwell (in the south). Controversy still exists as to whether his policy was primarily military or whether he anticipated urban growth from the start. About thirty *burhs* were established in and around Wessex, some of which failed: in Devon, for example, Halwell, which presumably occupied one of the earthwork enclosures surviving in that parish, was replaced by Totnes in the tenth century: this site, at a crossing-point of the Dart, had much more potential for urban growth.

Whether economic growth may have led to Exeter's revival without the stimulus of its Alfredian repair as a *burh* is a fascinating but unanswerable question. A strong argument has been made by John Maddicott that Alfred's motive in developing Exeter was not only defensive: it reflected his ambition to extend royal control of tin extraction in the region and to maximise his important south-western resources when assailed by vikings from the north and east. The suggestion of such particular royal patronage from Alfred conforms with Aethelstan's later interest in Exeter and may explain the city's pre-eminent position in the eleventh century. The mid-twelfth-century historian Henry, archdeacon of Huntingdon, listed the qualities for which some English cities were famous: Exeter was notable for its metals. The Exeter street which by the thirteenth century was called *Smythenestrete* – street of the smiths – could well have been the location of a zoned occupation in earlier centuries. Located behind Fore Street, in the less-densely-occupied west quarter, this would have been a good location for workshops. Exeter's probable early role in the administration of the tin industry was shared with Lydford, situated immediately adjacent to the mineral-rich environment of Dartmoor as well as close to Cornwall (which had no equivalent urban centre of its own). Although specific documentation on Lydford as an economic centre, for the moorland resources of tin and hunting, is Norman and later, it is hard to escape the conclusion that this was part of its original function, alongside its defensive role, in the late Saxon period. The notable output of coins from the Exeter and Lydford mints in the late tenth and early eleventh centuries (see below) may also reflect their importance in this context. From the later twelfth century, however, Exeter's involvement with tin was lost, and the role left to Lydford (itself eventually eclipsed by Cornwall's tin industry).

Domesday Book reveals that an overall separation of urban and rural economy had yet to take place, and that "urban agriculture" (though apparently a paradox) was a feature of life in all the *burhs*. At Exeter, studied by John Allan and others, the burgesses had land for twelve plough-teams outside the city, the implication being that it was worked corporately on behalf of the city. The bishop also had two and half acres, lying with the city's lands (presumably meaning two and a half acres within each parcel of land) said to "belong to the church". This land has normally been

4.9: The four *burhs* of late Saxon Devon, viewed from the air (a) Exeter (b) Lydford; *Opposite*: (c) Barnstaple (d) Totnes. Despite subsequent developments, the main outlines of the defended areas and their street plans are still evident. Photographs: Frances Griffith (in order: 22/3/87; 26/6/84; 18/8/84; 10/7/90), copyright Devon County Council.

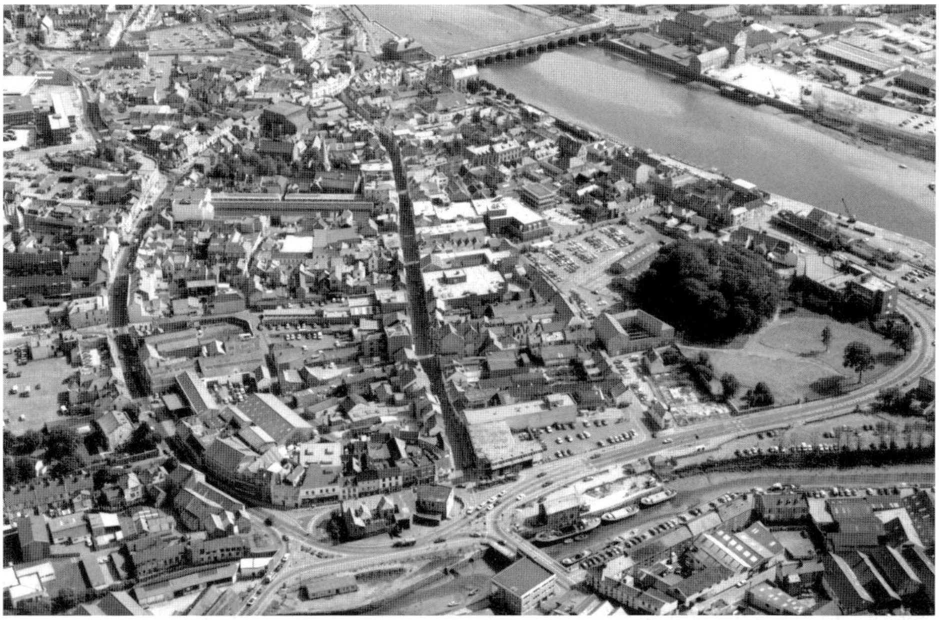

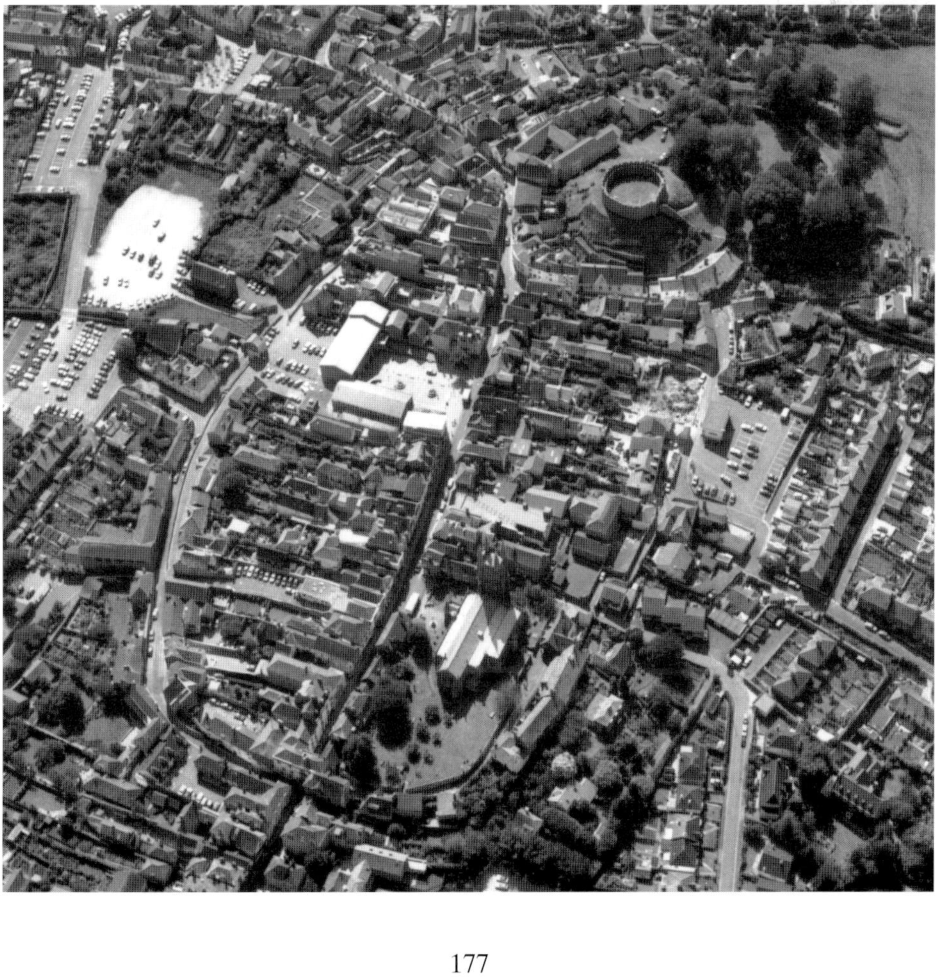

identified with St Sidwell's parish, documented as an episcopal manor by the thirteenth century. The city's lands were almost certainly in the manor of Duryard, largely equivalent to St David's parish, documented as the city's possession also by the thirteenth century. The occupants of Devon's other towns also maintained interests beyond their walls in 1066. Domesday Book reveals that at Lydford the burgesses had two plough-lands outside the borough, and the majority (41 out of 69) of its total burgess population lived outside the borough (perhaps occupying its Dartmoor hinterland as miners and foresters?). At Barnstaple, 40 burgesses lived within the borough and 9 outside it. At Totnes, 95 burgesses lived within the borough and 15 worked land outside it: perhaps the build-up of the area between the *burh* and the (presumed) bridge across the river Dart may have been in progress. Only Exeter's population (see above) was of significant size at this time: the Domesday estimations for Totnes, Barnstaple and Lydford number only a few hundreds each.

While the *burhs* still had agricultural interests, in other respects – such as their defences, mints and markets – they had very distinctive characters. This is easy to appreciate with respect to Exeter, the shire town with a long and prosperous future, but it should not be under-estimated for the three smaller places at this date, even though their futures as towns were less notable (and, in the case of Lydford, specialised and relatively short-lived). In addition to distinctive military service (below) it seems that powerful groups of influential Devon townsfolk had achieved a status which was unusual, as James Tait noted long ago, for small *burhs* at this time. The *burhwitan* of Exeter, Lydford, Barnstaple and Totnes were referred to in 1018, in a letter written by bishop Eadnoth about a land transaction near Newton St Cyres. These people presumably convened in their own *burh* courts, whereas the institution of the *burhgemot*, mentioned in Edgar's laws (see above), is generally thought to have existed only in the larger towns (the smaller ones being attached to rural hundred courts). That Eadnoth informed not just the city of Exeter, but also the three smaller urban centres, must also reflect the significance of their leaders within the society of the shire. By this date, the *burhs* of Alfred and Edward the Elder had clearly become the boroughs later described in Domesday Book. By the later twelfth century, the *burhwitan* of Exeter had become a group of influential citizens, with a reeve (*praepositus*), who assembled in their guildhall to transact legal and other business.

The relations of the late Saxon *burhs* with their rural hinterlands were interesting not just in terms of engagement in agriculture (above) but also in terms of what must have been a gradual process of disengagement from the administration of whatever royal estate they originally formed part. In the Burghal Hidage list, the place we know as Lydford – from the *Anglo-Saxon Chronicle* in 997, from the coins minted there and later from Domesday Book – was known as *Hlidan*, which looks like a territory name based on the name of the river Lyd (and this sort of name had earlier occurred, with royal grants of land to the church, in relation to the rivers Torridge and Creedy: see Chapters 2, 3). At Lydford, the status of the church as something less than a full minster (see Chapter 3) suggests that disengagement from the wider territory of Lifton hundred was never fully achieved. At Exeter, the extra-mural parishes belonging to the bishop and burgesses in the middle ages (see above and Chapter 3) may give clues as to the minster's early jurisdiction. Exeter was within the hundred of Wonford, and the royal manor of Wonford itself was very close to the city. It included Heavitree, traditionally regarded as the original hundred meeting-place, whose name may, as W.G. Hoskins thought, have been *heafod-treow* – "the tree where criminals' heads are displayed". In the late Saxon period the city-based authority developed very close to the centre of this ancient rural one, and eventually became independent of it. At the same time, Exeter became the court site for the whole shire, and, by the twelfth century, regarded itself as a hundred in its own right.

The Burhs and military organisation *(Figs. 4.10, 4.11)*

The military arrangements of the *burhs* are revealed mainly through two sources. First, Domesday Book reveals that Exeter paid half a mark of silver as geld *ad opus militarem*, in other words as tax to support the royal mercenaries. In addition, when royal armies were raised in the shires, for service on land or sea, Exeter's provision was the equivalent of five hides of land in the countryside: that is, a trained warrior and his maintenance. Barnstaple, Totnes and Lydford shared service to royal armies equal to Exeter's: despite their modest size, they had been drawn specifically into the framework of royal military service, which was often not the case with such small places in other southern shires (though Dorset's boroughs were also hidated for provision of royal service). Second, the defence of the *burhs* themselves is revealed in the document known to historians as the Burghal Hidage, much studied by David Hill, Nicholas Brooks, Jeremy Haslam and others. This is a list, perhaps dating from the early tenth century but clearly including information dating back to Alfred's reign,

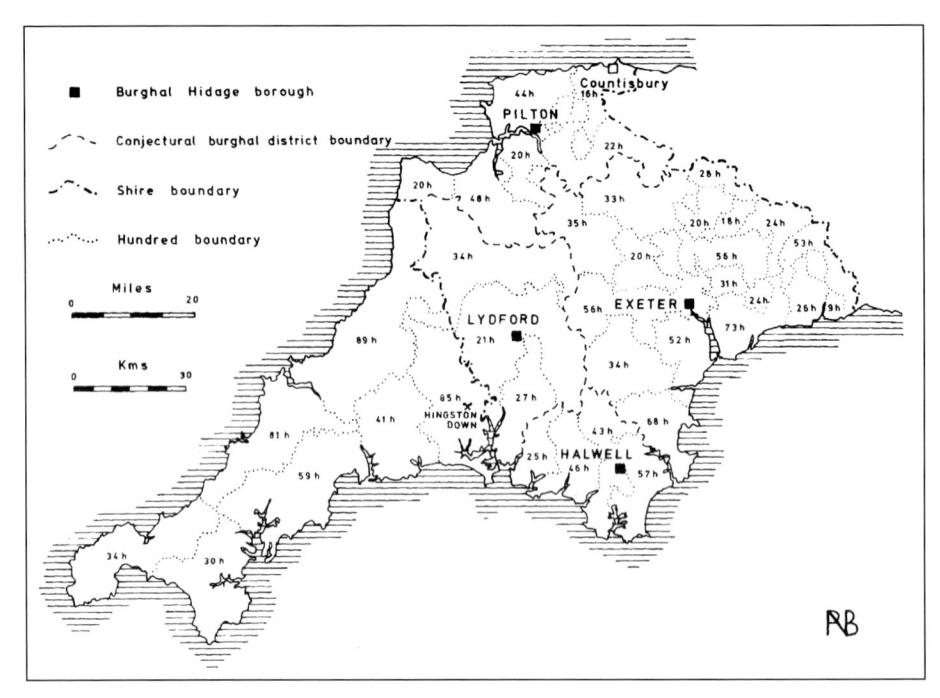

4.10: The hundreds, *burhs* and suggested *burghal* districts of Devon, from Brooks 1996. By permission of the author.

relating to *burhs* in Wessex and its Mercian fringe. Opinion is divided as to whether Alfred's *burhs* were built over a drawn-out period or to a shorter time-scale. Jeremy Haslam has argued, for example, that the *burhs* named in the Burghal Hidage arose in a concerted campaign of building in 878-879. The list does not relate to all parts of southern England: it names no places either in Cornwall or Kent. Kent certainly had defensible places at this time, but Cornwall seems not to have. The list gives not only the names of the *burhs* in Wessex, but also the number of hides of land alloted to each for their maintenance and defence (hence the name given to the document by historians). At this stage in their development, they were dependent on rural manpower: their own populations cannot have been sufficient. Because the numbers of hides was directly related to manpower raised, and the relationship of manpower to length of defences was stated, much time and effort has been expended in comparing the lengths of the notional perimeters thus suggested with those actually surviving on the ground. Sometimes, the calculations coincide, and sometimes not. At Exeter, for example, the Roman circuit, which we assume to have been repaired throughout, is actually longer than the notional circuit provided for in the Burghal Hidage arrangements. But the best way to view the southwestern situation seems not to be through concentrating on individual calculations, but by looking at the region as a whole, as Nicholas Brooks has emphasised.

Since Domesday Book later reveals that the combined hidation of Devon and Cornwall (some 1534 hides) totalled all the hides earlier allocated for support of the four *burhs*, it would appear that the two shires in combination maintained and manned them: according to the Burghal Hidage list, Exeter had 734, Halwell had 300, Lydford had 140, and Barnstaple/Pilton had 360. In other words, what mattered was the actual total hidation available in the region, which produced a smaller number of men for guarding the *burhs* than the theory of the Burghal Hidage list supposed. If this interpretation of a combined Devon-Cornwall hidation and organisation of the four *burhs* is correct (and it has much appeal) then not only does it have interesting implications for the mobility of labour and armed men over considerable distances, but also implications for the chronology of Cornwall's incorporation into Wessex: it means that Cornwall was already hidated along English lines by Alfred's reign at the latest (quite probably following Egbert's victory in 838) and not as a result of Aethelstan's campaign against the Cornish some thirty years later. Oddly, the Burghal Hidage list omits any reference to the shires and ealdormen which provided the framework of overall military organization. This may simply emphasise the specialised and restricted nature of what the list records. On the other hand, the eleventh-century practice of giving the earls (of Cnut's enlarged earldoms) a third of the profit of the *burh* courts could have originated in payments made to their predecessors, the ealdormen, in return for duties in administering the *burhs*.

Nicholas Brooks has suggested that, as at some other important West Saxon *burhs*, Exeter's allocation of 734 hides was an earlier arrangement, not one created for the purpose of burghal defence in Alfred's time. This idea is based on the exact nature of the 734 figure (those for the other Devonian *burhs* having a more "rounded" nature). If true, it would certainly explain why the length of Exeter's actual defences did not conform to 734 hides according to the formula given in the Burghal Hidage list: this formula was an Alfredian creation which did not always match the resources actually available. But the idea also raises an important issue: in what context, and for what purpose, had this earlier allocation existed? Was pre-Alfredian Exeter more important than we know? Did this hidation relate to circumstances pre-dating the eventual hundreds: to an earlier

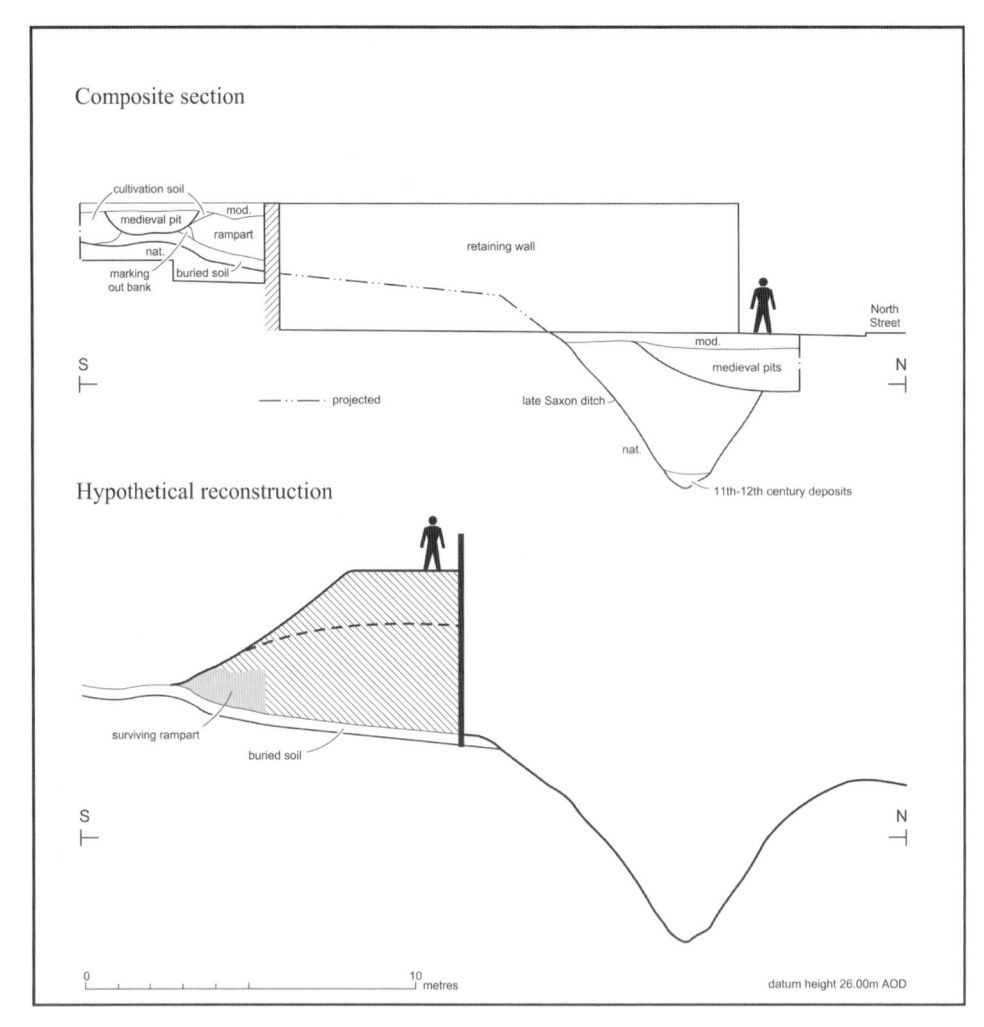

4.11: The defences of late Saxon Totnes, from Dyer & Allan 2004.
By permission of the authors and Devon Archaeological Society.

West Saxon *regio* attached to the city, or even to a territory inherited from Dumnonian times? As Nicholas Brooks has also pointed out, however, 734 hides is notably close to the 730 which Domesday Book reveals as the total for nineteen of Devon's hundreds, situated in the east and centre of the shire, leaving about 800 elsewhere in Devon and Cornwall for the support of Lydford, Barnstaple-Pilton and Halwell-Totnes. The evidence of Domesday Book also reflected this proportion in other ways: as noted above, by that time, the three smaller places together owed the same military service to the king as did Exeter alone.

An instructive way to view the situation is that, in the late ninth century, Devon and Cornwall were regarded as one administrative area for military purposes, despite their different histories as parts of Wessex. It is often said that Cornwall had no *burh*, which is true in the sense that the old Dumnonian region contained two territories (the suggestion, made many years ago, that a late tenth-century mint in east Cornwall at St. Stephen's, the predecessor of Launceston, was succeeded by one in the south at Castle Gotha, remains controversial). But Aethelstan's fixing of the Tamar boundary, which finalised this tradition in terms of distinct West Saxon shires, had yet to occur when the Burghal Hidage arrangements were made: Lydford was simply the *burh* for westernmost Wessex, situated near the junction of more-English and less-English territories. On the other hand, the Burghal Hidage hidation for Lydford (140 hides) and the Domesday hidation for Cornwall (some 400 hides) are very different, revealing that Cornwall was not simply allocated to the support of its nearest *burh*. Alfred's will stated that some of his British lands (that is, in Cornwall) belonged to his estate of Lifton, which may therefore have been the successor to an earlier unit of West Saxon royal administration cutting across the traditional boundary. The Devon part of this estate, which emerged as a hundred in the tenth century, was also to contain a monastery, founded at Tavistock in 980, probably in replacement of an earlier minster church. Lifton itself was immediately east of the Tamar, that is as far west in Devon as it could be. It is in this slightly fluid definition of what later became the Devon-Cornwall distinction that Lydford's role as a defensive *burh* is best understood, as well as in its economically-important Dartmoor hinterland (see above). The fact that an earlier settlement had existed at Lydford on this naturally defensive promontory may also have influenced its choice for a *burh*. It is possible that the English battle with the Cornish in 825, at nearby Galford (see Chapter 2), was accompanied by a development in Lydford's importance. The defences existing not later than Alfred's reign were effective against Danish attack in 997, which followed the sack of Tavistock abbey. They have been shown by Peter Addyman's excavations to have comprised a rampart and palisade around the whole spur-sited settlement, together with a rampart, palisade and multiple ditches across the neck of the spur.

The *burh* at Halwell, some five miles south of its successor, Totnes, presumably occupied one of the two earthwork enclosures known at Halwell itself and nearby Stanborough. Pilton, was situated immediately adjacent to its successor, Barnstaple, though opinion is divided as to whether they had always been one and the same place. The positions of Barnstaple,

Making Anglo-Saxon Devon

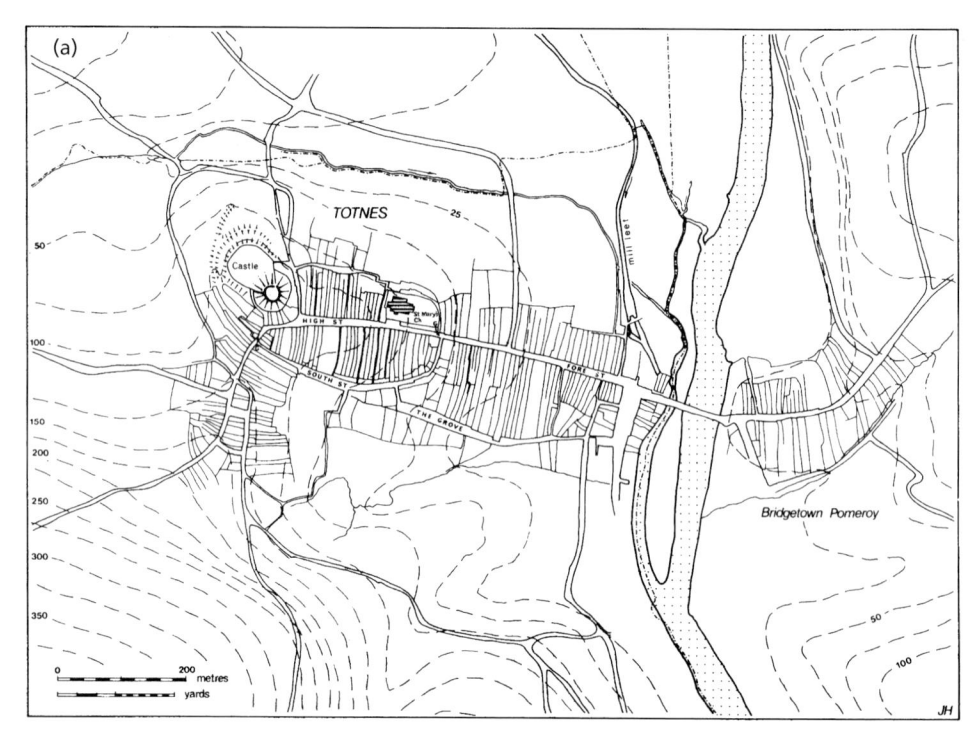

4.12: Plans of (a) Totnes and (b; *opposite*) Barnstaple showing developed topography around Saxon *burhs*, from Haslam in Haslam (ed) 1984. By permission of Jeremy Haslam.

situated on the major northern estuary of the Taw, and Totnes, near the major southern estuary of the Dart, reflected issues of coastal security and communication. How early these places received the bridges known in later times is not clear. The defences of these places were considerable. Excavation has shown that the ditch at Totnes was ten metres wide and five deep, the rampart being nine wide and perhaps four high. The primary defences of the burhs at Totnes and Lydford were of earth and timber, with later stone phases. Cautiously, these phases have been correlated with the Alfredian and Aethelredian periods respectively, both reigns when viking attack was a real threat.

Burghal planning (Figs. 4.5, 4.9, 4.12, 4.13)

More research deserves to be carried out on the early planning of these *burhs*, which evolved into the boroughs (*burgi*) of Domesday Book. On the basis of places with better documentation, for example Worcester and

Government and Towns

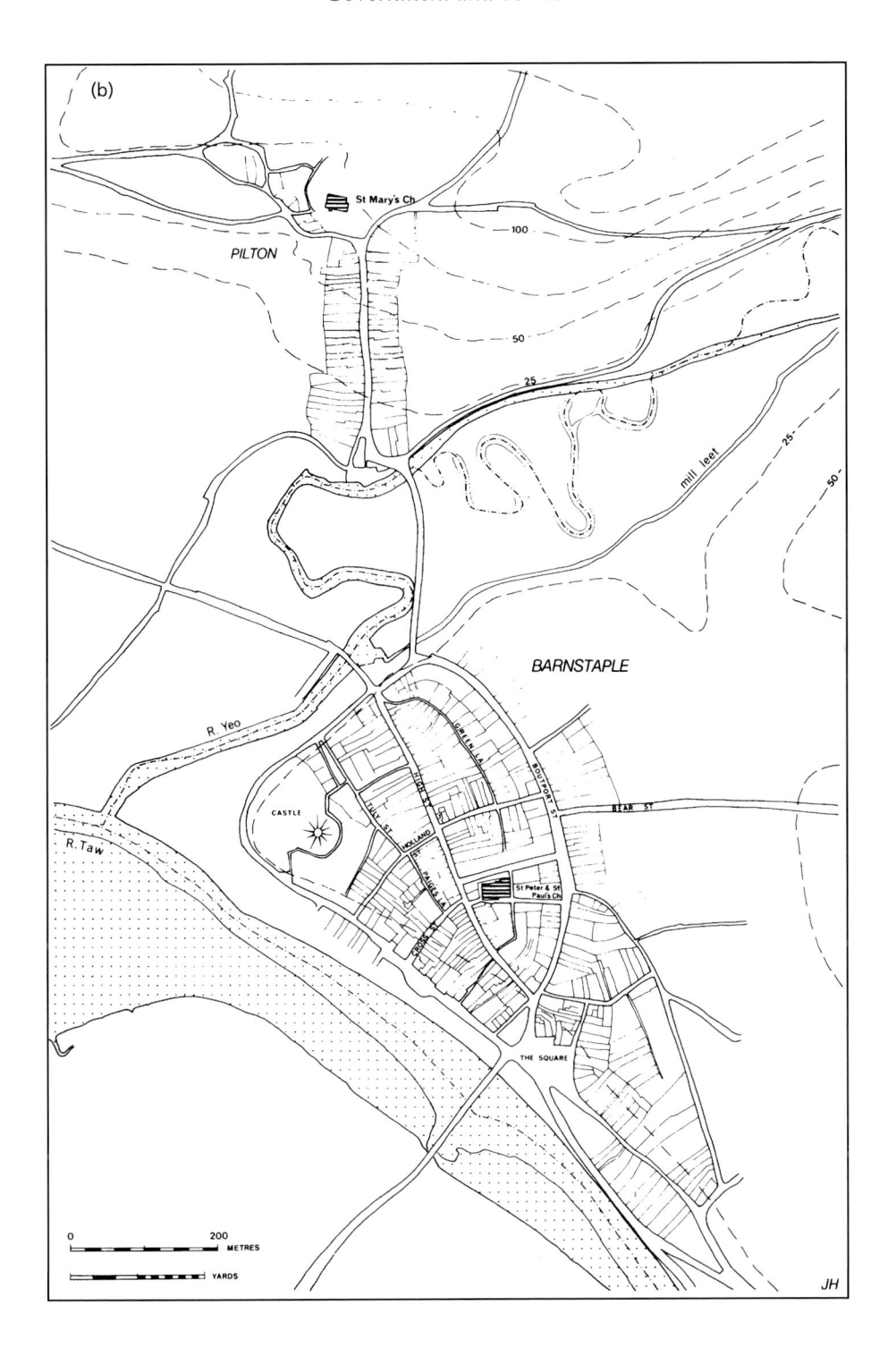

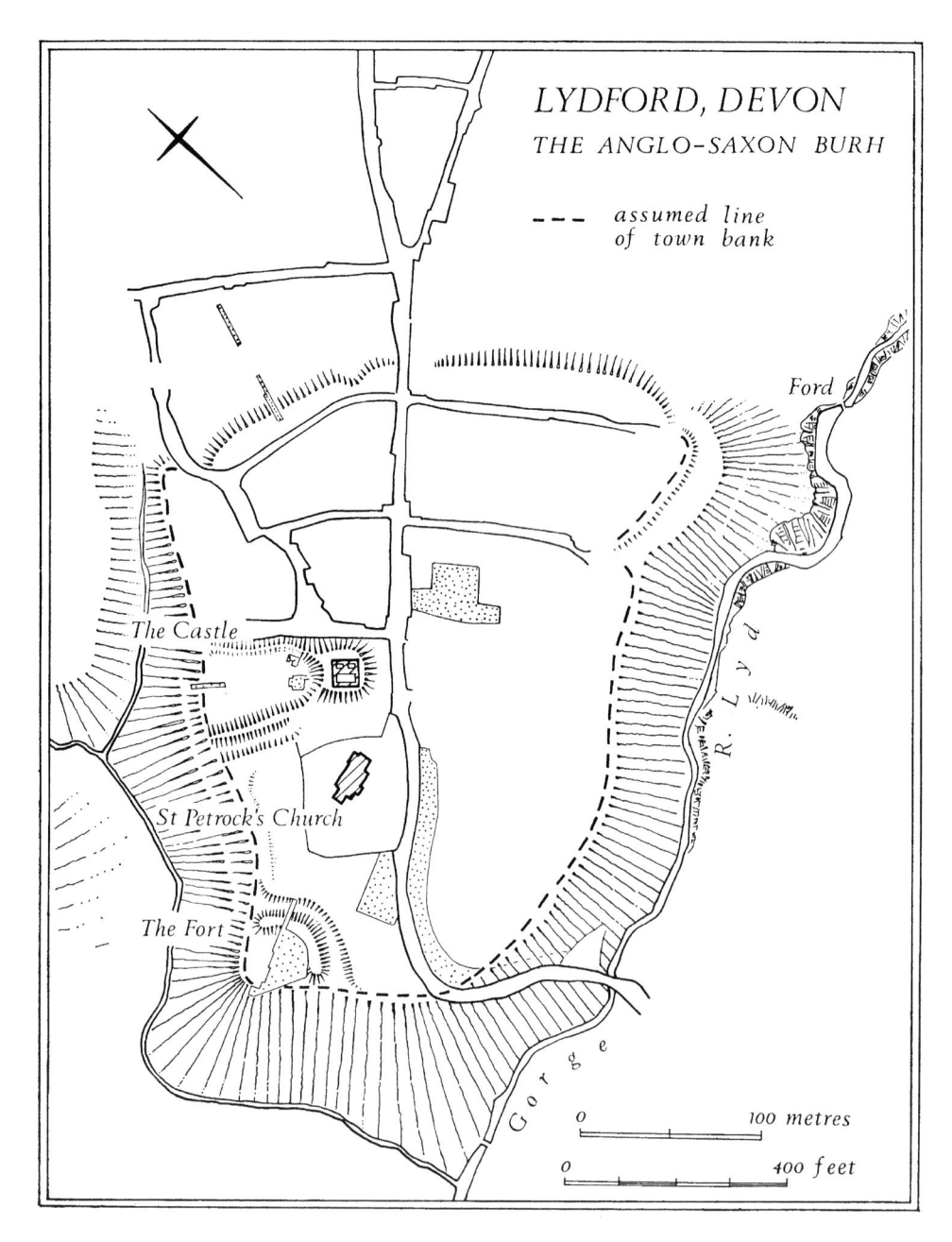

4.13: Plan of Lydford, from Radford 1970. Here, in the least subsequently-developed of Devon's *burhs*, the late Saxon framework is very clear. By permission of the Society for Medieval Archaeology and Maney Publishing, Leeds.

Rochester, it is now generally argued that townscapes of multiple, long, narrow tenements, characteristic of medieval towns, were not primary features of the burghal period. They probably developed, under pressure of population growth and economic activity, from the late tenth century onwards. In the first century of their existence, the walled areas had comprised a smaller number of much larger properties, for which the contemporary word *haga* was employed. At Lydford, we may still be able to see these larger blocks because subsequent development was so limited. They comprise the areas limited by the single spine street and the small number of narrow side streets (now lanes) running away from it. Such blocks may also have existed where these side streets are not apparent: the church and church yard may occupy one, the first Norman castle another, and the later medieval castle yet another. At Barnstaple, which eventually had a more complex street pattern, the original plan probably also comprised a few side streets running away from a spinal street, creating similar blocks of land. Totnes is more difficult to analyse, because if there was a system of streets running away from the spinal street, this was obscured by the later development of medieval burgage plots. But the north-east sector, occupied by the parish church and priory site, may reflect an original *haga*: it is bounded by a straight, narrow lane which runs from High Street to the back of the defences. While the castle motte may have occupied another block of plots, its creation was also destructive of earlier boundaries since the streets which reflect its curving base are clearly post-castle features.

At Exeter, perhaps entire blocks of land on either side of the High Street – Fore Street line, bounded by the side streets running out towards the defences, were the primary property blocks, the back lanes which developed in some parts being a result of subsequent burgage plot development. If this is true, it is tempting to regard the block where St Olave's church stood as the *haga* revealed in a twelfth century source as *Irlesbyri* (the earl's *burh*). This name probably reflected a large property held by the Godwinson family, earls of Wessex, for whose use St Olave's was founded as a chapel. Since the earls presided over the shire courts in the eleventh century, it is even possible that this was their location. Situated in lower Exeter, towards the river Exe, and bounded by the city wall and the streets later known as Fore Street, St Mary Arches Street and Friernhay (which supplanted the name *Irlesbyri*) it may also have been the nucleus of a small Scandinavian trading community (St Olave's, Chester, near the river Dee, is an obvious comparison). William the Conqueror, who inherited the property from the Godwinsons, used it for the foundation of St Nicholas's Priory. Another example of an early *haga* in Exeter may be revealed by the street name recorded in the thirteenth century as *Doddehaystrete*, which was later to become Catherine Street. The root of the name is likely to have been late Saxon, as *Dodda's haga*, revealing a detail of tenurial history in the *burh* relating probably to a thegn who held a substantial property there. Thirteenth-century sources also refer to a piece of land in Exeter called *Bilebury*, in which houses stood adjacent to High Street. Given the analogy with the name *Irlesbyri* (above) it is tempting to see this also as a *haga* of late Saxon origin. In one corner of the city, the Norman castle may have been laid out to conform with the limits of one or more existing *hagae*. Domesday Book mentions houses destroyed, but since it is known that the Conqueror's occupation of the city was negotiated (though after a protracted siege) rather than enforced, it may be that the outer lines of the castle site respected existing tenurial boundaries. Lack of knowledge of this area in the late Saxon period is a major gap in our understanding of late Saxon Exeter. Was it occupied not just by houses, but also by some "royal" building swept away by the Normans? In what sort of building was Edward the Confessor's party accommodated in 1050 when they attended the installation of bishop Leofric? Excavations within the castle in 2006 have revealed burials of pre-Norman date, suggesting this area may earlier have contained a church site. There is still much to learn about the topography of Exeter on the eve of the Norman Conquest.

Other possible defended and marketing places (Figs. 4.14, 4.15)

Despite the determination of tenth-century kings to concentrate trade in the *burhs*, some rural marketing undoubtedly existed. Royal insistence on having witnesses to rural trade can be traced back to Ine's law-code. Aethelstan's Grately code allows for exchange in the countryside, for example of livestock: perhaps this regulation, which insisted on transactions being witnessed by the lord, reeve or priest of the estate in question, catered for barter. Edgar's fourth code insisted that rural transactions should have twelve witnesses (reduced to four in Cnut's second code) provided by the Hundred: perhaps revealing markets at hundred centres themselves. It seems fairly safe to assume that local markets grew to serve minster communities (see Chapters 3 & 5) and there may thus have been a level of proto-urban activity, too low to have left imprint in documentary sources, hidden beneath the boroughs or markets which emerged from the thirteenth century onwards at such places as Crediton, Tiverton, Axminster and Cullompton. At Tavistock, whose market function is not documented until around 1100, it is likely that economic growth had been developing from the abbey's foundation in the late tenth century. In Devon, Domesday Book mentions a market at Okehampton, a new creation in conjunction with a Norman castle and incipient borough, and also one at Otterton, a manor by then belonging to the abbey of Mont St Michel. In Cornwall, the Domesday markets noted at St Germans and Bodmin were presumably of pre-Norman origin, at important ecclesiastical centres, as was that at St. Stephen's, which had been subsequently moved to nearby Launceston where a castle was built. As in other matters, it is generally accepted that Domesday under-records the important activity of marketing in the local rural economy.

Generally unknown also is the number of places which may have developed some wider urban characteristics at an early date but without formal identification as *burhs* and thus not mentioned in the Burghal Hidage list or other sources. This line of analysis has been usefully pursued for Devon by Jeremy Haslam. It is widely accepted that the Burghal Hidage list, concerned primarily with defensive and military matters, is not a full guide to late Saxon urbanism: Dorchester, for example, Dorset's shire town, does not figure in the Burghal Hidage. It is nevertheless difficult to gauge both the extent of rural markets and the development of "anonymous" *burhs*. The precise date of the Burghal Hidage list has been a matter of argument: a cautious conclusion is that, while it contains information on West Saxon arrangements which applied in Alfred's reign, the list as it stands is a product of Edward the Elder's reign when West Saxon power had spread into southern Mercia. Thus, if it was, as sometimes argued, Edward the Elder who replaced Halwell with Totnes (and perhaps Pilton with Barnstaple), these changes post-dated the original compilation of the data in the Burghal Hidage list. Other arguments have been put forward for Aethelstan's reign as the period of changes. It is hard to see how, on available evidence, these issues can be resolved.

It has been suggested by Jeremy Haslam that the royal estates at Kingsteignton, Kingsbridge and Plympton contained proto-urban centres founded as royal *burhs* in the tenth century by Edward the Elder or Aethelstan. These occupied important estuarine locations, like Totnes and Barnstaple. Plympton and Kingsteignton also became hundred centres. Edward the Elder specifically acquired the estate and minster of Plympton from bishop Asser, in exchange for three properties in Somerset: perhaps a Devon example of a wider southern English trend in which he acquired former church properties in places felt to be of potential military significance (Portchester in Hampshire was another). The original name of the hundred containing (Kings)teignton was probably Teignbridge, indicating the significance of this estuary and its crossing by an early bridge in conjunction with an important royal manor. In his study of south Devon, Paul Luscombe has reminded us that king Aethelwulf's charter of 847, concerning land in the South Hams, refers to a fort of some sort (perhaps already ancient?) in the Kingsbridge area. Jeremy Haslam has suggested this may have been the nucleus of a later *burh*. Moreover, in the charter of King Edgar, granting land at Sorley in 962, a bridge at Kingsbridge was specifically mentioned. Bridges are assumed to have played important roles in the planning of most Devon *burhs* (as in many other shires) even though specific documentary reference to them does not occur until much later. It has also been suggested that, whatever urban future Alfred may have intended for all but the smallest *burhs*, it was only in the reigns of his tenth-century successors that town life, as opposed to fortress organisation, really took hold. This holds true for Exeter, Lydford, Totnes and Barnstaple, whose urban characteristics are made clear by Domesday Book. But

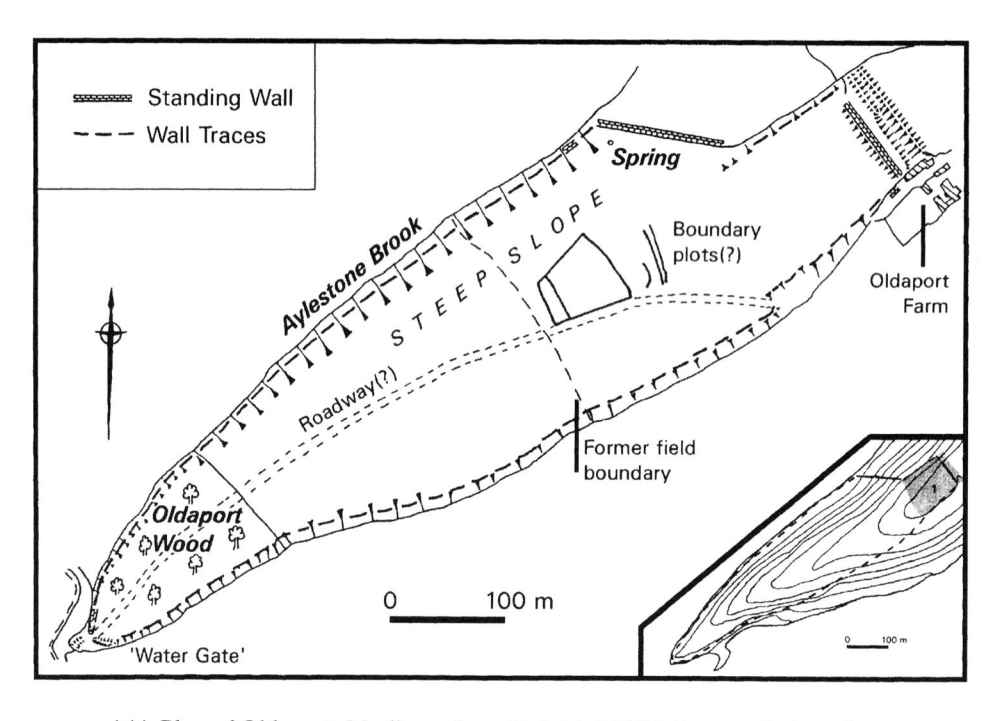

4.14: Plan of Oldaport, Modbury, from Rainbird 1998. By permission of the author and Devon Archaeological Society.

if other places had earlier possessed urban characteristics, they had disappeared by 1086 or at least did not meet Domesday Book's borough criteria (though it is well known for being less than consistent in its coverage of urban matters). Plympton had a minster church, but there is no evidence for this at Kingsbridge. At Kingsteignton, a sub-oval enclosure lay at the settlement core, not unlike some minster settlements in southern England, and a minster is a strong probability (see Chapters 3 & 5). Plympton and Kingsbridge became boroughs of a later sort in the twelfth and thirteenth centuries, Plympton on a new site determined by a Norman castle. Kingsteignton did not become a later borough: this developed at nearby Newton Abbot. Excavations at Kingsteignton produced limited evidence of late Saxon activity, and no indication of defences. Nevertheless, its early importance cannot be denied and it was chosen for attack by vikings in 1001. It lay in a very important royal estate whose reconstruction, by Peter Weddell, suggests it had originally included the land both north and south of the Teign, enhancing its control of the estuary.

The enigmatic promontory site at Oldaport, near Modbury, studied by Paul Rainbird and others, continues to provide interesting discussion. Carbon dating of mortar from its cross-spur wall, originally a hundred metres long, suggests it was added between the late ninth and early eleventh centuries to a site of probably much earlier origin (perhaps Dumnonian). Perhaps, like South Cadbury, Somerset, its fortification marked a re-occupation against viking threat in the reign of Ethelred II. In a Devon context, its location near an estuary (the river Erme) provides a parallel with other sites with royal connections, but, if it was fortified at this time it may not have seen much use: unlike South Cadbury, it did not become a mint site.

Mints and minting *(Figs. 4.15, 4.16, 4.17)*

Edward the Elder's second law-code, which was issued at a council in Exeter in 924, stipulated the witnessing of trade in the *burhs* (there called a *port*) by a royal *portreeve*. Aethelstan's law-code issued at Grately, Hampshire, reveals a fully-developed royal attitude to those *burhs* which had become towns. Their defences were to be repaired annually, significant trading was to be confined to them, and the minting of coins also confined to them. The minting of silver pennies had become an important attribute of urban life as well as a major feature of royal government. This coinage had been introduced by king Offa of Mercia in the eighth century and later became

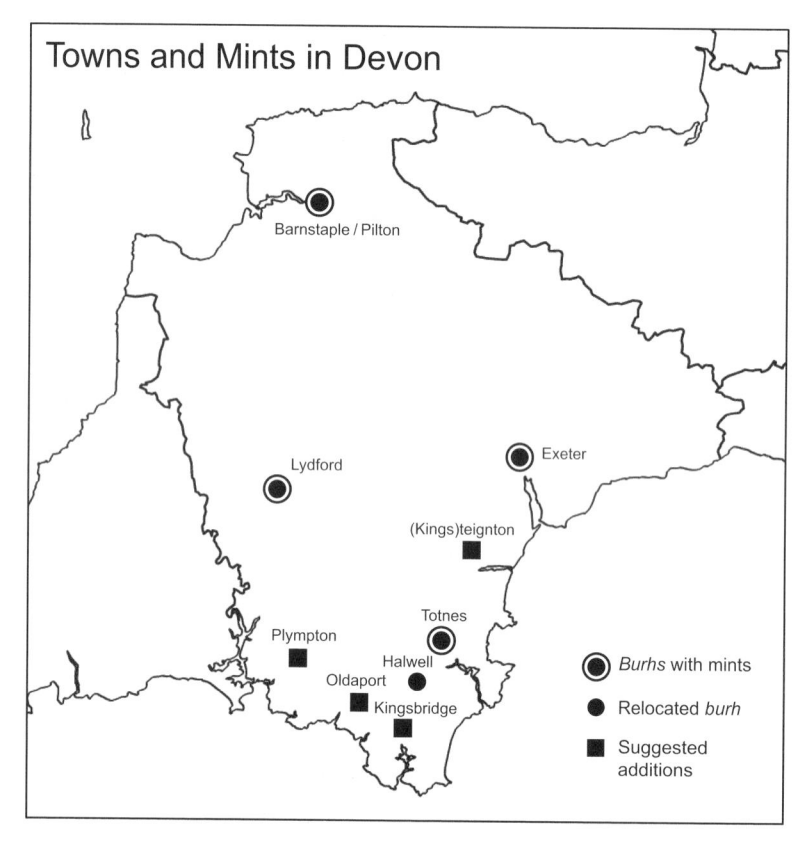

4.15: Towns and mints in Saxon Devon.
Map by Robert Higham and Oliver Creighton.

widespread. Its importance has long been recognised thanks to the early work of Michael Dolley and subsequently of other numismatists. Exeter was minting from around 895, Barnstaple and Totnes by the 950s and Lydford from around 973. Only a few pennies survive from Exeter's first mint (identified by their EXA mark), established by king Alfred. The location of this mint and its successors is not known ("The Mint" street name is a much later creation). According to Aethelstan's law-code, Exeter had two moneyers, like some other tenth-century Wessex mints: lesser *burhs* had only one moneyer. With Edgar's reform of the coinage, around 973, came greater standardisation of design, including the regular inclusion of mint-name and moneyer's name, making the coins more informative (to us) as historical documents. England now had the most sophisticated coinage system in western Christendom. At least fifty mints were in operation, striking and distributing huge numbers of coins on a local basis, using iron dies purchased by the moneyers but controlled by kings, engraved in London or Winchester, or sometimes in regional centres such as Exeter. Old coins were withdrawn and new coins were issued at intervals, at least nominally, of three or six years. No coin hoards have been found in Devon, and a mere handful of individual coin finds. As for English coins in general, the bulk of Devon's surviving coins come from Scandinavia (which drew massively from England in this period) and significant finds also come from Dublin, attesting on-going economic links in the Irish Sea zone. The peak of Exeter's coin production was in the reigns of Aethelred II and Cnut, from which the bulk of surviving pennies date, and during which about twenty-five moneyers' names are known. Though the other Devon *burhs* also had mints, production at Exeter's was more continuous (it closed down, with other provincial mints, late in the thirteenth century). At times, Exeter's mint ranked fifth in national importance, measured by output (see above).

A recent study by John Allan of Lydford's modestly-ranking mint, which flourished from the 970s to 1020s but then declined, suggests that it produced about a million pennies in this period (of which some 400 survive). The output from a major mint such as Exeter was proportionately greater. Some moneyers worked in consecutive reigns, reflecting a stable system. At Exeter and elsewhere these names are mainly English, though some Scandinavian ones also occur. It seems probable that the profession of moneyers was drawn from men with related skills – the silversmiths and others engaged in metal-working activities. Through the coins from different mints we can follow the movements of these men, whose profession often took them to work in various places, especially in the reigns of Aethelred II and Cnut. Goda, Godwine and Aelfstan, for example, minted at Exeter, Totnes and Lydford. Aelfwine and Hunwine, on the other hand, appear at mints not only in Devon but also in Somerset and Dorset. These coins provide a fascinating route into a world of named individuals, who were at least partly literate, but of probably neither clerical nor landowning status (though we do not know for certain that moneyers may not also have been minor clerics or merchant burgesses). In contrast, the craftsmen who produced all other aspects of the period's material culture – in stonework, woodwork, metalwork and ceramics – have remained anonymous. Together with the evidence of Domesday Book and the witness-lists to charters, the coins provide a very important source for pre-Norman personal names in Devon.

The quantity of coins produced, and the tightly-controlled system which produced them, are also major indicators of England's immense overall

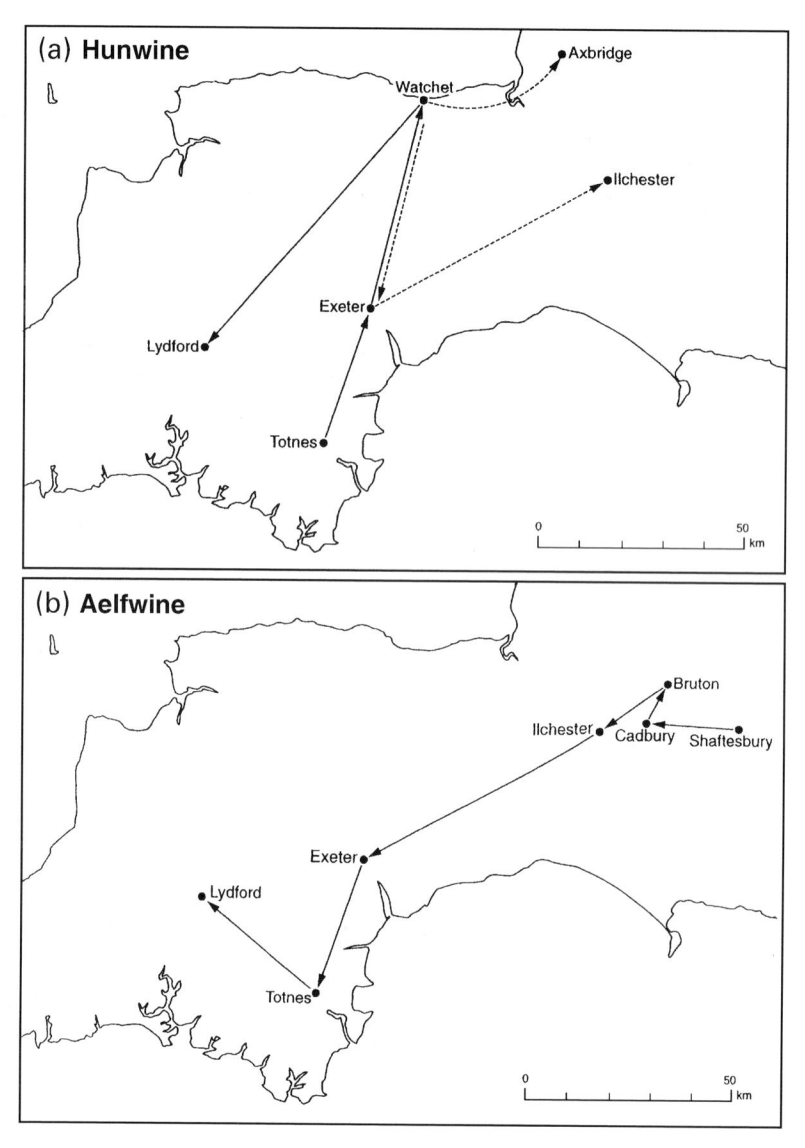

4.16: The careers of two south-western moneyers (a) Hunwine and
(b) Aelfwine as indicated by their coins, from Allan 2002.
By permission of the author and the Devonshire Association.

prosperity in the later tenth and eleventh centuries: a most important feature of its attractiveness to Scandinavian and Norman conquerors. It is striking how easily the compilers of Domesday Book could describe landed property in terms of monetary value. It has been suggested by Peter

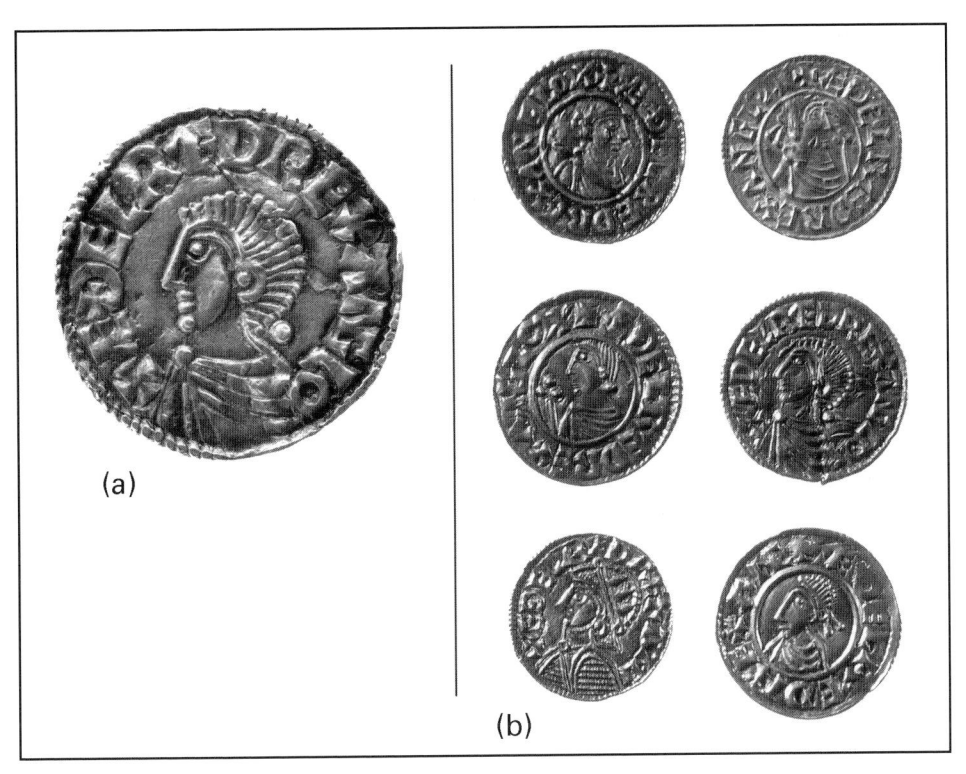

4.17: Silver pennies minted in late Saxon Devon (a) Aethelred II's issue of 997-1003 (Lydford mint) and (b) the six issues of Aethelred II (Exeter mint). Photographs: Royal Albert Memorial Museum and Art Gallery, Exeter. (a) and (b) not same scale.

Sawyer that the supply of silver needed, in addition to that produced from the limited English sources and from melting down the withdrawn coinage, was imported from Germany via the Low Countries in exchange for the export of English wool. The general silence of Domesday Book on English livestock makes this hypothesis difficult to pursue, but it is feasible: the Exon Domesday gives (demesne) livestock data, from which it is clear that sheep were very important in the south west (see Chapter 5). Devon, while not amongst England's richest shires, may thus have made a significant contribution to the national prosperity upon which the stability of the coinage rested.

Landowners and towns

Remarkable though these urban developments seem, they did not occur overnight simply because Alfred established *burhs*. Asser, his biographer, noted a certain reluctance shown by the king's subjects in building fortifications, and the reliance on rural areas for manpower for defence, revealed in the Burghal Hidage list, reflects very low urban populations in the first instance. By what stages these communities grew remains unclear. There may have been some enforced, or at least heavily induced, movement of people from the countryside. The *Anglo-Saxon Chronicle*'s description of the army raised by king Alfred in 893 says this army included "the king's thegns who were then at home at the fortresses", implying that rural lords had properties and/or responsibilities there. Though the *burhs* remained royal establishments, it seems fair to assume that local thegns acquired urban properties, probably in three contexts: first, in conjunction with duties relating to organisation of defence which they owed there; second, as a source of income, through rents, from the growing urban populations; third, and particularly in Exeter, as private residences for use when attending the shire courts. In Exeter, while some founding of lesser churches by the minster/cathedral cannot be ruled out, it is hard to explain the origin of all the eventual urban "parish" churches unless some had started as chapels in secular urban properties (see Chapter 3). The eventual boundaries of these parishes deserve more study as a guide to the city's early social and tenurial history.

Unfortunately, it is impossible to identify the general pattern of urban tenures which had applied in 1066. In Lydford, all properties seem to have been royal, since no specific information on holdings of tenants-in-chief is given for 1086: this may reflect this small *burh*'s very particular economic function (see above). Totnes had been given by the Conqueror to the Breton, Judhel, and Domesday Book does not describe any distinctions within its earlier tenures, which by 1086 were probably wholly Judhel's. In 1086, three tenants-in-chief held property in Barnstaple alongside the royal properties; thirteen secular and four ecclesiastical tenants-in-chief held property in Exeter alongside the royal properties. It is likely that this diversity reflected something similar before the Norman Conquest, but it is impossible to go further than that limited inference. First, some changes of balance between royal and other holdings had occurred since the Norman Conquest. For example, in 1086 the bishop of Coutances held houses in Exeter and Barnstaple which had been royal properties in 1066. Second, and related, is the complexity of land transference from Saxon thegns to Norman lords in Devon, where there seems to have been much sub-division of old estates and re-constitution of new ones. Historians have emphasised the difficulty here of reconstructing the holdings of the Devonian late

Saxon *thegnly* class. And the problem of this countryside-based task in Devon extends also to its towns. Contrasting examples, ecclesiastical and secular, suffice to illustrate the difficulties. First, in Exeter in 1086, the biggest property-holder after the king was Osbern, the bishop of Exeter, who had about 50 houses (nine of which were attached to the manor of Bishopsteignton). It is hard to imagine that, before 1066, bishop Leofric's cathedral had not held some Exeter property (and perhaps, before 1050, the minster had done likewise?), especially as the bishop had an interest in the city's extra-mural fields (see above). But whether such properties had passed unaltered through this period, or had been subject to loss or augmentation, seems impossible to determine.

Second, when we speak of *thegnly* properties in towns, there is an assumption that such properties were attached to the rural manors held by *thegns*. Domesday Book refers to non-royal urban holdings within each list of lands of individual tenants-in-chief, rather than within its descriptions of the royal towns themselves, but normally without linking them to named manors. In a few cases, however, this link is revealed. Some of the Exeter houses of Baldwin de Meules, the king's sheriff, were said to have formerly belonged to Edward the Confessor. But his other Exeter houses belonged to his rural manor of Kenn, south of Exeter, whose lord in 1066 had been Brictmer. His Barnstaple properties were said to belong to his manor of Shirwell, in north Devon (the manor was held in 1086 by his tenant Robert of Beaumont), whose lord in 1066 had also been Brictmer. So here we have a glimpse of rural-urban property connections which may have been more general, as well as the identity of one late Saxon thegn who had urban properties attached to manors located not far from the *burhs* in question. Domesday illuminates few other details. In 1086, Walter of Douai held houses in Exeter which had been held in 1066 by Asgar. A manorial connection for these houses is not stated, but in 1066 Asgar held several manors later held by Walter, including Goodrington and Stoke (Fleming). In 1066, Harold (Godwinson) had houses in Exeter attached to his manor of Tawstock. One house in Exeter was attached to the manor of Ilsington, held in 1086 by Ralph Pagnell (its lord in 1066 not being identified). As in later centuries, though the preferred life-style of the gentry was rural, urban interests played a part in their overall activities and income. Indeed, since the early eleventh-century treatise on social status (referred to earlier) reveals that one way to achieve thegnhood was to be a very successful merchant, it is also possible that some of the gentry of 1066 had achieved that status from urban, merchant origins in the tenth century.

Conclusion: urbanism on the eve of the Norman Conquest (see Figs. 4.18, 4.19, 4.20)

It is tempting, from the modern view-point, to assume that the growth of towns was a "natural" progression. But it is important to remember that the towns were originally artificial, and that the apparently natural place in medieval society which they eventually held had to be won, by their founders and by their occupants. The spread of mints beyond Exeter created some economic stimulus to urbanism, as did tightening royal control of urban trade and administration in the post-Alfredian period. Urban populations grew, especially in the later tenth century. Originally spacious *hagae* were progressively sub-divided into the familiar long, narrow urban tenements of later times: the numbers of houses in the towns mentioned in Domesday Book is testimony to this process, especially in Exeter. The merchant class familiar in the later middle ages was by now established. Gradually, responsibility for defence shifted from the countryside, as described in the Burghal Hidage, to the urban communities themselves, a process analysed at national level by Oliver Creighton and the present author. At Exeter, the urban militia, known from later centuries, came into being, as did the urban wards within which, alongside legal and tax matters, the militia was organised. There is a strong likelihood that the four wards, divided by the main streets (often known as "quarters" – north, south, east and west – in later sources) were developing here by the eleventh century, as in some other English cities. In his account of Exeter's resistance to William the Conqueror's siege in 1068, Orderic Vitalis said the city was defended by its citizens. Thus, urban defences, which had originally been an artificial creation whose maintenance had to be deliberately stimulated by kings (as well as manned from the countryside), gradually became the matter of civic pride and organisation which they subsequently remained for many centuries.

At the same time, the period saw the entrenchment of an enduring feature of English urban life whose roots lay in Alfred's *burhs*: a strong link between towns and kings. The political independence sought by towns and cities in some European countries did not become characteristic of English medieval history. Domesday Book clearly states that Edward the Confessor and William the Conqueror possessed Devon's towns (though the status of Totnes was different by 1086) and this must also have been true of earlier kings. Even when resisting William the Conqueror in 1068, Exeter was seeking not independence but simply a continuation of its

4.18: Eleventh-century rubbish pits excavated behind house tenements on the south side of High St, Exeter (Princesshay re-development scheme). Photograph: Exeter Archaeology.

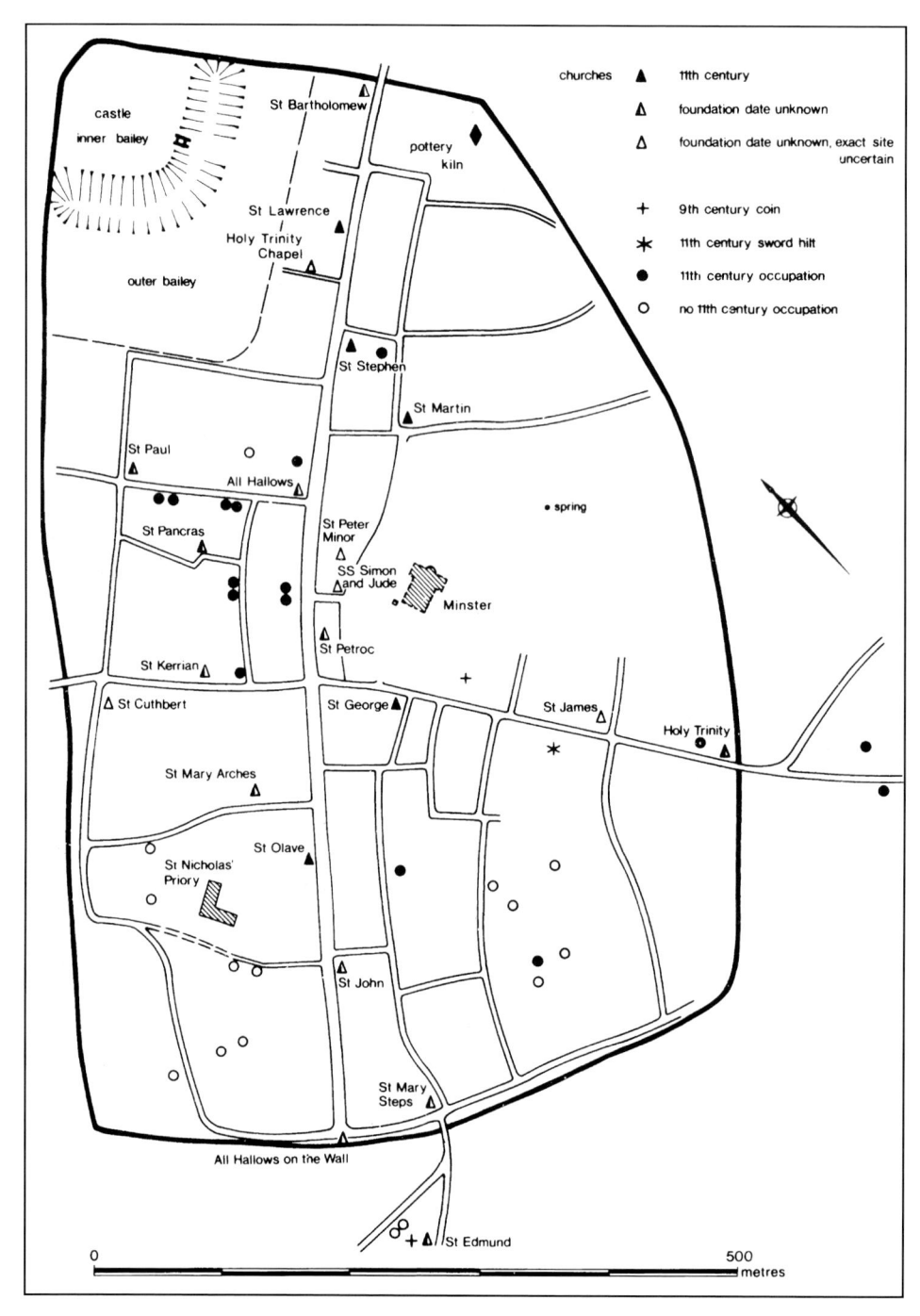

4.19: Exeter in the eleventh century. From Allan, Henderson & Higham in Haslam (ed) 1984. By permission of Jeremy Haslam. The distribution of datable finds has been supplemented since this survey was published, for example by the excavations in Princesshay (see 4.18).

existing obligations to England's kings. This could also help explain the "Anglo-Saxon" features (long and short quoining and triangular-headed windows) in the "Norman" castle gatehouse: perhaps not simply a symbol of conquest, but also of partnership between the old order and the new ?

Archaeological evidence from Exeter, the best-understood of these late Saxon south-western towns, suggests, however, that the prosperous city which resisted William the Conqueror in 1068 may have been fully recognisable only by the late tenth century. It was at this time that the output of its mint increased, that local pottery became available, that the earliest smaller churches appeared, and the spread of domestic occupation revealed by excavations became considerable. In the post-1945 excavations carried out by Aileen Fox, a kiln site was discovered near Bedford Street, which had produced wheel-thrown vessels, some glazed. At first thought to be of later medieval date, these were subsequently recognised as a tenth- and eleventh-century industry whose products were different from the contemporary coarse-wares made near the Devon-Somerset border (see illustrations in Chapter 2). Further quantities of what is often called "Bedford Garage Ware" in Exeter's archaeological circles have been found in the excavations carried out in 2006 in the Princesshay re-development area, south of High Street. It is known from these investigations that plentiful rubbish pits (classic indicators of urban occupation) of the eleventh century lay not simply along the High St – Fore St spine of the city, as previously understood, but also stretched back from High St towards the city walls. This was an area from which urban occupation had retracted by the thirteenth century, so making it available for occupation by the Dominican friary. From the late tenth to twelfth centuries, Exeter's citizens also used pottery manufactured in and around Normandy and Brittany: its import was presumably the by-product of regular trading links in other, less archaeologically-visible, goods. There is no doubt that in the very late Saxon and early Norman periods Exeter was enjoying one of the most prosperous periods in its history. Orderic Vitalis, the Anglo-Norman chronicler, said that the citizens of Exeter engaged the services of foreign merchants resident in the city to help their resistance to William the Conqueror's siege. This "international" quality to Exeter in the eleventh century is entirely consistent with the picture provided by a variety of evidence.

4.20: The gatehouse (with its original entry later blocked) of Exeter castle. Begun in 1068, this structure shows a mixture of some late Saxon (the triangular-head openings, the long-and-short quoins) with some Norman (the arch shape, the cushion capitals) architectural features. Photograph: Exeter Archaeology.

SOURCES USED AND FURTHER READING

Abels 1988; Alexander 1919–1922; Alexander 1931; Allan *et alii* 1984; Allan 2002; Barlow 1991; Barlow 2002; Birch 1885–1899; Blackburn (ed) 1986; Brooks 1996; Burrow 1977; Campbell 2000; Clarke 1994; Creighton & Higham 2005; Crick forthcoming; Darby & Welldon Finn (eds) 1967; Davies 1982; Darby 1977; Dolley (ed) 1961; Dyer & Allan 2004; Faith 1997; Farley & Little 1968; Finberg 1953; Fleming 1993; Fleming 2000; Fox 1952; Gillingham 1995; Glendining 1970; Gover *et alii* 1931–32; Greenway (ed) 1996; Harmer 1989; Haslam (ed) 1984(a); Haslam 1984(b); Haslam 2006; Henderson 1999; Henderson 2001; Higham 1987; Higham 1992; Hill 1981; Hill & Rumble (eds) 1996; Hollister 1962; Hooke 1990; Hooke 1994; Hoskins 1954; Jackson 1972; Kemble 1839-48; Keynes & Lapidge (eds) 1983; Liebermann (ed) 1903–1916; Luscombe 2005; Maddicott 1989; Morris 1927; Napier & Stevenson 1895; O'Donovan 1988; Padel 1999; Palliser (ed) 2000; Pounds 2000; Radford 1970; Rainbird 1998; Rainbird & Druce 2004; Reynolds 1999; Robertson 1939; Rose-Troup 1923; Rose-Troup 1937; Sawyer 1965; Sawyer 1983; Sharpe 2003; Sheldon 1928; Slater 1991; Stafford 1997; Stenton 1947; Swanton 1999; Tait 1936; Thorne & Thorne (eds) 1985; Thorne 1991; Weddell 1987; Whitelock (ed) 1930; Whitelock (ed) 1955; Williams 2003; Wormald 1999; Yorke 1995.

5

Land and Rural Folk

See Fig. 5.1 (map of places not mentioned in other chapters)

Land and Resources *(see Figs. 1.1, 5.2)*

In eleventh-century England, despite the growing significance of towns, the vast majority of the population was (including some burgesses) engaged in agriculture. In a region such as the south west, with very long coastlines, the exploitation of resources in estuaries was also very important. In view of the daily pursuit of rural and riverine activities, we might expect their study to be an easy task. But this is far from the case. Although the boundaries of some rural estates were described in charters, and aspects of agriculture were mentioned in other sources, we have few documents from the Saxon period itself through which to examine rural life. Thus, much weight must be placed upon the testimony of Domesday Book, written for William the Conqueror, in which rural society and its resources were described in detail. Because information was recorded both for 1086, when it was compiled, and for 1066, when Edward the Confessor died, it provides a view of Anglo-Saxon, as well as Norman England. The latter was here described in terms of the new conditions, framed in the landed endowments, or *fiefs*, of the now-dominant class from Normandy, Brittany and Flanders. But beneath this society we can also see an older one, whose *thegnly* landlords had been extensively displaced but which otherwise survived the Conquest. The data which the Normans inherited came from the English organisation of the shires and hundreds (see Chapter 4). Thus Domesday Book displays contrasting elements: from the old order, administrative and from the new order, feudal. It is ironic that this illumination of society comes from a source produced not by its own masters but by their conquerors. Without

Land and Rural Folk

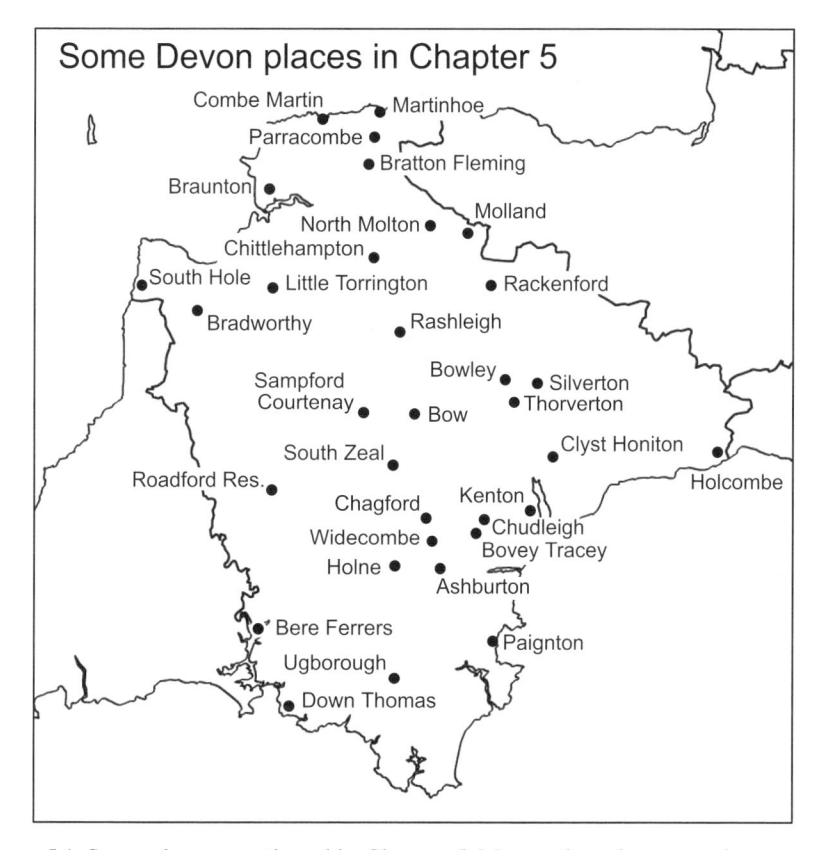

5.1: Some places mentioned in Chapter 5. Many other places are shown in other maps. See 1.1 (river-names); 3.7 (church-related); 4.1, 4.2 (royal-property-related); 4.3 (Anglo-Saxon charters). Map by Robert Higham and Oliver Creighton.

the Conquest, we would know far less about earlier rural society and its economy. Nevertheless, understanding the details of pre-Norman times poses many challenges, particularly in Devon. This was (and is) a very large shire with a great many small places, with frequent recurrence of identical or similar names for the Saxon lords of 1066, as well as extensive dismemberment of their estates by the Normans: all are barriers to reconstructing earlier patterns of land-holding.

The commonly-used phrase "Domesday Book" is in fact an umbrella term (of later creation) for a collection of sources which were not initially bound as books at all, but as collections of booklets. Its Devonian content can be conveniently studied in the edition by Caroline and Frank Thorne, and numerous commentaries on it have been published, for example those

5.2: The *Exon* Domesday Book (Exeter Cathedral Archives).
Photograph: Seán Goddard; by permission of the Dean and Chapter.

by Frank Barlow and others in the Alecto edition. The compilation of this *descriptio* of England (literally, a description) for William the Conqueror arose from a complex mixture of political, tenurial and tax-related motives. The Exchequer Domesday, made at Winchester, was the final abstract of data gathered from six of the seven regional circuits into which England was divided for the purpose of data-gathering. The Little Domesday, covering the seventh circuit (East Anglia), contains material never incorporated in the Exchequer version. The Exeter Domesday (often known as *Exon*) is the fuller version of circuit II, containing much of the data originally gathered in its five shires (Wiltshire, Dorset, Somerset, Devon, Cornwall). It contained information on land-holding running across these shires, where the Exchequer version re-ordered the material by individual shires. Historians are undecided whether an intermediate stage (like Little Domesday) existed between the Exeter and Exchequer versions. A particular *Exon* Domesday feature was that, as well as describing for manors the classes and numbers of rural society and the extent of arable, meadow and pasture, it also included demesne livestock (but not tenants' livestock). This data was omitted from the Exchequer abstract. Pig-rearing was clearly significant in the Devon economy, with about 3,700 pigs mentioned and 366 *porcarii* (swineherds) distinguished within the rural occupations, a feature shared (though to a lesser extent) with Somerset and Wiltshire. The number of cattle and goats mentioned in Devon was about 7,500 each; the large number of sheep mentioned, at around 50,000, was notable. It has been suggested that a major source of England's wealth by the eleventh century was a wool trade from eastern England to Europe, bringing in, amongst other things, silver from Germany to sustain the country's plentiful coin supply (see Chapter 4). Devon may have been significant in the wool production which lay behind such a trade.

Eleventh-century society enjoyed a climatic optimum, which had started in the later Saxon period and lasted until around 1300. There was a rise in summer temperatures and a drop in overall rainfall, one indicator of which was significant viticulture in southern England which was specifically mentioned for Wiltshire, Dorset and Somerset in Domesday Book (the recent growth of wine-production in the south, now including Devon, is thus not a new phenomenon). In Devon, this society occupied landscapes with significantly distinctive features. The rivers were not navigable except in important estuaries: the Exe, Dart, Plym, Teign, Taw and Torridge. The lower reaches of the Axe and Otter, in the south-east of the county, were broader than in modern times. Coastal communications must have been very important in the south west as a whole (see also Chapter 2). The interior was broken by the upland mass of Dartmoor and north Devon shared Exmoor with neighbouring Somerset. The richer soils of Devon lay in the Exe valley and adjacent areas, based on geological deposits less ancient than those to the west: the latter included the so-called Culm Measures which continued into Cornwall. Estimating from Domesday Book the actual populations which occupied these environments is complex, but relative distributions do emerge from the data. The most densely populated areas, on a par with some other English regions, were the lower Exe and Creedy valleys and the area between the rivers Teign and Dart. Dartmoor had the thinnest population (not, of course, evidence that its resources were not in regular use) but Exmoor somewhat more. But even on the moorlands, settlement was found at high altitudes: Willsworthy, at 900ft on west Dartmoor; Natsworthy at 1200ft on east Dartmoor; Belstone, at 1000ft on north Dartmoor; Radworthy at 1200ft on Exmoor. Devon and Cornwall together were less populous than southern and midland England, and Cornwall was uniformly a shire of very thin population. We cannot believe that this overall situation had developed only on the eve of the Norman Conquest: driven largely by differential natural environments, it probably had ancient roots. But whether what survived was simply a pattern inherited from Dumnonia, or whether it was significantly affected by the region's gradual absorption in Wessex, we cannot easily distinguish.

The human, agricultural and other resources revealed in Domesday Book have been intensively studied by many scholars. It has been estimated from Domesday and later evidence for England as a whole, that by the eleventh century the overall quantity of land in arable use was much the same as it was to be around 1900 (which is not to say that it was exactly the *same* land). Medieval and later expansion certainly involved some new arable (apparently at its greatest extent in the thirteenth century) but had generally more effect on the creation of pasture and meadow, through improvement of waste and woodland. *Exon* Domesday's constant reference not only to land for ploughing, but also to considerable pasture, reveals a mixed land use in the south west which corresponds to the frequent reference to sheep. And the same is true of the regular inclusion of reference to woodland: this was a major managed resource, not primeval forest, crucial both for timber and for pannage for the pigs which Domesday records.

Domesday also reveals other important economic features, though less systematically recorded: it is widely accepted that we can observe the range and nature of activities rather than their true extent. Salt-pans operated on the south Devon rivers, as well as the Taw-Torridge estuaries (they were also mentioned near the mouth of the Teign in a charter of 1044 relating to Dawlish). About eighty places in Devon had (water) mills, mainly on the south-eastern rivers: Exe, Culm, Clyst, Otter and Axe. This was certainly an under-represented feature, since more are mentioned in Somerset and Dorset, and it is hard to imagine there existed in north Devon only the handful which are mentioned there. But in Cornwall, a mere six were mentioned, so it is possible that mill technology (as opposed to grinding with querns) had spread slowly from east to west. Horse-breeding occurs in the south west, as elsewhere in England, occurring in Somerset, Devon and Cornwall. The horses referred to at Brendon and Lynton were presumably what would later be known as Exmoor ponies. It is also hard to credit Domesday's single reference (compared with several in Somerset) to iron-working in Devon: at North Molton, a royal estate inherited from the West Saxon dynasty, the agricultural population included four smiths (*ferrarii*). Perhaps the Domesday compilers had access here to recorded details for a royal estate which went un-noticed elsewhere: archaeological evidence for iron-working has now come from a variety of locations (see below).

Fisheries were mentioned in Domesday on the major estuaries – the Exe, Dart, Avon, Plym, Tavy, Taw and Torridge – but it has always seemed inconceivable that the population of a county with such extensive coastlines did not have more fishing by this date, and long before. Harold Fox argued that far more fishing was actually carried out by the eleventh century. First, we know of fisheries, not specified in 1086, such as that at Axmouth referred to in a charter around 1100, and that at Braunton referred to in king Aethelwulf's charter granting the estate to Glastonbury abbey in the ninth century. Second, other features may conceal fishing activity. Some manors near the south coast had high numbers of people known as *bordarii* in 1086 (see below): perhaps some of these occupied temporary dwellings on the coast, at certain times of year, from which fishing was pursued. Some later parishes had small, detached portions immediately on the coast, as if specifically to provide a maritime resource, and these "outliers" presumably originated in earlier manorial arrangements. Harold Fox showed that for many centuries fishing was a seasonal activity pursued from temporary coastal shelters; permanent fishing settlements, which became an important south-western feature, emerged only later on.

Rural Society

Broadly speaking, Anglo-Saxon (secular) society consisted of three major classes: nobles, ordinary but free people, and slaves. Some aspects of the noble, land-owning class, have been discussed above (Chapters 2, 3, 4). The class of ordinary but free people contained several variations. In Wessex generally, few peasants were specifically described as of free legal status (*liberi homines*) in Domesday Book's language. These were, however, numerous in the eastern and midland shires: the distinction may have arisen from faster processes of manorial development in the south or from different experiences on either side of the Danish-English divide in the ninth-tenth centuries. In Devon, therefore, according to the evidence of Domesday, the most numerous classes were the *bordarii* and *villani*, the latter comprising nearly half the rural peasant population (whereas in Cornwall, *bordars* were the largest group). Bordars (and their largely equivalent cottars elsewhere) were smallholders, whereas the *villani* (on whom, see also below) held larger amounts of land. There was also the third category, of slaves, called *servi* in Domesday Book, that is people who were the personal property of individuals or institutions. In England their history has been illuminated by David Pelteret. Early medieval Europe as a whole had an extensive system of slavery, which was not seen as inconsistent with Christianity. It was fed not only by warfare, conquest and subjugation but also by trade and by social demotion through extreme poverty or legal punishment. Some have questioned, however, how close the Domesday situation was to modern notions of "slavery" : thus "serf" is preferred to "slave" by some commentators. In Wessex as a whole, like most of England, slaves may have comprised around 10% of the population by the mid-eleventh century. It has been suggested that the numbers of slaves given in Domesday Book may be real numbers (as they were property) whereas for other social classes the numbers given are more probably heads of households (creating challenges in estimating overall population figures). In westernmost Devon and in Cornwall, slave numbers were particularly high, at around 20% of the population. Somerset, Devon and Cornwall between them had about 25% of all the slaves recorded in England by Domesday Book. This may reflect the legacy of the West Saxon suppression of western British society. But it may alternatively reflect the regional workings of manorial economy: where landlords worked much of their land as demesne, they needed large labour forces. So Domesday Book may simply be revealing that in the south-western region landlords had been less inclined in the late Saxon period to lease manors to other men than was the case in more easterly shires (see below).

From wills and other sources, we know that kings, bishops and thegnly land-owners regularly freed slaves as an act of piety. Bishop Aelfwold of Crediton, for example, freed all slaves on his episcopal estates through his will (1012). Cornwall and Devon provide much of our knowledge of this practice in England generally, from records of manumissions of various dates entered in the Bodmin Gospels and in bishop Leofric's "Missal" (helpfully summarised with Della Hooke's collection of charter bounds). They are interesting not only because they reveal pious acts, but also because they reveal slaves – both men and women – as real people with personal names and places of origin. Around 1045, for example, a slave called Edwy (together with his wife and child) won his freedom at Topsham from his master, Hunewine, presumably a thegn. The ealdorman Ordgar, who died in 971, freed slaves from various estates when anticipating death in his sick-bed at Bradstone. These included Cunsie from Lifton, Leofric from Sourton, Aelfgyth from Buckland, Small from Okehampton, Wifman from Bradstone, Byrhflaed from Trematon and Aelflaed from

Land and Rural Folk

Climsland. These last two were from Cornwall, the others from west Devon. Manumissions coincided with a religious occasion, and priests were normally present: this has implications for the locations of minster churches (see Chapter 3). Cross-roads (symbolic of freedom of choice?) may have been favoured locations for manumissions, since "at the four ways" was sometimes specified: Huna was freed at such a spot in Okehampton, as was Aethelgyfu at High Bray. Birhtric (presumably a thegn) freed Hroda at Coryton on the day after Pentecost mass; the eve or day of midsummer mass is mentioned in other instances. The Normans steadily abandoned traditional slavery, but in earlier times it had been prominent. Nevertheless, despite the impression which might be deduced from Domesday Book, Anglo-Saxon society did not consist of castes: there had been upward and downward mobility of individuals and families. Not only might slaves be freed, but ordinary freemen might fail and become slaves or might prosper and become *thegns*. And, despite these flexible social categories, as well as the growing importance of lordship over men, the role of kinship in society also remained significant. In Anglo-Saxon law, kin-groups remained important in the pursuit of justice for victims and in raising compensation when members were convicted of crimes.

In the Latin terminology and Norman framework of Domesday Book, we may look for English equivalents (see below), but it is not always easy to find everyday reality within the vocabulary of the sources. Behind Domesday's use of Latin lay data provided in English to administrators who spoke Norman-French: and thus the study of eleventh-century society has produced many challenges for many historians. One problem, mentioned above, lies in the paucity of "freemen" in Wessex according to Domesday Book: it is hard to imagine that the Conquest had seen the wholesale suppression of a class which, to judge from earlier and later sources, was numerous. The likely solution lies in a flexible definition of *villani* in 1086, compared with the stricter definition, which had emerged a century later, of villeins as a wholly unfree class. Domesday Book probably used the term as an inclusive description of various ranks which had in common the holding of some land. Some were descendants of the free men of earlier times, whose variants included *ceorls* and *geneats*. Other members of this class may have been the descendants of slaves who had been granted their freedom. To the compilers of Domesday, a *villanus* was the occupant of a *villa*, or vill. The word has been rendered in modern English by some commentators as "villager" but by others as "villan" so as not to assume the sort of settlement which these people occupied: a point significant in a Devon context (below). W.G. Hoskins thought that most of the Devon freeholders visible in later medieval records had emerged during agricultural expansion in the twelfth and thirteenth centuries. But Harold Fox argued that large numbers of freemen's families were of earlier origin, hidden within Domesday's terminology of *villani*, or simply not mentioned at all: when they emerge in later medieval sources they often lived in farms whose names contained Old English elements, often personal names, but which were not identified by name in Domesday Book. Such farm-names would not be created much after about 1100 and must have been part of the late Saxon landscape (see also below).

Estate Organisation

Early signs of manorialism (a word coined by historians from the medieval word *manerium*, manor) can be seen in Ine's law-code of around 690, which distinguished various rural classes, and it was re-inforced in the ninth and tenth centuries by growing emphasis on lordship: in this period appears the term *landhlaford,* landlord, which was to be a building-block of rural society for the next thousand years. It was in the century and a half before the Norman Conquest that we find an enlarged thegnly class as landlords of the smaller estates whose creation, out of earlier and larger territories, was often recorded in charters (see Chapter 4). Under local and resident lords manorialism evolved further, the distinction between the demesne and tenants' lands, and the obligations of tenants towards their lords, becoming defining features. But manorialism did not develop uniformly in all parts of England. An early eleventh century tract, *Rectitudines Singularum Personarum* (loosely, "the rights and ranks of people") outlines rural society and appended to it was a text entitled *Gerefa* describing the work of the manor reeve and related agricultural routines (though this is as much a piece of literary composition as of practical estate management). From these and other sources, Old English terms can be broadly equated with the Latin language of Domesday Book: *geneat* with *liber homo; kotsetla* with *bordarius* or *cottarius*; *gebur* with *villanus*; *theow* and *thrall* with *servus.* The category of *ceorl*, well-known from earlier times, probably embraced various groups of the free rural population. In the later pre-Norman period, we can easily appreciate that fragmentation of large estates into smaller ones, with a more local and resident landlord class concerned about estate management and productivity, led to the emergence of written tracts with more specific definitions of rural society. In the twelfth century, legal

Land and Rural Folk

developments placed great emphasis on distinguishing the free from the unfree: thus an extensive class of "serfs" emerged in manorial society: but they were not slaves in the older sense, their servility lying in the services they owed and restrictions imposed on them by their lords.

Another line of continuous development can be seen in the way large numbers of estates were administered at this time. Whereas later, from the thirteenth century, land-owners commonly exploited their estates directly through manorial officials, in the Norman period it was common for estates to be leased out to intermediaries. These "landlords" drew as much profit as they could from the land, and paid fixed sums in return to the land-owners. This practice had started in pre-Norman England and is well-documented from the tenth century. As explained earlier (see Chapter 4) all land originally belonged to kings, and thus their kingdoms, and was called *folcland*. Such land might be granted out and held by a charter, thus becoming bookland (from *boc* – the charter). The church or thegnly family who held bookland might lease some of it out for fixed periods, in which case it was known as loanland (from Old English *laen*). These practices were well-established by the ninth century: they occur in a famous passage in king Alfred's Preface to St. Augustine's Soliloquies. In Norman England, leasing was further developed and became a very popular method of land management.

The compilers of Domesday Book may have struggled with harmonising real places and the names of the manor in which they lay. The population of such places included *villani*, so the places were, in that sense, vills (see above). But whereas the *Exchequer* Domesday simply gives the place-name, *Exon* called each a *mansio*: it is hard to see what this meant if not the "manor" at some stage in its evolution: something characterised by a house, presumably belonging to a landlord or his representative. We can see, from later sources, that manors did not always coincide with discrete settlements, especially in regions of dispersed settlement. But the situation was also more complex still: when Domesday tells us, with apparent simplicity, that in 1086 a Norman lord had either retained a manor in demesne or sub-let it to a tenant, the situation was often more elaborate, as revealed by other sources or the later history of an estate. First, the manor sub-let might be held for feudal tenure (personal, especially military service) or it might be held for rent. If the latter, it was analogous with a lease. Second, sub-tenancies might become hereditary, or they might be held for one life (during which the year 1086 fell). Again, if the latter, this was analogous with a lease. Third, where a sub-tenancy became hereditary, its holders might lease it out to other parties. Fourth, and important, probably large numbers of manors said by Domesday to be held in demesne by their lords were actually leased out to (un-named) third parties for fixed rents, in continuation of an Anglo-Saxon practice: thus a whole layer of society crucial to land management is not identified in Domesday Book at all.

It is impossible to say in detail how these various and sometimes semi-visible practices applied in Devon around 1066. The high level of slavery in Devon and Cornwall, probably linked to demesne farming (see above), may reveal that leasing had been less popular here and that rural society remained somewhat old-fashioned. Leases were not, however, wholly absent, particularly with ecclesiastical lords: early in the eleventh century, Holcombe (Rogus) was leased out by Sherborne and Uffculme was leased out by Glastonbury. Later evidence of lingering rural conservatism appears in a fascinating episode from around 1180, illuminated by Frank Stenton and H.P.R. Finberg. In a charter of Tavistock Abbey, the twelve jurors referred to were said to come "from four neighbouring *bochaland*". Elsewhere in England, and probably in the south west by this date, the origins of jurors would be given as vills or as manors. Here we see an on-going identification of manors, in the vernacular culture, with the "booklands" of the Anglo-Saxon period from which they had earlier arisen. The Domesday compilers, too, sometimes equated old and new terminology. *Exon*'s description of the manor of Bovey (Tracey) reveals that the lands of fifteen thegns had been added to it: these lands were called not only manors (*mansiones*) but also booklands *(bochelandis)*. In Devon, some lands held by *boc* had also created their own place-names: there are fourteen Buckland names, and it is significant that nine were later parish names, underlining the sequence discussed elsewhere (see Chapter 3) of: grant, estate, private church and parish.

Estate bounds (see Fig. 5.3)

The background to this situation lay in the lands described in Anglo-Saxon charters (see Chapter 4). In Devon and Cornwall, fewer charters survive than in areas further east and those with boundary clauses are mainly of tenth- and eleventh-century date. The charter was evidence of a grant but did not constitute the grant itself (presumably made in a witnessed ceremony): thus some charters are "forgeries" in the sense that they were written long after the purported date of the grant, but sometimes to demonstrate genuine title for which no evidence survived. Some boundary clauses are not of the same date as their charter. Charters could be lost: Exeter's minster library was destroyed, probably in the Danish attack on the city in 1003, which lead to the later "re-creation" of charters under bishop Leofric. Despite all these difficulties, charters are a crucial source in several respects. They illuminate the growth of Saxon land-holding and, later, the relationship with parish evolution (see Chapters 3 & 4). They provide us with early names of estates and individual places, as well as of man-made and natural features in the countryside. The real rural environment emerges in their boundary clauses, whereas in Domesday Book it has been disaggregated. We read, in the Devonian boundary clauses assembled by Della Hooke, of valleys and prominent trees, of old sites such as barrows and hill-forts, and of contemporary communications – river fords (*ford*), bridges (*brycg*), lanes and paths (*lane; path*), streets (*straet*), simple roads (*weg*) and more major highways (*herepath*). The charter boundaries contain a variety of topographical and land-use terms, as well as plant and animal names, which illuminate the living countryside. Animals and birds make frequent appearances: eel, calf, cock, crow, deer, eagle, fox, vixen, hawk, hen, raven, rook, lamb, ram, sheep, pig, wolf and snake are all referred to. Relating to agriculture, we encounter Old English words for: acre, grove, hedge or fence, boundary, woods and clearings in them, mills, moors, pools and waste. A whole array of tree- and plant-life appears, including: oak, apple, ash, alder, broom, birch, elder, fern, bramble, hazel, heather, holly, ivy, lime, maple, reed/rush, crab-apple, thorn and willow.

It seems fair to assume that the various uses of hedges known in later times emerged in Anglo-Saxon times. Hedge species were of value for making medicines, food and drink, they could be used for making dyes, as well as being essential sources of material for wooden artefacts and building supplies. Hedges were far more than simply land divisions: they were a considerable resource. Some features which appear in charter boundaries marked the edges of, or divisions within, fields and field-systems (the word *landscearu* evolved into the later word "landscore"). But, in Devon, charter references to hedges are not common, though points on the boundaries described are quite often single trees or clumps of trees (as, for example, in the charters for Crediton, Topsham, Uplyme, Culmstock, Ipplepen and Clyst St Mary). In the charter for Sandford (930), reference is made to a *haga* at *broom leah* and another *haga* at Downhayne. The word *haga* also occurs in the Ashford/Boehill charter (958) and in another Sandford charter (997). Although one translation of this word is "hedge" it can also mean an enclosure (that is, what a hedge or fence achieves). It is difficult to know what this paucity of

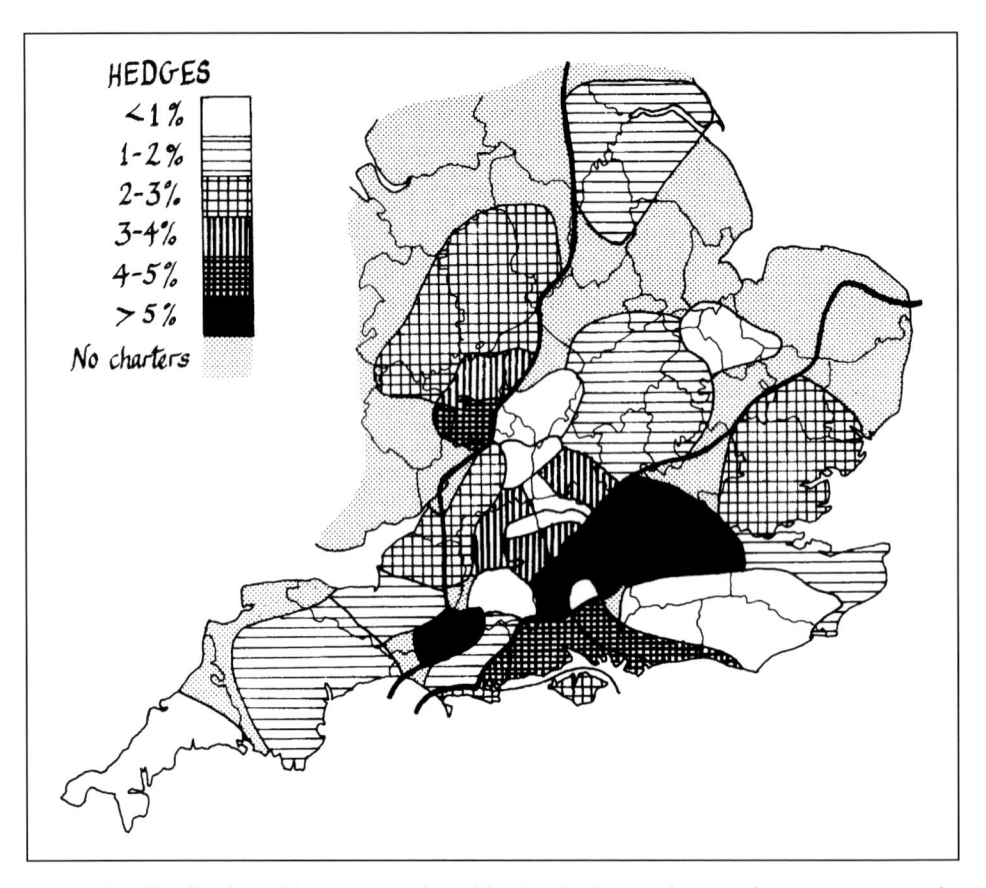

5.3: The distribution of hedges mentioned in Anglo-Saxon charters (as a percentage of all features mentioned in boundaries), mapped in Rackham 1986. By permission of the author and J.M. Dent, a division of The Orion Publishing Group. In common with some other shires, Devon's figure is a low one.

references to hedges in Devon at this time actually means: was there a real paucity of hedges, or alternatively a custom of not referring to them in this way, perhaps because, in contrast, they were so numerous that they could not be used as distinctive points in the landscape? It is also difficult to relate this issue to the appearance of hedges which is presumed to have accompanied the emergence of the historic landscape of farms and hamlets in this period (see below). The distribution of hedges referred to in English charter bounds, as proportions of points named on boundaries, has been mapped by Oliver Rackham. He noted variety in the density of distributions between shires: Devon's low numbers are matched in some others and are not, in themselves, unusual; there were even fewer in Cornwall.

Another way to approach the emergence of hedges is through their dating by botanical species counting. This methodology, promoted and described by Pollard, Hooper and Moore, has been much quoted, mis-quoted, applied and mis-applied: and it remains controversial. Despite the *caveats* emphasised by the pioneers, and despite their own subsequent refinement of ideas, it became widely believed that a new species of tree or shrub becomes established in a thirty-metre length of hedge approximately every hundred years. But, in practice, there are several important variables: variations in soils and local woodland *flora;* variations in new hedge-building practices (single or multi-species planting); variations in subsequent practices of hedge-management; a fundamental distinction between woodland-relic hedges and newly-created ones; a tempting, but dangerous, assumption that a still-living hedge is a primary feature of a boundary which appears in a dated document. Case-studies in Devon were amongst those which Max Hooper and others first used in testing hedge-dating, but W.G. Hoskins was drawing public attention to the subject even before their own work was published: for example, hedges at Chumhill Farm, Bratton Fleming, seemed to be datable from the tenth century onwards. Lesley Chapman has pursued studies at Sampford Courtenay and Braunton and has suggested that some hedges here were first laid in the eleventh century. A balanced view of the problems and possibilities of hedge studies by Barnes and Williamson suggests, however, that seeking "century-specific" dates may be pointless, given all the inherent complexities of the methodology. It is better to regard species-counting simply as a way of distinguishing relative hedge chronology in a particular location, as well of establishing *possible* origins for hedges: medieval, early modern and modern. It is probably best of all not to regard hedge-study as primarily a dating method, but to regard the botanical evidence provided by hedges as indicators of vegetational history in particular areas, as well as indicators of regionally-variant hedge-building traditions. A detailed examination by Michelmore and Proctor at Farleigh Farm, Chudleigh, where the hedges are probably of later medieval origins onwards, has demonstrated the value of this more ecological approach in a Devonian case-study.

Comparisons of charters with Domesday evidence can reveal considerable continuity in the history of some estates, as Della Hooke has shown. Relating the boundary clauses of Saxon charters to the Domesday and later landscape can be pursued through comparison of the hidation of an estate give in Domesday Book and the number of hides (called *mansi* or *cassati*) given in a charter relating to the same place: the figures are sometimes identical. The mapping of estate boundaries against the modern map creates a very vivid link with conditions more than a thousand years old: notable Devon examples where significant continuity is found, either of boundary courses or recognisable boundary points, include Crediton, the South Hams, Sandford, Topsham, Uplyme, Stoke Canon, Upton Pyne, Ottery St Mary, Seaton, Dawlish and several others. The fascination of estate reconstruction from charters and Domesday Book, in Devon as elsewhere, goes back a very long way and continues to attract new effort, as seen, for example in Paul Luscombe's recent study of south Devon. It was suggested by W.G. Hoskins that some of the earlier and larger estates, pre-dating this more fragmented tenurial landscape (on which, see also Chapter 4), may be hinted at in place-name evidence, particularly where these reveal related name-forms. Examples put forward by him include (Bishop's) Tawton and Tawstock in north Devon, Plympton and Plymstock in the south, and Cullompton and Culmstock in the east. Such names, applied eventually to tenurially unrelated places (sometimes even in different hundreds), may indicate earlier and very extensive estates, occupying rich valley locations, dating from the very beginning of the Saxon period and conceivably even of Damnonian origin. This fascinating possibility is deserving of further examination.

Domesday: limitations and strengths (see Fig. 5.4)

As well as revealing rural society, Domesday Book also tells us a little of the settlement pattern which it occupied. But here, major problems of interpretation are encountered because Domesday was a record not of real landscapes but of dismembered ones: it broke the environment down into its components of estates, their occupants and resources, but without revealing the topographical context in which they lay or the nature of the settlements themselves. While it is notable that Domesday gives us the first occurrence of so many place-names, much debate has been pursued, from the late nineteenth century to the present day, as to what these names actually represented. It is now generally agreed that they were the "umbrella" labels for rural estates which often contained far more settlement components than were identified individually: we are seeing, through these names, the vills and manors which emerge more fully in documentation of later centuries, and which were the framework of land-holding and tax liability. Thus there have arisen fascinating, but often controversial, debates involving historians, archaeologists and geographers concerning the rural landscapes of the eleventh century.

The limitations inherent in Domesday Book sometimes emerge directly from its own data. A classic Devon example is Crediton, discussed in this context also by W.G. Hoskins, whose description in 1086 can be linked to its charter and boundary clause, and thence to an extensive tract of countryside (see also Chapters 3, 6 and Appendix 2). Domesday Book gives us the overall name of Crediton and perhaps four hundred rural occupants. It is inconceivable that all these people lived in the settlement which had grown around the minster church there: they must surely have lived mainly in the numerous settlements scattered around this enormous estate, not separately identified in 1086 but emerging by name only at a later date. In England generally, we find numerous settlement names in twelfth- and later-century sources which did not appear in 1086. This used to be much-quoted to support the idea that the twelfth and thirteenth centuries saw a massive expansion of rural settlement, with hitherto unoccupied waste land being colonised for the first time. But the evidence for extensive exploitation of the English countryside in prehistoric, Romano-British and early medieval times, which has accumulated in the last thirty years, makes this hypothesis an inadequate general explanation. There was certainly growth of agriculture and settlement, sustained by a period of strong economy and population growth, between the eleventh and thirteenth centuries. But research based on the appearance of place-names whose form actually *suggests* new settlements, as well as on cautious comparisons of Domesday population estimates with those derived from fourteenth century tax records, has shown that this growth varied regionally: in Devon the apparent rate of growth had been less than in Cornwall and in areas to its east. The situation in Devon is made more complicated because the county is less well-provided than some others with twelfth- and thirteenth-century sources which can reveal this growth in detail. And this, in turn, makes assessing the true situation in the eleventh century more challenging. But it seems likely that, as in some other shires, many of the Devon places which emerge only in later sources had long existed: in 1086 they had simply been parts of an estate which had a single name for tenurial and tax purposes. Many such places had, in any case, Old English name elements. Harold Fox emphasised this line of argument for Devon, highlighting the pre-Norman period, rather than later, for the creation of many of the countryside's farms (see above). In Devon, Domesday names about 1,000 "places", but it has been estimated that this disguises a true figure of between 2,000 and 3,000.

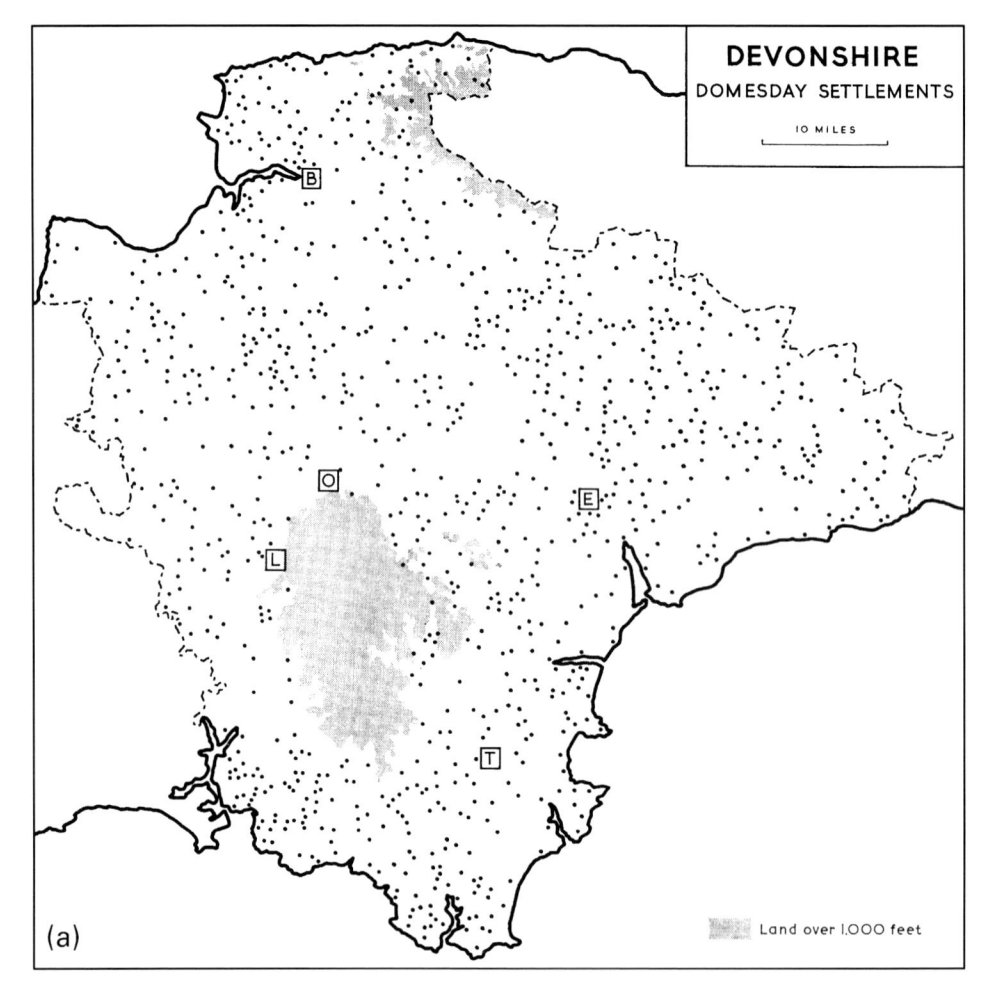

5.4: The Devonian distributions in 1086 of (a) named places and (b; *opposite*) population mapped by G.R. Versey from the data of Domesday Book in Darby and Welldon Finn (eds) 1967. By permission of Cambridge University Press.

When located on a map, however, the Domesday names provide our first overall view of Devonian settlement history (as elsewhere). In Devon, the majority of those names still survive in our present-day landscapes, applied to a parish, village, or (more frequently, given the predominantly dispersed settlement pattern) to a hamlet or farm. The Domesday names, despite difficulties in their interpretation, remain a very vivid link with the Anglo-Saxon past.

The "land behind Domesday Book" was everywhere subject to many variations in its agricultural applications, in its tenure, its physical form and

DEVONSHIRE
DOMESDAY POPULATION
10 MILES

POPULATION PER SQUARE MILE

10 – 15
5 – 10
2·5 – 5
UNDER 2·5

(b)

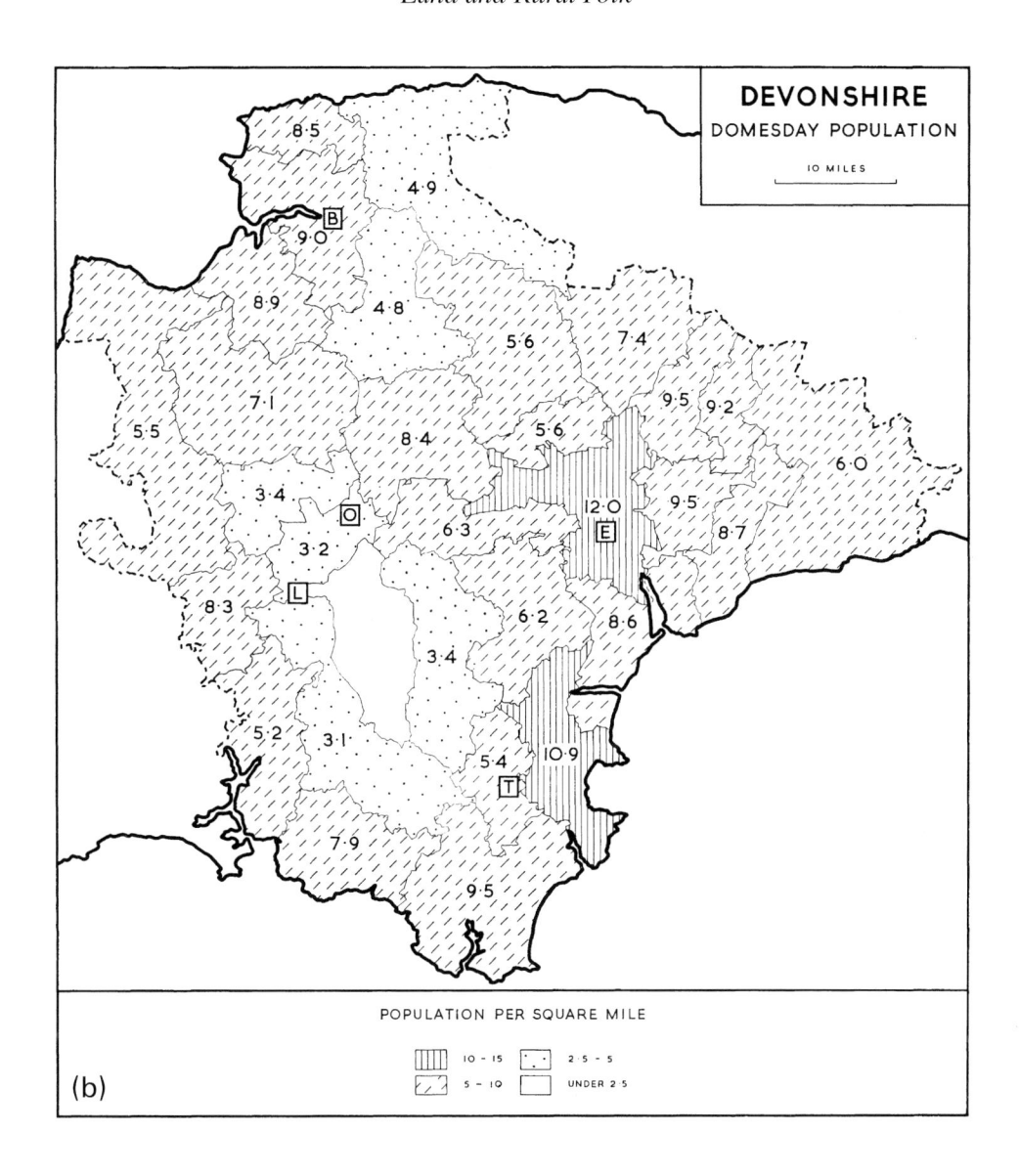

in the society which it contained. Because shires were the basic building-block of the English state by the eleventh century, it is tempting to seek generalisations about a shire in comparison with others. But within a shire, particularly a large one such as Devon with major variations in topography, there were also internal contrasts, in population, land-use, social classes and much else, deriving from differences in the underlying geology and surface soils, in the nature of the topography, altitude and drainage. The maps published in Henry Darby and Rex Welldon Finn's *Domesday*

Geography of South West England, illustrating population distribution and named places, as well as land use and agricultural resources, are immensely revealing. Two are reproduced with this chapter. They achieve, despite some simplification inherent in their complation, a visual and spatial rendering of data which was not construed in these terms when compiled in the eleventh century. Across England as a whole, Domesday Book reveals a great many variations in regional economy and society. These include, for example, considerable variety in the size of peasant land-holdings. Earlier in the eleventh century, from the tract known as *Rectitudines Singularum Personarum*, we have an outline of a society in which the roles of rural classes and occupations are described, as on a great working estate. Manorial organisation was clearly well-advanced, but variations in practice from one place to another were acknowledged – "The estate-law is fixed on each estate: at some places . . . it is heavier, at some places, also, lighter, because not all customs about estates are alike." The rich variety of English country life, apparent in later and better-documented periods, was well-established before the Norman Conquest.

Land-use (see Fig. 5.5)

Revealing though the mapping of rural resources described in Domesday Book may be, more detailed observations about the actual organisation of agriculture in specific places are more difficult to make. It has been noted that in both Devon and Cornwall the number of plough-lands recorded by Domesday was far greater than that of plough-teams. In Cornwall, there were only half as many teams as lands and, in Devon, three-quarters. It has also been noted that in west Somerset and Devon, the numbers of ploughlands seem excessive, by general English standards, in relation to the hidation of the manors. An interpretation suggested by Michael Costen is that the hidation survived from assessments imposed early in the Saxon absorption of the area whereas the extent of ploughlands reflected an expansion of agriculture which had occurred later on in the pre-Norman period. Considerations of land-assessment apart, however, a strong likelihood is that these discrepancies reveal extensive infield-outfield agriculture, where not all the available land for arable was in use at any one time. In 958, king Eadwig granted lands at Ashford and Boehill (near Sampford Peverell, east Devon) to a certain Eadheah. The description concluded "there are many hills (*manega hylla*) there that one may plough (*man erien maeg*)" – indicating land available for arable but not always in use: perhaps an indication of infield-outfield practice, or perhaps of what is now called convertible husbandry (see below). The use of infield/outfield agriculture is supported by later documentary references to this practice, as well as by vestiges of the distinction seen on early maps and in the landscape itself. At the Exmoor site of Badgworthy (just on the Devon side of the border with Somerset) studies by Hazel Riley and Robert Wilson-North have noted that the remains of a deserted hamlet are accompanied not only by intensively-used adjacent fields but also by enclosures taken in from the moorland which bear signs of more sporadic ploughing. Its name – meaning Baga's Farm – is of Saxon origin and so might be the core of its field systems. At Holne Moor, on the eastern side of Dartmoor, fieldwork by Andrew Fleming and Nicholas Ralph on a relict landscape also identified intakes of land, possibly of tenth-century date, from lower-lying farms in the Venford valley. These new lobe-shaped fields, which were divided into strips for cultivation, were the first stage in a sequence of developments culminating in thirteenth-century boundaries which can be correlated with documented events. The tenth-century origin is thus an estimation, rather than independently datable.

Other broad deductions may be made about the period in question, such as the importance of transhumance, that is the seasonal movement of people and their livestock, in the economy of estates having access both to upland and lowland topographies. The early, but brief, physical description of Britain given by Gildas (on whom, see Chapter 2) included two pertinent observations on his contemporary environment. First, there was "vigorous agriculture", by which he presumably meant arable cultivation. Second, he noted "mountains well suited to alternating the pastures of livestock", by which he presumably meant transhumance. Exmoor certainly had documented transhumance in later times, and perhaps with much earlier origins. Peter Herring has pointed out its importance in early medieval Cornwall, using evidence of place-names, upland hut-groups and the apportionment of upland resources amongst the Cornish hundredal divisions. It has been noted by Susan Pearce and others that some estate (later parish) boundaries around the fringe of Dartmoor seem deliberately to have been formed so as to include complementary types of upland and lowland resource. Here, the movement of livestock to upland pasture in the summer months, which was documented in later centuries, no doubt had a long evolution stretching back to the Saxon and perhaps Dumnonian periods. Another form of transhumance (some would say, its true form) involved movement to land linked with, but quite separate from the home

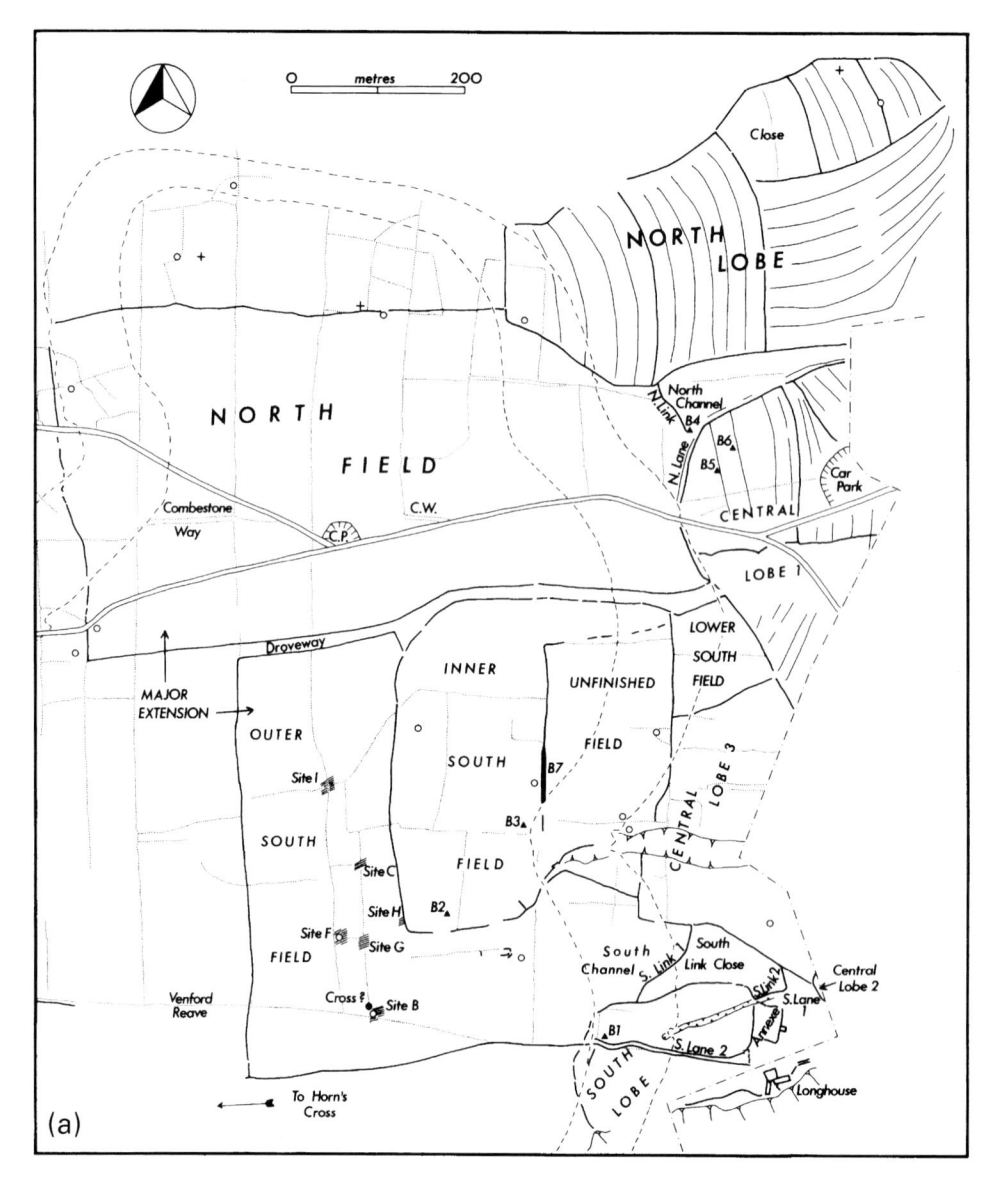

5.5: (a) Survey and (b; *opposite*) chronological interpretation from Fleming's and Ralph's 1982 study of the field systems at Holne Moor. These grew from tenth-century or earlier origins to their full extent of c. 1300.
By permission of the authors, the Society for Medieval Archaeology and Maney Publishing, Leeds.

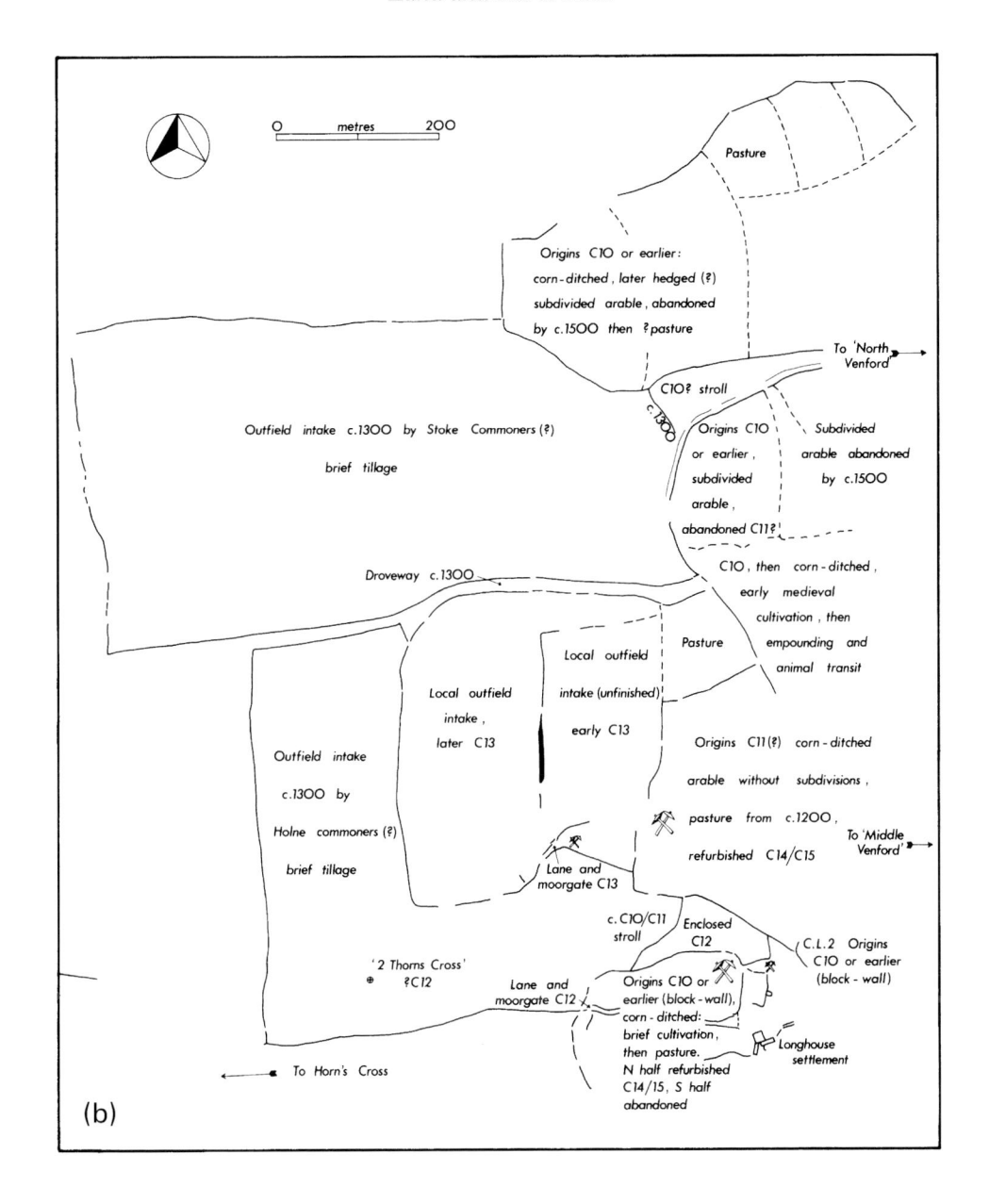

manor, land where people and livestock actually stayed for part of the year. The charter of king Cnut, recording a grant of land at Meavy in 1031 to the thegn, Aethelric, referred to "the way of the people of Buckland [Monachorum]", probably a route used by Buckland's inhabitants to take livestock up to Dartmoor for grazing. Some Dartmoor land, within a (difficult-to-date) charter boundary for *Peadingtun*, later belonged to

Paignton manor: from this, it was suggested by Harold Fox that Paignton had an upland summer pasture resource, separate from its main centre, from an early date. It is notable, as Susan Pearce has pointed out, that the *Peadingtun* estate did not give rise to a (surviving) place-name: whereas its southern boundary conforms to later parishes (including Ashburton) its northern one does not – here the eventual parishes (including Widecombe and Manaton) extend deeper into the moorland, revealing further moorland colonization subsequent to the earlier definition of the charter boundary. Harold Fox argued that the arrangement found at Paignton applied at other lowland south Devon places in the pre-Norman period, including Kenton, Cockington and Ipplepen, whose manors also had detached territories on Dartmoor. In the 1960s, the excavators of deserted hamlets at Hound Tor, and elsewhere on the moorlands, argued that the permanent thirteenth-century settlements had been preceded by less substantial, seasonally-occupied structures, perhaps of late Saxon origin. But this idea has been controversial and other excavations have suggested that the archaeological features in question may not be earlier at all, but contemporary with the later stone long-houses. Nevertheless, transhumance arrangements may well have been more widespread than we can know. Another indicator may be the fragmented nature of some hundreds (see Chapter 4) which had outlying portions in different terrains, as noted by Frank Thorn. The hundreds of Kerswell (later Haytor) and Exminster, for example, had detached Dartmoor portions, in the vicinities of Widecombe and Chagford respectively. Such considerations can now be matched by other evidence: study of preserved Dartmoor pollens from the Merrivale and Royal Tor areas, by Ben Geary and others, has suggested use of the moorland for pastures in the period before the expansion of arable agriculture there in the thirteenth century. This, however, could simply reflect the general practice of Dartmoor grazing which was available to virtually all Devonians. Harold Fox considered that this right, documented in the later middle ages, had much earlier origins. This seems highly likely, and provides another useful illumination of the rural situation in the Anglo-Saxon period.

Oddly, Dartmoor (now Devon's most famous landscape) does not appear by name in Domesday Book (it is named a century later), which reminds us of Domesday's specific tenurial and financial purposes. It may be a reasonable assumption, from their later status as royal forests, that both Dartmoor and Exmoor had provided royal-controlled hunting resources in the pre-Norman period, but this is not absolutely clear. Though neither territory had a royal hunting lodge (as at Cheddar in Somerset) the *burh* at

Lydford would have provided a suitable base for Dartmoor and Withypool (in the Somerset part of Exmoor) was said by Domesday Book to have been held by three "foresters" in 1066. Dartmoor and Exmoor seem not to have been designated as Norman royal forests by 1086, though they had been by 1130 (presumably by Henry I). The new forest law enhanced the high-status character of hunting wild animals, no longer available to poorer people. Harold Fox observed that the development of markets on the fringe of Dartmoor in the later Anglo-Saxon period was likely to have been stimulated by transhumance: at the end of each summer, livestock would be brought down from the higher ground, and any not destined for return to its home estate would be sold. Thus places such as Tavistock and Lydford would receive further economic stimulus to that already provided by their (respectively) ecclesiastical and administrative functions. Lydford's market certainly existed given its status as a *burh*. Tavistock's, though not actually documented until around 1100, probably had earlier origins (see below).

Evolution of Settlement (see Figs. 5.6, 5.7)

Challenging but crucial though Domesday Book and related documentary evidence is to our view of pre-Norman rural Devon, we can also approach this difficult subject through general comparisons with developments elsewhere in England as well as through archaeological methods (fieldwork, excavation and environmental evidence) and historical geography (especially comparing the present-day landscape with early maps). The twentieth century witnessed a massive re-assessment of English settlement history. At its start, much faith was placed in cultural explanations of settlement variations. It was confidently supposed that the late Romano-British and western Celtic-speaking populations had managed their agriculture in small, individually-owned fields whilst living in scattered farms and hamlets. With the arrival of the Anglo-Saxons, it was believed, came also very quickly nucleated villages and larger open-field systems – classic indicators of "Englishness". This interpretation was based largely on a back-projection of regional differences which were known in later centuries, on the known history of post-medieval open-field enclosure, and on the evidence of Ordnance Survey mapping which, by the late nineteenth century, had provided an unprecedented view of settlement form and distribution. It was enormously influential down to the 1960s and it coloured everything written down to that time, including ideas about the south west of England. W.G. Hoskins's enormously important *Making of the English Landscape* (1955) came towards the end of that period. Slightly earlier, in 1952, Hoskins had already published an essay about Devon entitled "The Making of the Agrarian Landscape". Though it now seems somewhat dated in some of its assumptions (for example, about the nature of early "English" impact and of later "expansion") it remains a remarkable composition, written with great empathy for its subject-matter. It illuminates the character of the Devonshire countryside, with its variety of landscapes, farms, hamlets, villages and field-systems. It also laid out discussion of major research themes which, fifty years later, are still under scrutiny: for example, the origin of large estates and their evolution, through fragmentation, into smaller ones and eventually into parishes.

From the 1970s onwards, many lines of enquiry, pursued by many people, changed the normally accepted picture in basic ways and with two major effects, one chronological, the other geographical. Christopher Taylor's commentaries in his 1988 edition of Hoskins's famous book, for example, reveal many advances in knowledge in the intervening years. First, it became clear that the early Anglo-Saxon period witnessed no settlement or agrarian revolution: the fifth, sixth and seventh centuries were characterised largely by continuity, under the ownership of new land-owning classes, in landscapes dominated by dispersed settlement. But starting as early as the seventh century in some areas, and developing more obviously by the ninth and tenth, parts of England (especially the midlands) underwent big changes organised by land-owners: populations aggregated into nucleated settlements surrounded by open-fields in which all had a share. This was probably driven by awareness that land could be farmed more profitably in this way in a period of rising population and increasing economic prosperity: in its later stages it coincided also with the growth of towns and trade. Creation of nucleations was not, however, confined to the pre-Norman period: planned villages were being laid out in some areas in the twelfth and thirteenth centuries (for example, following William the Conqueror's "harrying of the north"). But, second, and equally important, was the geographical re-assessment of the subject. Whereas at first, the village with open fields had been regarded as the norm against which dispersed settlement was regarded as peripheral, eventually the true and peculiar nature of nucleated settlement was emphasised. The latter was never "typically English" but dominated a central belt of England, orientated north-south, a territory of rich soils with flexible arable and pasture applications. In Kent, in East Anglia, in the south-west, along the Welsh border, and in parts of the north, landscapes were never dominated by nucleated villages but by a network of dispersed settlement, the principle of which was inherited from very early times. The latter was really the national norm, with nucleation added to it in some regions. Thus, the visible differences were not ethnic and cultural in origin, but rather the product of complex economic and agrarian processes stretching over many centuries.

In applying to Devon this overview of England, some complications arise. First, English influence was irrelevant in what, elsewhere, was the early Anglo-Saxon period. Devon's absorption in Wessex was begun in the seventh century but completed only in the eighth, so that issues of early continuity, or a lack of it, are as much Dumnonian as West Saxon. Second, there is the complete lack of excavated data from early medieval "English" settlements to put alongside that from some early post-Roman Dumnonian sites. Third, despite its location outside the classic "nucleated settlement zone" of central England, and despite an overwhelmingly dispersed settlement pattern, Devon is not wholly without nucleated villages and these need explanation. Fourth, research has in some cases shown that dispersed settlement can, in its surviving form, be the product of relatively recent change, and we must beware the temptation of uncritically assuming the "ancientness" of the Devon countryside. The complexity of Devon's patterns of settlements and fields emerges clearly when viewed against national overviews of settlement and its regional variations, for example as carried out by Roberts and Wrathmell.

Aerial reconaissance in Devon, much of it by Frances Griffith, has shown the importance of Romano-British rural settlements in sub-rectilinear enclosures, now revealed from the air as crop-marks, especially in the south and east of the county. How long this settlement form outlived the Roman period is not clear. The example (illustrated) near Ashburton and Buckfastleigh poses interesting questions. In later prehistoric and early historic times, small embanked settlements were also characteristic of Devon landscapes. In Cornwall, such sites are called "rounds" because of their commonly circular form. In Devon, they were less regular in shape, and their upland counterparts, on and around Exmoor, were hillslope enclosures of various types. They survive in great numbers, fossilized in hedgebanks, or as earthworks, or as ploughed-out remains visible from the air, and their use extended over a very long period. A recently excavated example near Parracombe, north Devon, was occupied in the Bronze Age. The site at Rudge, Morchard Bishop, excavated by Malcolm Todd,

5.6: Aerial photograph of a double-ditched enclosure between Ashburton and Buckfastleigh, now surviving as a crop-mark. Although we do not know its date of occupation, Frances Griffith observed that the earthworks must have been upstanding into the medieval period, since the site's perimeter clearly influences the line of the subsequent field boundary in the historic landscape. Photograph: Frances Griffith (20/7/84), copyright Devon County Council.

was occupied in the Romano-British period. At Hayes Farm, near Clyst Honiton in Devon, excavation of a complex of features by Shirley Simpson and others revealed occupation from the Bronze Age down to the early post-Roman period. The Romano-British farm was represented by a sub-rectilinear enclosure; over this lay a curvilinear ditch, dated between the fifth and seventh centuries, which represented another settlement form: a sub-circular enclosure. A site at Dunkeswell, east Devon, was excavated on the presumption of a late prehistoric date but turned out to be a thirteenth-century domestic enclosure. Other examples of enclosed farms dating from as late as the thirteenth century are also known, as at West Wortha (Germansweek, Cornwall) and those excavated in advance of construction of the Roadford reservoir in west Devon. The most fully studied individual

Land and Rural Folk

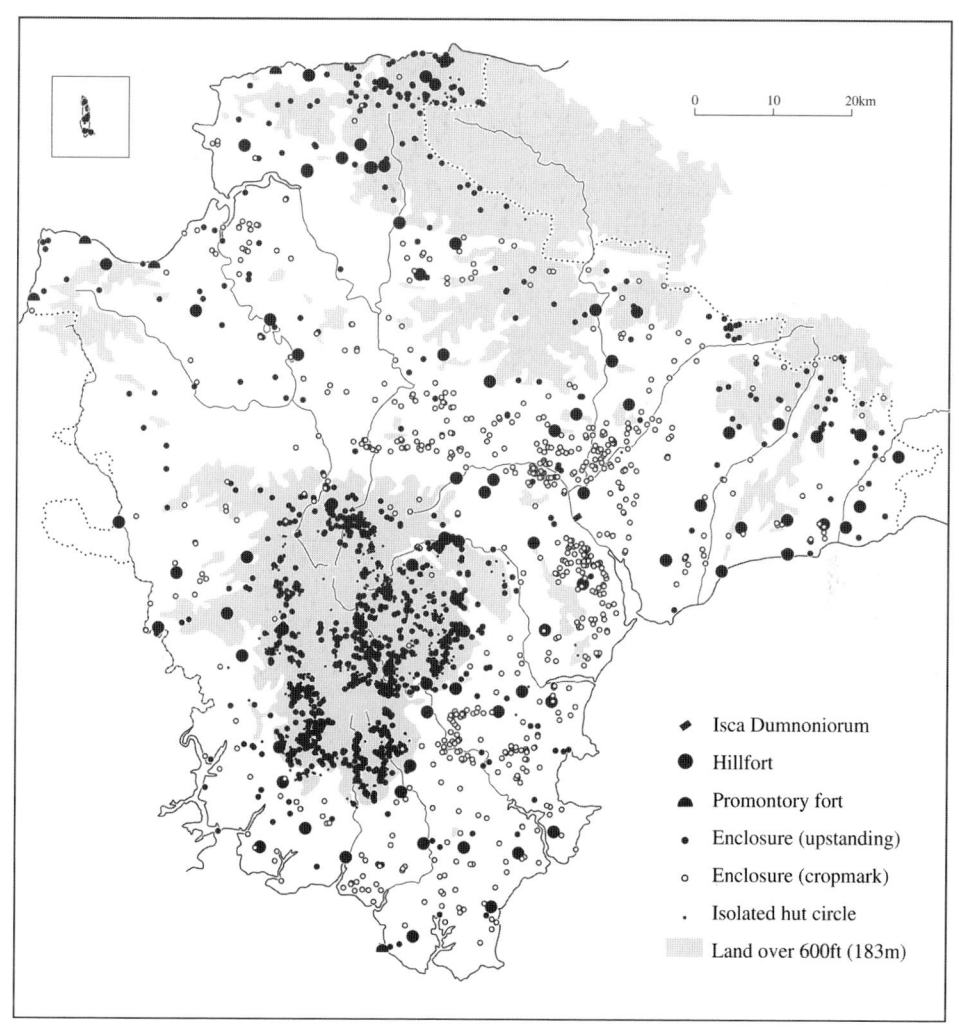

5.7: Settlement in Devon from c. 2,500 BC to AD 600, mapped by Frances Griffith and Henrietta Quinnell in Kain & Ravenhill (eds) 1999. By permission of the authors, University of Exeter Press and Roger Kain. The enclosure sites (upstanding or cropmarks) are particularly relevant to the broad theme of early medieval rural settlement, though the numbers occupied at that time cannot be determined.

site of this form in the south west, that excavated at Trethurgy in Cornwall by Henrietta Quinnell, was occupied from the second to sixth centuries. Its occupants built very substantial oval-shaped houses with roof-spans equivalent to those of much later medieval timber-framed buildings. Whether this evidence indirectly illuminates contemporary Devon, or is particular to Cornwall, is not clear.

In both counties, however, the general impression is that this form of settlement, an enclosed farmstead or small group of farms, eventually went out of use during the post-Roman period, to be replaced by the unenclosed farms and hamlets which were the foundation of the medieval settlement pattern. This process can be regarded as the south-western equivalent of what elsewhere is sometimes called "the middle Saxon shift" of settlement. The argument involves, however, a major methodological difficulty: we cannot be certain that the south-western enclosed sites had stood alone. They may have been accompanied by unenclosed farms which were abandoned and have left no trace. Putative earlier unenclosed farms may conceivably have been the precursors of some of the later known settlements, so that our impression of settlement shift may be slightly skewed. We suffer major ignorance of the chronology, causes and cultural context of rural change in Devon in this period. In Cornwall, research by Peter Rose, Ann Preston-Jones, Peter Herring and Oliver Padel has suggested that the shift from "rounds" to a pattern of hamlets and farms (commonly with *tre* place-names) started in the seventh century, with subsequent expansion of settlement producing more Celtic place-names and eventually some English ones. The historic Cornish landscape of small hamlets with field systems ploughed in strips, seems to have been born in this period. In Cornwall, change obviously developed within a Dumnonian context since it was totally uninfluenced by Wessex at that date. Indeed, the fact that in Cornwall, "rounds" were abandoned just as comprehensively as were their equivalents in Devon, despite the significantly later influence of West Saxon lordship in Cornwall, may be an indication that the change in both counties related to developments within indigenous, rather than in-coming society.

Comparable developments in Devon may have been already well advanced, under Dumnonian lordship, within the estates which Saxon landlords took over in the later seventh and eighth centuries. Perhaps the figures whose names occur on inscribed memorial stones (see Chapters 2 & 3) represented a class of landlord who, for whatever reason, began some re-organisation of habitation on their lands, just as landlords in parts of England did in the Saxon period and again in the later middle ages. Amongst the possible functions which these memorials may have had, it has been suggested that they may have been an important visible expression of the Dumnonian landlords' imprint on land ownership and land organization. Increasingly, settlement and related social studies have emphasised the role of lordship in the evolution of both the Anglo-

Land and Rural Folk

Saxon and later medieval landscape: Rosamund Faith has published a fine overview of this theme, of equal value to both historians and archaeologists. We should not be surprised if this important theme had its roots, in Devon, in the pre-English era. Equally, we should not overlook the possible impact on rural settlement created by circumstances beyond human control, such as the plagues recorded in the sixth and seventh centuries (see chapter 2). If any depopulation resulted from death or emigration, landlords as well as peasant families might introduce changes as part of subsequent re-population and economic recovery (we may bear in mind here the analogy of some later medieval settlement changes, in areas affected by the various disasters of the fourteenth century). On the other hand, it is impossible to be certain what the actual effects of such changes may have been and palaeo-environmental evidence in some places suggests much continuity in land-use (see below).

Up until the shift away from enclosed settlements, in whatever circumstances it occurred, there seems to have been a continuous evolution of settlement from prehistoric times onwards. The landscapes of west Somerset and Devon bore little imprint of Romanisation except for the city of Exeter and a few villa estates such as those known at Crediton, Holcombe, Otterton and Seaton (the last variously interpreted as villa, road-station or port settlement). Frances Griffith and Henrietta Quinnell, surveying the overall pattern of Romano-British settlement, have suggested that in Devon we should think more in terms of "Roman-style buildings" than in terms of classic "villas". The overview by Jeremy Taylor, of rural settlement in Roman Britain, has underlined the distinction between the south-western region, with its small, dispersed settlements, limited urban and villa growth, and the more developed settlement forms found further east. Dumnonia had been conservative in the Romano-British period, and so, at first, it probably remained under its post-Roman rulers and land-owners. Whether the eventual shift from enclosed sites to new farms and hamlets was solely driven by economic motives within Dumnonian society, whether there was some imitation of conditions further east, perhaps perceived to be more efficient, or whether the gradual arrival of new English landlords was a crucial development, we cannot easily tell. It is interesting, nevertheless, that people felt able to abandon the relative security of enclosed settlement (which they had valued even under the *pax Romana*) and this must reflect a fairly well-ordered society in Dumnonian and early West Saxon times, despite the more turbulent impression of the period which easily arises from historical study. Of fundamental importance is the fact that nothing of great significance seems to have changed in the Devonian countryside as a result of the "end" of Roman Britain in the fifth century. Indeed, as discussed above (see Chapter 2), the south west simply continued with a second "Roman" experience, and, in one sense, Roman Britain here did not "end".

Sadly, severe difficulties of interpretation remain. We do not know exactly how late some enclosed settlements in Devon may have been occupied, and, although it is generally not assumed to be the case, we do not know for certain whether any Romano-British or post-Roman farms underlie those of the later landscape. A mere handful of examples amongst the known enclosed sites have any real dating evidence. New West Saxon lords, and the immigrants who came with them, may have added to the development of a new type of farmstead which gradually superseded the old. But details of the shift from enclosed sites, with no obvious attached field systems, to the farms and hamlets, surrounded by fields, which created (as in Cornwall) the historic landscape in Devon, remain generally obscure. The process noted in Cornwall, in which land originally abandoned along with enclosed settlements was later re-colonised as the farms and hamlets with *tre* names grew in number, may well have occurred in Devon. Since a very small number of *tre* place-names survived the subsequent and widespread English re-naming of the Devon countryside, it is possible that here, too, the creation of at least the earliest new farms and hamlets took place in a Dumnonian rather than an English context.

Finally, it is worth noting that some commentators have stressed continuity of settlement location, across very long periods of time. In this approach, attention is paid not to the form of the settlement sites, but to the sorts of topographies which they occupied, chosen for pragmatic reasons of land exploitation. Pioneering studies of Devon and Cornwall by William Ravenhill revealed a consistent popularity of valley-sites, including valley-heads and sides, and particularly inter-fluvial spur ends, for settlements and land-use widely ranging in date, from later prehistoric to later medieval times. Sam Turner's examination of historic landscapes in Cornwall, Devon and Western Wessex has also shown that, regardless of apparently British or English origin, the early medieval focus of settlement, agriculture and church was the valley. There was no obvious cultural or ethnic difference in landscape use once the earlier landscape of enclosed settlements had gone. These approaches are a useful reminder that farming communities – regardless of period, social culture, political and economic organisation, race, religion, language and all the other criteria by which archaeologists, historians and geographers analyse societies – face the common challenge of extracting from their surroundings a viable means of survival.

In analysing early society in Devon, a major methodological barrier comes to the fore. South-western material culture of this period available to archaeologists is very thin indeed: it comes from some hillforts with post-Roman occupation and from a few excavated "rounds" of this date. Thereafter, there occurs a blank in the record until occupation in the later Saxon urban *burhs* is encountered. We have absolutely nothing from so-called "English" rural settlement of early date. The putative pre-Norman phases of Dartmoor farmsteads, once thought to be primary structures related to transhumance, have probably been discredited as a result of further excavation (see above). Devon has had no Anglo-Saxon rural settlement excavations such as occur in central Wessex; no royal palace excavation, as at Cheddar in Somerset; nothing excavated in the Anglo-Danish context, as at the coastal site of Mawgan Porth in north Cornwall; no medieval settlement evolution project, as at Shapwick in Somerset. We can only assume that the thegnly and peasant buildings of pre-Norman Devon had mainly employed the stone, timber and cob technology which we see in the excavated and standing structures of later centuries. The problem of identification is made worse by the absence from Devon of a native rural pottery industry in the immediately post-Roman centuries, which removes the common occupation-indicator, of date and cultural context, heavily relied upon by fieldworkers and excavators and so important in counties to the east, as well as in Cornwall, which had more continuous native pottery traditions. But in Devon, it was only in the late Saxon period that ceramic production resumed. By the later tenth century, Exeter had a Saxo-Norman pottery industry and pottery was also being produced on the Devon-Somerset border: both types are found also in other Devon *burhs* in the eleventh century. The population's presumed reliance, in earlier centuries, on wooden, metal and leather vessels is an interesting cultural phenomenon, but an unhelpful one to academic rural studies.

However, research in palaeo-environmental studies (which interpret preserved pollens, plant and animal remains) has now been drawn into the debate in a most productive manner, particularly with regard to pollen evidence. Earlier work of this sort was concentrated on the uplands of Dartmoor and Exmoor, frequently revealing more about the prehistoric than later periods. The implications of pollen analysis for the historic period on the Exmoor highlands are, however, significant: development of scrubland on the high moor in the fifth and sixth centuries suggests a decline in established pastoral farming in the very early post-Roman period, with such areas being re-colonised later, for both arable and pastoral exploitation, in the thirteenth century. But Dartmoor and Exmoor cannot be said to be typical of the countryside as a whole. Other pollen studies backed up by scientific dating, by Ralph Fyfe, Anthony Brown and Stephen Rippon, in contrast, have been concentrated in mid-Devon and on the fringe of Exmoor (Molland, Rackenford and Parracombe). These have revealed that in the late prehistoric, Romano-British and immediately post-Roman centuries, there was a little arable cultivation, but land-use was dominated by pastoral farming. The implication is that the enclosed settlements and hillslope enclosures of this period were the nuclei of a mainly pastoral rural economy and their apparent lack of associated field systems is thus explicable. The steeper valley sides had some woodland cover, though the extent to which this was actively managed is unclear. In the lowlands of mid-Devon, this situation remained unchanged until some time in the seventh or eighth century, when the proportions of cereal pollens increased markedly: now the growing of wheat, oats, rye and barley became significant alongside management of grass pasture and woodland. This trend to a major arable component appeared on the Exmoor fringes somewhat later, in the tenth century. Thus, over several generations, agriculture was being both intensified and diversified. But extrapolation from this agrarian evolution to inferences about settlement evolution has to be cautious: in the first instance, agricultural change presumably began from old settlements and a period of transition may have been lengthy. It has, however, been tentatively suggested by Stephen Rippon and his collaborators that this is when the historic landscape of the medieval period was born: the earlier pattern of enclosed settlements giving way to that of the farms, hamlets and associated fields of later centuries. It has also been suggested that this may also have been when south-western farming practices, known or deduced from written sources in the later middle ages, may have developed. In particular, the late medieval practice which agrarian historians call convertible husbandry may now have taken hold. This involved rotational use of fields, producing alternately cereal and grass crops, in a variation of the infield-outfield system which could be applied both to small enclosed fields and to small open field systems. Whether or not this hypothesis about the origin of convertible husbandry is valid, it is certainly the case that the practice was eminently suited to the settlement pattern of the south west which was to emerge: its flexibility was adaptable to a range of farm, hamlet and village occupation.

This palaeo-environmental research, however, raises a crucial question. Since the lowland change occurred mainly in the eighth century, starting in the seventh, how do we (or indeed, should we?) separate the contributions to it made by Dumnonian and West Saxon society? This was precisely when, according to historical record (see Chapter 2) English landlordship in Devon was established more widely throughout the shire, from its seventh-century beginnings and through its eighth-century consolidation. Did new landlords complete a process begun by their Dumnonian predecessors, establishing new farms and hamlets, now with new fields supporting a mixed economy and a major arable component? Or were the new Saxon landlords themselves the innovators? It has long now been accepted that, in eastern, central and southern England, the English did not immediately change the countryside which they took over in the fifth and sixth centuries. But in the south-west, the relative lateness of English influence may mean that two processes coincided: first, the extension of English influence into British territory in Devon; second the implementation here of rural changes by native society which were now made more complex – and perhaps faster? – by increasing changes in lordship. Hopefully, further palaeo-environmental work, if suitable deposits can be found around Devon, might refine our view of these processes. In such a large county, with many different environments ranging from the moorlands to the rich soils of the Exe valley and south Devon, agrarian and settlement change would not have progressed in identical ways nor at the same rate. Is it fanciful to imagine that, in some parts of Devon at some stage in this period, there was a coincidence of agrarian and broader cultural themes? Perhaps new English landlords, and forward-thinking British ones, regarded not only the older settlement pattern, but also its inhabitants, as old-fashioned and inferior. They would have found in this attitude an additional motivation and justification for the pursuit of landscape change, just as was to be the case with improvers and modernisers of agricultures and industries in more recent centuries.

Farms, hamlets, villages (Figs. 5.8, 5.9, 5.10, 5.11, 5.12)

Finally, a fundamental issue must be faced: the relationship and relative antiquity of farms, hamlets, villages and their associated field systems. As mentioned earlier, Domesday Book does not help here since it disaggregates real places into their various components. Only in later centuries do some documents, especially rental surveys, become more specific about the

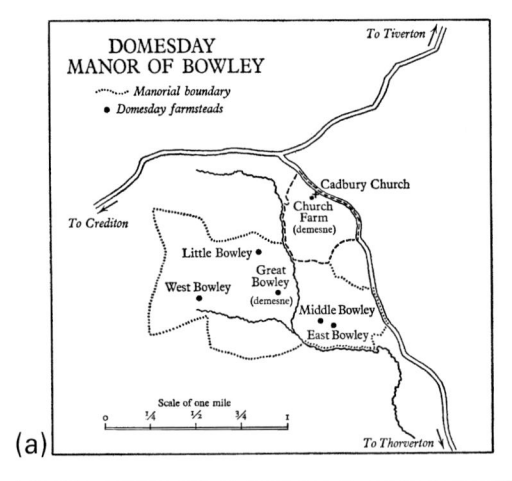

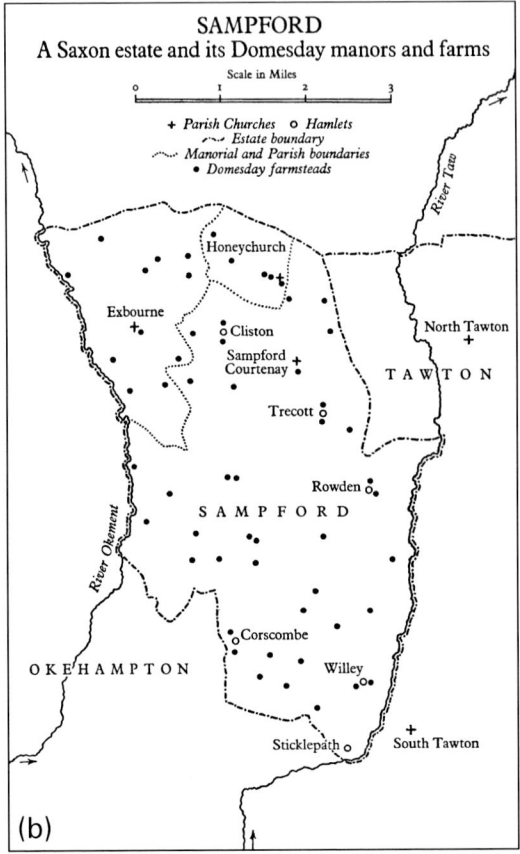

5.8: Two of Hoskins's case-studies illustrating his 1963 "Highland Zone in Domesday Book" essay at (a) Bowley and (b) Sampford Courtenay. Hoskins argued continuity of single farmstead siting over many centuries. By permission of Palgrave-Macmillan.

Land and Rural Folk

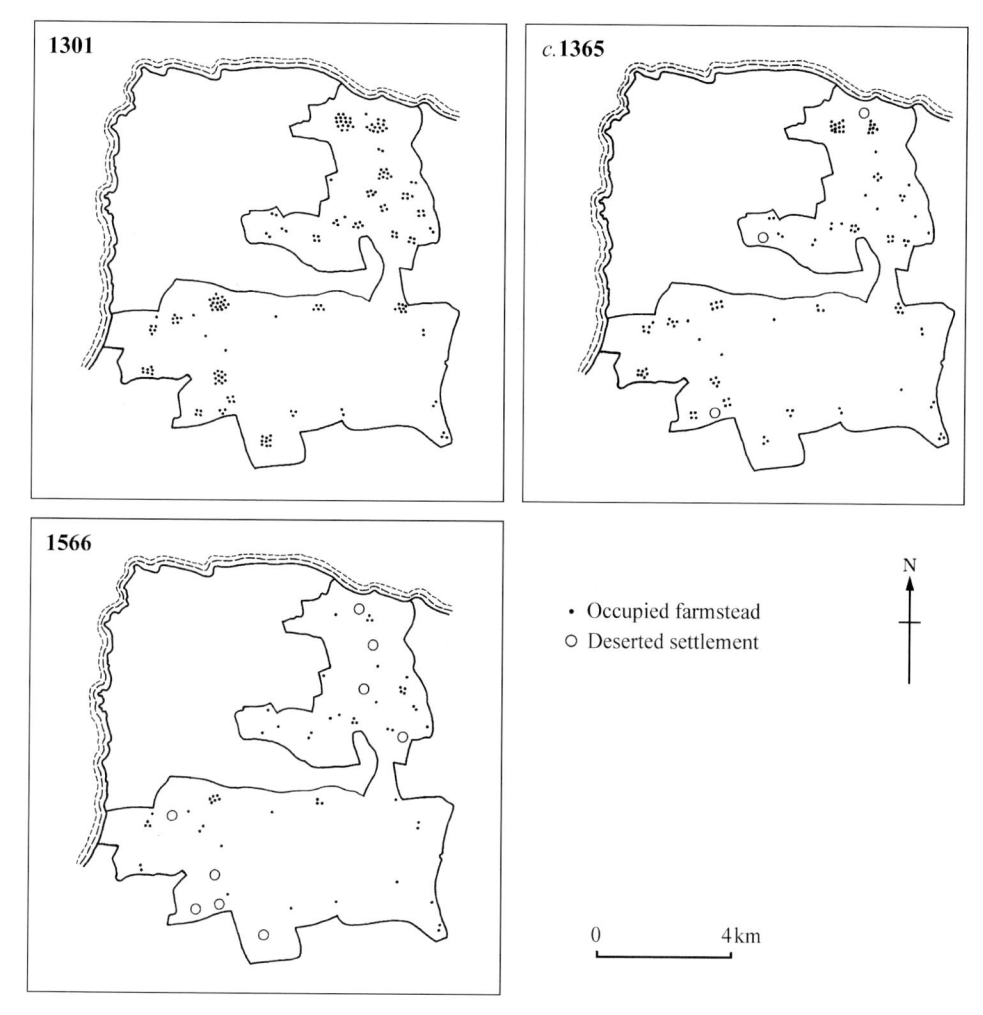

5.9: Fox's 1983 study of Hartland revealed that individual farmsteads can be the end-result of shrinkage of settlements which, in the middle ages, had been larger nucleated hamlets. By permission of the author.

actual groupings of habitations. While we can be confident that a Domesday description of a holding with a tiny number of people and resources must, by definition, relate to a farm or the smallest of hamlets, descriptions of more populous places leave crucial questions unanswered: did the population live scattered around the estate in numerous farms and small hamlets? Or in a smaller number of bigger hamlets? Or mainly in one nucleation – a village? A traditional method of addressing these problems was to look at Tithe Maps and early Ordnance Survey maps of the nineteenth century and see

239

what these places were like immediately prior to modern landscape changes. On this basis, for example, it was argued by W.G. Hoskins that, since the numbers of *villani* in a Domesday description sometimes correlated with the numbers of early nineteenth-century farms, the surviving patterns of farms might be very ancient indeed, revealing to us where the late Saxon population actually lived. This hypothesis was explored both in relation to some small manors, such as Bowley (north of Exeter), Eggbeer (west of Exeter), Rashleigh (in the Taw valley) and Rockbeare (in east Devon), and to some large ones such as Sampford Courtenay and Chittlehampton. The demesne farm of 1066/86 was commonly identifiable as the "Barton" farm of modern times, and in some cases groups of cottages arranged around a small open space might be the direct successors to habitations of Domesday cottars.

Using these case-studies, Hoskins suggested that a high proportion of Devon's farms had late Saxon antecedents, and possibly earlier origins still. This is quite likely to be true in some cases, but case-studies of different sorts, in both Cornwall and Devon, have emphasised the original importance of hamlets rather than the farms we now see. In Hartland, for example, examined by Harold Fox, documentary sources (particularly rental surveys) dating from the thirteenth to sixteenth centuries reveal shrinkage and disintegration of nucleated hamlets, of which the isolated farms of the modern landscape are but the surviving remnants. Demonstration of this process, through contemporary documents, provides a major warning against assuming that from a nineteenth-century map (or even from the landscape itself) we can leap backwards a thousand years. Archaeological fieldwork on Exmoor, where there are considerable remains of relict settlement within a living environment, has also suggested that single farms still in use, or abandoned in modern times, may often be the surviving remains of medieval hamlets, though the date of origin of the latter is still unknown. A similar pattern has been observed in the Wolf valley, in west Devon, where surviving farmsteads were studied in advance of construction of the Roadford reservoir. From the late thirteenth century, when written sources are more plentiful for Devon's countryside, we can see the existence of the farms and hamlets, which still dominate today's landscape, in great numbers. It is a reasonable assumption that both forms of settlement had also been plentiful in pre-Norman times. We are accustomed to posing questions about "village origins" in England, but questions about "hamlet origins" are equally as valid. Hamlets have been increasingly recognised as the basic building block of the historic landscape in south west England, but

5.10: Aerial photograph of the hamlet at South Hole, near Hartland. The hamlet has been increasingly recognised as the crucial building-block of settlement patterns in those parts of England, such as Devon, which did not develop many large nucleated villages. Photograph: Frances Griffith (22/12/86), copyright Devon County Council.

the processes of their formation are imperfectly understood. They may have been organic growths as farms proliferated close to each other over a period of time. The farms of a hamlet may have resulted from the fragmentation of an original, single unit. Or they may have been settlements created in this form under the influence of landlords. A Devon example at South Hole, near Hartland, is illustrated here.

Villages in Devon are yet another challenge. Hamlet- and farm-dominated though Devon's landscape became, there also developed some nucleated villages: for example, North Lew, Bradworthy and Hartland in the west, Silverton, Thorverton and Kentisbeare in the east, Braunton in the north, and Ugborough in the south. As these examples reveal, they are not confined to a particular area, soil-type or population-density zone. Such places, however, were never the only settlement within their immediately surrounding landscape, as was sometimes the case with midland English villages. Earlier commentators on Devon, including W.G. Hoskins, thought these villages were primary features of the West Saxon settlement, a new and planned form imposed by kings for new settlers in a hostile environment: many lay in large estates, identified through charter or Domesday evidence, which were sometimes hundredal centres with minster churches. Similar processes were assumed to lie behind villages in Cornwall, though at a slightly later date, such as Callington and Kilkhampton. According to this theory of Devon villages, virtually all the population listed in the Domesday description of such places could be identified safely as village inhabitants of settlements whose overall form, laid out by the mid-eighth century at the latest, had survived to modern times.

Attractive though this idea was, it has not withstood advances in knowledge of English rural settlement (outlined above). If Devon's villages are indeed pre-Norman in origin, they are much more likely to have been created in the tenth century by what a later age would call "improving landlords". This is the view now held about some parts of England, including eastern and southern Somerset: this area became part of England's village zone, but the very small settlements which survive in the west of Somerset reflect the Dumnonian tradition shared with Devon. Fieldwork directed by Michael Aston and Christopher Gerrard at Shapwick (and nearby

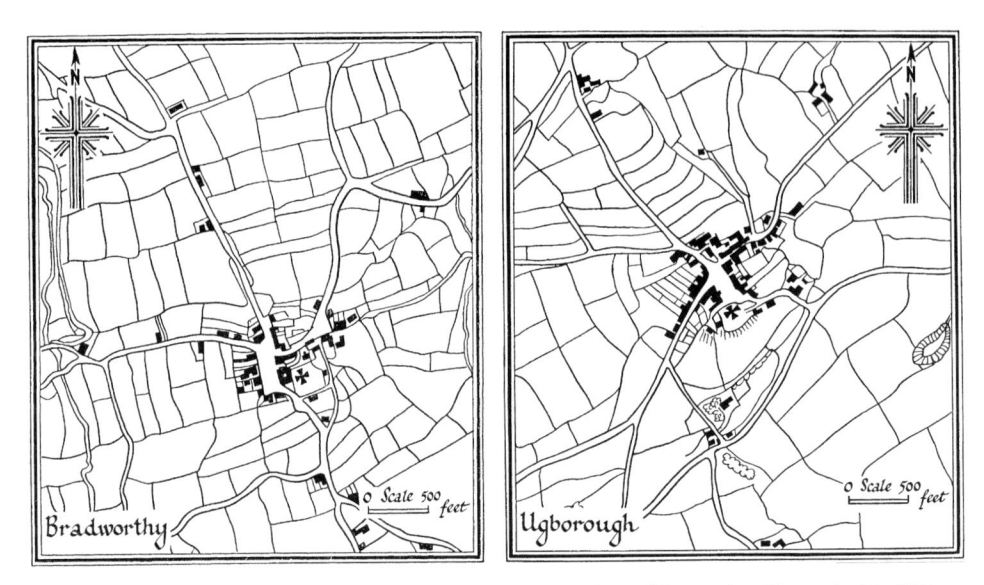

5.11: Two of Hoskins's examples from his 1952 discussion of Devon's villages in his "The Making of the Agrarian Landscape" essay: (a) Bradworthy and (b) Ugborough.

5.12: Aerial Photograph of Ugborough village, viewed from opposite direction to its orientation as illustrated in 5.11 (b). Photograph: Frances Griffith (13/7/84), copyright Devon County Council.

villages in Somerset) has suggested their creation in the tenth century, under the influence of its lords, the abbots of Glastonbury, out of earlier estates dominated by farmsteads, one of which had its name transferred to the new village. It may be no coincidence that one of Devon's villages, Braunton, was also a Glastonbury property in the ninth and tenth centuries (it was resumed by king Edgar in 973). So one way to think of Devonian village origins is as the result of particular processes within the history of estates, rather than as broad developments with a cultural basis. But we have no independent dating evidence for when the nucleated form of these Devon places originated. We must allow the possibility that they arose from seigneurial manipulation of landscapes and populations spread over long periods, perhaps starting in the late Anglo-Saxon period but also extending to the twelfth and thirteenth centuries, as elsewhere in England.

It was recently argued by Harold Fox that documentary sources may reveal some Devon settlements to have been villages in the later middle ages. But here we meet another complication, for in the latter period both Devon and Cornwall had many small boroughs, for which there is seigneurial charter or other documentary evidence, drawn to public attention many years ago by Maurice Beresford. While some grew into towns many remained very small and eventually failed. As settlements today, places in Devon such as South Zeal and Bow retain their borough plan and burgage plots but in a rural context. Such places were no bigger than the developed villages of some other shires, sometimes even smaller. So another possibility, for at least some of Devon's "villages", is that they represent settlements on their way to being given borough status, but lacking documented history which reveals this (presumably failed) objective to us. A critical need here is for more morphological analysis of these village plans, on the ground as well as from early maps and documents. This might show whether each was laid out in one operation or whether, as was often the case elsewhere in England, they evolved over time, with separate nuclei merging together or with secondary components added. Brian Roberts has drawn attention to the interest of Devon's villages in this respect in his discussion of settlement analysis at national level. In conjunction with further analysis in Devon, attention should be given to the functions of houses and house-plots at various dates within these settlements. Were they ever "villages" in the midland English sense of having all the farms in one place, surrounded by the fields? Or did they comprise, as they did in later centuries, a mixture of farms and cottages? In the midlands, farms were re-located as the fields were enclosed in relatively recent times. We should not overlook the possibility that some of Devon's farms also originated with the enclosure of formerly open fields, but at the much earlier date when enclosure was occurring (see below).

Fields and Field Systems *(see Figs. 5.13, 5.14, 5.15)*

We may also ask what sorts of field systems accompanied the late Saxon pattern of farms, hamlets and possibly villages? Fields and ploughing are the often-unsung heroes of history, without which settled populations could not have existed. It is a paradox, therefore, that fragments of early ploughs are a great rarity in the archaeological record: their wooden frames and metal tips were always valuable as re-cycled material. Very occasionally we see their imprint directly. Early medieval plough-marks, scored into the underlying sub-soil in the ninth and tenth centuries, were identified long ago by Peter

Fowler and Charles Thomas, excavating the early medieval settlement at Gwithian in Cornwall. This evidence reveals the use of the developed plough, with mould-board and coulter, by this date, which is very significant because there is still much debate about when and where this type of plough was developed (another field at Gwithian, first published as ploughed ridge and furrow, is now regarded as having spade-dug ridges). Mainly we see the history of ploughing through the fields which it created, and fields come in many shapes and sizes. They are also notoriously difficult to date, unless they have documentary evidence or clear stratigraphic relationships with independently datable landscape features. It is not surprising that theories on the evolution of different sorts of fields, expounded by Christopher Taylor and others, have been as contentious as those relating to the various types of settlement they accompanied.

The implications of Domesday Book and other sources for the use of infields and outfields in Devon was mentioned earlier, together with moorland landscape evidence for creation of new fields as intakes. The likely evolution of settlement described above suggests that the field systems of the medieval period began their evolution as the pastorally-based enclosed settlements of early times were replaced by a more arable-based economy centred on farms and hamlets. Individual farms might have one or two simple fields held as complete units by their owners or tenants. But hamlets of more than minimal size required fields with some level of co-operative organisation. In such a landscape it is not long before a network of roads, lanes and tracks is required and an early view of their development in Devon is provided by the mentions of roads and fords in Saxon charter boundaries (see above). It was shown many years ago by H.P.R. Finberg that, contrary to earlier arguments that the south west had no "open fields", open fields of sorts had certainly existed in many parts of Devon and Cornwall. Generally, however, these were not the large two- or three-field systems, with complex regulations, of the midland counties. They are more accurately described as field systems with sub-divided arable, for which there is plenty of medieval documentary evidence in Devon. Their fossilized remains can be seen in the Devon landscape today, where the curving courses of hedges preserve outlines of former groups of strips. And such features are vivid on some Tithe Maps, compiled when fewer of these fossilized remains had been destroyed. Whereas midland arable open fields were enclosed in relatively modern times, we know from studies of documentary evidence by Harold Fox that those of the south west were being enclosed at an early date. His work included an important

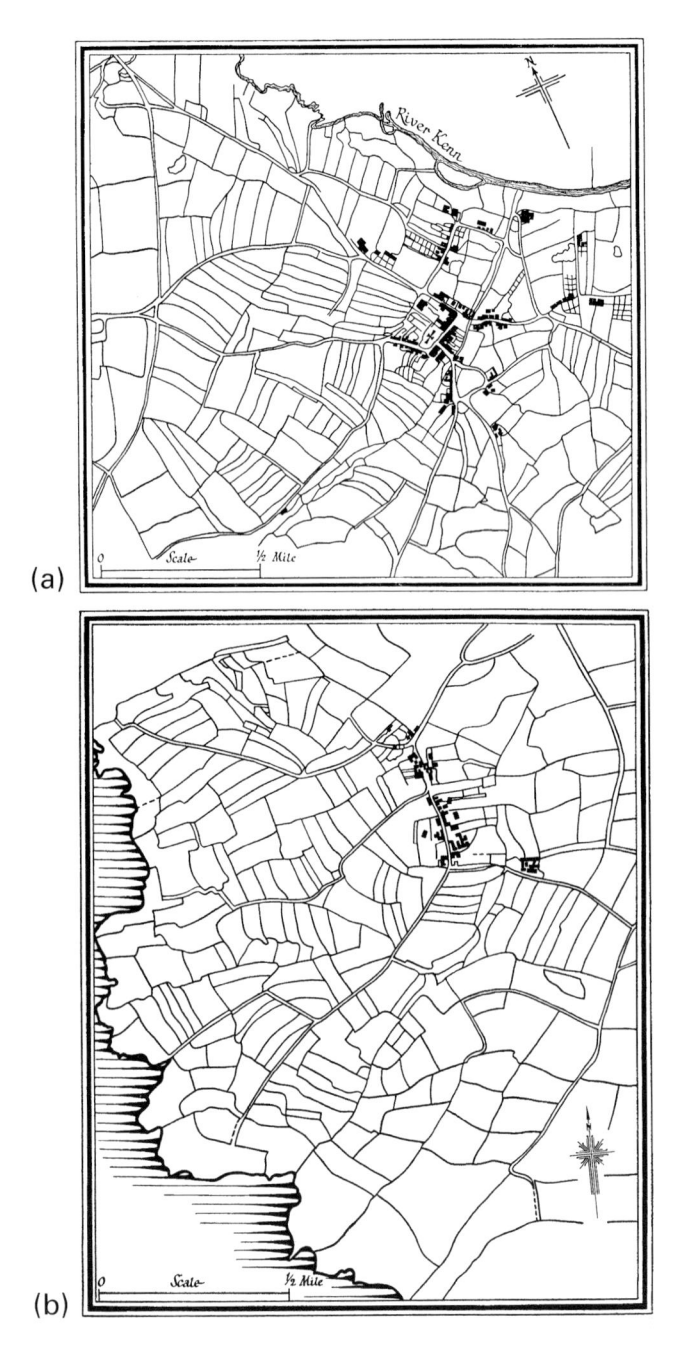

5.13: (a) the village of Kenton and (b) the hamlet of Down Thomas (near Wembury) as illustrated by Finberg in his 1952 "The Open Field in Devon" essay. This study, using map and documentary evidence, showed that sub-divided arable had been a common feature in medieval Devon, though this was not an area of midland-type classic open fields.

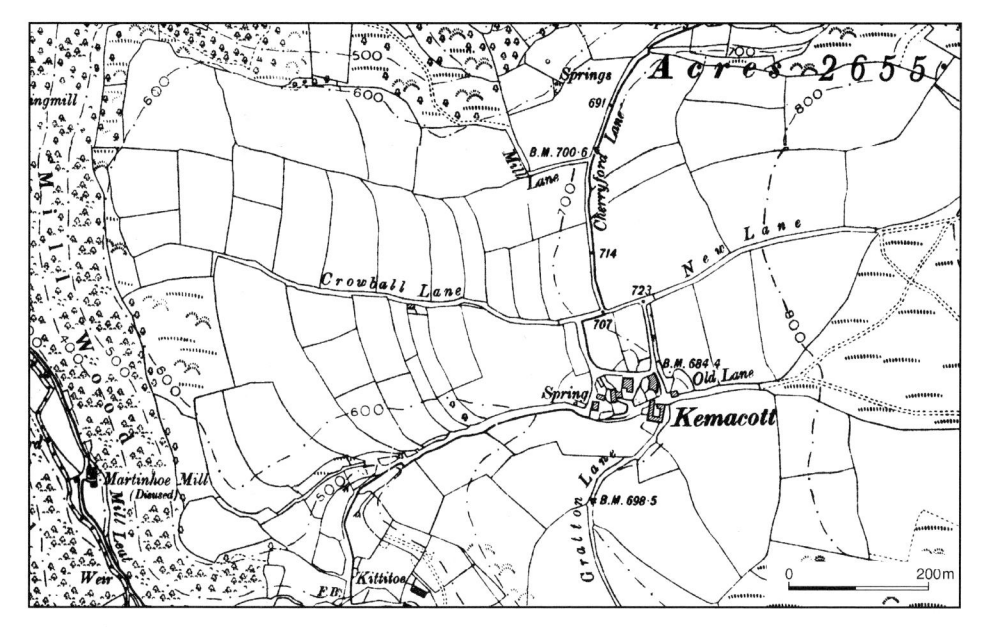

5.14: Kemacott, near Martinhoe, north Devon, as depicted by the Ordnance Survey around 1900, and studied by Martin Gillard, who comments: The Tithe Map of 1840 showed six different tenements whose holdings were interspersed among the narrow, curving strip-fields, and this pattern was still largely intact in the late nineteenth century. Kemacott was first mentioned in the Lay Subsidy Roll of 1330, but nearby Martinhoe had been named in Domesday Book. Many places first appearing in later medieval sources were probably much older, "hidden" within the descriptions of Domesday manors. Perhaps a hamlet such as Kemacott (whose name contains the Old English element –*cott*) existed by the late Anglo-Saxon period, occupied by some of Martinhoe's Domesday ploughlands, villeins and smallholders?

reminder, that we should not assume uniform developments within a shire, especially a large one such a Devon. Sub-divided arable in open fields had developed further in east and south Devon than in central and northern Devon. Neither was the documented process of arable enclosure uniform: it extended, in various phases, from the thirteenth to sixteenth centuries, and subsequent enclosure affected mainly wastes and pasture.

Evidence in the landscape and on maps also shows that these simple open fields had been developed not only at villages but, on an appropriate scale, at many hamlets. H.P.R. Finberg argued this, for example, at Kenton and Down Thomas (near Wembury) respectively. Since enclosure was in operation in some areas by the thirteenth century, there is at least a good chance that their origins lay in the Saxon period. Indeed, the burgage plots at some small thirteenth-century boroughs (see above) seem to have been created out of strips in fields, already therefore of some antiquity by this date. Sam Turner has quoted finds of thirteenth-fourteenth-century pottery from the enclosing field banks at Little Torrington, revealing the date at which the former open fields here were rendered obsolete. But such archaeological contributions are dependent upon chance finds and are not common. Finberg's study of open fields in Devon (above) showed them to have been associated with hamlets as well as villages, and subsequent studies have confirmed this impression. Research by Martin Gillard in north Devon (in an unpublished doctoral thesis) has shown that nineteenth-century maps depicted the fossilised forms of what had been very small open-field systems, for example at Kemacott, Martinhoe. Kemacott appears in documentary record only in the fourteenth century. It may well, however, have been a component of Martinhoe (which was named in Domesday Book) centuries before this. Its strip fields could similarly be of pre-Norman origin. Recent commentators on both Devon and Cornwall have been inclined to conclude that, while specific and independent dating evidence is elusive, the small open fields, ploughed in strips of sub-divided arable, later known to be associated with much of the hamlet-dominated settlement pattern, began their development as part of the same historic landscape in the eighth and subsequent centuries. They presumably did not develop simultaneously in all areas, and their creation was probably a long, drawn-out process. Equally, they never totally dominated Devon's early agrarian organisation: there was also plentiful use of small, enclosed fields in individual ownership or tenancy, associated with the farms and smaller hamlets in particular.

Limited evidence for open-field principles can be seen in Ine's law-code, around 700, but its interpretation is difficult. In tenth-century charters, in Wiltshire, Oxfordshire and Berkshire, characteristic features of fully-fledged open-field farming are mentioned: interspersed arable acres, headlands, furlongs and so on. It is now believed that open-field farming, on a bigger scale than seen associated with hamlets, developed in some parts of England in the late Saxon period, along with nucleated villages. One was the inevitable result of the other; the landlord putting all the peasant farmers together in one place would have made earlier agrarian arrangements redundant and necessitated a more communal approach. The village which stimulated this line of enquiry in the south west is Braunton. Here survives the Great Field, part of an originally more extensive open field system, in which unenclosed parcels of arable, separated by unploughed baulks, occupy a large flat terrain. In the early twentieth century it was argued that

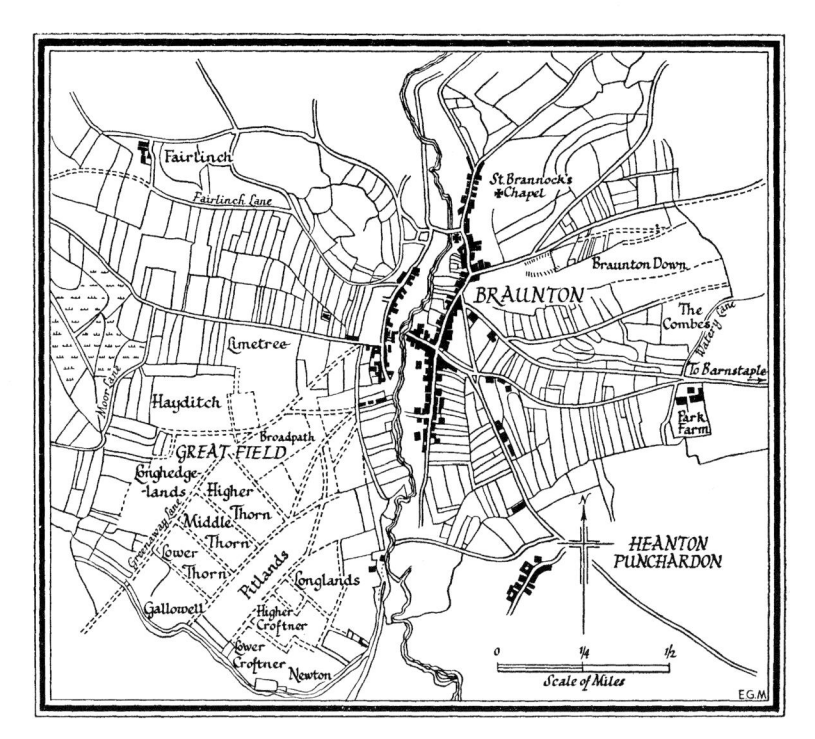

5.15: Braunton and its Great Field around 1900, as illustrated by Finberg in his 1952 "The Open Field in Devon" essay. Parts of the open fields of this nucleated village were long ago enclosed, but the Great Field retained its early character into modern times.

this field was a peculiar and "late" addition to Devon's landscape. But it was subsequently demonstrated by H.P.R. Finberg that the surviving portion, as well as the topography of adjacent areas, could be correlated in detail with a fourteenth-century survey. This showed a two-field system, spread across the two manors of which Braunton by then consisted, with the nucleated village at its centre. By that date, it was clearly well-established and Finberg suggested it was already ancient. Around Shapwick in Somerset, (quoted above, and also a Glastonbury abbey property) open fields were laid out with tenth-century villages. It is possible that Braunton's open fields arose with its village at the same time.

Countryside and Church *(See Figs. 5.16, 5.17)*

Some important aspects of landscape and settlement evolution have an ecclesiastical dimension. An obvious one is the way that large secular estates fragmented into smaller ones which, with the addition of private churches, paved the way for the medieval parishes (see Chapter 3). Another, expounded in a fascinating way by Sam Turner, concerns Christian perceptions of the environment. The historic landscape analysis of the south west and western Wessex, whose implications he has explored in various ways, suggested three zones identifiable from around the eighth century onwards: farmland, woodland and rough ground. The core agricultural zone contained most of the habitative place-names: *tre* names in Cornwall and a variety, including *tun* and others, in the (eventually) more English territories. This zone also contained the most popular situations for building churches: this was equally true in all territories. Turner has argued that contemporary society saw this situation not only in functional and practical terms, but also in spiritual ones. Thus, the core agricultural land, containing the churches, represented a "safe" and Christian environment. In contrast, the rough, less-managed ground on the peripheries of estates represented not only areas with a physical threat from wild animals and lawless people, but also areas with a cultural threat: containing the spirits of monsters associated with a distant pagan past as well as the spirits of criminals whose execution and burial places were often near estate boundaries. The various stone monuments which, especially before churches were numerous, were physical symbols of Christian society, perhaps helped to establish its authority over land in a very visible way: equally true of Dumnonian inscribed stones and of later Anglo-Saxon crosses (see Chapter 3). Where situated near roads and boundaries, as they sometimes were, perhaps they were intended to help extend protective Christian authority at the expense of the wild and unknown. Clearly, such arguments could be pursued to unrealistic lengths. But when handled cautiously, they contain an appealing way of linking religion and land, spirituality and practicality.

Another aspect of the on-going debate about settlement, landscape and the church concerns minsters (see Chapter 3) which, in England generally, are now seen as an important influence on the development of specialised nucleations before the later Anglo-Saxon expansion of towns and, in some regions, villages. It seems likely that they often attracted rural markets which crop up only sporadically in written sources: the market mentioned in Domesday Book at St. Stephen's (later Launceston) is a south-western example. Many places in England with known or probable pre-Norman minsters were rural market centres or small towns in the later middle ages: Devon examples include Tiverton, Cullompton, Axminster, Tavistock, Crediton and Plympton (though Plympton's growth arose also from the foundation of a Norman castle there). At Tavistock, whose early

Land and Rural Folk

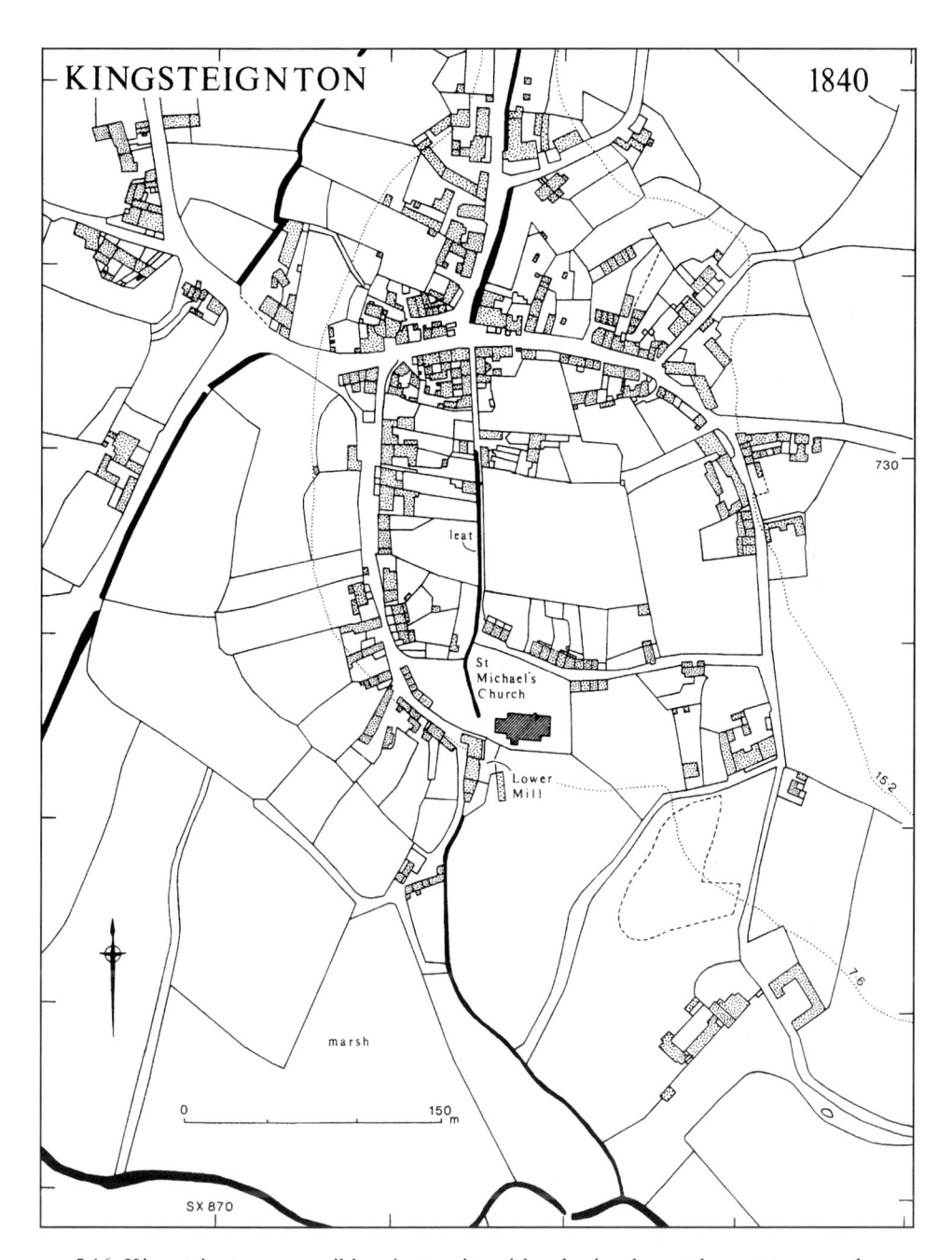

5.16: Kingsteignton: a possible minster site with sub-circular settlement topography. Re-drawn from the Tithe Map of 1840 by Peter Weddell; published in Weddell 1987. By permission of the author and Devon Archaeological Society (with amendments).

development was studied by H.P.R. Finberg, a charter for its market was received by the abbey around 1105 and in the thirteenth century Tavistock was classed as a borough. Finberg regarded Tavistock's commercial rise, like that of Okehampton (based on a new castle), as initiatives of the Norman period which competed with the existing market at the *burh* of Lydford. It seems highly likely, however, that the foundation of Tavistock abbey in the late tenth century had attracted some market function long before this was formalised in its charter. Similarly, it seems highly likely that when Crediton's minster was the centre of the see, for the century and half before 1050, some marketing would have been attracted to its community.

Because of their relevance to settlement and economic issues, minster sites have been subject to morphological analysis. Teresa Hall's study of Dorset minsters has made a valuable contribution to the south-western aspect of the subject. John Blair and others have pursued it on a wider front. Minster-related settlements display various trends. Some, found equally in "Germanic" England and the "Celtic" west, were curvilinear, planned in and around oval enclosures using old or newly-built earthworks, now apparent from the street-patterns which they influenced. More rectilinear forms seem to have emerged where the influence of underlying Romano-British structures, or even surviving structures, was relevant. Although we know nothing of the lay-out of the buildings which must have accompanied Exeter's minster, the origins of the site, in the Roman forum basilica and bounded by Roman streets, suggest it is likely to have fallen into this category.

In Devon, two general (and connected) observations are pertinent (see also Chapter 3). First, there is the relatively low number of churches with full minster status currently identifiable, in relation to Devon's large area. Second, given the longer survival of an independent Dumnonian church in Devon (and Cornwall) a greater contribution to the eventual pattern of churches, and church-related settlements, may have been made by sites of pre-English origin. When, however, we turn to those places in Devon with known or likely pre-Norman minster churches, precious little can currently be said about their form or settlement topography. Where such places are now larger rural "villages" or rural market towns, we sometimes find (or can see on nineteenth-century maps) roads skirting around the area in which the church stands, perhaps indicating an original sub-circular minster enclosure: this could be the case at Axminster, Colyton or Cullompton, for example. At Axminster, this hypothesis seems a likely explanation for the later settlement form, whose central element occupies the higher ground

Land and Rural Folk

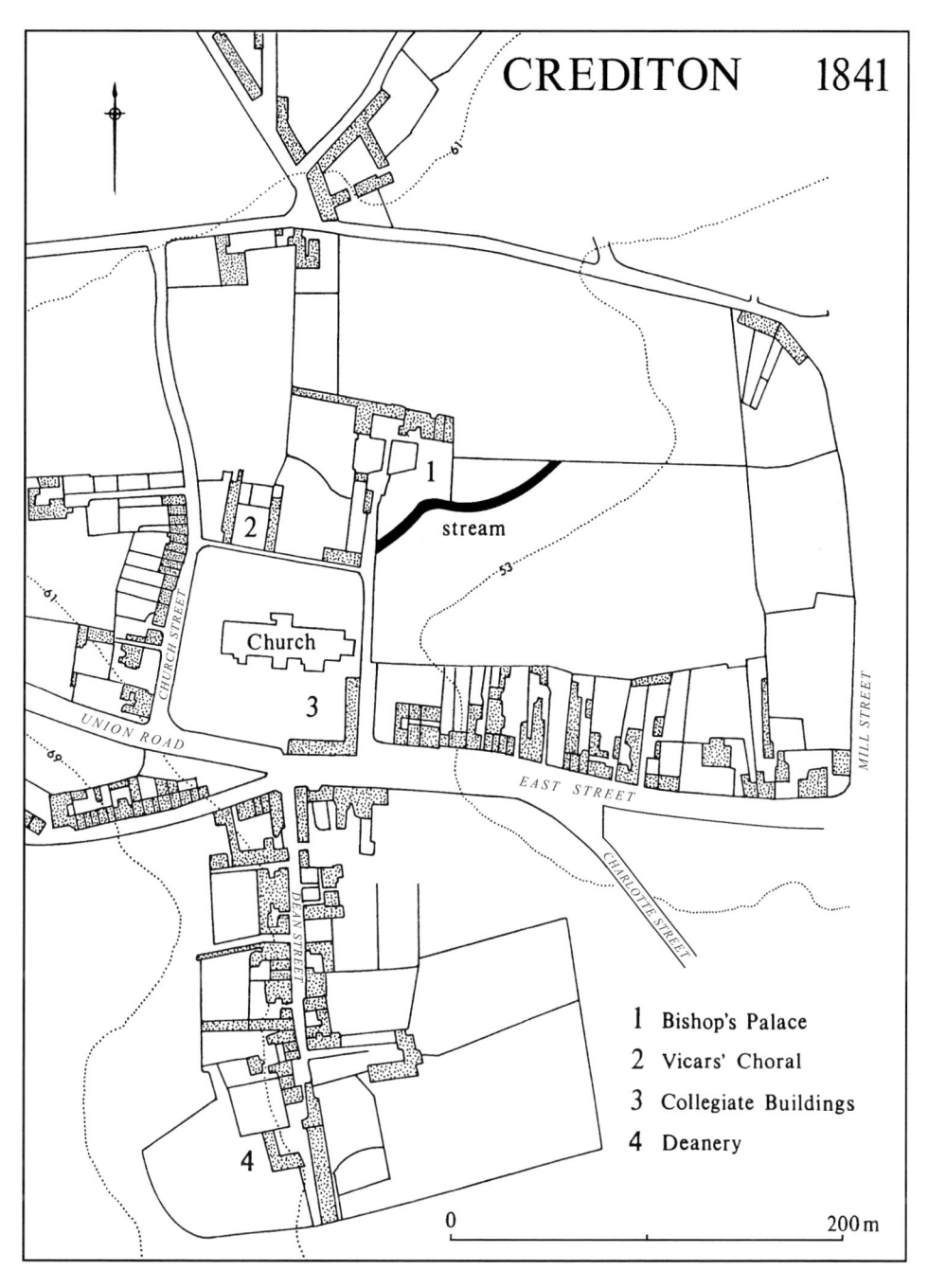

5.17: Crediton: a minster site with sub-rectilinear settlement topography. Re-drawn from the Tithe Map of 1841 by Peter Weddell and published in Henderson & Weddell 1985. By permission of the author and Exeter Archaeology (with amendments).

and is (now) bounded by West Street, South Street and Church Street. This putative enclosure (now also truncated by another street) has the church at one side. At Kingsteignton (not certainly a minster, though a very good case can be made) the street pattern also suggests a large sub-circular enclosure around the church. At Hartland and Braunton, it has been suggested that nineteenth-century maps reveal traces of originally British monastic enclosures later taken over when these places became English minsters. But all such observations have to be made with caution, since, in the absence of specific dating evidence for individual settlement components, their juxtaposition can easily lead to varying interpretations. At Axminster, for example, Susan Pearce has suggested a more extensive enclosure than the one postulated above. In some cases, for example Tiverton, later urban growth may simply have destroyed vestiges of early minster-related plans; at others, for example Tavistock, early elements may have been destroyed by later growth of a major church site. Moreover, many of the places amongst Devon's known or possible rural minster sites are now small, with essentially unplanned settlement-cores, including Exminster, which actually has a "minster" name.

There is, however, potential for further analysis of early Crediton, which is deserving of more attention than it has received. Here, the "west town" was a later medieval growth stretched along a road (it had a market from the thirteenth century) and the earlier "east town" lay around the church: they were quite distinct in form until brought together by the development of Union Road in 1836. In "east town", the approximate positions are known of the later medieval collegiate buildings and other structures associated with Crediton's post-cathedral history. There is no hint here of any early curvilinear enclosure, at least surviving in the modern topography. In contrast, the churchyard and alignments of adjacent streets have a sub-rectilinear character: this is shown not just on nineteenth-century maps but also on a map of 1598 by John Norden, which is preserved in a Victorian copy, now in the Devon Record Office. This sub-rectilinearity is enhanced if the modern road additions are removed: Union Road, Charlotte Street, Exhibition Road and the present southward loop of the Exeter Road. Thus Church Street, Dean Street and Mill Street ran north-south, while East Street ran east-west through the settlement. On the east, prior to the development of the estate around Downes House, the old route in the Exeter direction, in continuation of East Street, is suggested by surviving vestiges of lanes. Viewed in this way, the plan may give an impression of a primary enclosure, containing a church in one corner, with a secondary addition extending southwards. Three interesting possibilities are worth consideration. First, the plan of "east town" may be largely of later medieval origin, evolving during the life of the (post-cathedral) collegiate church, and all earlier traces of Crediton's lay-out may have been obscured. Second, in contrast, the Romano-British tile found in excavation in 1984 (see below) may indicate the influence of earlier occupation: we may have the survival of an early medieval plan of the eighth century influenced by an underlying Romano-British settlement. A "villa" site, identified from the air by Frances Griffith and tested by excavation, lies two miles to the south-east, near the River Yeo. Third, the presumed eighth-century minster may have attracted little settlement, the town plan developing largely from the tenth century when Crediton was established as a cathedral.

There is also a strong tradition, going back to Norden's time and transmitted via Ordnance Survey maps, that to the north-east of the church lay the episcopal palace site known to have existed in the later middle ages: Norden labelled this "The Pallace" and the building now on the site retains the name, "The Old Palace". Although a change of location may have occurred, it is also possible that this occupies the same site as the (presumed) tenth-century residence of Crediton's first bishops. Excavations conducted by Christopher Henderson and Peter Weddell in 1984, when a new vicarage was under construction to the north of the church, revealed wall foundations from a timber building of late Saxon or early Norman date. In a thirteenth-century grant, a plot of land between the churchyard and the bishop's garden was called *Godmaneshay*, preserving the Old English personal name Godman and perhaps originally a tenth- or eleventh-century canon's residence. A priest of this name and period is known, witnessing Exeter cathedral's foundation charter and holding land in 1066 at Brampford Speke and Clannaborough (see Chapters 3 and 4).

Conclusion: Rural Industries (see Fig. 5.18)

Finally, we must not forget the highly significant role of the rural industries which were practised alongside agriculture. From today's perspective it is too easy to equate industry with urbanism and forget its rural evolution: industry in the countryside was a crucial part of Devon's history for many centuries. Unfortunately, it is not possible to discuss this subject, on available evidence, in the detail which its importance at the time actually merits. The exploitation of tin, and its export, was clearly very important in Dumnonia and tin was later also highly significant to West Saxon royal

Making Anglo-Saxon Devon

interest in the south west (see Chapters 2 & 4). The burh at Lydford not only protected the kingdom's western extremity, but was also a centre for control of this Dartmoor resource and well-placed as an administrative centre for Cornish tin extraction before such centres developed in Cornwall itself. Studies of environmental profiles on Dartmoor by Ben Gearey and others have shown a marked increase in charcoal, from around the ninth century onwards, in the Merrivale area. It has been suggested that the human interference represented by this evidence could relate to tin-working activity, for which the Walkham valley was very important in later centuries. Disappointingly little can be said about other important activities. The emergence of stone churches and sculpture reflects the growth of quarrying and carving industries (see Chapter 3). By the mid-tenth century, pottery was being produced in Exeter and on the Somerset-

5.18: Excavation in progress at Blacklake Wood iron-smelting site, in the Barle Valley near Dulverton (on the Somerset side of the shire boundary). Gill Juleff comments: the site comprises a substantial slag heap and a levelled working area (foreground). Charcoal collected during initial survey gave a date of the 5th-6th centuries AD, suggesting the rare survival of an early medieval smelting site, but subsequent excavation and dating places the core activity here during the 4th century. The shaft furnaces used at the site were considerably smaller than those employed at the major Romano-British smelting sites on Exmoor. Photograph: Gill Juleff.

Devon border (see Chapter 4) and is found in the other urban *burhs*: this must reflect a growing market economy. In addition, we may suggest that some other industries, known only in later centuries, probably had earlier origins lacking historical record. The extraction of lead and silver at Combe Martin, in north Devon and Bere Ferrers in south Devon, is recorded only from the late thirteenth century but could well have an earlier beginning. This industry is currently the subject of research projects pursued in north Devon and at Exeter University.

Another industry which has received fruitful attention is ironworking. In the 1990s, Frances Griffith and Peter Weddell pursued a programme of work in the Blackdown Hills on behalf of Devon County Council and Exeter Archaeology. Ironworking evidence in the field, in the form of extraction pits, smelting sites and slags, was correlated with maps, field-names, documentary study, geophysical and aerial survey: the resulting impression is of a widespread industry from Romano-British times onwards, eventually contracting in the later middle ages. Scientifically-dated sites in Hemyock and Dunkeswell revealed activity in the Romano-British period and seventh-to-ninth centuries respectively. The publication by Steve Reed, Gill Juleff and Oliver Bayer of three iron-smelting furnaces excavated at Burlescombe (between the Blackdown Hills and Tiverton) has added further detail to industrial activity in this area. Of simple bowl-construction, and with plentiful evidence of slags and charcoal, these furnaces were used for making iron blooms as well as for re-heating them prior to smithing (presumably at immediately adjacent sites). The charcoal fuel employed came mainly from oak, as well as from some other species (notably ash). In its surviving form, this fuel reveals the management of local woodland through coppicing. Scientific dating of these furnaces placed their use between the seventh and tenth centuries: the charcoal was subject to carbon fourteen assessment and the fired clay furnace-linings to archaeomagnetic dating.

Another Exeter University-based project currently concerns iron extraction in north Devon and Somerset. The single mention in Domesday Book of iron-workers at North Molton has always been regarded an inadequate record of an activity in Devon which must have been much more widely-based. In recent years, Gill Juleff has organised a programme of fieldwork and excavation at furnace and slag-heap sites, backed up by scientific and artefactual dating, in and around Exmoor. This has revealed a fascinating history for this important industry. At Sherracombe Ford, Clatworthy and Brayford, iron-extraction was active in the Romano-British period; at Blacklake Wood, in the Barle valley, initial dating suggested the fifth to seventh centuries, but recently-revised dating suggests slightly earlier, in the late Romano-British period; at three other sites in the Barle valley, including Shercombe Slade, furnaces and workshops of medieval date survived. We must envisage a valuable and thriving industry, first controlled by the Romano-British authorities, then by a succession of kings: perhaps Dumnonian (though in this period the evidence is thin), then West Saxon and English. Investigating this early iron industry in Devon and Somerset also suggests other activities for further enquiry. One which the Exmoor iron project has also explored is the charcoal industry which produced a crucial raw material for the production of iron: a charcoal-burning platform has recently been excavated in Horner Wood, on the National Trust's Holnicote Estate. Another is the management of the woodland for charcoal production: at Blacklake Wood the charcoal remaining on site was analysed, revealing deliberate coppicing of oak, often on a 15-year cycle, between the third and fifth centuries. This was supplemented by the use of natural oak, and sometimes by birch. At Sherracombe Ford and Brayford in contrast, coppiced woodland was also managed in the Romano-British period, predominantly oak and hazel, but there was also significant use of resources from natural woodland. Thus the evidence of rural industry can also assist in the reconstruction of local variations in vegetation and its management.

SOURCES USED AND FURTHER READING

Allan 1994; Aston 1989; Aston & Gerrard 1999; Barlow 1991; Barnes & Williamson 2006; Beresford 1967; Blair 1992(a); Darby & Welldon Finn (eds) 1967; Chapman 2001; Costen 1992; Darby 1977; Darby 1987; Faith 1997; Finberg 1952(a); Finberg 1952(b); Finberg (ed) 1972; Fleming & Ralph 1982; Fleming 2000; Fowler & Thomas 1962; Fowler 2002; Fox 1975; Fox 1983; Fox 1989; Fox 1991; Fox 1996(a); Fox 1996(b); Fox 2001; Fox 2004; Fox 2006a; Fox 2006(b); Fyfe & Rippon 2004; Fyfe, Brown & Rippon 2004; Gearey *et alii* 1997; Griffith 1988(a); Griffith 1988(b); Griffith & Weddell 1995; Griffith & Weddell 1996; Griffith & Quinnell 1999(a); Griffith & Quinnell 1999(b); Hall 2000; Hallam (ed) 1988; Hamerow 1991; Hatcher 1988; Henderson & Weddell 1985; Henderson & Bidwell 1994; Herring 1996; Herring 2006; Higham (ed) 1989; Holdsworth (ed) 1986; Holt (ed)1987; Hooke 1994; Hoskins 1952; Hoskins 1955; Hoskins 1963(a); Hoskins 1967; Juleff 2005; Juleff 2006; Kain & Ravenhill (eds) 1999; Lennard 1959; Luscombe 2005; Maddicott 1997; Michelmore & Proctor 1994; Miller (ed)

1991; Orchard 2002; Padel 1999; Pearce 1982(b); Pearce 1985(a); Pearce 1985(b); Pearce 2004; Pelteret 1995; Pollard, Hooper & Moore 1974; Quinnell 2004; Rackham 1986; Rackham 1990; Ravenhill 1969(a); Ravenhill 1969(b); Reed *et alii* 2006; Reynolds 1999; Riley & Wilson-North 2001; Rippon 2006; Rippon *et alii* 2006; Roberts 1987; Roberts & Wrathmell 2002; Rose & Preston-Jones 1995; Sawyer 1965; Simpson *et alii* 1989; Stenton 1955; Taylor 1983; Taylor (ed) 1988; Taylor 2007; Thorne & Thorne (eds) 1985; Turner 2006(a); Turner (ed) 2006(b); Warren 1883; Whitelock (ed) 1955; Welldon Finn 1964; Williams & Erskine (eds) 1987.

6

Epilogue
The Legacy of Anglo-Saxon Devon

See Figs. 6.1, 6.2, 6.3; also various Figs. in Chapters 2, 3 and 4.

In the Preface to this book, the tentative nature of much of its content was emphasised. The changing character of archaeological evidence as well as the thin quantity of direct documentary evidence (before Domesday Book) conspire to leave us with many uncertainties and much scope for new advances in knowledge and understanding. It is perhaps disappointing that clear solutions to so many big and important questions have so far proved elusive. How many people of more-or-less-Germanic background settled in Devon in the late seventh and eighth centuries? How long did the Dumnonians in the shire continue to speak a British language and to what extent did the latter influence everyday speech in Old English? When and how did the shire bounds with Somerset and Dorset come into existence? How, why and when was the older Dumnonian settlement pattern replaced by the early historic landscape and how might this have varied from one part of Devon to another? How and when did existing names of older rural settlements give way to an overwhelmingly Old English pattern of names? Over what period did large rural estates break down into the smaller units familiar in later centuries? How many church sites had pre-English origins? How dominant and numerous in early Devon were minster churches? When did the later process of local church foundation begin and how were church sites chosen in regions of dispersed settlement? To what extent was Exeter inhabited in pre-Alfredian times? What was the lay-out of *hagae* like in all the *burhs* before they were sub-divided into numerous urban tenements? By what processes, and by whom, were Exeter's numerous local churches established? What was the full extent of Devon's urban and rural industries? How important was trade and the use of coinage in the lives of most of its inhabitants? In the foregoing chapters, these and other major issues have been explored, but often with very incomplete explanations. It is a daunting thought that the early history of but one English shire could occupy the efforts of numerous authors and postgraduate thesis-writers for many years to come. It is also (somehow) simultaneously depressing and comforting that so many of these issues have been in the public academic arena for at least the last fifty years.

With so many important matters imperfectly understood, it is tempting to see pre-Norman Devon as remote and with no modern connections. But this is not true. Exeter cathedral (as an institution though not as a building) has had a continuous history since 1050, and a history as a minster from the late seventh century, possibly earlier. Tenth- and eleventh-century royal government, with its reeves and courts, contributed much to the later framework of the shire, and Exeter has been Devon's shire town continuously since the late Saxon period. The present-day clergy of some city and rural parish churches are successors to the priests of churches of the tenth and eleventh centuries, and congregations at such places are successors to the urban and rural Christian communities of a thousand years ago. The modern practice of organising parishes together under team-ministries has revived something of the spirit of early minster churches and their groups of priests. Local politicians, traders and businessmen in Exeter, Totnes and Barnstaple are successors to the burghal officers and merchants who founded urban prosperity and faced both vikings and Normans. But this prosperity was not shared by all: there were poor and homeless then, just as there are, tragically, still in Devon today. All over Devon, farmers occupy land tilled by the people described in Domesday Book and by their ancestors. And great numbers of the rural population still occupy farms, hamlets and villages which lie on, or very near, the sites of early medieval settlements. Place-names with Old English (and a few British) elements confront us on maps and road signs in enormous numbers. The commonly-spoken form of Old English, possibly influenced by earlier British speech patterns, was the foundation on which later medieval and modern English was built. Although impossible to quantify, there must also be biological links between the early and modern populations of Devon, despite the considerable inward and outward movement of people in subsequent centuries. The blood-lines of Dumnonians and Saxons from

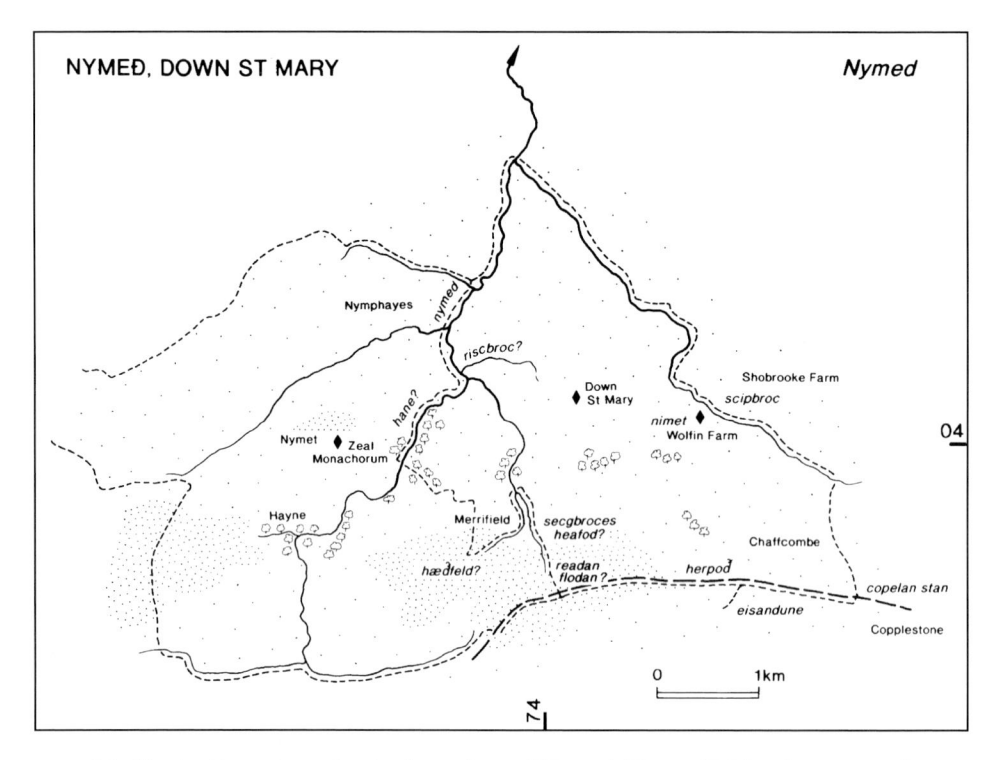

6.1: The tenth-century charter boundary of Nymed (Down St Mary) as mapped in Hooke 1994 (by permission of the author); the cross-shaft at Copplestone, a surviving marker (*copelan stan*) on that boundary, appears in 3.17.

all social classes contributed to the later societies. These included not only nobles, thegns, burgesses and peasants, but also slaves. In the period of this book's writing, there has been much discussion of more recent forms of slavery and of the living descendants of slaves. We easily overlook the indigenous dimension of this subject, safely cleansed and distanced from us by the passage of time. Any of us might have ancestors who were of any rank, from kings to slaves.

In broad terms, the notion of "community of the shire" which we recognise more clearly in later centuries, had its origins in the Anglo-Saxon period and significant elements of early social organisation have left a legacy to modern Devon. On the other hand, what we can actually see of Saxon Devon is more limited. Old though Devon's rural landscapes and many of its buildings are, their present form arises from centuries of continuous evolution in which significant change occurred in the later middle ages: we must beware the temptation to identify an impression of

Epilogue: The Legacy of Anglo-Saxon Devon

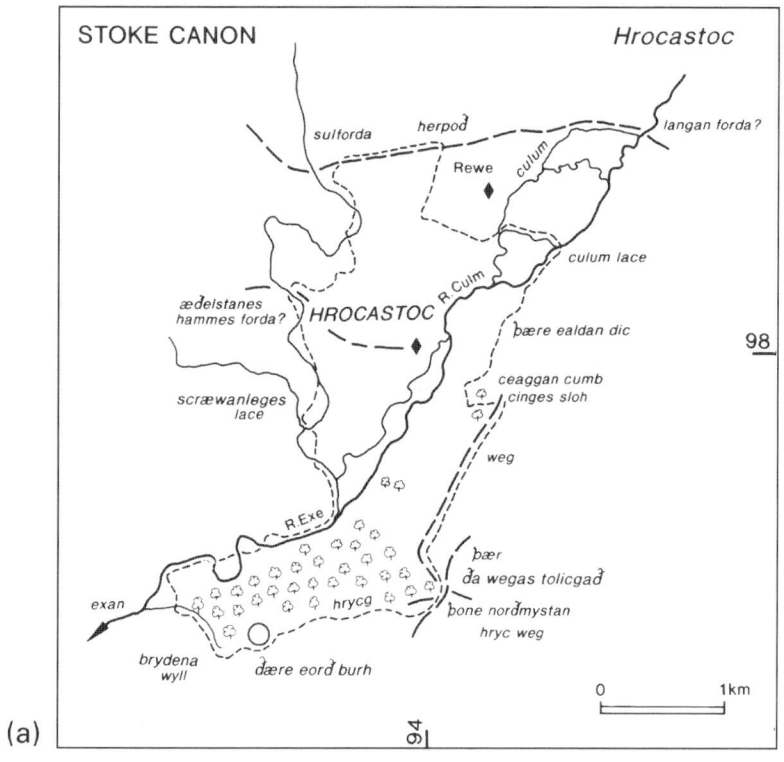

6.2: (a) the eleventh-century charter boundary of Stoke Canon as mapped in Hooke 1994 (by permission of the author), and (b) aerial photograph of Stoke Hill Camp, a surviving marker (*eorth burh*) on that boundary. Photograph: Bill Horner (23/8/95), copyright Devon County Council. See 4.4 for the charter itself.

Making Anglo-Saxon Devon

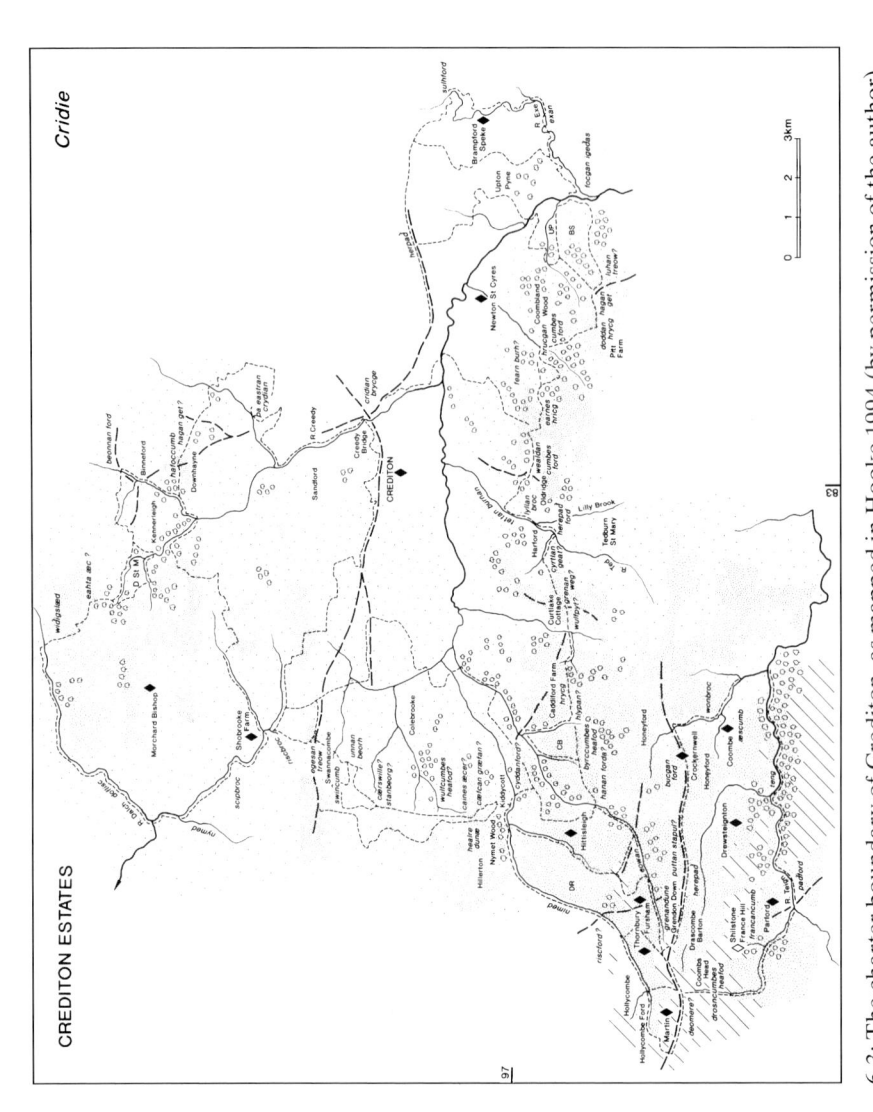

6.3: The charter boundary of Crediton, as mapped in Hooke 1994 (by permission of the author). Recorded in the eleventh century, this reflected enlargements of the eighth-century estate (see Appendix 2). It encompassed a wide territory covering Crediton hundred but also extending beyond.

Epilogue: The Legacy of Anglo-Saxon Devon

"ancientness" automatically with the Anglo-Saxon period. In 1955, in his *Making of the English Landscape*, W.G. Hoskins argued that Saxon estate boundaries, described in land charters, can be identified with banks and lanes in the present-day landscape, for example around Thorverton, Stoke Canon and Shobrooke, between the Exe and Creedy valleys. More recent work on charter boundaries has cast doubt on the specifics of some earlier proposed identifications and has suggested alternatives. It is nevertheless true, in general terms, that Saxon land boundaries have left their legacy in the evolution of Devon's lanes and hedgebanks, as well as in the parish boundaries which were often their direct successors and which have existed ever since. Moreover, the landscapes referred to in boundary clauses contained elements which are still identifiable in our own landscapes: Nymed (Down St Mary) and Stoke Canon are illustrated here, as examples. The charter recording king Aethelheard's grant in 739 of land at Crediton for building a minster, re-worked for bishop Leofric, serves as another example: its boundary clause, describing its eleventh-century extent rather than its original eighth-century extent, refers to many details which still survive, as Della Hooke has demonstrated. Its description starts at a bridge over the river Creedy (*cridian brycge*), north-east of present-day Crediton, where there is still a (later) bridge today. Its description ends with an old road (*eald herepath*) running near a stream called *east crydian,* now known as as Holly Water. It corresponds in part with present-day lanes in the vicinity of Stockleigh English, East Village and Priorton Barton. Along the way, the names of several boundary points have given rise to names which still exist, for example: Beonna's ford (*beonnan ford*) produced Binneford in Sandford; Franca's combe (*francancumb*) produced France Hill near Drewsteignton; the sheep brook (*scipbrok*) produced Shobrooke Farm near Morchard Bishop; the enclosure gate (*hagan get*) produced Downhayne on the Sandford-Stockleigh English boundary.

Exeter City Council's "Time Trail" website illustrates several aspects of the city and its environs, including a hedge and bank on the boundary of an eleventh-century charter for Topsham. Multi-species hedges in Devon were amongst the case-studies through which, many years ago, W.G. Hoskins, Max Hooper and others brought hedgerow dating to public attention. Although their dating has remained controversial, hedgebanks can preserve the shapes of field systems of great antiquity, especially where their curving lines reflect former strips in sub-divided fields. Some Devon hedges may well be of late Saxon origin. Braunton Great Field, now famous as a most unusual survival of a later medieval open field, was perhaps first laid out in the tenth century. Hundreds of miles of Devon's rural roads and lanes may have begun their long evolution in the Saxon period, to serve the growing pattern of farms and hamlets. Their deep profiles, flanked by enormous banks, so distinctive in some parts of the county, are the accumulation of various influences at work over many centuries: soil creep in hilly terrains with high rainfall; erosion from constant movement of livestock leading to regular cleaning out of lanes, the upcast adding even further to the banks; and the geology of the Culm Measures, occupying much of the county, whose slates are prone to erosion and gullying.

Visible material culture of early date is not plentiful, but nevertheless important. Saxon stone fabric is visible in a few Exeter churches and in the city wall in Northernhay Gardens. Some Saxon stone cross-shafts survive in Devon, as well as earlier inscribed stone memorials of the Dumnonian period. Street plans laid out in the late ninth or tenth centuries are still in use in Exeter, Lydford, Barnstaple and Totnes. In museums and archives, artefactual and manuscript products of late Saxon Devon may be viewed: including metalwork, silver pennies minted in the *burhs* and pottery manufactured in rural and urban kilns. The Exeter Book, on public display at the Cathedral Library, is a forceful reminder of England's early literary achievements. Alongside it, the *Exon* Domesday, dating from the early Norman period, was a product of administrative machinery created in late Saxon times. Both are manuscripts of international significance.

The name of "Devon" derives from a name with Romano-British (and earlier) origins in the tribal name of the *Dumnonii*. We are accustomed now to thinking of Cornwall's "Celticness". But we should not forget that early Devonians were of Dumnonian origin, though supplemented by others of ultimately Germanic background. The Dumnonians eventually slid down the social scale and disappeared from view in an English-speaking and English-dominated society. Devonian Englishness emerged from racial and cultural mixing over several centuries in which one political structure and one language were accepted. The Devonian society which we know in later times, characterised by a blend of conservatism and radicalism, has been modified in the modern period by population movement. But its roots, in the early medieval centuries, are more than a thousand years old. The creation of Anglo-Saxon Devonshire, though leaving the eastern extremity of Dumnonia in Somerset, perpetuated an already existing cultural distinction from the Cornovian Dumnonians to the far west, in what became Cornwall. In the twelfth century, in his *Description of Wales*

(Book I, Chapter 6) Gerald of Wales noted that the Cornish and Bretons spoke a language which was closer to the ancient British tongue than was the Welsh of his own day. He also observed that the English spoken in northern England had developed as a result of Scandinavian influence, whereas that of the south was a purer English, preserving more ancient features, particularly so in Devon.

In reflecting on Devonian roots, we might finally ask a question pertinent to Britain in the twenty-first century. In studying British history, we happily talk of "Romanization" and "Normanization", terms which acknowledge significant survival of indigenous culture under the major influences of conquering immigrant minorities. On the other hand, we seem not to speak of "Saxonization" or of "Anglianization". Use of such terms would be logical, since recently it has become customary to play down the numbers of Germanic immigrants and to play up the importance of social fusion. Such a view of events is particularly relevant to south west Britain, where Saxon influence was fairly late and considerable survival of native society a safe assumption. Even here, however, English modernisers won both the battles and the debates with British traditionalists. Perhaps the discrepancy in common terminology reflects something slightly distorted in our own view of our past. Whereas we can readily accept the "contributions" made by Rome and Normandy (as well as, in some British areas, by Scandinavia), we may be wedded to a notion of "Englishness" which subconsciously denies that it was created, to varying degrees, through the suppression and absorption of an indigenous people. Perhaps this stark reality sits awkwardly with our normal self-assessment as a tolerant and liberal-minded nation?

In contrast, king Alfred and his contemporaries had no problem with creating a picture of a conquering English race, whose victories over the British were celebrated in the *Anglo-Saxon Chronicle* long after the English had become the dominant element. This self-promoted "Englishness" had, of course, an important political motive: to bolster a powerful image when the English were seriously threatened by viking invaders. A sort of multiculturalism which had probably characterised the earlier Saxon period now gave way, out of necessity, to a stronger but more narrowly-defined sense of what it was to be English. This was carried through in the tenth century, as the viking-occupied areas in the midlands and north were conquered and, for the first time, a kingdom of England was created. In a Devonian context, the emergence of an English shire, first within a West Saxon kingdom, and later within an English one, provides a fascinating story with an important legacy to later times. Now, at the beginning of the twenty-first century, there is much debate, in contemporary culture and politics, about what it means to be "English" or "British". That debate could benefit from a fuller understanding of an issue much discussed in recent years by historians and archaeologists: how "Englishness" was created in the Anglo-Saxon period. Another important part of early Devon's legacy to the present is its relevance to that issue.

Appendices

Appendix 1: St Boniface – Devon's best-known Saxon

Around 675, somewhere not far from Exeter a boy called Wynfrith was born to a West Saxon family of probably noble status who held Dumnonian land. He was sent by his parents to the monastery in Exeter, ruled by abbot Wulfheard, a few years later. The monastery was a symbol of the West Saxon influence in Devon which had also brought Wynfrith's family here. In Exeter, he received some education and began what was later to be a career of international repute. Wynfrith soon moved to the monastery at Nursling in Hampshire, ruled by abbot Wynbert. Here, he extended his education, becoming a scholar and teacher. He was ordained a priest at thirty. He became king Ine's envoy to the archbishop of Canterbury. In 716, he went to preach in Frisia, returning to England in 717. In Rome in 718, he sought papal support for more missionary work. Three years in Frisia followed, during which, probably in 719, he adopted the name of a Roman martyr, Boniface. Appointed a bishop in Rome (722) he moved to Hesse and Thuringia (Germany) where his conversions and monastic foundations (with libraries and schools) were many. Pope Gregory III made him archbishop for Germany in 732: as archbishop of Mainz, he created several bishoprics. In the 740s he presided over Carolingian church reforms. An old man, he returned to Frisia where, in parts, paganism was still practised. He was killed, with a large party of followers, by a pagan band in 754, near Dokkum. His body was taken to the monastery at Fulda (Germany) which he had founded ten years previously. Here his burial place became the centre of his cult.

Though eventually revered in England, it was on the continent that his veneration was (and is) concentrated. An English priest called Willibald, connected with the German missions, wrote the first *Life* of Boniface some fifteen years after his death: it contained an account of his early years at the monastery in Exeter (*Ad-Escancastre*). Boniface was a contemporary of Bede (c. 673–735), but did not figure in the latter's writings (which were known to Boniface in Germany, where he sought them out). Although highly-esteemed by English church leaders, Boniface was not ranked as a major saint in early medieval England. In the 1330s, John Grandisson, bishop of Exeter, who introduced significant reforms into the collegiate church at Crediton (as he did also in the 1360s), mentioned an altar at Crediton church dedicated to Boniface. In a collection of lessons prepared (in the 1330s) for daily use at Exeter cathedral, Grandisson pronounced that Boniface had been born at Crediton: this occurs in the readings for 5th June, the date of Boniface's martyrdom which became the celebration of his feast as a saint. We do not know why he thought so, and there is no evidence of a Boniface cult or other association at Crediton before this time. Perhaps he had read a *Life* of Boniface, knew of his early education in Exeter and chose this local birth-place because it had an ancient church. In Boniface's time the actual name *Crediton*, which related only to the later settlement, had not emerged, and at the time of Boniface's birth it is not certain that territory west of the Exe was controlled by the English (see Chapter 2). Grandisson's creation may simply have been intended to boost the image of Crediton's church. It should also be seen in the context of his general interest in saints' lives. Grandisson's promotion of a Boniface-Crediton link has certainly proved very influential in modern times.

Boniface was the product of a "frontier" society, born when the English had influence as far as the Exe valley. His neighbours were Dumnonian as well as Saxon. The monastery at Exeter, where he was first educated, stood within a crumbling Roman city. He devoted his life to missionary work amongst the Frisian and Germanic peoples from whom some English people were ultimately descended. He was influential in shaping early medieval Europe through conversions, the foundation of monasteries and bishoprics, and his skilful employment of allied papal and imperial patronage. He was an international figure and a "European": not just Devon's best known Saxon, but one of England's most significant and famous sons of all time.

Sources: Cook 2004; Emerton 1940; Farmer 1992; Greenaway 1955; Reuter 1980 (ed); *Oxford Dictionary of National Biography* (2004), vol. 6 (Boniface), vol. 23 (Grandisson); Yorke 2007. I am grateful to Nicholas Orme for helpful discussion of the Grandisson-Boniface issue.

Appendix 2: The Minster church at Crediton before and after 909

We are informed by a charter that in 739 the church at Sherborne was endowed with twenty hides (*cassati*) in mid-Devon by king Aethelheard of Wessex (Birch, *Cartularium Saxonicum*, no. 1331 – hereafter *BCS*; Sawyer 1968, no. 255). This land, the charter stated, was granted to bishop Forthhere for the building of a minster at a place called *Cridie* (*in loco ubi dicitur Cridie*). Because the cathedral established around 909 for Devon and Cornwall by Edward the Elder was situated at Crediton, and because the boundary clause of the charter describes a swathe of territory which includes Crediton, the name *Cridie* has always been regarded as indicating Crediton. It has therefore been assumed by most historians that a minster was built by Sherborne, in the place later known as Crediton, soon after the grant of 739. The possibility that a British church (and its territory?) was being re-founded does not seem to have been much considered, though in the context of parallels at Sherborne and (perhaps?) Exeter this possibility should not be dismissed. The name *Cridie* was, in fact, the (British) name of a river, which had presumably given its name to a wider territory (this particular naming process may have been a general phenomenon: see Chapter 2). Aethelheard's grant of ten hides to Glastonbury in 729 had been *in Torric* (a river Torridge territory) and Lydford's name in the Burghal Hidage list had been *Hlidan* (perhaps a river Lyd territory). The town of Crediton, despite its name, did not grow directly on the river: the Creedy runs slightly to its east.

The "charter of 739" (as it will be referred to here, to indicate that its purported date is not that of the document itself) was analysed by Pierre Chaplais (1966) and H.P.R. Finberg (1968) and has been commented upon more recently by Heather Edwards (1988, 255-258). Despite its content, the surviving document is not a "Sherborne source", nor a "Crediton" one, but an "Exeter" one (though it later became part of the collections of the Bodleian Library, Oxford). It is an eleventh-century document written at Exeter in the time of bishop Leofric. Chaplais dated it to *circa* 1069: it was written by the same hand which wrote another Exeter document in 1069, a confirmation by king William I of lands, in Oxfordshire and Devon, granted to the Exeter canons by Leofric. The charter seems, however, to be based on an authentic model with reliable elements, including its witness-list. It is regarded as evidence of a real eighth-century grant of which record had been preserved first at Sherborne, later at Crediton (whose archive would have been inherited by Exeter in 1050, when it became the cathedral; unlike Exeter's archive, lost in the viking attack of 1003, Crediton's had presumably survived). Had it been a complete fabrication of the eleventh century, we might expect more anachronisms, including the name Crediton itself – current by that time (see below) – to have been used rather than the name *Cridie*: this does look like a preserved name of much earlier origin. The evolution of the place-name can, however, be observed in subsequent endorsements of the charter noted by Birch: first *Cridian*, then later, *Criditonia*.

The boundary clause of the Crediton charter (mapped in Hooke 1994, 86ff), however, is an eleventh-century creation, replacing an earlier description of a smaller area and reflecting an enlarged tenth- and eleventh-century estate belonging to Crediton church in its time as a cathedral: it includes far more than the original grant would have covered, as observed by Finberg and other commentators, who have also noted that its very detailed form reflects its late creation and would not have been found in an eighth-century charter. Finberg (1968) and Edwards (1988) have argued that the charter written for Leofric was based on an authentic earlier one (which no longer exists) but that the boundary clause of the latter was replaced by another, which was more detailed and took in a larger territory. In the initial copying, Chaplais (1966) observed that the original hidation (had it been ten, as with Glastonbury's land in the Torridge valley?) of the eighth-century grant had been reproduced, but the scribe then erased it and entered twenty hides: this was more like the contemporary assessment of the territory now described. The motive for Leofric's production of the new charter, as Finberg suggested and Edwards has enlarged upon, may have been a dispute over the ownership of Newton (St Cyres) which Exeter claimed and which was still ongoing at the time of Domesday Book. The larger boundary clause now employed was (very conveniently) available in a separate and earlier eleventh-century document which had been written at Crediton (Sawyer 1968, no. 255; *BCS*, nos. 1332, 1333) and was by then at Exeter. Finberg (1968) argued that this had been produced to reflect the growth of the Crediton estate since the eighth century, perhaps in the context of its additional definition as an episcopal ship-soke in the reign of Aethelred II (on which, see Chapter 4).

O'Donovan's (1988, xlii, xlvii-xlviii) edition of the Sherborne sources notes that, in a late medieval list of that church's royal benefactions, although Aethelheard's grant of 739 did not figure, there was a record of a grant of thirty-five hides at *Cridiaton* from Cynewulf (757-786). Perhaps this grant, if it was not a wholly late invention – and its hidation certainly seems quite unreal in relation to the other evidence – was an early stage in the process of enlargement (the form of the place-name used in this list reflects, of course, its late medieval date). Various writers, including Finberg, the *Place-names of Devon* editors (vol. II, 402) and Della Hooke (1994, 97) have noted that the eleventh-century boundary clause also embraced a bigger territory than just the administrative unit which had emerged as Crediton hundred: at its eastern and south-western limits, the estate here described also extended into Wonford hundred, which is probably also evidence of enlargement of an originally smaller territory (see fig. 6.3).

In 933, king Aethelstan granted privileges to bishop Eadwulf and his new see at Crediton, confirming freedom of the episcopal estates from all burdens due to the king except service in the army and work on fortresses. Interestingly, this charter referred to *ecclesia Cridiensis*, using a place-name similar to that in the "charter of 739" (*BCS*, no. 694; Sawyer no. 421). The creation of this new see based on Crediton was described in correspondence to king Aethelred II, in the late tenth century, perhaps written by Dunstan, archbishop of Canterbury (see Whitelock 1955, 822-823). This was motivated by a dispute between the (then) dioceses of Devon and Cornwall about ownership of three manors in Cornwall originally given to Sherborne on Egbert's defeat of the Cornish in the early ninth century. It was related how Edward the Elder and Plegmund, the archbishop of Canterbury, appointed on one occasion five bishops to West Saxon sees: Winchester, Ramsbury, Sherborne, Wells and Crediton. As Whitelock noted, these last two were new creations, and the most likely date was 909: Denewulf, bishop of Winchester, had died in 908; Asser, bishop of Sherborne, died in 909. The choice of Crediton as the new see in 909 certainly makes sense as the elevation of an earlier church belonging to Sherborne, out of whose diocese the new see was made. But, in the 890s, when (according to Asser's *Life* of that king) Alfred gave Asser a jurisdiction which, in effect, made him a suffragan of Sherborne for Devon and Cornwall, he had made Exeter its centre: perhaps, this arrangement, superceded when Asser became bishop of Sherborne, had proved unsatisfactory.

There is no specific evidence of a church at Crediton before 909 apart from the intention to build stated in "the charter of 739". There are no references to a minster in this period, and no known names of abbots or priests. The abbot Duddus (Duddo) who witnessed the "charter of 739" was presumably from another house since at that stage the foundation of Crediton lay in the future. Whether he was the same abbot Duddo to whom Boniface wrote (from Germany) in 735 cannot be determined, though Edwards (1988) suggested he might be. This man was a former pupil of Boniface to whom the latter wrote to enquire about a biblical text and about a detail of Roman law: so wherever Duddo was abbot of, his house had a good library (Emerton 1940, 63-64, who suggested Duddo may have been in Rome itself). It is tempting, but probably too fanciful to speculate that John Grandisson already knew of Duddo in Boniface's letter, then (in Exeter) saw the Crediton charter's witness-list and thus made his Boniface-Crediton connection. Grandisson had been educated in Paris, had been chaplain to Pope John XXII on whose behalf he made diplomatic missions, and was consecrated bishop in Avignon (Audrey Erskine in *ODNB*, vol. 23, 266-268). Whether he had enjoyed access to copies of Boniface's letters is not, I think, known (early locations of these copies mentioned by Emerton (1940) are Mainz, Fulda and Cologne). Another suggestion relevant to the Crediton-Boniface connection has been made by Charles Insley (1998, 174, n.5). Since the *Anglo-Saxon Chronicle* tells us that bishop Forthhere accompanied Frithogyth, queen of king Aethelheard, to Rome in 737, is it possible that on this trip the bishop actually met Boniface, or someone close to him, learned of his Devonian origins and later persuaded the king to grant to Sherborne an estate in Boniface's home territory?

None of this, of course, in any way disproves the existence of a minster, since many known or probable minster churches in Anglo-Saxon England have no (surviving) contemporary supporting data. But it does at least raise the possibility that the minster whose building was intended in 739 was not actually built at this time (as tentatively suggested by Nicholas Orme in Reuter [ed] 1980). If this was so, then the choice of Crediton in 909 was presumably made because it was the centre of an estate belonging to Sherborne, suitably situated (and a little more centrally than Exeter) in the new see's territory. There is, theoretically, the possibility (but unlikely since there is no evidence for it) that a connection of Crediton with St Boniface was already in circulation by around 900, giving the estate some wider reputation. On the whole, the choice of Crediton as the see in 909 makes more sense if a church already existed there: otherwise, the permanent elevation of Exeter (where there certainly was one) would have been simpler to effect. It is also possible is that in 909 Edward the Elder wished to keep the crucial *burh* of Exeter, at the head of the Exe estuary, under exclusively royal control (which its ancient minster probably already was). Perhaps Crediton's minster was also at this time better endowed with land than was Exeter's minster and thus more suitable for supporting a bishopric. Between 936 and 939, the bishop of Crediton, Aethelgar, announced papal and episcopal indulgences for those who would contribute to building works at Crediton's minster church (*BCS*, 732; the *ministre* of St Mary at *Cridinton/Criditon*). Davidson (1878), however, queried whether these indulgences had been real. He suggested, on the basis of general European evidence, that they reflected eleventh- rather than tenth-century practice and had been "created" much later to boost the image of a church which, after 1050, had lost its cathedral status.

Apart from the appearance of *Cridie* in "the charter of 739" and of *Cridiaton* in the late medieval Sherborne list, the only reference to Crediton relating to circumstances pre-dating 909 may be in two charters, purporting to be of king Egbert, concerning land in Hampshire and Wiltshire, at Martyr Worthy and Alton Priors respectively, granted to the Old Minster in Winchester (*BCS*, 389, 390). The content of these charters tells us that their writing was in two stages: it began, in August 825, when the king was with his army at *Creodantreow* in a campaign conducted against the British; it was completed in Southampton in December 825. Because there is a superficial resemblance between this place-name and Crediton, at least with respect to their first elements, there has been some speculation about whether it was in Crediton's vicinity: that is, whether Egbert's army stopped near Crediton while conducting a south-western campaign. The charters survive only in versions written in the twelfth century, at Winchester, centuries after the grants described, and later became part of the British Museum collections (Sawyer nos. 272, 273). Some credence was given to their content by Whitelock, though without comment on the location of *Creodantreow*, because, she argued, they may corroborate but also correct the evidence of the *Anglo-Saxon Chronicle*. The latter records that the men of Devon (though without specifying Egbert's personal participation) fought the British at Galford, which is near Lydford in the extreme west of Devon. But the *Chronicle*'s date at this point (823) is out of synchronisation with the actual date, which was 825 as described in the two charters. Thus, Whitelock suggested (1955, 171, 342) in her discussion of the *Chronicle* and other sources, that whatever the truth of the claim to the estates in question at that early date, it seems the Winchester records had preserved not only narrative detail but also a (correct) date, both of which were from a source independent of the *Chronicle* as we know it. Perhaps this was a version of the *Chronicle* which is thought to have been at Winchester but which has not survived (Whitelock 1955, 113).

More recently, however, the analysis of these charters by Edwards has cast doubt on whether these connections are plausible (1988, 150-155). The Martyr Worthy charter (the place is near Winchester in Hampshire) is based on a reliable and early one, though having a later boundary clause attached to it. Its dating clause, including the *Creodantreow* reference, is authentic. But the campaign against the British referred to may not necessarily be that which led to the battle at Galford, as Whitelock assumed. The dating clause states "the beginning of this charter was written when king Egbert moved the army of the West Saxons (*exercitum Gewissorum*) against the British (*contra Brettones*) at the place called Creoda's Tree (*ubi dicitur Creodantreow*)". Egbert, however, was not mentioned in the *Anglo-Saxon Chronicle's* description of the battle at Galford, so perhaps two separate campaigns took place in 825, one by the king and the other by the men of Devon? The other issue is that of the name *Creodantreow*. Beyond any reasonable doubt, it actually means "Creoda's Tree": it is based on a personal name, not a river name (as is Crediton and its earlier forms). No-one has suggested a surviving place-name based on Creoda in Devon which might represent either an army assembly-point or somewhere on the itinerary of Egbert's army, but the name Creoda does give rise to place-names, as Gelling pointed out (1984, 150, 170), including Credenhill (Herefordshire) and Long Crendon (Bucks). Finally, Edwards has shown that the Alton Priors (the place is a few miles from Marlborough in Wiltshire) charter is a fabrication concocted from various other charters, one of which was the Martyr Worthy charter, so it adds nothing independently to the arguments. Curiously, however, its boundary clause (itself copied from another document relating to the estate) includes a point called "Creodan hylle". The published discussion of this boundary (Grundy 1919, 159-164) offers no identification on the ground for a "Creoda's Hill". Also in Wiltshire (near Malmesbury) there is Crudwell, whose name means "Creoda's spring, stream or well" (Gover, Mawer & Stenton 1939, 56). Tempting though it might be to imagine Egbert's army pausing near Crediton at a place called "Creedy Tree" – perhaps an early hundred centre (for which the name form would be appropriate) – all the evidence points to *Creodantreow* being a place called "Creoda's Tree" somewhere else, as yet unidentified, but quite possibly in Wiltshire. Here places had been named after an important person called Creoda, perhaps some mythical figure, or perhaps a local land-owner, or perhaps the figure of that name who appeared in the early West Saxon royal dynasty (see the list in the *Anglo-Saxon Chronicle*, 855). *Creodantreow* was thus perhaps where Egbert's army was assembled in 825 in central Wessex for its move south-westwards against the British.

The editors of the *Place-Names of Devon* (who did not include Egbert's charters amongst their quoted sources: vol. II, 404) noted that the specific place-name "Crediton" (*Crydiantun* and similar) appears only in sources of tenth century and later date – that is, after the establishment of the see in 909. In a mortgage of land (identified as Lower Creedy, near Newton St Cyres: Sawyer no. 1387; see Davidson 1878; Napier & Stevenson 1895) by bishop Eadnoth in 1018, distinction was drawn between the river-name (*Cridia*) and the place-name for Crediton itself (*Cridiamton*). This was the transaction of which the bishop informed the communities of the four *burhs* (see Chapter 4). Crediton's wider ecclesiastical history from this period onwards has been described by Nicholas Orme (in Reuter 1980). In its cathedral (and later) days, Crediton church was supported by a group of clergy, not by monks. From the tenth to thirteenth centuries, the church was dedicated to St. Mary; thereafter, to Holy Cross. In accordance with its earlier elevated status, the estate of Crediton was administered separately from the rest of the medieval diocese. Having ceased to be a cathedral in 1050, it was a collegiate church and parish church throughout the later middle ages and simply a parish church from the sixteenth century.

Unless excavation around the church at Crediton ever reveals early and datable evidence, the question of its precise origin is unlikely to be resolved. The traditional assumption, that a church followed the grant of 739, is perfectly plausible. Indeed, if the intention to build a minster was stated in the original grant of land it is difficult to imagine how Sherborne could easily have avoided this obligation for too long, especially as the nature of the grant, in specifying this particular detail, seems to have been unusual in Devon. Also, if no church had been built before 909 this would have been well-known in Crediton and Exeter circles, perhaps making Leofric's reproduction of the early charter less plausible. Whereas other Saxon minsters in Devon are known to have been associated with royal estates at hundred-centres whose territories were their "parishes", Crediton's circumstances seem particular in pre-Norman Devon in that such a large estate, whose growth was to embrace, then exceed, an entire hundred actually belonged to the church. The foundation of an important minster is more easily explained in such a context, despite the absence of specific reference to Crediton church before the tenth century.

Scepticism about the building of an early minster at Crediton might be supported if the crucial phrase of the eleventh-century "charter of 739" – *ad construendum monasterium* – was suspect. If that had been the case, consideration might be due to the possibility that, like the boundary clause of the charter, the mention of early minster-building had been an eleventh-century interpolation intended to suit contemporary circumstances. But the phrase also occurs (in this or similar form) in up to ten other charters dating from, or purporting to have original sources dating from, the later seventh- and eighth centuries. Some are regarded by various commentators as spurious but several are regarded as authentic: the Sawyer no. first; the *BCS* no. second: 45 (78); 46 (211); 48 (198); 53 (85); 84 (139); 232 (64);

235 (72); 241 (101); 252 (74). It is unlikely that all of these contain later fictions involving the same phrase, and the phrase seems not to occur much after the middle of the eighth century (the overall span of those quoted is from 673 to 762). In her discussion of the Crediton charter, Edwards (1988) thought this phrase was unexceptional and its employment did not undermine the charter's authenticity on this point. On balance, therefore, it seems reasonable to support the traditional view that Aethelheard's original charter had included the stated intention to build a minster/monastery and that one was actually built at some point thereafter. But *proving* beyond all doubt that a church was built at this time seems impossible (at least on historical grounds).

The issue therefore remains an archaeological and topographical one. The influence of minster churches on the growth of rural market-centres in England was very important. At Crediton there are several possibilities of settlement evolution: involving slow and continuous growth from the 8th century onwards (or even earlier), or more rapid growth, with the foundation of the see from the 10th century. The church was the focus of the "east town", a local name for which is also Kirton (known from 14th century onwards – see *PND*, 405), perhaps derived from "church-town" (though apparently in the local view, Kirton derives from Crediton). In the narrative of the rural to urban, Crediton to Exeter shift, which was included in bishop Leofric's "Missal", it was described, in Latin, as *villa* and its diminutive, *villula* (Warren 1883, 2). Domesday Book also described Crediton as a rural territory. The Crediton estate illustrates (as Nicholas Orme, in Reuter 1980, observed) how the development of smaller parishes was slower where a mother church was of particularly high status. Its large territory, occupied by many hamlets and farms, had several dependent chapels by the thirteenth century. But only two of these – at Sandford and Kennerleigh – ever gave rise to separate parishes, and then not until the sixteenth century. In other contexts, the existence of dependent chapelries in a large parish is taken as evidence of an earlier minster church at its centre (see Chapter 3). The possible lines of Crediton's topographical evolution as a minster settlement are discussed in more detail elsewhere (see Chapter 5).

Appendix 3: some influential people in pre-Norman Devon

This list is confined to the "English of high status" in early Devon society. English kings are named (as are some Dumnonian ones) in the appropriate chapters. It is the first portion of what I had hoped would be a wider-ranging assemblage of early Devonian people. Such an assemblage could include: first, all the names which occur on the Dumnonian inscribed memorials, belonging to people of British and Irish descent; second, all the thegns who attested royal charters (though distinguishing Devonians from others who attested, at royal gatherings attended by men from many shires, would be a challenge); third, all the people whose personal names, a few British but mainly English, contributed to the formation of the place-names, mainly recorded for the first time in Domesday Book (though this would be a generic list, since the same names would recur many times); fourth, all the English-named lords whose tenure of land in 1066 is recorded in Domesday Book, some of whom still figured in 1086; fifth, all the English and Scandinavian names of the moneyers who appear on the coinage. Such a collection would provide more flesh for the skeleton of society with which this book has been concerned: this remains a task, for someone, in the future. It would be facilitated by the growth of data on individuals named in early sources which are now available in on-line sources. These sources, whose scope continues to develop, include: The Prosopography of Anglo-Saxon England (through *pase.ac.uk*); an up-dated version of Sawyer's 1968 charter-listing (through *esawyer.org.uk*); and full texts of charters and their witness-lists (through *anglo-saxons.net*).

N.B. Some dates given in what follows are approximate.

A. **Leading Churchmen pre-dating the see of Crediton**
(a) **Bishops of Winchester**: Wini (662–663); Leutherius (670–676); Haeddi (676–705)
(b) **Bishops of Sherborne**: Aldhelm (705–709); Forthhere (709–736); Hereweald (736–766x778); Aethelmod (766x778–789x794); Denefrith (793–796x801); Wigheort (796x801–816x824); Eahlstan (816x824–867); Heahmund (868–871); Aethelheah (871–881x889); Wulfsige (881x889–892x901); Asser (892x901–909).

B. Abbots of the minster church at Exeter *(few are known by name)*
Wulfheard – in the late seventh century – mentioned in Willibald's *Life* of St. Boniface
Sideman – 968–973 – he was bishop of Crediton from 973
Leofric – 973–993 – in an agreement on Stoke Canon with an abbess Eadgyfu
Byrhtelm – witnesses charters of Aethelred II in 993 and 997
Aethelwold – abbot at the time of Cnut's charter to Exeter's minster in 1019
?Wulfweard – witnesses charters of Edward the Confessor up to 1050 (identity not certain)

C. Bishops of Devon, at Crediton *(abbots of earlier minster not known by name)*
Eadwulf – 909–934
Aethelgar – 934–953
Aelfwold I – 953–972
Sideman – 973–977
Aelfric – 977–985x988
Aelfwold II – 985x988–997

Aelfwold III – 997–1012
Eadnoth – 1012–1027
Lyfing – 1027–1046; former abbot of Tavistock; also bishop of St. German's & Worcester)
Leofric – 1046–1050; also bishop of St German's; later bishop of Devon and Cornwall at Exeter

D. Bishop of Devon and Cornwall, at Exeter
Leofric – 1050–1072

E. Ealdormen of Devon
- ? one of the three *praefecti* witnesses of the Crediton charter, 739 (Herefryth, Ecgfrith, Puttoc)
- Ceorl – mentioned in the *Anglo-Saxon Chronicle* and Asser's *Life* of Alfred (851)
- Odda – mentioned in Aethelweard's version of the *Anglo-Saxon Chronicle* (878)
- Aethelred – his death mentioned in the *Anglo-Saxon Chronicle* (899)

F. Ealdormen of the western shires of Wessex
Ordgar – 964–971 (father of Ordulf, founder of Tavistock abbey)
Aethelweard I – 973–998
Aethelmaer – 998–1014 (Aethelweard's son)
Aethelweard II – 1014–1020 (Aethelmaer's son-in-law; founded Buckfast abbey; it was presumably this man who was incorrectly named as *Aethelberht dux* in the charter written for bishop Leofric which re-created a charter to the church at Exeter granted by king Cnut in 1019).

G. Earls of Wessex in the eleventh century
Godwin – 1018–1053
Odda of Deerhurst – 1051–1052 (during exile of Godwinson family)
Harold – 1053–1066 (king Harold II in 1066; defeated by Duke William of Normandy)

H. Sheriffs of Devon
- Kola or Eadsige (*Anglo-Saxon Chronicle* 1001)
- Wada (in Edward Confessor's writ re. Axminster, 1060x1066)
- Heca (mentioned in Domesday Book as lord of West Portlemouth in 1066)
- *given the importance of this office, remarkably few known names are associated with it; but perhaps sheriffs also appeared as thegns, without distinction, in charter witness-lists?*

I. Abbots of Tavistock
- First abbot ?– name unknown (occurs in Aethelred's 981 charter, but not by name)
- Aelfmaer – ?990–?
- Lyfing – 1009–1027 (accompanied Cnut to Rome; later Bishop of Crediton)
- Ealdred – 1027–1043 (later bishop of Hereford/Worcester; then archbishop of York)
- Sihtric – 1043–1082 (occurs in a documented 1045 shire court case in Exeter)

J. Abbots of Buckfast
Either one abbot (Aelwinus/Aelfwine) from foundation c.1018 to 1066 + (occurs in *Exon* DB)
Or (a) first abbot unknown, and (b) Aelwinus from before 1045 (when named in a shire court case in Exeter) to 1066 +.

Sources Used: the foregoing is based largely on standard printed sources. In addition to specific references to narrative and other sources given against individual items, see generally Powicke and Fryde 1961, Birch 1885–99 (*BCS*), Sawyer 1968; Barlow 1963 on the churchmen; Finberg 1951 and Holdsworth 2003 on Tavistock. Some names have also been checked against the *pase* database.

Bibliography

The following is not a full academic Bibliography of the Devonian subject and its wider context, but a list of items found helpful in the writing of this book. Some are cited at the end of each chapter as aids to further reading and as indications of the sources used.

Abels, R.P. 1988: *Lordship and Military Obligation in Anglo-Saxon England* (London. British Museum)

Abrams, L. 1996: *Anglo-Saxon Glastonbury: Church and Endowment* (Woodbridge. Boydell Press)

Alexander, J.J. 1916: The Aethelstan Myth, *Transactions of the Devonshire Association*, 48, 174-179

Alexander, J.J. 1919–1922: When the Saxons came to Devon; Part I, *Transactions of the Devonshire Association*, 51, 152-168; Part II, 52, 293-309; Part III, 53, 168-179; Part IV, 54,187-198

Alexander, J.J. 1931: The beginnings of Lifton, *Transactions of the Devonshire Association*, 63, 349-358

Alexander, J.J. 1932: Presidential Address. The Saxon Conquest and Settlement, *Transactions of the Devonshire Association*, 64, 75-112

Alexander, L. 1995: The legal status of the native Britons in late seventh century Wessex as reflected in the law-code of Ine, *Haskins Society Journal*, 7, 31-38

Allan, J.P., Henderson, C.G. & Higham, R.A. 1984: Saxon Exeter, in Haslam, J. (ed), 385-414

Allan, J.P. 1994, Medieval Pottery and the Dating of Medieval Settlements on Dartmoor, *Proceedings of the Devon Archaeological Society*, 52, 141-147

Allan, J.P. 2002: The Anglo-Saxon Mint at Lydford, *Transactions of the Devonshire Association*, 134, 9-32.

Aston, M. 1989: The development of medieval rural settlement in Somerset, in Higham (ed), 19-40

Aston, M. & Lewis, C. (eds) 1994: *The Medieval Landscape of Wessex* (Oxford. Oxbow)

Aston, M. & Gerrard, C. 1999: 'Unique, traditional and charming'. The Shapwick Project, Somerset, *Antiquaries Journal*, 79, 1-58

Baker, N. & Holt, R. 1998: The Origins of Urban Parish Boundaries', in Slater, T.R. & Rosser, G. (eds), *The Church in the Medieval Town* (Aldershot. Ashgate), 209-235

Barber, C. 1993: *The English Language: a historical introduction* (Cambridge University Press)

Barlow, F. 1963: *The English Church 1000–1066: a Constitutional History* (London. Longmans)

Barlow, F. et alii 1972: *Leofric of Exeter* (University of Exeter Press)

Barlow, F. 1991: An Introduction to the Devonshire Domesday, in *The Devonshire Domesday* (Alecto Historical Editions), 1-25

Barlow, F. 1996: *English Episcopal Acta. XI. Exeter 1046–1184.* (Oxford University Press for the British Academy)

Barlow, F. 2002: *The Godwins* (Edinburh, London. Longman Pearson)

Barnes, G. & Williamson, T. 2006: *Hedgerow History: Ecology, History and Landscape Character* (Windgather Press)

Baugh, A.C. & Cable, T, 1993: *A History of the English Language* (London. Routledge. 4th Edition)

Beresford, M.W. 1967: *New Towns of the Middle Ages* (London. Lutterworth Press)

Biek, L. *et alii* 1994: Tin ingots found at Praa sands, Breage, in 1974, *Cornish Archaeology*, 33, 57-70

Birch, W. de Gray, 1885-1899: *Cartularium Saxonicum* (4 vols. London)

Blackburn, M.A.S. (ed) 1986: *Anglo-Saxon Monetary History* (Leicester Univ. Press)

Blair 1985: Secular minster churches in Domesday Book, in Sawyer, P. (ed), *Domesday Book: a re-assessment* (London. Edward Arnold), 104-142

Blair, J. 1987: Local churches in Domesday and before, in Holt (ed), 265-278

Blair, J. (ed) 1988: *Minsters and Parish Churches: the local church in transition 950–1200* (Oxford University Committee for Archaeology. Monograph No. 17)

Blair, J. 1992(a): Anglo-Saxon Minsters: a topographical review, in Blair & Sharp (eds), 226-266

Blair, J. 1992(b): The Making of the English Parish, *Medieval History*, 2, pt.2, 13-19

Blair, J. 1995: Ecclesiastical organization and pastoral care in Anglo-Saxon England, *Early Medieval Europe*, 4, 193-212

Blair, J. 2002: A saint for every minster? Local cults in Anglo-Saxon England, in Thacker & Sharpe (eds), 455-494

Blair, J. 2005: *The Church in Anglo-Saxon Society* (Oxford University Press)

Bibliography

Blair, J. & Sharpe, R. (eds) 1992: *Pastoral Care before the Parish* (Leicester Unversity Press)

Blair, J. & Orme, N. 1995: The Anglo-Saxon Minster and Cathedral at Exeter: twin churches, *Friends of Exeter Cathedral, Annual Report,* 65, 24-26

Blake, D.W. 1974: Bishop Leofric, *Transactions of the Devonshire Association,* 106, 47-57

Blaylock, S.R. & Westcott, K.A. 1989: Late Saxon fabric in St. Martin's church, Exeter, *Proceedings of the Devon Archaeological Society,* 47, 119-122

Boggis, R.J.E. 1922: *A History of the Diocese of Exeter* (Exeter)

Branscombe, R. 2004: *A Guide to the church of Saint Winifred, Branscombe* (Branscombe Parish Council; 2nd ed.)

Breeze, A. 2005: The Anglo-Saxon Chronicle for 661 and Posbury, Devon, *Devon and Cornwall Notes and Queries,* 39 (pt.vii), 193-195

Brooks, N.P. 1996: The administrative background to the Burghal Hidage, in Hill & Rumble (eds), 128-150

Bruce-Mitford, R. 1997: *Mawgan Porth: A settlement of the late Saxon period on the north Cornish coast. Excavations 1949–52, 1954, and 1974* (ed. R.J.Taylor; English Heritage Report no. 13)

Burrow, I.C.G. 1973: Devon 300–700 AD, in *Archaeological Review for 1972* (CBA Groups XII & XIII), 46-47

Burrow, I.C.G. 1977: The town defences of Exeter, *Transactions of the Devonshire Association,* 109, 13-40

Cambridge, E. & Rollason, D. 1995: The pastoral organization of the Anglo-Saxon Church: a review of the "minster hypothesis", *Early Medieval Europe,* 4, 87-104

Cameron, K. 1979-80: The meaning and significance of Old English *walh* in English place-names, *Journal of the English Place-name Society,* 12, 1-53

Campbell, A. 1962: *The Chronicle of Aethelweard* (London. Nelson)

Campbell, J. 2000: Some Agents and Agencies in the late Anglo-Saxon State, in idem (ed), *The Anglo-Saxon State* (Hambledon), 201-225

Cave, W. 1899: Notes on the Saxon crypt, Sidbury church, Devonshire, *Archaeological Journal,* 56, 74-76

Chadwick, N. K. 1969: *Early Brittany* (Cardiff. University of Wales Press)

Chaplais, P. 1966: The authenticity of the royal Anglo-Saxon diplomas of Exeter, *Bulletin of the Institute of Historical Research,* 39, 1-34

Chapman, L. 2001: *The Living History of our Hedgerows* (Chudleigh, Devon. Orchard Publications)

Charles-Edwards, T. 1995: Language and society among the insular Celts 400–1000, in Green, M.J. (ed), *The Celtic World* (London. New York. Routledge), 703-736

Charles-Edwards, T. 2004: The making of nations in Britain and Ireland in the early middle ages, in Evans. R. (ed), 11-37

Cherry, B. & Pevsner, N. 1989: *The Buildings of England: Devon* (Harmondsworth. Penguin Books)

Clarke, P. 1994: *The English Nobility under Edward the Confessor* (Oxford. Clarendon Press)

Coates, R., Breeze, A. & Horovitz, D. 2000: *Celtic Voices, English Place-Names. Studies in the Celtic Impact on Place-Names in England* (Stamford, Lincs. Shaun Tyas)

Colgrave, B. & Mynors, R.A.B. (eds) 1969: *Bede's Ecclesiastical History of the English People* (Oxford. Clarendon Press)

Collis, J. 2003: *The Celts: Origins, Myths, Inventions* (Stroud. Tempus Books)

Conner, P.W. 1993: *Anglo-Saxon Exeter. A Tenth Century Cultural History* (Woodbridge. Boydell)

Cook, D. 2004: *St Boniface, 675–754: the first European* (Crediton. Crediton Church Corporation)

Costen, M. 1992: *The Origins of Somerset* (Manchester University Press)

Cramp, R. 2006: *Corpus of Anglo-Saxon Stone Sculpture, Vol. VII: South West England* (Oxford University Press for the British Academy)

Creighton, O. & Higham, R. 2005: *Medieval Town Walls: an archaeology and social history of urban defence* (Stroud: Tempus)

Crick, J. 2004: *Pristina Libertas*: Liberty and the Anglo-Saxons re-visited, *Transactions of the Royal Historical Society*, 6th series, 14, 47-71

Crick, J. forthcoming: Exeter in Devon: a shire town in the Anglo-Saxon and Norman periods

Darby. H.C. & Welldon Finn, R. (eds) 1967: *The Domesday Geography of South West England* (Cambridge University Press)

Darby, H.C. 1977: *Domesday England* (Cambridge University Press)

Darby, H.C. 1987: Domesday Book and the Geographer, in Holt (ed), 101-119

Dark, K.R. 1994: *Civitas to Kingdom. British Political Continuity 300–800* (Leicester. Leicester University Press)

Darlington, R.R. & McGurk, P. (eds) 1995: *The Chronicle of John of Worcester*, Vol. II (Oxford. Clarendon Press)

Davidson, J.B. 1878: On some ancient documents relating to Crediton minster, *Transactions of the Devonshire Association*, 10, 237-254

Davies, W. 1982: The Latin charter tradition in western Britain, Brittany and Ireland in the early medieval period, in Whitelock, D. et alii (eds), *Ireland in Eraly Medieval Europe: studies in memory of Kathleen Hughes* (Cambridge University Press), 258-280

Davies, W. 1992: The myth of the Celtic church, in Edwards & Lane (eds), 12-21

Dolley, R.H.M. (ed) 1961: *Anglo-Saxon Coins: Studies presented to F.M.Stenton* (London. Methuen)

Dyer, M. & Allan, J.P. 2004: An excavation on the Defences of the Anglo-Saxon

Burh and Medieval Town of Totnes, *Proceedings of the Devon Archaeological Society*, 62, 53-77

Edwards, H. 1988: *The Charters of the Early West Saxon Kingdom* (British Archaeological Reports, British Series, 198)

Edwards, N. & Lane, A. (eds) 1992: *The Early Church in Wales and the West* (Oxbow monograph, 16)

Ekwall, E. 1960: *The Concise Oxford Dictionary of English Place-Names* (Oxford. Clarendon Press. 4th edition)

Elworthy, F. T. 1875-1877: *The dialect of West Somerset (and) an outline of the grammar of the dialect of West Somerset* (English Dialect Society; Series D. Miscellaneous; two volumes in one)

Elworthy, F.T. 1886: *The West Somerset Word-Book: a glossary of dialectical and archaic words and phrases used in the west of Somerset and east Devon* (English Dialect Society; two vols)

Emerton, E. 1940: *The Letters of Saint Boniface* (New York. Columbia Press)

Erskine. A.M. et alii 1988: *Exeter Cathedral: a short history and description* (Exeter. Dean & Chapter, Exeter Cathedral)

Evans, R. (ed) 2004: *Lordship and Learning: Studies in Memory of Trevor Aston* (Woodbridge. Boydell Press)

Faith, R. 1997: *The English Peasantry and the Growth of Lordship* (Leicester University Press)

Faith, R. 2004: Cola's *tun:* rural social structure in late Anglo-Saxon Devon, in Evans, R. (ed), 63-78

Farley, M.E. & Little, R.I. 1968: Oldaport, Modbury: a re-assessment of the fort and harbour, *Proceedings of the Devon Archaeological Society*, 26, 31-36

Farmer, D.H. 1992: *The Oxford Dictionary of Saints* (Oxford University Press. 3rd edition)

Filppula, M; Klemola, J; Pitkanen, H. (eds) 2002: *The Celtic Roots of English* (Studies in Languages, 37; University of Joensuu, Finland)

Finberg, H.P.R. 1951: *Tavistock Abbey* (Cambridge University Press)*)*

Finberg, H.P.R. 1952(a): The Open Field in Devon, in Hoskins & Finberg, 265-288

Finberg, H.P.R. 1952(b): The borough of Tavistock: its origin and early history, in Hoskins & Finberg, 172-197

Finberg 1953: *The Early Charters of Devon and Cornwall* (Leicester. Department of English Local History. Occasional Papers, No. 2; with Supplement in Hoskins 1960)

Finberg, H.P.R. 1964: Sherborne, Glastonbury and the Expansion of Wessex, in idem, *Lucerna* (London. Macmillan), 95-115

Finberg, H.P.R. 1964(a): The Making of a Boundary, in idem, *Lucerna* (London. Macmillan), 161-180

Finberg, H.P.R. 1964(b): Hyple's Old Land, in idem, *Lucerna* (London. Macmillan), 116-130

Finberg, H.P.R. 1968: Some Crediton documents re-examined, *Antiquaries Journal*, 88, 59-86 (re-printed as Fact and Fiction from Crediton, in Finberg 1969, 29-69)

Finberg, H.P.R. 1969: *West Country Historical Studies* (Newton Abbot. David & Charles)

Finberg, H.P.R. (ed) 1972: *The Agrarian History of England and Wales. Vol I. Part II. AD 43-1042* (Cambridge University Press)

Fisher, E.A. 1962: *The Greater Anglo-Saxon Churches: an Architectural-Historical Study* (London. Faber & Faber)

Fisher, E.A. 1969: *Anglo-Saxon Towers* (Newton Abbot. David & Charles)

Fleming, R. 1993: Rural elites and urban communities in late Saxon England, *Past and Present*, 141, 3-37

Fleming, R. 2000: The new wealth, the new rich and the new political style in late Anglo-Saxon England, *Anglo-Norman Studies*, XXIII, 1-22

Fleming, A. & Ralph, N. 1982: Medieval settlement and land-use on Holne Moor, Dartmoor: the landscape evidence, *Medieval Archaeology*, 26, 101-137

Foot, S. 1996: The making of *Angelcynn*: English identity before the Norman Conquest, *Transactions of the Royal Historical Society*, 6th Series, 6, 25-49

Foot, S. 1999: Remembering, Forgetting and Inventing: Attitudes to the Past in England at the End of the First Viking Age, *Transactions of the Royal Historical Society*, 6th Series, 9, 185-200

Foot, S. 2000: *Veiled Women: the disappearance of nuns from Anglo-Saxon England* (Aldershot. Ashgate. 2 vols)

Fowler, P.J. & Thomas, A.C. 1962: Arable fields of the pre-Norman at Gwithian, *Cornish Archaeology*, 1, 61-84

Fowler, P.J. 2002: *Farming in the First Millennium AD* (Cambridge University Press)

Fox, A. 1952: *Roman Exeter* (Manchester University Press)

Fox, A. 1973: *South-West England* (2nd ed. Newton Abbot. David & Charles)

Fox, A. 1995: Tin ingots from Bigbury Bay, South Devon, *Proceedings of the Devon Archaeological Society*, 53, 11-23

Fox, H.S.A. 1970: The boundary of Uplyme, *Transactions of the Devonshire Association*, 102, 35-47

Fox, H.S.A. 1975: The chronology of enclosure and economic development in medieval Devon, *Economic History Review*, 2nd series, 28, 181-202

Fox, H.S.A. 1983: Contraction, desertion and dwindling of dispersed settlement in a Devon parish, *Medieval Village Research Group, Annual Report*, 31, 40-42

Fox, H.S.A. 1989: Peasant farmers, patterns of settlement and *pays*, in Higham (ed), 41-73

Fox, H.S.A. 1991: Devon and Cornwall, in Miller (ed), 152-174; 303-323; 722-743

Bibliography

Fox, H.S.A. (ed) 1996(a): *Seasonal Settlement* (University of Leicester)

Fox, H.S.A. 1996(b): Transhumance and Seasonal Settlement, in Fox (ed) 1999(a), 1-23

Fox, H.S.A. 2001: *The Evolution of the Fishing Village: landscape and society along the south Devon coast, 1086-1550* (Oxford. Leopard's Head Press)

Fox, H.S.A. 2004: Taxation and settlement in Medieval Devon, in *Thirteenth Century England*, X (Proceedings of the Durham Conference, 2003; Boydell Press), 167-185

Fox, H.S.A. 2006(a): Foreword, in Turner (ed), xi-xvi

Fox, H.S.A. 2006(b): Fragmented manors and the customs of the Anglo-Saxons, in Keynes, S. & Smyth, A.P. (eds), *Anglo-Saxons: studies presented to Cyril Roy Hart* (Dublin. Four Courts Press), 78-97

Fyfe, R. & Rippon, S.J. 2004: A landscape in transition? Palaeoenevironmental evidence for the end of the "Romano-British" period in Southwest England, in Collins, R. & Gerrard, J. (eds), *Debating late Antiquity in Britain AD 300–700* (BAR. British Series, 365), 33-42

Fyfe, R., Brown, A.G. & Rippon, S.J. 2004: Characterising the late prehistoric, "Romano-British" and medieval landscape and dating the emergence of of a regionally distinct agricultural system in South West Britain, *Journal of Archaeological Science*, 31, 1699-1714

Galliou, P. & Jones, M. 1991: *The Bretons* (Oxford. Blackwell)

Gameson, R. 1996: The origin of the Exeter Book of Old English Poetry, *Anglo-Saxon England*, 25, 135-185

Gearey, B.R. *et alii* 1997: The landscape context of medieval settlement on the south-western moors of England: recent palaeoenvironmental evidence from Bodmin Moor and Dartmoor, *Medieval Archaeology*, 41, 195-208

Gelling, M. 1978: *Signposts to the Past* (London. Dent)

Gelling, M. 1984: *Place-Names in the Landscape* (London. Dent)

Gelling, M. 1993: Why aren't we speaking Welsh?, in *Anglo-Saxon Studies in History and Archaeology*, 6, 51-56

Gelling, M. & Cole, A. 2000: *Landscape of Place-Names* (Stamford. Shaun Tyas)

Gem, R. 1988: The English parish church in the 11th and early 12th centuries: a great re-building?, in Blair, J. (ed), 21-30

Gillingham, J. 1995: Thegns and Knights in Eleventh Century England: who was then the gentleman?, *Transactions of the Royal Historical Society*, 6th series, V, 129-153

Giot, P-R; Guignon, P; Merdrignac, B. 2003: *The British Settlement of Brittany* (Stroud. Tempus)

Glendining & Co. 1970: *Catalogue of the R.P.V. Brettell Collection of Coins of Exeter* (London)

Gore, D. 2001: *The Vikings and Devon* (Exeter. The Mint Press)

Gore, D. 2004: Britons, Saxons and Vikings in the South-West, in Adams, J. &

Holman, K. (eds), *Scandinavia and Europe 800–1350: Contact, Conflict and Co-existence* (Turnhout. Brepols), 35-41

Gover, J., Mawer, A. & Stenton, F. (eds) 1931–32: *The Place-Names of Devon* (2 vols. English Place-name Society)

Gover, J., Mawer, A. & Stenton, F. (eds) 1939: *The Place-Names of Wiltshire* (English Place-name Society)

Grant, N. 1995: The occupation of hillforts in Devon during the late Roman and post-Roman periods, *Proceedings of the Devon Archaeological Society*, 53, 97-108

Green, M.J. (ed) 1995: *The Celtic World* (London. New York. Routledge)

Greenaway, G.W. 1955: *Saint Boniface: three biographical studies for the twelfth centenary festival* (London. Black)

Greenway, D. (ed) 1996: *Henry, Archdeacon of Huntingdon: The History of the English People* (Oxford. Clarendon Press)

Griffith, F.M. 1986: Salvage observations at the Dark Age site of Bantham Ham, Thurlestone, *Proceedings of the Devon Archaeological Society*, 44, 39-57

Griffith, F.M. 1988(a): *Devon's Past: an aerial view* (Devon County Council. Devon Books)

Griffith, F.M. 1988(b): A Romano-British villa near Crediton, *Proceedings of the Devon Archaeological Society*, 46, 137-142

Griffith, F.M. 1994: Changing perceptions of the context of prehistoric Dartmoor, *Proceedings of the Devon Archaeological Society*, 52, 85-99

Griffith, F.M. & Weddell, P. 1995: Ironworking in the Blackdown Hills, in Crew, P. & Crew, S. (eds), *Iron for Archaeologists: a review of recent work on the archaeology of early ironworking sites in Europe*, 13-15

Griffith, F.M. & Weddell, P. 1996: Ironworking in the Blackdown Hills: results of recent survey, *Mining History. The Bulletin of the Peak District Mines Historical Society*, 13, no.2, 27-34

Griffith, F.M. & Quinnell, H. 1999(a): Settlement 2500 BC to AD 600, in Kain, R., and Ravenhill, W. (eds), 62-68

Griffith, F.M. & Quinnell, H. 1999(b): Iron Age to Roman Buildings, Structures and Coin and other Find Spots, in Kain, R. and Ravenhill, W. (eds), 74-76

Griffith, F.M. & Wilkes, E.M. 2006: The land named from the sea? Coastal archaeology and place-names of Bigbury bay, Devon, *Archaeological Journal*, 163, 67-91

Grundy, G.B. 1919: The Saxon land charters of Wiltshire, *Archaeological Journal*, 76, 143-301

Gunn, J.D. (ed) 2000: *The Years without summer: tracing AD 536 and its aftermath* (British Archaeological Reports, International Series, no. 872)

Hall, T. 2000: *Minster Churches in the Dorset Landscape* (BAR. Brit. Ser. No. 304)

Bibliography

Hall, T. 2005: Sherborne: Saxon Christianity *be Westanwuda*, in Barker, K. et alii, (eds), *St. Wulfsige and Sherborne* (Oxford. Oxbow Books), 133-148

Hallam, H.E. (ed) 1988: *The Agrarian History of England and Wales. Vol II. 1042–1350* (Cambridge University Press)

Hamerow, H. 1991: Settlement mobility and the "middle Saxon shift", *Anglo-Saxon England*, 20, 1-17

Handley, M.A. 2001: The Origins of Christian Commemoration in Late Antique Britain, *Early Medieval Europe,* 10, no. 2, 177-199

Harmer, F.E. 1989: *Anglo-Saxon Writs* (Manchester University Press 1st ed. 1952; Stamford. Paul Watkins. 2nd edition 1989)

Hase, P.H. 1994: The Church in the Wessex Heartlands, in Aston & Lewis (eds), 47-81

Haslam, J. (ed) 1984 (a): *Anglo-Saxon Towns in Southern England* (Chichester. Phillimore)

Haslam, J. 1984 (b): The Towns of Devon, in Haslam, J. (ed), 249-283

Haslam, J. 2006: King Alfred and the Vikings: strategies and tactics, 876–886AD, in *Anglo-Saxon Studies in Archaeology and History,* 13, 122-154

Hatcher 1988: South-western England, in Hallam (ed), 234-245; 383-398; 675-685

Henderson, C.G. 1999: The City of Exeter from AD 50 to the Early Nineteenth Century, in Kain, R. and Ravenhill, W. (eds), 482-498

Henderson, C.G. 2001: The development of the South Gate of Exeter and its role in the city's defences, *Proceedings of the Devon Archaeological Society*, 59, 45-123

Henderson, C.G. & Bidwell, P.T 1982: The Saxon minster at Exeter, in Pearce, S. (ed), *The Early Church in Western Britain and Ireland* (British Archaeological Reports, British Series, 102), 145-175

Henderson, C.G. & Weddell, P.J. 1985: Archaeological Investigations at Crediton Vicarage, 1984: preliminary report (Exeter Museums Archaeological Field Unit report)

Henderson, C.G. & Weddell, P.J. 1994: Medieval settlements on Dartmoor and in West Devon: the evidence from excavations, *Proceedings of the Devon Archaeological Society*, 52, 119-140

Herring, P. 1996: Transhumance in medieval Cornwall, in Fox (ed) 1996(a), 35-44

Herring, P. 2006: Cornish Strip Fields, in Turner (ed), 44-77

Higham, N. J. 1991: Old light on the dark Age landscape: the description of Britain in *De Excidio Britanniae* of Gildas, *Journal of Historical Geography,* 17, no. 4, 363-372

Higham, N.J. 1992: *Rome, Britain and the Anglo-Saxons* (London. Seaby)

Higham, N.J. 1994: *The English Conquest: Gildas and Britain in the Fifth Century* (Manchester University Press)

Higham, R.A. 1987: Public and Private Defence in the Medieval South West:

Town, Castle and Fort, in idem (ed), *Security and Defence in South-West England before 1800* (University of Exeter Press), 27-49

Higham, R.A. (ed) 1989: *Landscape and Townscape in the South West* (University of Exeter Press)

Hill, D. 1981: *An Atlas of Anglo-Saxon England* (Oxford. Blackwell)

Hill, D. & Rumble, A. (eds) 1996: *The Defence of Wessex: the Burghal Hidage and Anglo-Saxon Fortifications* (Manchester University Press)

Hills. C. 2003: *Origins of the English* (London. Duckworth)

Holdsworth 1980: Saint Boniface the Monk, in Reuter, T. (ed), 49-67

Holdsworth, C. (ed) 1986: *Domesday Essays* (University of Exeter Press)

Holdsworth, C. 1986(a): The church of Domesday, in Holdsworth, C. (ed), 51-64.

Holdsworth, C. 1991: From 1050 to 1307, in Orme, N. (ed), 23-52

Holdsworth, C. 1999: Ecclesiastical institutions in 1086 and monastic houses c. 1300, in Kain, R. and Ravenhill, W. (eds), 206-211

Holdsworth, C. 2003: Tavistock Abbey in its late tenth century context, *Transactions of the Devonshire Association*, 135, 31-58

Hollister, C.W. 1962: *Anglo-Saxon Military Institutions* (Oxford. Clarendon Press)

Holt, J.C. (ed) 1987: *Domesday Studies* (Woodbridge. Boydell Press)

Hooke, D. 1990: Studies on Devon charter boundaries, *Transactions of the Devonshire Association*, 122, 193-211

Hooke, D. 1994: *Pre-Conquest Charter Bounds of Devon and Cornwall* (Woodbridge. Boydell)

Hooke, D. 1999: Saxon conquest and settlement, in Kain, R. and Ravenhill, W. (eds), 95-104

Hooper, M. 1970: Hedges and History, *New Scientist* (31 December), 598-600

Hoskins, W.G. 1952: The Making of the Agrarian Landscape, in Hoskins & Finberg, 289-333

Hoskins, W.G. 1954: *Devon* (London. Collis; revised edition, Devon Books 1992)

Hoskins, W.G. 1955: *Making of the English Landscape* (London. Hodder & Stoughton; 2nd ed. 1988)

Hoskins, W.G. 1960: *The Westward Expansion of Wessex* (Leicester. Department of English Local History. Occasional Papers, No. 13)

Hoskins, W.G. 1963(a): The Highland Zone in Domesday Book, in idem (ed) 1963(b), 15-52

Hoskins, W.G. (ed) 1963(b): *Provincial England: essays in social and economic history* (London. Macmillan)

Hoskins, W.G. 1967: *Fieldwork in Local History* (London. Faber & Faber)

Hoskins, W.G. & Finberg, H.P.R. 1952: *Devonshire Studies* (London. Jonathan Cape)

Bibliography

Insley, C. 1998: Charters and Episcopal Scriptoria in the Anglo-Saxon South West', *Early Medieval Europe*, 7.2, 173-197

Jackson, A. 1972: Medieval Exeter, the Exe and the Earldom of Devon, *Transactions of the Devonshire Association*, 104, 57-79

Jackson. K. 1994: *Language and History in early Britain* (2nd ed. Dublin. Four Courts Press; first published 1953)

Jankulak, K. 2000: *The Medieval Cult of St Petroc* (Studies in Celtic History, XIX; Woodbridge: Boydell)

Juleff, G. 2005: Exmoor Iron, in *Exmoor National Park Authority: Historic Environment Review 2004*, unpaginated

Juleff, G. 2006: Exmoor Iron, in *Exmoor National Park Authority: Historic Environment Review 2005*, unpaginated

Kain, R. & Ravenhill, W. (eds) 1999: *Historical Atlas of South West England* (University of Exeter Press)

Kain, R. (ed) 2006: *England's landscapes: the South West* (English Heritage)

Kemble, J.M. 1839–1848: *Codex Diplomaticus Aevi Saxonici* (6 vols. London)

Keynes, S. & Lapidge, M. (eds) 1983: *Alfred the Great: Asser's Life of King Alfred and other contemporary sources* (Harmonsworth. Penguin)

Knowles, D. et alii 2001: *The Heads of Religious Houses: England and Wales, Vol. I. 940–1216* (revised edition, C.N.L. Brooke; Cambridge University Press)

Lapidge, M. 1984: Gildas's education and the Latin culture of sub-Roman Britain, in Lapidge, M. & Dumville, D. (eds), *Gildas: new approaches* (Studies in Celtic History, V; Woodbridge. Boydell Press), 27-50

Lennard, R. 1959: *Rural England 1086–1135* (Oxford. Clarendon Press)

Lepine, D. & Orme, N. 2003: *Death and Memory in Medieval Exeter* (Devon and Cornwall Record Society, new series, vol. 46)

Liebermann, F. (ed) 1903–1916: *Die Gesetze der Angelsachsen* (3 vols)

Luscombe, P. 2005: Charters, place-names and Anglo-Saxon settlement in South Devon, *Transactions of the Devonshire Association*, 137, 89-137

Maddicott, J.R. 1989: Trade, Industry and the Wealth of King Alfred, *Past and Present*, 123 (May), 3-51

Maddicott, J.R. 1997: Plague in seventh century England, *Past and Present*, 156, 7-54

Manning, P. & Stead, P. 2002-2003: Excavation of an early Christian cemetery at Althea Library, Padstow, *Cornish Archaeology*, 41-42, 80-106

Michelmore, A.P.G. & Proctor, M.C.F. 1994: The Hedges of Farleigh farm, Chudleigh, *Transactions of the Devonshire Association*, 126, 57-84

Miles, T. 1986: The excavation of a Saxon cemetery and part of the Norman castle at North Walk, Barnstaple, *Proceedings of the Devon Archaeological Society*, 44, 59-84.

Miller, E. (ed) 1991: *The Agrarian History of England and Wales, Vol. III. 1348–1500* (Cambridge. Cambridge University Press)

Morris, J. 1980: *Nennius: British History and the Welsh Annals* (Chichester. Phillimore)

Morris, R. 1989: *Churches in the Landscape* (London. Dent)

Morris, W. A. 1927: *The English Medieval Sheriff to 1300* (Manchester Univ. Press)

Muir, B. J. (ed) 1994: *The Exeter Anthology of Old English Poetry: an edition of Exeter Dean and Chapter MS 3501* (Exeter University Press, 2 vols; 2nd edition 2000; DVD edition 2006)

Mynors, R.A.B., Thompson, R.M., Winterbottom, M. (eds) 1998-99: *William of Malmesbury: Gesta Regum Anglorum. The History of the English Kings* (Oxford. Clarendon Press. 2 vols).

Napier, A.S & Stevenson, W.H. 1895: *The Crawford Collection of Early Charters and Documents now in the Bodleian Library* (Oxford. Clarendon Press)

Okasha, E. 1993: *Corpus of Early Christian Inscribed Stones in South-west Britain* (Leicester University Press)

Oliver, G. 1846: *Monasticon Dioecesis Exoniensis* (London & Exeter)

Olson, L. 1989: *Early Monasteries in Cornwall* (Studies in Celtic History, XI; Woodbridge. Boydell Press)

Orchard, N. (ed) 2002: *The Leofric Missal* (London: Bradshaw Society, 113-114; 2 vols)

Orme. N.I. 1980, The church in Crediton from St. Boniface to the Reformation, in Reuter, T. (ed), 97-131

Orme, N. 1986: The medieval parishes of Devon, *Devon Historian*, 33, 3-9

Orme, N. 1991(a) (ed), *Unity and Variety: a History of the Church in Devon and Cornwall* (University of Exeter Press)

Orme. N. 1991(b): From the beginnings to 1050, in idem (ed), 1-22

Orme, N. 1995: Two unusual Devon saints, *Devon Historian*, 51, 10-13

Orme, N. 1996: *English Church Dedications: with a survey of Cornwall and Devon* (University of Exeter Press)

Orme, N. & Henderson, C.G. 1999: Exeter Cathedral, in Kain, R. and Ravenhill, W. (eds), 499-502

O'Donovan, M.A. 1988: *Charters of Sherborne* (Oxford University Press for the British Academy)

Padel, O.J. 1978: Two new pre-conquest charters for Cornwall, *Cornish Studies*, 6, 20-27

Padel, O.J. 1985: *Cornish Place-name Elements* (Nottingham. English Place-Name Society)

Padel, O.J. 1988: *A Popular Dictionary of Cornish Place-Names* (Penzance. Hodge)

Padel, O.J. 1999: Place-names, in Kain, R. and Ravenhill, W. (eds), 88-94

Padel, O.J. 2002: Local Saints and Place-names in Cornwall, in Thacker & Sharpe (eds), 303-360

Bibliography

Padel. O.J. 2005: The charter of Lanlawren (Cornwall), in O'Brien O'Keeffe, K. & Orchard, A.. (eds), *Latin Learning and English Lore: Studies in Anglo-Saxon Literature for Michael Lapidge* (Toronto, 2 vols), 74-85

Page, W. (ed) 1906: *Victoria History of the County of Devon, Vol. I* (London)

Page, W. 1915: Some remarks on the churches of the Domesday Survey, *Archaeologia*, 2nd series, XVI, 61-102

Palliser, D. (ed) 2000: *The Cambridge Urban History of Britain, Vol. I, 600–1540* (Cambridge University Press)

Pearce, S.M. 1978: *The Kingdom of Dumnonia* (Padstow. Lodenek Press)

Pearce, S.M. 1982 (a) (ed): *the Early Church in Western Britain and Ireland* (British Archaeological Reports. British Series, 102)

Pearce, S.M. 1982 (b): Church and Society in South Devon AD 350–700, *Proceedings of the Devon Archaeological Society*, 40, 1-18

Pearce, S.M.. 1985 (a): The Early Church in the Landscape: the evidence from North Devon, *Archaeological Journal*, 142, 255-275

Pearce, S.M. 1985 (b): Early medieval land-use on Dartmoor and its flanks, *Devon Archaeology*, 3, 13-19

Pearce, S.M. 2004: *South-Western Britain in the Early Middle Ages* (Leicester University Press)

Pelteret, D.A.E. 1995: *Slavery in Early Medieval England* (Woodbridge. Boydell Press)

Petts, D. 2002: Cemeteries and Boundaries in Western Britain, in Lucy, S. & Reynolds, A. (eds) *Burial in early Medieval England and Wales* (London. Society for Medieval Archaeology), 24-46

Pollard, E., Hooper, M.D.& Moore, N.W. 1974: *The New Naturalist: Hedges* (London. Collins)

Pounds, N.J.G. 2000: *A History of the English Parish* (Cambridge University Press)

Powicke, F.M. & Fryde, E.B. (eds), 1961: *Handbook of British Chronology* (London. Royal Historical Society. 2nd edition).

Preston-Jones, A. 1992: Decoding Cornish Churchyards, in Edwards, N. and Lane, A. (eds), 104-124

Quinnell, H. 1993: A sense of identity: distinctive Cornish stone artefacts in the Roman and post-Roman periods, *Cornish Archaeology*, 32, 29-46

Quinnell, H. 2004: *Trethurgy. Excavations at Trethurgy Round, St. Austell: Community and Status in Roman and Post-Roman Cornwall* (Truro. Cornwall County Council)

Rackham, O. 1986: *The History of the Countryside* (London. Dent)

Rackham, O. 1990: *Trees and Woodland in the British Landscape* (London. Dent. 2nd ed.)

Radford, C.A.R. 1957: Sidbury Church, *Archaeological Journal*, 114, 166-167

Radford, C.A.R. 1970: The later pre-conquest boroughs and their defences, *Medieval Archaeology*, 14, 83-103

Radford, C.A.R. 1975: The Pre-Conquest Church and the Old Minsters of Devon, *Devon Historian*, 11, 2-11

Rainbird, P. 1998: Oldaport and the Anglo-Saxon defence of Devon, *Proceedings of the Devon Archaeological Society*, 56, 153-164

Rainbird, P. & Druce, D. 2004: A late Saxon date from Oldaport, *Proceedings of the Devon Archaeological Society*, 62, 177-180

Rattue, J. 1995: *The Living Stream: Holy Wells in Historical Context* (Woodbridge. Boydell Press)

Ravenhill, W. 1969(a): The evolution of settlement in Celtic, Saxon and medieval times, in Barlow, F. (ed), *Exeter and its Region* (Exeter University & British Association for the Advancement of Science), 150-163

Ravenhill, W. 1969(b): The early settlement of South-West England, in *South West England* (eds. Shorter, Ravenhill & Gregory. London. Nelson), 81-111

Ravenhill, W. 1999: Population distribution from the Domesday Book of 1086, in Kain, R. and Ravenhill, W. (eds), 107-109

Reed, S.J., Juleff, G., Bayer, O.J. 2006: Three late Saxon iron-smelting furnaces at Burlescombe, Devon, *Proceedings of the Devon Archaeological Society*, 64, 71-122

Reichel, O.J. 1939: The church and the hundreds of Devon, *Transactions of the Devonshire Association*, 71, 331-342

Reynolds, A. 1999: *Later Anglo-Saxon England* (Stroud. Tempus)

Reynolds, A. & Turner, S. 2003: Excavations at Holy Trinity, Buckfastleigh, *Society for Medieval Archaeology Newsletter*, 28, 5-6

Reuter, T. (ed) 1980: *The Greatest Englishman: Essays on St. Boniface and the Church at Crediton* (Exeter. Paternoster Press)

Riley, H. & Wilson-North, R. 2001: *The Field Archaeology of Exmoor* (English Heritage)

Rippon, S. J. 2006: Landscapes of pre-medieval occupation, in Kain, R. (ed), *England's Landscape: the South West* (English Heritage), 41-66

Rippon, S. J., Fyfe, R.M., & Brown, A.G. 2006: Beyond villages and open fields: the origins and development of a historic landscape characterised by dispersed settlement in south west England, *Medieval Archaeology*, 50, 31-70

Roberts, B.K. 1987: *The Making of the English Village* (Harlow. Longmans)

Roberts, B.K. & Wrathmell, S. 2002: *Region and Place: a Study of English Rural Settlement* (Swindon. English Heritage)

Robertson, A.J. 1939: *Anglo-Saxon Charters* (Cambridge University Press)

Rose, P. & Preston-Jones, A. 1995: Changes in the Cornish countryside AD400–1100, in Hooke, D. & Burnell, S. (eds), *Landscape and Settlement in Britain AD400–1100* (Exeter. Exeter University Press), 51-68

Bibliography

Rose-Troup, F. 1923: *Lost Chapels of Exeter* (Exeter. History of Exeter Research Group, monograph no. 1)

Rose-Troup, F. 1929: The new Edgar charter and the South Hams, *Transactions of the Devonshire Association*, 61, 249-280

Rose-Troup, F. 1937: Exeter manumissions and quittances of the eleventh and twelfth century, *Transactions of the Devonshire Association*, 69, 417-445

Rosser, G. 1988: The Anglo-Saxon Gilds, in Blair, J. (ed), 31-34

Rosser, G. 1992: The cure of souls in English towns before 1000, in Blair, J. & Sharpe, R. (eds), 267-284

Sawyer, P. 1965: The wealth of England in the eleventh century, *Transactions of the Royal Historical Society*, 5th series, 15, 145-164

Sawyer, P. (ed) 1968: *Anglo-Saxon Charters. An Annotated List and Bibliography* (London. Royal Historical Society)

Sawyer, P. 1983: The royal *Tun* in pre-conquest England, in Wormald, P. (ed), *Ideal and Reality in Frankish and Anglo-Saxon Society* (Oxford. Blackwell), 272-299

Searle, W.G. 1897: *Onomasticon Anglo-Saxonicum* (Cambridge University Press)

Sharpe, R. 2003: The use of writs in the eleventh century, *Anglo-Saxon England*, 32, 247-291

Sheldon, G. 1928: *From Trackway to Turnpike an illustration from East Devon* (Oxford University Press)

Simpson, S.J., Griffith, F.M., Holbrook, N. 1989: The prehistoric, Roman and early post-Roman site at Hayes Farm, Clyst Honiton, *Proceedings of the Devon Archaeological Society*, 47, 1-28

Sims-Williams, P. 1990: *Religion and Literature in Western England, 600–800* (Cambridge University Press)

Slater, T.R. 1991: Controlling the South Hams: the Anglo-Saxon *Burh* at Halwell, *Transactions of the Devonshire Association*, 123, 57-78

Snyder 2003: *The Britons* (Oxford. Blackwell)

Stafford, P. 1997: *Queen Emma and Queen Edith* (Oxford. Blackwell)

Stenton, F.M. 1947: *Anglo-Saxon England* (Oxford. Clarendon Press. 2nd edition)

Stenton, F.M. 1955: *Latin Charters of the Anglo-Saxon Period* (Oxford. Clarendon Press)

Stephan, J. 1970: *A History of Buckfast Abbey from 1018 to 1968* (Bristol. Burleigh Press)

Stevens, C.E. 1976: The Sacred Wood, in Megaw, J.V.S. (ed), *To Illustrate the Monuments: essays on archaeology presented to Stuart Piggott* (London. Thames & Hudson), 239-244.

Swanton, M. (ed) 1996: *The Anglo-Saxon Chronicle* (London. Dent)

Swanton, M. 1999: King Alfred's ships: text and context, *Anglo-Saxon England*, 28, 1-22

Swanton, M. & Pearce, S.M. 1982: Lustleigh, South Devon: its inscribed stone, its churchyard and its parish, in Pearce, S.M. (ed) 1982, 139-143

Sykes-Balls, H. 1978-79: Viking Treasure, *Transactions and Proceedings of the Torquay Natural History Society,* 18, Part I, 10-13

Tait, J. 1936: *The Medieval English Borough* (Manchester University Press)

Taylor, H.M. & Taylor, J. 1965: *Anglo-Saxon Architecture,* Vol. II (Cambridge University Press)

Taylor, C. 1983: *Village and Farmstead: a history of rural settlement in England* (London. George Philip)

Taylor, C. (ed) 1988: *W.G. Hoskins: The Making of the English Landscape* (London. Guild Publishing)

Taylor, J. 2007: *An Atlas of Roman Rural Settlement in England* (Council for British Archaeology Research Report, 151).

Thacker, A. & Sharpe, R. (eds) 2002: *Local Saints and Local Churches in the Early Medieval West* (Oxford University Press)

Thomas, A.C. 1981: *Christianity in Roman Britain to AD 500* (London. B.T. Batsford)

Thomas, A.C. 1994: *And Shall These Mute Stones Speak? Post-Roman Inscriptions in Western Britain* (Cardiff. University of Wales Press)

Thomas, A.C. 1999: Early Christian Dumnonia, in Kain, R. and Ravenhill, W. (eds), 82-87

Thorne, C. & F.(eds) 1985: *Domesday Book: Devon* (2 vols. Chichester. Phillimore)

Thorne. F. 1991: Hundreds and Wapentakes, in *The Devonshire Domesday* (Alecto Historical Editions), 26-42

Thorpe, L. (ed) 1978: *Gerald of Wales: The Journey through Wales and the Description of Wales* (Harmondsworth. Penguin Books)

Todd, M. 1987: *The South West to AD 1000* (London. Longman)

Todd. M. 1999(a): Classical sources for Roman place-names, in Kain, R. and Ravenhill, W. (eds) 1999, 80-81

Todd, M. 1999(b): The latest inscriptions of Roman Britain, *Durham Archaeological Journal,* 14-15, 53-58

Todd, M. 2005: Baths or Baptisteries? Holcombe, Lifton and their analogies, *Oxford Journal of Archaeology,* 24.3, 307-311

Turner, S. 2003: Making a Christian Landscape: early Medieval Cornwall, in Carver, M. (ed), *The Cross goes North: processes of Conversion in Northern Europe (*Woodbridge. York Medieval Press), 171-194

Turner, S. 2006(a): *Making a Christian Landscape: the countryside in early medieval Cornwall, Devon and Wessex* (University of Exeter Press)

Turner, S. (ed) 2006(b): *Medieval Devon and Cornwall: shaping an ancient countryside* (Macclesfield. Windgather Press)

Wade-Evans, A.W. 1959: *The Emergence of England and Wales* (Cambridge. Heffer & Son; second edition)

Ward-Perkins, B. 2000: Why did the Anglo-Saxons not become more British?, *English Historical Review*, 115 (no. 462), 513-533

Warren, F.E. 1883: *The Leofric Missal* (Oxford. Clarendon Press)

Watts, V. (ed) 2004: *The Cambridge Dictionary of English Place-Names* (Cambridge University Press)

Weddell, P.J. 1987: Excavations within the Anglo-Saxon Enclosure at Berry Meadow, Kingsteignton, in 1985, *Proceedings of the Devon Archaeological Society*, 45, 75-96

Weddell, P.J. 2000: The excavation of a post-Roman cemetery near Kenn, *Proceedings of the Devon Archaeological Society*, 58, 93-126

Welldon Finn, R. 1964: *The Liber Exoniensis* (London. Longmans)

Whitelock, D. (ed) 1930: *Anglo-Saxon Wills* (Cambridge University Press)

Whitelock, D. (ed) 1955: *English Historical Documents, I, c. 500-1042* (London. Eyre & Spottiswoode)

Williams, A. & Erskine, R.W.H. (eds) 1987: *Domesday Book Studies* (London. Alecto)

Williams, A. 2003: *Aethelred the Unready: the ill-counselled king* (London & New York. Hambledon)

Williams, H. 2006: *Death and Memory in Early Medieval Britain* (Cambridge University Press)

Winterbottom, M. (ed) 1978: *Gildas: The Ruin of Britain* (Chichester. Phillimore)

Wormald, P. 1999: *The Making of English Law: King Alfred to the Twelfth Century. Vol. I* (Oxford. Blackwell)

Yorke, B. 1995: *Wessex in the Early Middle Ages* (Leicester University Press)

Yorke, B. 1997: *Kings and Kingdoms of early Anglo-Saxon England* (London. Routledge)

Yorke, B. 1999: *The Anglo-Saxons* (Stroud. Sutton)

Yorke, B. 2006(a): The Saints of Anglo-Saxon Wessex, in Meek, M. (ed), *The Modern Traveller to our Past: Festschrift in honour of Ann Hamlin* (Dublin. DPK), 177-183

Yorke, B. 2006(b): *The Conversion of Britain, 600–800* (London. Pearson Longman)

Yorke, B. (2007): The insular background to Boniface's continental career, in Felton, F.J., Jarnut, J. and von Palberg, L.E. (eds), *Boniface – Leben und Nachwirken* (Mainz)

Yorke, B. forthcoming: Dorset, 400–700, in Gardiner, K. (ed), *Kings, Tyrants and Priests: the south west c. AD 400–700*

Indices

As emphasised in the Preface, I have written this book as a text to be read for its overall coverage rather than to be consulted for specific information. How to index it to best effect poses something of a problem, in addition to which I lack the professional skills needed to produce a detailed and thematic index which draws all the possible threads together. I hope the reader will find, instead, the following two indices helpful. The first is a list of sub-section titles from the four central chapters, giving guidance as to where, allowing for much inter-connection, discussion of particular subjects is to be found. The second is a place-name list which readers may find helpful in locating discussion of particular places. It includes, for the most part, settlement names rather than shire, topographical and other names, and it covers all such places mentioned, whether in Devon or elsewhere. This data is given in raw form: unaccompanied by thematic labels about the information given where these place-names occur in the text. The second list, like the first, relates only to the four central chapters. The Prologue and Epilogue – which are of a more general nature – and the Appendices – which are of a more technical nature – are excluded since they are of different character. Place-names are given in their modern form, with which readers will be familiar. A complementary index of personal names has not been included: I judged that most of the readers at whom this book is aimed would probably not know enough of these names beforehand to make such a list very useful.

I: Chapter sub-sections

Chapter 2: People and Place

Social groups, language and culture 13
Kingdoms and conflict 26
Emigration and immigration 42
Language and place-names 49
Shire bounds 57
Scandinavian influences 63
"Englishness" and the archaeological record 69

Chapter 3: Church and Society

Dumnonia 74
English minsters 86
Urban minsters 100
Reformed monasteries 103
The dioceses 104
Local rural churches 107
Local churches in Exeter 116
Early church fabric 119
Exploitation and use of stone 128
Church culture on the eve of the Norman Conquest 135

Chapter 4: Government and Towns

Shires and royal lands 139
Hundreds, ealdormen and earls 144
Royal households and councils 150
Military service 152
Estates and charters 156
Sheriffs and law-courts 162
Exeter's re-emergence 167
The *burhs* of king Alfred and his successors 174
The *burhs* and military organisation 179
Burghal planning 184
Other possible defended and marketing places 188
Mints and minting 191
Landowners and towns 195
Urbanism on the eve of the Norman Conquest 198

Chapter 5: land and Rural Folk

Land and resources 204
Estate organization 212
Estate bounds 214
Domesday: limitations and strengths 218
Land-use 222
Evolution of settlement 227
Farms, hamlets, villages 237
Fields and field-systems 244
Countryside and church 249
Rural industries 255

Indices

II: Place-Names Referred To

Abbotskerswell:162
Abingdon: 89, 105
Ashford: 26, 215, 222
Athelney: 65
Axminster: 87, 88, 90, 113, 142, 147, 151, 188, 250, 252, 254
Axmouth: 88, 142-143, 147, 209

Badgworthy: 223
Bampton: 42, 142
Bantham: 35
Barnstaple: 65, 100, 110, 130, 142, 174, 178-179, 181, 183, 187, 190, 192, 196
Bath: 16, 134
Belstone: 129
Bere Ferrers: 257
Bickleigh (south Devon): 151
Bickleigh (Exe valley): 111
Bigbury: 63, 148
Bindon (Devon): 28
Bindon (Dorset): 28
Bishopsteignton: 197
Bishop's Tawton: 93, 218
Blacklake Wood: 258
Blatchford: 159
Bodmin: 79, 80-81, 94, 102, 135, 189, 210
Boehill: 26, 215, 222
Bolham: 42
Bovey Tracey: 214
Bow: 244
Bowley: 240
Bradstone: 94, 210
Bradworthy: 241
Brampford Speke: 26, 155, 162, 167, 255
Branscombe: 57, 88, 101, 109, 125, 143
Braunton: 80, 86-88, 91, 98, 113, 115, 130, 134, 142, 161, 209, 241, 243, 248, 249, 254

Brayford: 257, 258
Breazle: 52
Bridestowe: 94
Brixham: 57
Broadclyst: 102
Buckfast: 81, 88, 103-104, 120, 132, 148, 160, 167
Buckfastleigh: 229
Buckland (near Dolton): 132
Buckland (elsewhere): 210
Buckland Monachorum: 225
Burlescombe: 257
Butterleigh: 42

Cadbury (Devon): 36
Cadbury, South (Somerset): 67, 191
Callington: 28, 64, 242
Cambridge: 107
Cannington: 79
Canterbury: 135, 171
Carhampton: 64
Carley: 52
Chagford: 226
Challacombe: 55
Chardstock: 62
Charford: 115
Charles: 52
Cheddar: 235
Chercombe: 114
Cheristow: 91, 114-115
Cheriton Bishop: 55, 114, 162
Cheriton fitzPaine: 114
Cheriton (near Payhembury): 114
Cheriton (near Brendon): 114
Cherubeer: 133
Chester: 107, 118, 169, 187
Chichester 107
Chillington: 92, 94, 148
Chippenham: 65

Chittlehampton: 98, 240
Chivelstone: 92
Chudleigh: 217
Churchstanton: 62
Churchstow: 92, 114
Churston Ferrers: 114
Cirencester: 16
Clannaborough: 167, 255
Clatworthy: 257
Climsland: 211
Clyst St George: 102, 162
Clyst Honiton: 72, 230
Clyst St Mary: 162, 215
Clovelly: 26
Cockington: 226
Coleridge: 148
Colyton: 89-90, 102, 113, 130, 134, 142, 147, 151, 252
Combe Martin: 257
Copplestone: 130, 134
Cornwood: 23, 111, 159
Coryton: 211
Countisbury: 37-38, 65
Cowley: 42
Crediton: 55-56, 88-93, 98, 104-106, 130, 136, 155-157, 160-162, 167, 188, 210, 215, 218-219, 233, 250, 252, 254-255
Creechbarrow: 26
Crook: 52
Crooke: 52
Croyde: 55
Cullompton: 72, 88, 113, 143, 188, 218, 250, 252
Culmstock: 62, 93, 137, 161-162, 215, 218

Dainton: 162
Dalwood: 62
Dartington: 26, 111
Dartmouth: 149
Dawlish: 113, 137, 207, 218

Deerhurst: 149, 167
Denbury: 37
Dinnaton: 159
Diptford: 92, 142, 148
Dolton: 52, 130, 132-134
Dorchester (Dorset): 140, 163, 189
Dorchester (-on-Thames): 104
Doulting: 134
Dowland: 132
Downhayne: 215
Down St Mary: 162
Down Thomas: 247
Dublin: 149
Dunchideock: 26, 52
Dunkeswell: 257
Dunterton: 52
Dyrham: 16

East Budleigh: 142
East Ogwell: 86
Edington: 65
Eggbeer: 240
Egloshayle: 30, 51
Englebourne: 55
Exbourne: 114
Exeter: 17, 19, 28, 32, 38-39, 65, 67, 69-70, 72, 74, 77, 81, 88-90, 93, 97-99, 102, 104-107, 110, 112-113, 116, 118, 120-121, 124, 126, 128, 130, 134-137, 139-140, 149, 151, 154-155, 162-163, 167, 169, 171-175, 178-180, 182, 187-188, 190-192, 196-198, 201, 215, 235, 252
Exmouth: 102
Exminster: 87-88, 93, 142-143, 226, 254

Fardel: 23, 111, 159
Fowey: 36

Galford: 28, 33, 183
Galsworthy: 57

Germansweek: 230
Glastonbury: 32, 41, 59, 88-89, 131-132, 135, 161, 209, 214, 243
Gloucester: 16, 69
Goodrington: 67, 197
Grately: 191
Grimston: 67
Gripstone: 67
Gwithian: 245

Halsdon: 130
Halsford: 102
Halstock: 84
Halwell: 65, 67, 92, 100, 174-175, 181, 183, 189
Hamwic: 169
Harberton: 55, 92-93, 100
Hartland: 57, 80, 86, 88, 90-91, 98-99, 100, 110, 113, 115, 143, 145, 240-241, 254
Harton: 91
Hatherleigh: 132
Hawkchurch: 62, 114
Hayle: 30
Hayridge: 148
Hayes: 230
Haytor: 148, 226
Heavitree: 90, 113, 179
Hemyock: 52, 89, 142, 257
Hereford: 69
High Peak: 34
Hingston Down: 28, 64
Holcombe (south-east Devon): 37, 74, 233
Holcombe (Rogus): 156, 167, 214
Hollacombe: 81, 94
Holne: 223
Honeychurch: 114
Horner Wood: 258
Hound Tor: 226
Huntingdon: 175

Ilchester: 104
Ilsington: 197
Instow: 83, 99
Ipplepen: 162, 215, 226
Ivybridge: 23

Jacobstowe: 83, 132

Kelly: 52
Kemacott: 248
Kenbury: 67, 161
Kenn: 77, 79, 197
Kentisbeare: 241
Kentisbury: 52
Kenton: 93, 150, 226, 247
Kerswell: 148, 226
Kigbeare: 57
Kilkhampton: 62, 242
Kingsbridge: 72, 114, 173, 189-191
Kingskerswell: 94, 113, 142
King's Tamerton: 142, 151
Kingsteignton: 66, 93, 142, 147, 189-191, 254

Landcross: 52, 83
Landkey: 52, 80, 83, 99
Langport: 29
Launceston: 90, 183, 189, 250
Lew Trenchard: 33
Lichfield: 107
Lifton: 88, 94, 101, 143, 145, 150-152, 179, 183, 210
Lincoln: 69, 77
Littleham: 162
London: 77, 169, 193
Lydford: 65-67, 81, 84, 94, 100-102, 142, 174-175, 178-179, 181, 183-184, 187, 190, 192-193, 196, 227, 252
Lynmouth: 38
Lynton: 21
Lustleigh: 23, 84, 143

Maindea: 52
Manaton: 226
Maker: 41, 62, 104, 156
Malmesbury: 17, 19, 79, 89, 97, 137, 151, 169
Mamhead: 52
Marlborough: 92
Martinhoe: 248
Marystow: 94
Mawgan Porth: 235
Meavy: 115, 162, 225
Milton Damarel: 55
Modbury: 67, 94, 148, 191
Molland: 236
Monkton: 137, 162
Morchard Bishop: 52, 229
Mothecombe: 35
Muchelney: 89

Natsworthy: 207
Newton Abbot: 191
Newton St Cyres: 178
Newton St Petrock: 81, 94
North Huish: 92
North Lew: 241
North Molton: 150, 208, 257
North Tawton: 142
Norwich: 169
Nutwell: 102

Ogwell: 114
Okehampton: 84, 95, 130, 167, 189, 210-211, 252
Oldaport: 67, 191
Oldstone: 67
Old Sarum: 105, 107
Otterton: 189, 233
Ottery St Mary: 89, 162, 218

Padstow: 66, 79, 80
Paignton: 112, 226
Parracombe: 21, 229, 236

Penn: 28
Penselwood: 28
Petherwin: 63
Petrockstow: 81, 132
Pilton: 174, 181, 183, 189
Pinhoe: 28, 66, 113, 164
Plymouth: 109, 151
Plympton: 62, 88, 91-93, 100, 105, 110, 113, 142, 145, 162, 189, 191, 218, 250
Plymstock: 92, 134, 218
Poltimore: 72
Poole: 65
Porlock: 134, 149
Portchester: 189
Posbury: 28, 37
Poughill: 113
Prescott: 115
Prescombe: 115
Prestacott: 115
Preston: 115
Priestacott: 115
Priestaford: 115
Priestland: 115

Rackenford: 236
Radworthy: 207
Ramsbury: 132
Rashleigh: 240
Rewe: 42
Roborough: 148
Rochester: 187
Rockbeare: 240
Roseland: 62
Ruan Lanihorne: 103
Rudge: 229

St. Austell: 135
St. Germans: 79, 105-106, 152, 189
St. Marychurch: 113
Salcombe: 92
Salisbury: 93
Sampford Courtenay: 114, 240

Indices

Sampford Peverell: 26, 162, 222
Sandford: 162, 215, 218
Seaton: 162, 218, 233
Selsey: 107
Shapwick: 235, 242, 249
Shaugh: 92
Sherborne: 32, 41, 62, 79, 86, 88-89, 92-93, 104-105, 107, 143, 148, 156, 167, 214
Sherford: 67, 92, 161
Sherracombe Ford: 257-258
Shirwell: 197
Shobrooke: 137
Sidbury: 101, 109, 123, 130, 134
Sidmouth: 102
Silverton: 42, 88, 142-143, 148, 241
Somerton: 140, 163
Sorley: 190
Sourton: 23, 82, 134, 210
South Brent: 115
South Hole: 241
South Huish: 92
South Milton: 92
South Molton: 88, 113, 142
South Zeal: 244
Stanborough: 148, 183
Stockland: 62
Stokenham: 92, 94, 99
Stoke Canon: 42, 98, 137, 155, 162, 218
Stoke Fleming: 99, 197
Stoke St Nectan: 91
Stowford: 83
Stratton: 57, 143
Sutton: 109, 142, 151
Swimbridge: 115

Taunton: 29
Tavistock: 21, 55, 84, 88, 94, 98, 101, 103-104, 114, 120, 132, 135-136, 148, 155, 160, 167, 183, 189, 214, 227, 250, 252, 254
Tawstock: 93, 161, 197, 218

Teignbridge: 148, 173, 190
Teignmouth: 113, 125
Thetford: 169
Thorncombe: 62
Thorverton: 241
Thurlestone: 63
Tintagel: 34, 38, 102
Tiverton: 42, 88-89, 91, 110, 143, 147, 188, 250, 254
Topsham: 137, 155, 162, 169, 210, 215, 218
Torrington: 145, 248
Totnes: 67, 100, 110, 113, 142, 175, 178-179, 184, 187, 189, 190, 192, 193, 196
Treable: 52, 56
Trebick: 52
Trellick: 52, 57
Trematon: 210
Trethurgy: 231
Trewhiddle: 135
Trigg: 36, 143
Trusham: 52
Truro: 99

Uffculme: 214
Ugborough: 241
Uplyme: 37, 41, 62, 162, 215, 218
Upton Pyne: 162, 218

Walkhampton: 115, 142, 148, 151
Walland: 55
Wallover: 55
Walreddon: 55
Wareham: 23, 65, 86
Weekaborough: 64
Welcombe: 91
Wells: 105
Wembury: 92, 247
Werrington: 63
West Alvington: 89, 92-93, 142
West Wortha: 230

Westminster: 150
Whimple: 52
Whitchurch: 55, 114
Whitestone: 102
Widecombe: 226
Wigborough: 65
Willsworthy: 207
Wilton: 150
Winchester: 69, 88-89, 104-105, 148, 150, 169, 193

Winkleigh: 129
Withypool: 227
Wonford: 90, 163, 169, 179
Woodbury: 102, 113
Woodleigh: 92
Worcester: 119, 137

Yealmpton: 93, 113, 142
York: 77, 104, 169